FINITE MATHEMATICS

WITH APPLICATIONS IN THE SOCIAL AND MANAGEMENT SCIENCES

FINITE MATHEMATICS
WITH APPLICATIONS IN THE SOCIAL AND MANAGEMENT SCIENCES

LOUIS O. KATTSOFF

PROFESSOR OF MATHEMATICS, BOSTON COLLEGE

ALBERT J. SIMONE

ASSOCIATE PROFESSOR OF BUSINESS ADMINISTRATION, BOSTON COLLEGE

McGRAW-HILL BOOK COMPANY

NEW YORK ST. LOUIS SAN FRANCISCO TORONTO LONDON SYDNEY

FINITE MATHEMATICS
With Applications in the Social and Management Sciences

Copyright © 1965 by McGraw-Hill, Inc. All Rights Reserved. Printed in the United States of America. This book, or parts thereof, may not be reproduced in any form without permission of the publishers.
Library of Congress Catalog Card Number 64-8417

33381

1234567890MP7210698765

To our wives, Hilda and Carolie,
for their invaluable assistance

PREFACE

We have tried to steer a course through the Scylla and Charybdis of too much theory and not enough theory. We are sure we shall be criticized for both, but the result is our considered judgment of what is desirable. Too much theory for the nonprofessional mathematician tends to prevent the achievement of one important objective, viz., the ability to *use* these mathematical concepts in the modern world of business, government, and research. We do not subscribe to the unsupported hope that students equipped only with theory will know how to make the appropriate applications. On the other hand, too little theory fashions a student who may know how to apply techniques without a true comprehension of why these techniques do work. Without a basis in theory, the creative use of mathematics is almost impossible. To provide some experience in application and understanding, we have worked some of the applications in along with the theory, while others are provided in the form of straightforward use of techniques.

What we have tried to write is basically a mathematics book with applications in the social and management sciences. The early part of the book is relatively easy. As the student develops some maturity, the level of the work is raised. We have indicated from time to time certain portions of the book that may be omitted, either on first reading or by students whose level of maturity is not high. Accordingly, the book is very flexible and lends itself to a number of types of courses:

1. A liberal-arts course in finite mathematics
2. A course in a college of business administration either for freshmen or for more advanced students who need acquaintance with basic mathematical concepts

In addition, it is useful as a supplementary text in the following courses:

3. A course, at the senior or first-year graduate level, for students of the social and management sciences in preparation for quantitative analysis in their research courses and thesis work to come
4. A course in linear programming which requires a review of basic mathematics

Each instructor, naturally, will select from the material those chapters he finds most suitable for his particular students. For example, an instructor of students who fall in the third category above would want to go at a relatively fast pace and include Chaps. 12 and 13, which apply the theory of vectors and matrices developed in Chaps. 7, 10, and 11 to linear programming. It is the availability of these chapters which also makes our text suitable to students falling in the fourth category.

On the other hand, an instructor offering a course to average students falling in either of the first two categories could omit these chapters, without disturbing the continuity of the text, and concentrate on the basic mathematics.   In this event, the instructor will find ample opportunity to treat applications in these mathematical core chapters, since they contain examples, problems, and entire sections on application.

Again, within each chapter we have sought to provide flexibility by placing the application sections in such a position (usually at the end) that they can be omitted without affecting the continuity of the text. Examples of this are the sections dealing with logical models in production management (Chap. 1), Bayes theorem and binomial probabilities (Chap. 4), break-even analysis (Chap. 5), an introduction to linear programming (Chap. 6), the Leontief input/output model (Chap. 7), learning curves (Chap. 8), and capital theory and product failure (Chap. 9).

Above-average students at the first and second-year undergraduate level can, of course, be held responsible for some, or all, of the chapters excluded above.

There are certain distinctive features of the book that must be recorded:

1. Wherever possible, computational formulas are given in a form adaptable to machine programming.

2. Very often, a single problem recurs in more than one context. This enables the student to see the various aspects of a given problem.

3. The integrated and cohesive nature of mathematics is illustrated by the use of mathematical concepts developed in earlier chapters in the applications of later chapters.   For example, the various probability definitions and theorems of Chap. 4 and the exponential function introduced in Chap. 8 are used in conjunction with the subject matter of Chap. 9 (sequences and progressions) in a product-life application presented at the end of Chap. 9, and the concepts of a random variable, probability distribution, and expected value introduced in Chap. 4 are applied in Chap. 10 to a decision-theory problem involving matrices.

4. Some nonfinite mathematics is introduced (e.g., Chaps. 5, 8, 9) which we thought important for further work. This material is organized so that it can be treated or not, at the discretion of the instructor.

5. We provide a self-contained development of linear programming.

6. Our examples and problems treat situations arising in economics, management, sociology, psychology, education, and political science. Most of these applications are from the fields of economics and business. Nonetheless, they are so constructed that they form paradigms for

structurally identical problems in any of the other sciences, both social and natural.

7. The chapters on linear programming have been put at the end of the book because of their complexity and the degree of maturity they demand for comprehension. We think that they are not above the level which we hope the student will have reached, but they do require rather sustained attention.

8. A rather complete study of linear algebra is included because of its importance.

9. We have introduced a fair amount of analytical geometry, where it occurs naturally.

10. We introduce, at an early stage, the concepts of sets and functions and use them as consistently as possible, departing from them only for pedagogical reasons.

11. Ample examples and problems are provided, in the belief that students can learn best by "doing." Those students who want to pursue further a given topic will find additional concepts, both theoretical and in the area of application, in these problem sections.

12. We have introduced topics with a view toward preparing the student for work in the calculus.

13. We have tried to conform as far as possible to the recommendations of the Committee on Undergraduate Programs in Mathematics for Biology, Management, and Social Sciences of the American Mathematical Association[1] and to the recommendations of M. D. Richards and R. Carzo in their Ford Foundation sponsored monograph "Mathematics in Collegiate Business Schools."[2] Most of the topics recommended by the above studies are discussed. Naturally, however, all we can do is lay the groundwork for further work. We therefore consider the book suitable for the modern student and presuppose only a good secondary school background in mathematics.

14. To enhance the teachability of the text, answers to odd numbered problems are provided in an answer section appearing at the end of the book, and an Instructor's Manual containing fully worked out solutions to most problems is available to instructors.

We wish to thank the administration of Boston College for their encouragement and assistance while this project was in progress.

LOUIS O. KATTSOFF

ALBERT J. SIMONE

[1] Committee on the Undergraduate Program in Mathematics, "Tentative Recommendations for the Undergraduate Mathematics Program of the Students in the Biological, Management, and Social Sciences," Mathematical Association of America, 1964.

[2] M. D. Richards and R. Carzo, "Mathematics in Collegiate Business Schools," South-Western Publishing Co., Cincinnati, 1963.

CONTENTS

1 STATEMENTS

1.1 INTRODUCTION

Certain procedures are fundamental to all correct reasoning.
Students of any field whatever should be aware at least of the
basic ideas and rules of correct reasoning. However, since
mathematics is itself a system of procedures for arriving at valid
conclusions, it may be looked upon as a system of logic. The
student should therefore realize that what he will study in this
book are rules and methods for arriving at valid conclusions on
the basis of given data. The conclusions may or may not be
applicable to actual situations, but they may still give valuable
insight into what may or may not be possible.

The formulation of logical concepts and rules of reasoning in symbolic form constitutes what is called *symbolic logic*. The applications of symbolic logic will be found to be quite numerous in many fields.

1.2 STATEMENTS: ATOMIC AND COMPOUND

Statements are the foundations upon which logic is built. A statement may be defined as a declarative sentence. The following sentences are statements: "The essence of money is typified by paper currency." "Profits are the earnings of enterprise."

If a statement has other statements as component parts, it is said to be *compound* (or *molecular*); otherwise it is *atomic*. The two statements given above are atomic, but "Every businessman seeks to maximize his profits and increase the size of his firm" is compound, being really two statements:

1. Every businessman seeks to maximize his profits.
2. Every businessman seeks to increase the size of his firm.

Notice that the statement "John and Joe enter into partnership" is an atomic statement. (Why?)

The following three examples will show how we can form compound statements from atomic ones.

Example 1.1. We can unite two or more atomic statements by the word "and." We can use the symbol & to denote "and." So if p and q are statements, we can write $p \& q$. The result of combining two or more statements by & will also be a statement. If p, q, and r are statements, then $p \& q$ is a statement and $(p \& q) \& r$ will also be a statement. The result of combining statements into a single statement by & is called a *conjunction*.

Example 1.2. We can unite two or more statements by the expression "either . . . or . . . ." We use the symbol $\vee$ to denote "either . . . or . . . ." If p and q are statements, then $p \vee q$ will be a statement. The result of combining two or more statements by $\vee$ is called an *alternation*. For example,

Either *every businessman seeks to increase sales revenue*, or *every businessman seeks to reduce unit costs*

If the above statements were intended to mean "either . . . or . . . but not both," the result would be called an *exclusive alternation*.

Example 1.3. A third way of constructing compound statements is to use the expression "if . . . then . . . ." We use an arrow $\rightarrow$ to designate this expression. If p and q are statements, then $p \rightarrow q$ (read "If p, then q") will also be a statement. $p \rightarrow q$ is called a *conditional statement*.

The statement "If every businessman seeks to increase his sales revenue, then every businessman seeks to reduce his unit costs" is a conditional statement.

In this case p is replaced by "Every businessman seeks to increase his sales revenue," and q is replaced by "Every businessman seeks to reduce his unit costs." p is called the *antecedent* and q the *consequent*.

Example 1.4. In the following statement, indicate the atomic statements, and show the form of the complete statement:

If you spend less than your income, then your net saving is positive and you add to your assets or reduce your liabilities.

Solution. We note the "if . . . then . . . ," which tells us to use an arrow. The atomic statements are symbolized as follows. Let

$$p = \text{you spend less than your income}$$
$$q = \text{your net saving is positive}$$
$$r = \text{you add to your assets}$$
$$s = \text{you reduce your liabilities}$$

We see that the consequent, i.e., everything after the word "then," is the conjunction $q \& (r \lor s)$. The statement is then

$$p \to [q \& (r \lor s)]$$

The meaning of the statement and its punctuation tell us where to put the parentheses.

PROBLEM SET 1.1[1]

1. Which of the following are statements?
   a. Money is expensive.
   b. Buy Standard Oil!
   c. If you diversify your investments, your risk is lessened.
   d. The high cost of living!

2. Let p be the statement "Inflation hurts people with fixed money incomes," q be the statement "Inflation is destructive of purchasing power," and r be the statement "The lower the level of government spending, the less the danger of inflation." Write the statements represented by
   a. $p \& r$
   b. $r \& q$
   c. $(p \lor r) \to q$
   d. $q \to (p \& r)$
   e. $(p \& q) \to (p \to r)$
   f. $(p \lor q) \& r$

[1] Answers to odd-numbered problems are shown at the back of the book.

1.3 TRUTH TABLES

It is important to define the conditions under which we shall call compound statements true or false. These conditions, the "truth conditions," will be the truth or falsity of the atomic statements making up the compound statement. The truth tables (Figs. 1.1 to 1.6) may be viewed as definitions of the symbols used.

Let p and q be statements, and let T denote that a statement is true and F that it is false. We notice the following important facts:

1. p & q is *true* if and only if p is true and q is true (Fig. 1.1).
2. $p \vee q$ is *true* if and only if at least one of the two statements is true (Fig. 1.2).
3. $p \rightarrow q$ is *false* if and only if p (the antecedent) is true and q (the consequent) is false (Fig. 1.3).

These truth tables can be used to decide whether or not two compound statements constructed out of the same atomic statements are *logically equivalent*. By definition, two or more compound statements are logically equivalent if they have the same truth values under the same truth conditions. We denote logical equivalence by the symbols $p \equiv q$ or $p \leftrightarrow q$.

Example 1.5. Are p & $(q \vee r)$ and $(p$ & $q) \vee (p$ & $r)$ logically equivalent?

Solution. We construct the truth table shown in Fig. 1.4. The table of Fig. 1.4 is completed by using Figs. 1.1, 1.2, and 1.3 as basic definitions. For example, the third row from the bottom is constructed in the following way:

We have the combination of p true, q false, and r false. This makes $q \vee r$ false and p & $(q \vee r)$ false. Also p & q and p & r are both false. So $(p$ & $q) \vee (p$ & $r)$ is false. We notice that column A and column B have exactly the same entries for the same truth conditions of p, q, and r. They are therefore logically equivalent, and we write a T in the last column.

p	q	p & q
T	T	T
T	F	F
F	T	F
F	F	F

Fig. *1.1*

p	q	$p \vee q$
T	T	T
T	F	T
F	T	T
F	F	F

Fig. *1.2*

p	q	$p \rightarrow q$
T	T	T
T	F	F
F	T	T
F	F	T

Fig. *1.3*

				A			B	
p	q	r	$q \vee r$	$p \,\&\, (q \vee r)$	$p \,\&\, q$	$p \,\&\, r$	$(p \,\&\, q) \vee (p \,\&\, r)$	$p \,\&\, (q \vee r) \leftrightarrow (p \,\&\, q) \vee (p \,\&\, r)$
T	T	T	T	T	T	T	T	T
T	F	T	T	T	F	T	T	T
F	T	T	T	F	F	F	F	T
F	F	T	T	F	F	F	F	T
T	T	F	T	T	T	F	T	T
T	F	F	F	F	F	F	F	T
F	T	F	T	F	F	F	F	T
F	F	F	F	F	F	F	F	T

Fig. *1.4*

Example 1.6. In the following paragraph,

1. Symbolize all statements.
2. Indicate the forms of the statements.
3. Determine whether or not the two statements are logically equivalent.

The problem can be described as follows: Either consumers are saving too much or governments are spending too little and businessmen are not investing enough. This is logically equivalent to: "Consumers are saving too much or governments are spending too little, and businessmen are not investing enough or consumers are saving too much."

Solution. 1. Let

c represent "Consumers are saving too much."
g represent "Governments are spending too little."
b represent "Businessmen are not investing enough."

2. $c \vee (g \,\&\, b)$, $(c \vee g) \,\&\, (b \vee c)$.

3. See Fig. 1.5. Since columns A and B in Fig. 1.5 are alike, the two statements are logically equivalent. (Compare the symbolic expression in this example with that in Example 1.5.) The expression in the last column turns out to be true under all possible truth conditions of its component parts. Any expression which is true under all possible truth conditions is called a *tautology*.

We now define the negation of a statement by means of a truth table. If p is a statement, then $-p$ will denote its negation and can be read "p is false." This tells us that, if a statement is true, its negation is false and, if it is false, its negation is true.

Example 1.7. If p means "Business is good," then $-p$ means "It is false that business is good."

				A			*B*	
c	*g*	*b*	*g* & *b*	*c* ∨ (*g* & *b*)	*c* ∨ *g*	*b* ∨ *c*	(*c* ∨ *g*) & (*b* ∨ *c*)	*c* ∨ (*g* & *b*) ↔ (*c* ∨ *g*) & (*b* ∨ *c*)
T	T	T	T	T	T	T	T	T
T	F	T	F	T	T	T	T	T
F	T	T	T	T	T	T	T	T
F	F	T	F	F	F	T	F	T
T	T	F	F	T	T	T	T	T
T	F	F	F	T	T	T	T	T
F	T	F	F	F	T	F	F	T
F	F	F	F	F	F	F	F	T

Fig. *1.5*

We now show that the negation of the negation of a statement is the original statement; i.e., we want to discover the truth table for $-(-p)$ from

p	$-p$
T	F
F	T

Let q be $-p$, so that

q	$-q$
F	T
T	F

But this is the same as

$-p$	$-(-p)$
F	T
T	F

If we compare $-(-p)$ with p for the same truth value, we see that they are identical. Therefore $p \leftrightarrow -(-p)$.

PROBLEM SET 1.2

1. Construct a truth table for $p \rightarrow q$ and $-p \vee q$. Compare the two.
2. Construct a truth table
   a. For $p \vee q$ and for $-(-p \,\&\, -q)$
   b. For $p \,\&\, q$ and for $-(-p \vee -q)$
(These are known as *De Morgan's laws*.)
3. Construct truth tables
   a. For $p \rightarrow q$ and for $q \rightarrow p$
   b. For $(p \rightarrow q) \,\&\, (q \rightarrow p)$
4. Show that $p \leftrightarrow q$ if and only if p and q have the same truth values. Are $(p \leftrightarrow q)$ and $(p \rightarrow q) \,\&\, (q \rightarrow p)$ logically equivalent?

5. Construct the truth table for:
 a. $(p \lor q) \, \& \, (-p \lor -q)$
 b. $p \, \& \, -p$
 c. $p \lor -p$
 d. $p \, \& \, (q \lor r)$ and $(p \, \& \, q) \lor (p \, \& \, r)$
 e. $(p \, \& \, q)$ and $(q \, \& \, p)$
 f. $(p \, \& \, q) \to p$
 g. $(p \lor q)$ and $(q \lor p)$
 h. $(p \to q) \to -(p \, \& \, -q)$
 i. $(p \, \& \, q) \, \& \, r$ and $p \, \& \, (q \, \& \, r)$
 j. $-(p \, \& \, q) \leftrightarrow -p \lor q$
 k. $[p \, \& \, (p \to q)] \to p$
 l. $[-q \, \& \, (p \to q)] \to -p$

Select some logically equivalent expressions. Are (c), (h), (k), and (l) tautologies?

6. Construct a truth table for the following set of statements:

Every businessman seeks to maximize his profits, and every businessman seeks to minimize his losses. But every businessman will sell some things at a loss and will not seek to maximize his profits.

(A set of statements, false for all possibilities, is called a *contradiction*.)

1.4 THE NEGATION OF COMPOUND STATEMENTS

It is important to know how to write the negation of compound statements. We offer some examples.

Problem 2a in Problem Set 1.2 tells us that $p \lor q$ is logically equivalent to $-(-p \, \& \, -q)$. Therefore, $p \lor q$ is the negation of $-p \, \& \, -q$; that is, the negation of a conjunction is the alternation of the negation of the parts of the conjunction.

Example 1.8. Write the negation of "Costs are held down, and inflation will not result."

Solution. Let p represent "Costs are held down," and let q represent "Inflation will result." The compound statement is therefore $p \, \& \, -q$, and its negation is $-p \lor q$.

We can translate $-p \lor q$ as follows: "Costs are *not* held down, or inflation *does* result" or "It is false that costs are held down, or it is false that inflation will not result."

Problem 2b in Problem Set 1.2 tells us that $p \, \& \, q$ is logically equivalent to $-(-p \lor -q)$. Hence the negation of $-p \lor -q$ must be $p \, \& \, q$.

Example 1.9. Write the negation of "Costs are not down, or inflation is not increasing."

Solution. We let

p represent "Costs are down."
q represent "Inflation is increasing."

The given statement is $-p \lor -q$, and its negation is $p \, \& \, q$. The statement we seek is "Costs are down, and inflation is increasing."

In Sec. 1.3 it was pointed out that $p \rightarrow q$ is false if and only if p is true and q is false. This tells us that the negation of $p \rightarrow q$ is $p \& -q$. The student should construct the truth tables for $p \& -q$ and note that the conditions under which $p \rightarrow q$ is true (or false) make $p \& -q$ false (or true). This means that $p \rightarrow q$ and $-(p \& -q)$ are logically equivalent.

Example 1.10. Write the negation of "If costs continue to rise, then inflation will result."

Solution. Let p denote "Costs continue to rise" and q denote "Inflation will result." The compound sentence is, then, $p \rightarrow q$, and its negation is $p \& -q$, that is, "Costs continue to rise, and inflation will not result."

Example 1.11. Write the negation of "If costs continue to rise, then either inflation will result or wages will be frozen."

Solution. In this example there are three atomic statements. Let

p denote "Costs continue to rise."
q denote "Inflation will result."
r denote "Wages will be frozen."

Clearly the compound statement is

$$p \rightarrow (q \lor r)$$

The negation is $[p \& -(q \lor r)]$. To simplify, we note that $-(q \lor r)$ is the logical equivalent of $-q \& -r$. So $[p \& -(q \lor r)]$ is logically equivalent to

$$[p \& (-q \& -r)]$$

The negation is therefore

Costs continue to rise, and inflation does not result,
and wages will not be frozen.

PROBLEM SET 1.3

1. Write the negation of "We must either trade with or aid foreign nations."
2. Write the negation of "Either productivity is *not* increasing, or productivity is *not* being measured correctly."
3. Write the negation of "If our tariffs are lowered, our exports will increase."
4. Write the negation of "If the Federal government spends more on medical research, then either medical scientists' salaries will permanently increase or there will be many more such scientists."
5. Write the negation of "Our national income is *not* growing rapidly enough, and our government policies are *not* sufficiently resolute."
6. The negation of what compound statement is implied by the following? "Technical change is rapid, and unemployment is *not* high."

7. Write the negation of "Government should either regulate monopoly or allow free trade in monopolized commodities."

8. Show by the truth table that $-(p \& -q)$ is logically equivalent to $-p \lor q$. (Cf. Prob. 5j, Problem Set 1.2.)

9. Show by truth tables that $p \to q$ is logically equivalent to $-q \to -p$ but is not equivalent to $-p \to -q$.

1.5 VALID ARGUMENTS

An important application of truth tables is their use in checking for the validity of arguments. An argument is a sequence of statements that purport to imply another statement. The sequence of statements serving as evidence will be called the *premises*, and the statement inferred will be called the *conclusion*. An argument is valid if and only if, whenever the conjunction of the premises is true, the conclusion is also. If we let p_1, p_2, and p_3 be the premises and p_4 the conclusion, then "$p_1 \& p_2 \& p_3$ implies p_4" will be valid if and only if whenever $p_1 \& p_2 \& p_3$ is true, p_4 is also. We can reduce this to the conditional $\to$ as follows:

Definition 1.12. If $p_1, p_2, \ldots, p_n$ are premises and p is a conclusion, then $p_1, \ldots, p_n$ validly implies p if and only if $p_1 \& p_2 \cdots \& p_n \to p$ is true for all combinations of truth values of $p_1, \ldots, p_n$ and p. In other words, to decide whether an argument is valid, use the conjunction of the evidence as the antecedent of a conditional of which the conclusion of the argument is the consequent, and see whether or not a tautology results.

When we are dealing with arguments whose premises and conclusions are statements, we can use truth tables to decide whether or not the argument is valid.

Example 1.13. Is the following argument valid? "If the labor market is perfect, then the wages of persons in a particular employment will be equal. But it is always the case that wages for such persons are not equal. Therefore the labor market is not perfect."

Solution. If we neglect the rhetoric, the argument boils down to the following: Let

p_1 be "The labor market is perfect."
p_2 be "Wages of persons in a particular employment will be equal."

The premises then are
$$p_1 \to p_2$$
$$-p_2$$
and the conclusion is $-p_1$.

We formulate the argument
$$(p_1 \to p_2) \& -p_2 \text{ implies } -p_1.$$

1	2	3	4	5	6	7
p_1	p_2	$-p_2$	$-p_1$	$(p_1 \to p_2)$	$(p_1 \to p_2)$ & $-p_2$	$[(p_1 \to p_2)$ & $-p_2] \to -p_1$
T	T	F	F	T	F	T
T	F	T	F	F	F	T
F	T	F	T	T	F	T
F	F	T	T	T	T	T

Fig. *1.6*

The argument is valid if and only if

$$[(p_1 \to p_2) \text{ & } -p_2] \to -p_1 \tag{1.1}$$

is a tautology.   We construct the truth table as shown in Fig. 1.6.   In columns 1 and 2 we write the truth possibilities of p_1 and p_2.   In columns 3 and 4 we write the negations of p_2 and p_1.   In column 5 we denote the truth values of $p_1 \to p_2$ for the combinations in columns 1 and 2.   Column 6 is the conjunction of columns 3 and 5.   Column 7 contains the truth values for $6 \to 4$.   Since column 7 contains all T's, (1.1) is a tautology and the argument is valid.

Notice that whenever the conjunction of the premises is true (the fourth case in column 6) the conclusion is true (third and fourth cases in column 4).   As pointed out at the beginning of this section, this is an alternative method for determining the validity of an argument.

Since an argument is valid only if the resultant conditional is a tautology, it will be shown invalid if the conditional fails to be true in at least one case.   It is sometimes possible to find the case without constructing the entire truth table.

Example 1.14.   Show that the following is invalid:

If I buy stocks, I will lose money.   Therefore, if I lose money, I buy stocks.

Solution.   Let

s denote "I buy stocks."
m denote "I lose money."

The argument is therefore

$$(s \to m) \to (m \to s)$$

The argument is invalid because, if s is false and m is true, then

$s \to m$ will be true,

but $m \to s$ will be false,

by the table for the conditional.

Therefore, I will have a true statement $(s \to m)$ implying a false statement $(m \to s)$ which is false. Therefore $(s \to m) \to (m \to s)$ is not a tautology.

Evidently, whether or not a conditional is a tautology depends on its form and not on its subject matter. Therefore, the more tautological forms we know, the easier it will be to "spot" a valid argument. We therefore note a number of important forms of valid arguments. The student, by constructing truth tables, should check to see that the following six conditions are indeed tautologies:

$$-(-p), \text{ therefore } p \tag{1.2}$$

$$\left.\begin{array}{l} p \ \& \ q, \text{ therefore } -(-p \lor -q) \\ p \lor q, \text{ therefore } -(-p \ \& \ -q) \end{array}\right\} \text{ De Morgan's laws} \qquad \begin{array}{l} (1.3a) \\ (1.3b) \end{array}$$

$$(p \to q) \ \& \ p, \text{ therefore } q \tag{1.4}$$

$$(p \to q) \ \& \ -q, \text{ therefore } -p \tag{1.5}$$

$$(p \to q) \ \& \ (q \to r), \text{ therefore } (p \to r) \tag{1.6}$$

$$(p \lor q) \ \& \ -p, \text{ therefore } q \tag{1.7}$$

The following illustrate the valid-argument forms of (1.4) to (1.7), respectively:

Equation (1.4). Farm income will increase if farm prices rise. Farm prices are rising. Therefore, farm income will increase.

Equation (1.5). If national income is high, personal-income-tax collections are high. Tax receipts are low this year; therefore national income must be low.

Equation (1.6). If business investment increases, then national income rises. When national income rises, personal saving increases. Therefore, an increase in business investment will result in higher personal savings.

Equation (1.7). Either England must radically reorganize the Commonwealth trading system or prepare to join the Common Market. She is not at all concerned with Commonwealth reorganization; therefore, she is preparing to join the Common Market.

1.6 CONTRAPOSITIVE

Sometimes another form of the conditional helps to decide whether an argument is valid or invalid. The following tautology is a valid-inference form:

$$p \to q \text{ is logically equivalent to } -q \to -p \tag{1.8}$$

$-q \to -p$ is called the *contrapositive* of $p \to q$. The student should study the results of Prob. 9 of Problem Set 1.3.

Example 1.15.   Write the contrapositive of

   If prices do not rise, ·inflation will be controlled.

   Let

   p denote "Prices do rise."
   q denote "Inflation will be controlled."

The conditional is then $-p \rightarrow q$, and the contrapositive is $-q \rightarrow -(-p)$. Note the double negative. Since $-(-p)$ is logically equivalent to p, we can rewrite the contrapositive as $-q \rightarrow p$, which reads "If inflation is not controlled, prices will rise."

PROBLEM SET 1.4

In each problem (1) symbolize the argument; (2) decide whether or not the argument is valid either by reference to the valid forms (1.2) to (1.8), or by constructing a truth table. Where necessary, use (1.8) to put the argument into one of the forms (1.5) to (1.7).

1. Consumers buy more at higher incomes and less at higher prices. It is therefore false that they buy less at higher prices and more at higher incomes.

2. Either income taxes go up, or new excise taxes must be levied. Therefore income taxes cannot fail to increase and no new excise taxes levied.

3. If investments fail to increase per period, then income will decline several periods later. But investments are higher this period than last. Therefore no new decline is indicated.

4. If any industry is organized monopolistically to maximize group profits, then the individual firm will set its prices so that, over time, they will show a fixed relationship to those of other firms. But the facts are that prices charged by individual firms seldom show the same relationship from one month to the next. Therefore, the industry is not organized monopolistically to maximize profits.

5. If a country is poor, it cannot devote much of its income to technological development. Moreover, if a country cannot devote much of its income to technological development, its income will not change. Therefore, if a country is poor, it will not have any income change.

6. If United States exports do *not* increase faster than United States imports, then the gold flow to the rest of the world will continue. The gold flow stops. Thus exports have increased faster than imports.

7. What is the contrapositive of

   If property taxes are not lessened, then real-estate values will fall.

8. Banks hold cash reserves against their demand deposits or carry deposits at other banks in case of crisis. It is true therefore that a bank cannot have neither a cash reserve nor a deposit elsewhere.

9. If income increases, consumers' buying increases. When consumers buy more, businessmen invest more. Therefore, increase in income depends upon increase in investment.

10. What, if any, conclusion can be validly obtained from the following? Either taxes are equitable, or there is political discontent. There is no political discontent.

1.7 ADMINISTRATIVE ORGANIZATIONAL PATTERNS

The theory of compound statements may be used for the solution of problems other than those of logic and mathematics.   We now outline its application to administrative structural problems.   An administrative structure is an arrangement of paths of communication from the top administrator to the worker.   If a path of communication is open, then communication can result; if it is closed, no communication is possible.

Clearly, the simplest administrative structure consists of one administrator and one worker.   In this case there is a single path of communication.   We shall let "p is true" mean that the path is open and "p is false" that the path is closed.

Now, if we call the top administrator the president, let us suppose that there is one vice-president through whom the worker must communicate with the president.   We denote this in Fig. 1.7.   Let

p denote "The path from p to $v.p.$ is open."
q denote "The path from $v.p.$ to w is open."

For the worker to be able to communicate, p and q must both be true.   This administrative setup can be represented by $p \& q$.   In this case the worker can communicate only with the vice-president, who then can pass on the communication to the president.   If we want to allow for direct communication between the president and the worker, we can symbolize the situation as shown in Fig. 1.8.

We now add another letter r to designate "The path directly from p to w is open," and the new structure can be symbolized as

$$r \vee (p \& q) \text{ is true}$$

Notice that, if $r \vee (p \& q)$ is false, then $-r \& -(p \& q)$ is true (see Prob. 2*b* in Problem Set 1.2 and discussion on pages 7 and 8).   This is logically equivalent to $-r \& (-p \vee -q)$, that is, "The path from p to w is closed,

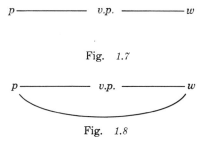

p——————— $v.p.$ —————————w

Fig.   *1.7*

Fig.   *1.8*

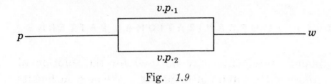

Fig. *1.9*

and either the path from p to $v.p.$ is closed or the path from $v.p.$ to w is closed or both are closed." Also note (see Prob. 5d in Problem Set 1.2) that $-r \mathrel{\&} (-p \lor -q) \leftrightarrow (-r \mathrel{\&} -p) \lor (-r \mathrel{\&} -q)$.

Therefore, to denote a breakdown in communication between p and w, we could write $-(p \mathrel{\&} q) \mathrel{\&} -r$ or $(-p \mathrel{\&} -r) \lor (-q \mathrel{\&} -r)$.

We shall now assume that no direct communication between p and w is desired and that the organizational structure involves two vice-presidents, each coordinate in authority with the other. Figure 1.9 is the structure diagram.

If we let

p_1 denote "The path from p to $v.p._1$ is open,"
p_2 denote "The path from p to $v.p._2$ is open,"
q_1 denote "The path from $v.p._1$ to w is open,"
q_2 denote "The path from $v.p._2$ to w is open,"

then the structure may be written as

$$(p_1 \mathrel{\&} q_1) \lor (p_2 \mathrel{\&} q_2)$$

i.e., communication between p and w is possible either through $v.p._1$ or through $v.p._2$.

PROBLEM SET 1.5

1. In Fig. 1.7, list the conditions under which no communication is possible. (*Hint:* When is $p \mathrel{\&} q$ false?)
2. In Fig. 1.9, list the conditions under which communication will be possible and when it will not be possible. (*Hint:* Construct a truth table from the expression representing Fig. 1.9.)
3. Represent the administrative structure given in Fig. 1.10.
4. Construct another application of the theory of compound statements.

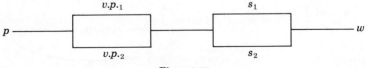

Fig. *1.10*

5. Interpret in terms of Fig. 1.8:
   a. $p \mathbin{\&} q \rightarrow p$
   b. $[(p \rightarrow q) \mathbin{\&} (q \rightarrow r)] \rightarrow (p \rightarrow r)$
   c. De Morgan's laws
   d. $(p \rightarrow q) \rightarrow (-p \vee q)$

1.8 A LOGICAL MODEL FOR A PROBLEM IN PRODUCTION MANAGEMENT[1]

In this section we shall show how the concepts we have studied can be applied to problems involving a changeover in production methods.

A chemical manufacturer produces a product which has three major ingredients. For a number of years he has been producing these ingredients from the same three basic materials. He now wishes to analyze the result of changing his methods of manufacture in order to use other, more recently developed materials. He is interested in improvement of quality and reduction of costs.

His research staff reports that there are four newly developed materials that he can use for ingredient 1, five for ingredient 2, and four for ingredient 3.

We shall assume the materials for each element to be numbered beginning with the number 1. So, for ingredient 1, we have materials 1, 2, 3, 4; for ingredient 2, materials 1, 2, 3, 4, 5; and for ingredient 3, materials 1, 2, 3, 4. There are therefore a total of 13 materials for the three ingredients. We shall use the symbol $x_{i,j}$, where i designates the ingredient and j the material, to denote the 13 materials. For example, $x_{2,1}$ denotes material 1 that can be used for ingredient 2. Evidently i and j are integers such that $1 \leq i \leq 3$ and $1 \leq j \leq 5$. Of course, the expression $x_{i,j}$ can be the same element as $x_{k,j}$ $(i \neq k)$; that is, the same material may be used for two different ingredients. There are, however, certain limitations upon the use of these materials.

Condition 1. One and only one material can be used from each group for each ingredient.

We wish to represent this condition as a compound statement.

Let $P_i(x_{i,j})$ denote the sentence "Ingredient i is produced from material $x_{i,j}$." For example, $P_2(x_{2,3})$ states that ingredient 2 is produced with the third material in that group of materials which can be used to produce ingredient 2.

If we use exclusive alternation, represented by $\underline{\vee}$, then we can write

---

[1] This section may be omitted on first reading. Cf. L. O. Kattsoff and A. J. Simone, A Logical Model for a Problem in Production Management, *APICS* (American Production and Inventory Control Society) *Quart. Bull.*, vol. 6, no. 2, 1965.

for ingredients 1, 2, and 3, respectively, three compound statements,

(a) $\qquad P_1(x_{1,1}) \vee P_1(x_{1,2}) \vee P_1(x_{1,3}) \vee P_1(x_{1,4})$

(b) $\qquad P_2(x_{2,1}) \vee P_2(x_{2,2}) \vee P_2(x_{2,3}) \vee P_2(x_{2,4}) \vee P_2(x_{2,5})$

(c) $\qquad P_3(x_{3,1}) \vee P_3(x_{3,2}) \vee P_3(x_{3,3}) \vee P_3(x_{3,4})$

The first condition is the conjunction of these three statements,

$$[P_1(x_{1,1}) \vee \cdots \vee P_1(x_{1,4})] \,\&\, [P_2(x_{2,1}) \vee \cdots \vee P_2(x_{2,5})]$$
$$\&\, [P_3(x_{3,1}) \vee \cdots \vee P_3(x_{3,4})] \quad (1.9)$$

All possible combinations of materials are summarized in this compound statement. For example, $P_1(x_{1,1}) \,\&\, P_2(x_{2,1}) \,\&\, P_3(x_{3,1})$ could be used to describe the materials employed. There are 80 acceptable combinations of materials from which to choose under condition 1. (We shall show how to compute this number in a later chapter.) The truth table would contain $2^{13} = 8,192$ rows. (Why?)

Research on the materials discloses that, because of electrical, chemical, mechanical, or other physical properties, certain materials are incompatible—i.e., if one of these is used for ingredient 1, for example, certain of the materials for ingredients 2 and 3 cannot be used. This second set of conditions is summarized below. We shall use the shilling bar (/) as a symbol to denote "is incompatible with," this being a symmetrical relation.

Condition 2

$P_1(x_{1,1})/P_2(x_{2,1})$ $\qquad$ $P_1(x_{1,1})/P_3(x_{3,1})$

$P_1(x_{1,1})/P_2(x_{2,2})$ $\qquad$ $P_1(x_{1,1})/P_3(x_{3,2})$

$\qquad\qquad\qquad\qquad\quad P_1(x_{1,1})/P_3(x_{3,3})$

$P_1(x_{1,2})/P_2(x_{2,1})$ $\qquad$ $P_1(x_{1,2})/P_3(x_{3,1})$

$P_1(x_{1,3})/P_2(x_{2,2})$ $\qquad$ $P_1(x_{1,3})/P_3(x_{3,1})$

$P_1(x_{1,3})/P_2(x_{2,3})$

$P_1(x_{1,3})/P_2(x_{2,4})$

$P_1(x_{1,3})/P_2(x_{2,5})$

$\qquad\qquad\qquad\qquad\quad P_1(x_{1,4})/P_3(x_{3,1})$

$\qquad\qquad\qquad\qquad\quad P_1(x_{1,4})/P_3(x_{3,4})$

$\qquad\qquad\qquad\qquad\qquad\qquad\quad P_2(x_{2,1})/P_3(x_{3,1})$

$\qquad\qquad\qquad\qquad\qquad\qquad\quad P_2(x_{2,1})/P_3(x_{3,2})$

$\qquad\qquad\qquad\qquad\qquad\qquad\quad P_2(x_{2,2})/P_3(x_{3,1})$

$\qquad\qquad\qquad\qquad\qquad\qquad\quad P_2(x_{2,5})/P_3(x_{3,3})$

Example 1.16. Suppose that we use $x_{1,2}$. Since $P_1(x_{1,2})/P_2(x_{2,1})$ and $P_1(x_{1,2})/P_3(x_{3,1})$, we cannot use $x_{2,1}$ and $x_{3,1}$. Therefore, let us select $x_{2,5}$ and $x_{3,2}$. This gives us the true statement $P_1(x_{1,2}) \,\&\, P_2(x_{2,5}) \,\&\, P_3(x_{3,2})$.

More generally, the statement

$$\{[P_1(x_{1,j})/P_2(x_{2,l})] \lor [P_1(x_{1,j})/P_3(x_{3,m})] \lor [P_2(x_{2,l})/P_3(x_{3,m})]\} \quad (1.10)$$

must be false (i.e., each factor must not appear under condition 2) for condition 2 to be satisfied for a given combination of three materials. Or, what is the same thing,

$$-\{[P_1(x_{1,j})/P_2(x_{2,l})] \lor [P_1(x_{1,j})/P_3(x_{3,m})] \lor [P_2(x_{2,l})/P_3(x_{3,m})]\} \quad (1.11)$$

must be true.

Condition 3 is a set of budget conditions imposed by the financial vice-president.

Condition 3. 1. No more than \$100,000 can be spent for new equipment associated with the introduction of a new material.

2. If the operating cost associated with new equipment is more than 10 per cent higher than present operating costs, the cost of the new material must be no more than 15 per cent higher than the cost of the present material.

Let $C(x_{i,j})$ represent the statement "The cost of the changeover of equipment for material $x_{i,j}$ is \$100,000 or less."

Let $R(x_{i,j})$ represent the statement "The ratio of the operating cost associated with new equipment for $x_{i,j}$ to the operating cost associated with the present equipment is 110 per cent or less."

Let $R'(x_{i,j})$ represent the statement "The ratio of the cost of the new material $x_{i,j}$ to the cost of the present material is 115 per cent or less."

For a given $x_{i,j}$ the cost conditions will be satisfied if

$$C(x_{i,j}) \ \& \ [R(x_{i,j}) \lor R'(x_{i,j})] \quad (1.12)$$

is true. In this case the symbol $\lor$ denotes ordinary alternation.

From logic (see Prob. 5*d* in Problem Set 1.2) we know that statement (1.12) is equivalent to

$$[C(x_{i,j}) \ \& \ R(x_{i,j})] \lor [C(x_{i,j}) \ \& \ R'(x_{i,j})] \quad (1.13)$$

Table 1.1 lists the relevant cost data. We see, for example, that

$$C(x_{1,4}) \text{ is true, while } C(x_{2,1}) \text{ is false.}$$
$$R(x_{1,4}) \text{ is false, while } R(x_{2,3}) \text{ is true.}$$
$$R'(x_{1,2}) \text{ is true, while } R'(x_{2,2}) \text{ is false.}$$

Note that $C(x_{2,4}) \ \& \ [R(x_{2,4}) \lor R'(x_{2,4})]$ is true since each factor is true.

The final set of conditions relates to quality requirements.

Condition 4. 1. All materials must meet quality standard Q_1.

2. All materials must meet quality standard Q_2 or Q_3.

TABLE 1.1

Material	Changeover cost	Ratio of operating cost of new equipment to present equipment, %	Ratio of new-material cost to present-material cost, %
$x_{1,1}$	\$ 81,000	89	102
$x_{1,2}$	70,000	74	111
$x_{1,3}$	105,000	109	99
$x_{1,4}$	93,000	123	87
$x_{2,1}$	101,000	119	119
$x_{2,2}$	100,000	111	144
$x_{2,3}$	93,000	106	98
$x_{2,4}$	82,000	104	104
$x_{2,5}$	98,000	100	114
$x_{3,1}$	101,000	119	106
$x_{3,2}$	72,000	109	108
$x_{3,3}$	89,000	79	104
$x_{3,4}$	121,000	121	101

Let $Q_1(x_{i,j})$ denote "$x_{i,j}$ meets quality standard Q_1," and similarly for $Q_2(x_{i,j})$ and $Q_3(x_{i,j})$. Then condition 4 is satisfied if, for a fixed i and j, the following statement is true:

$$Q_1(x_{i,j}) \mathbin{\&} [Q_2(x_{i,j}) \lor Q_3(x_{i,j})] \tag{1.14}$$

Table 1.2 indicates the result of testing for Q_1, Q_2, and Q_3. Only sentences which are true are included.

TABLE 1.2

$Q_1(x_{1,1})$	$Q_3(x_{2,1})$	$Q_2(x_{3,1})$
$Q_2(x_{1,1})$	$Q_1(x_{2,2})$	$Q_1(x_{3,2})$
$Q_3(x_{1,1})$	$Q_3(x_{2,2})$	$Q_1(x_{3,3})$
$Q_1(x_{1,2})$	$Q_1(x_{2,3})$	$Q_2(x_{3,3})$
$Q_3(x_{1,2})$	$Q_2(x_{2,3})$	$Q_2(x_{3,4})$
$Q_1(x_{1,3})$	$Q_1(x_{2,4})$	
$Q_2(x_{1,3})$	$Q_3(x_{2,4})$	
$Q_3(x_{1,3})$	$Q_1(x_{2,5})$	
$Q_1(x_{1,4})$	$Q_2(x_{2,5})$	
$Q_2(x_{1,4})$	$Q_3(x_{2,5})$	
$Q_3(x_{1,4})$		

We are now in possession of a set of conditions which enable us to select, from the 80 possible combinations, those that will be acceptable. **Example 1.17.** By Example 1.16, the combination $x_{1,2}$, $x_{2,5}$, and $x_{3,2}$ is feasible since it satisfies conditions 1 and 2. Does this combination satisfy the other conditions?

Solution. We need to decide the truth or falsity of

(a)
$$C(x_{1,2}) \& [R(x_{1,2}) \lor R'(x_{1,2})]$$
$$Q_1(x_{1,2}) \& [Q_2(x_{1,2}) \lor Q_3(x_{1,2})]$$

(b)
$$C(x_{2,5}) \& [R(x_{2,5}) \lor R'(x_{2,5})]$$
$$Q_1(x_{2,5}) \& [Q_2(x_{2,5}) \lor Q_3(x_{2,5})]$$

(c)
$$C(x_{3,2}) \& [R(x_{3,2}) \lor R'(x_{3,2})]$$
$$Q_1(x_{3,2}) \& [Q_2(x_{3,2}) \lor Q_3(x_{3,2})]$$

Equation (a). $C(x_{1,2})$ and $R(x_{1,2})$ are true from Table 1.1. Therefore, the cost condition for $x_{1,2}$ is satisfied. Also, $Q_1(x_{1,2})$ is true, and $Q_2(x_{1,2})$ is false, but $Q_3(x_{1,2})$ is true (Table 1.2). Therefore, the quality condition is also satisfied for $x_{1,2}$.

Equation (b). $C(x_{2,5})$ is true, and $R(x_{2,5})$ is true, thereby satisfying the cost condition for $x_{2,5}$. We note that $Q_1(x_{2,5})$, $Q_2(x_{2,5})$, and $Q_3(x_{2,5})$ are true, so that the quality condition is also satisfied for $x_{2,5}$.

Equation (c). $C(x_{3,2})$ and $R(x_{3,2})$ are true, and therefore the cost condition is satisfied. We note that $Q_1(x_{3,2})$ is true but $Q_2(x_{3,2})$ and $Q_3(x_{3,2})$ are false. Therefore the quality condition is not satisfied for $x_{3,2}$, and, as a result, this particular combination is not feasible.

In the present case, it turns out that only four combinations meet all four sets of conditions (see Prob. 2 of Problem Set 1.6). Accordingly, management need devote its attention only to these possibilities, determining which, if any, of these four combinations will be introduced on grounds other than those considered here.

The advantage of this procedure should be clear. A complex situation involving many individual variables and many combinations of variables, each having its own physical, cost, and performance characteristics, was systematically analyzed, the result being the straightforward determination of which combinations satisfied certain already specified physical, cost, and performance requirements.

1.9 ADDENDUM

In general, any combination of materials for which statements (1.9), (1.11), (1.12) or (1.13), and (1.14) are all true will be feasible combinations. These statements are collected below for the general case of n ingredients, each of which can be produced, respectively, by $n_1, n_2, \ldots, n_n$ materials.

$$[P_1(x_{1,1}) \lor \cdots \lor P_1(x_{1,n_1})] \& \cdots \& [P_n(x_{n,1}) \lor \cdots \lor P_n(x_{n,n_n})] \quad (1.9)$$

$$- \{[P_1(x_{1,j})/P_2(x_{2,l})] \lor \cdots \lor [P_1(x_{1,j})/P_n(x_{n,z})]$$
$$\lor [P_2(x_{2,l})/P_3(x_{3,m})] \lor \cdots \lor [P_2(x_{2,l})/P_n(x_{n,z})]$$
$$\lor \cdots \lor [P_{n-1}(x_{n-1,y})/P_n(x_{n,z})]\} \quad (1.11)$$
$$C(x_{i,j}) \ \& \ [R(x_{i,j}) \lor R'(x_{i,j})] \quad (1.12)$$
$$Q_1(x_{i,j}) \ \& \ [Q_2(x_{i,j}) \lor Q_3(x_{i,j})] \quad (1.14)$$

PROBLEM SET 1.6

1. A firm produces 11 products. In order to advertise each product more effectively, it has decided to devote its fixed advertising budget to just 9 products, completely eliminating 2 products from its product line. In deciding which products to drop, the following criteria are to be employed:

   a. If 20 per cent or less of the advertising budget is at present being spent on a product, do not consider dropping this product unless its unit profit margin is under 3 per cent and its sales revenue is under $100,000 per year. Table 1.3 summarizes these relationships.

   b. Consider dropping any product on which more than 20 per cent of the advertising budget is now being spent if either the unit profit margin is under 3 per cent or sales revenue is under $100,000 per year. Table 1.3 summarized these relationships.

   c. Since products D and E are by-products, respectively, of products A and B, do not consider dropping A and B unless D and E, respectively, also satisfy the first or second criterion.

Construct the compound statements which must be true if a product can be considered for elimination, and determine which products are involved. Indicate which criteria are not being satisfied for those products which are not considered for elimination.

TABLE 1.3

Product	Percentage of advertising budget at present expended on product	Per cent unit profit margin	Sales revenue
A	22	2	$150,000
B	5	2	50,000
C	6	1	80,000
D	3	8	101,000
E	8	2	40,000
F	10	0.5	86,000
G	3	5	110,000
H	3	10	70,000
I	21	25	186,000
J	13	1	160,000
K	6	1	96,000

2. Return to the situation discussed in the text.   Which of the following combinations are feasible?

    a. $x_{1,1}x_{2,3}x_{3,3}$

    b. $x_{1,2}x_{2,3}x_{3,3}$

    c. $x_{1,2}x_{2,4}x_{3,3}$

    d. $x_{1,3}x_{2,1}x_{3,1}$

    e. $x_{1,4}x_{2,3}x_{3,3}$

    f. $x_{1,4}x_{2,4}x_{3,3}$

    g. $x_{1,4}x_{2,5}x_{3,4}$

3. In the above problem, which conditions are being violated in those combinations which are unacceptable?

2 SETS

2.1 SETS AND THEIR ELEMENTS

Modern mathematics is based upon the concept of sets. The applications of the theory of sets are many and widespread. Indeed, business analysis is constantly analyzing sets of various kinds, from sets of data, to sets of manufactured goods, to sets of favorable outcomes of decisions. We need, therefore, to become acquainted with the basic terms and operations involved in the theory of sets.

We shall use the word *set* to denote any collection of things, and we shall demand that these things be well defined; i.e., in principle we must be able to tell whether or not a given thing is in a given set. If a thing is in a set, we shall say that it is an *element* of the set. If a denotes a thing and S the set in which a is an element, we write

$$a \, \epsilon \, S \text{ (read ``a is an element of S'')}$$

(The symbol ϵ is the lowercase Greek letter epsilon.)

In English, $a \, \epsilon \, S$ usually translates as "a is an S," for example, "IBM is a growth industry."   Here the set is the collection of growth industries (call it G), and IBM is an element in that set:

$$\text{IBM } \epsilon \, G$$

We shall use capital letters to denote sets.

Sets may be described in two ways:

1. We may list the elements of the set, writing them inside braces.

2. We may state some characteristic a thing must have to be an element in the set.

Example 2.1.

$$S = \{1,2,3,4\}$$
or
$$P = \{\text{Dwight Eisenhower, Harry Truman}\}$$

Here we list the elements of S and P.

Example 2.2. S is the set of integers between 0 and 5. We denote this as

$$S = \{x | x \text{ is between 0 and 5, and } x \text{ is an integer}\}$$

(read "S is the set of all x's such that x is an integer and is between 0 and 5")

$$P = \{x | x \text{ is a living former president of the United States}\}$$

(read "P is the set of all x's such that x is living and is a former president of the United States").

Notice that in the definition of S we replace x by integers. We call this fixed set of positive integers $\{1,2,3,4,5,6, \ . \ . \ .\}$ the *universe set* and denote it by U. The universe set, then, refers to the set of all possible elements in the group at present under study. As this group changes, so will U. For example, in the set P the universe set is the set of former presidents of the United States.

Example 2.3.   Let the universe set be the set of stocks on the New York Stock Exchange.   We define a set

$$P = \{x | x \text{ sells at a price greater than \$100}\}$$

Notice that, having stated what our universe set is to be, we do not need to state that in the definition of P.

We can also define P as follows:

$$P = \{\text{IBM, Zenith, etc., . . .}\}$$

We list all the stocks on the New York Exchange selling for more than $100.

If a is not an element of a set S, we shall write $-(a \, \epsilon \, S)$ or its equivalent $a \notin S$.

If, in principle, it is possible to list *all* the elements of a set, the set is said to be *finite;* otherwise, it is infinite.   So the sets P and S in Example 2.3 are finite sets.   But

$$N = \{x | x \text{ is a natural number}\}$$

is an infinite set because we cannot list all the elements of N.

PROBLEM SET 2.1

1.   Let the universe set be the set of positive integers.   Describe the set of positive integers less than 25, divisible by 3.

2.   Let U be the set of railroad corporations; list the elements of the set

$$B = \{x | x \text{ declared itself bankrupt in 1961}\}$$

3.   Is the set "$C = \{x | x \text{ is an industry, and } x \text{ made a profit in 1961}\}$" finite or infinite?

4.   A man is planning to invest $30,000 in stocks.   He wants a distribution among steels, electronics, and drugs.   Each is to be purchased in multiples of five.   Construct a set of possible distributions of purchases.

5.   A mail-order house is considering the listing of three products in their annual catalogue.   A product is listed if it passes a quality test administered by the mail-order house.   Describe two sets of possible outcomes of the tests.

6.   A committee of three is to be appointed from labor, management, government, and the general public.   There cannot be two representatives from any one group.   Assuming that one labor representative has been appointed, describe two possible sets satisfying the conditions for a committee.

2.2 SUBSETS

It is sometimes necessary to select those elements of a set having a special property.   For example, suppose that we consider the set of all numbers of the form p/q, where p and q are integers and q is different from zero.   These numbers are called *rational numbers*.   Suppose, further, we assume that every integer can be written as $p/1$.   Then the set of integers, say between 0 and 10, is called a *subset* of the set of rational numbers.

Definition 2.4. If all the elements of a set A are elements of a set B then A will be called a *subset* of B. We shall use the symbol $A \subseteq B$ to denote that A is a subset of B. Evidently any set is a subset of itself.

Example 2.5. Let A be the set containing as elements all *living* former presidents of the United States, and let $B = \{x|x$ is a former president of the United States$\}$. Then $A \subseteq B$.

Example 2.6. Let $B = \{x|x$ is an asset of a given corporation$\}$ and $A = \{x|x$ is a \$1,000 bond held by the corporation$\}$. Then $A \subseteq B$.

If $A \subseteq B$ means that every element in A is an element in B, then $(A \subseteq B)$ & $(B \subseteq A)$ is true if and only if A and B are the same set. We denote the fact that A and B are the same set by the symbol $A = B$.

Example 2.7. Consider the set of employees of General Electric. Let that be the universe set. We designate other sets as follows:

$$E = \{x|x \text{ is an engineer}\}$$
$$S = \{x|x \text{ is a salesman}\}$$
$$A = \{x|x \text{ is an accountant}\}$$
$$R = \{x|x \text{ is a repairman}\}$$

If we assume that all repairmen are engineers, then $R \subseteq E$. Moreover, if all salesmen are engineers, then $S \subseteq E$. If all engineers are also repairmen, then $E \subseteq R$ and that would mean that $E = R$.

We notice that, if a universe set is designated, then any subset A of elements of that universe divides the universe into two sets: the set of elements in A and the set of elements not in A. We call the set of elements of the universe U which are not in A the *complement* of A and denote it by $\bar{A}$. $\bar{A}$ is the same set as the set consisting of the elements of the universe without the elements of A. Together any set and its complement contain all the elements of the universe.

Example 2.8. Let $U = \{1,2,3\}$.

List all the subsets of U, and then indicate the complement of each subset.

Solution. Since every element of U is a subset of U, and since $U \subseteq U$, the subsets are

$$\{1,2,3\} \quad \{1\} \quad \{2\} \quad \{3\}$$
$$\{1,2\} \quad \{1,3\} \quad \{2,3\}$$

The complement of $\{1\}$ is $\{2,3\}$; of $\{2\}$ is $\{1,3\}$; of $\{3\}$ is $\{1,2\}$; of $\{2,3\}$ is $\{1\}$; of $\{1,3\}$ is $\{2\}$; of $\{1,2\}$ is $\{3\}$. This example show two things. First, if every set is to have a complement, then $\{1,2,3\}$ must also. But since $\{1,2,3\}$ contains all the elements of U, its complement cannot have any elements. A set without any elements will be called an *empty* set and will be designated by $\emptyset$ (a zero with a line through it). Second, we notice that, if A is the complement of B, then B is the complement of A.

If $A \subseteq B$ but A is not the same as B, then A will be called a *proper subset* of B.

We need to define one other set. Suppose that A is a set of elements $\{a_1, a_2, \ldots, a_n\}$. Then, if $B = \{b_1, b_2, \ldots, b_k\}$, $A - B$ (read "set A without set B") will be the set which results when we eliminate the elements of B that are in A.

Definition 2.9. $A - B = \{x | x \in A \ \& \ x \notin B\}$.

Example 2.10. Let $A = \{1,2,3,4,5,6\}$ and $U = \{x | x \text{ is a positive integer}\}$. Let $B = \{3,4,6\}$. Then $B \subseteq A$, and $A - B = \{1,2,5\}$. Notice that $A - B$ is the complement of B relative to A.

Example 2.11. Let $A = \{x | x \text{ is a Ford dealer}\}$ and $U = \{x | x \text{ is an automobile dealer}\}$. Now let $B = \{x | x \text{ is a Ford dealer and has sold over 1,000 cars}\}$.

Then $B \subseteq A$, and $A - B = \{x | x \text{ is a Ford dealer who has sold 1,000 cars or fewer}\}$.

PROBLEM SET 2.2

1. Argue for the following assertions:
   a. $\emptyset \subseteq A$ (i.e., the empty set is a subset of every set).
   b. If A, B, and C are sets such that $(A \subseteq B) \ \& \ (B \subseteq C)$, then $(A \subseteq C)$ (that is, the relation of being a subset is transitive).
   c. Every set is a subset of a universe set.

2. If $A \subseteq B$, is $B \subseteq A$? (*Hint:* Give an example to prove your reply.) Is $\bar{B} \subseteq \bar{A} = \bar{A} \subseteq \bar{B}$?

3. In Example 2.10, write $B - A$. On the basis of this, is $A - B$ equal to $B - A$?

4. Argue that the complement of the complement of a set A is the set A (that is, $\bar{\bar{A}} = A$).

5. Which of the following are true?
   a. $\emptyset \subseteq \emptyset$
   b. $\emptyset \in \emptyset$
   c. $\emptyset \subseteq U$
   d. $\emptyset = \{\emptyset\}$
   e. $\emptyset \in \{\emptyset\}$
   f. $\emptyset \subseteq \{\emptyset\}$
   g. $\emptyset \in U$
   h. $U \subseteq U$

6. Let $U = \{x | x \text{ is an American}\}$. Let $A = \{x | x \text{ is a native of New York}\}$ and $B = \{x | x \text{ is a millionaire}\}$. Write the following sets:
   a. $\bar{A}$
   b. $U - A$
   c. $A - B$
   d. $B - A$
   e. $\bar{B}$
   f. $U - \bar{B}$
   g. $U - (A - B)$

7. Let

$A = \{x|x$ is an employee of General Motors$\}$
$W = \{x|x$ is a female employee of General Motors$\}$
$M = \{x|x$ is a manager at General Motors$\}$
P denote the president of General Motors
r denote the vice-president in change of public relations

Using the ϵ and $\subseteq$, write all the relationships of which you can think. Also describe the sets $A - W$, $A - \{p\}$, $W - M$, $\bar{W}$ (if A is taken as U).

8. A company has two vice-presidents and two accountants on its payroll. A committee is to be formed from these four, consisting of two people. How many committees can be formed? (*Hint:* Construct the subsets of the set of these four people, containing two elements.)

9. A board of four members reaches its decision by a simple majority vote. What are the winning coalitions? (*Hint:* Winning coalitions are subsets of at least three elements.) What are the other coalitions?

2.3 UNION AND INTERSECTION OF SETS

It is often convenient to form new sets when two (or more) sets are given.

If A and B are sets, then the set $A \cap B$ (read "A intersection B") will be the set containing all elements common to the two sets. More formally, we have the following definition.

Definition 2.12. $A \cap B = \{x|x \epsilon A \ \& \ x \epsilon B\}$.

Example 2.13. Let $A = \{1,2,3,4,5,6\}$ and $B = \{2,3,4,5,6,7\}$. Then

$$A \cap B = \{2,3,4,5,6\}$$

Example 2.14. Suppose that $A = \{x|x$ is a member of the board of Standard Oil$\}$ and $B = \{x|x$ is a member of the board of General Motors$\}$. Then $A \cap B = \{x|x$ is a member of the board of Standard Oil *and* a member of the board of General Motors$\}$. (Where this occurs, we speak of an *interlocking directorate*.)

Evidently, if two sets have no elements in common, then their intersection is the empty set $\emptyset$.

Example 2.15. Let $A = \{x|x$ is a United States Senator$\}$ and

$$B = \{x|x \text{ is a United States representative}\}$$

Then $A \cap B = \emptyset$ since no Senator can also be a representative.

In this case $U = \{x|x$ is a United States congressman$\}$ and $U - A = B$, while $U - B = A$; so $\bar{A} = B$, relative to the set of United States congressmen.

On the other hand, if $C = \{x|x$ is a Southerner$\}$, then $A \cap C = \{x|x$ is a Southern Senator$\}$ and $B \cap C = \{x|x$ is a Southern representative$\}$.

If A and B are sets, we can form a new set whose elements are the elements of A or the elements of B. We call this the *union* of A and B and denote it by $A \cup B$.

Definition 2.16. If A and B are sets, then $A \cup B = \{x | x \, \epsilon \, A \vee x \, \epsilon \, B\}$.

The student should note that the intersection of A and B involves the conjunction of two sentences, $(x \, \epsilon \, A)$ & $(x \, \epsilon \, B)$, while the union involves the alternation of the two, $(x \, \epsilon \, A) \vee (x \, \epsilon \, B)$.

(The student should carefully distinguish between the symbol $\vee$, which connects sentences, and the symbol $\cup$, which connects sets.)

Example 2.17. Let $S = \{x | x \text{ is a negative integer}\}$, $T = \{x | x \text{ is a positive integer}\}$.

$S \cup T = \{x | x \text{ is a negative or } x \text{ is a positive integer}\}$; that is, $S \cup T$
$$= \{\ldots -5, -4, -3, -2, -1, 1, 2, 3, 4, \ldots\}.$$

Example 2.18. Let
$$S = \{x | x \text{ is a Ford sedan}\}$$
$$T = \{x | x \text{ is a Ford convertible}\}$$
$$S \cup T = \{x | x \text{ is a Ford sedan or a Ford convertible}\}$$

Example 2.19. Let

$$F = \{x | x \text{ is a fatal accident}\}$$
$$H = \{x | x \text{ is an accident at home}\}$$
$$A = \{x | x \text{ is an automobile accident}\}$$
$$F \cap H = \{x | x \text{ is a fatal accident at home}\}$$
$$F \cup H = \{x | x \text{ is a fatal accident or one that occurred at home}\}$$

What is $F \cup A$? What is $F \cap A$?

PROBLEM SET 2.3

1. Argue for the following: If A and B are sets:
   a. $A \cap B = B \cap A$
   b. $A \cup B = B \cup A$
   c. $A \cap (B \cap C) = (A \cap B) \cap C$
   d. $A \cup (B \cup C) = (A \cup B) \cup C$

2. Company Z is a multiproduct firm with sales divisions in this country and overseas. Let $A = \{x | x \text{ is a product on which the profit margin is greater than } 10\%\}$ and $B = \{x | x \text{ is a product sold overseas}\}$. What are $A \cap B$, $A \cup B$, $\bar{A} \cap B$, and $\bar{A} \cap \bar{B}$? If $A \cap B = \emptyset$, can company Z be accused of "dumping"?

3. In the above problem, if $A \cap B \neq \emptyset$ and if $A \cap \bar{B} = \emptyset$, can company Z be accused of "milking" the foreign market?

4. Suppose that we have a universe U, and let $A \subseteq U$, $B \subseteq U$, and $A \neq B$. Argue that, for every $a \, \epsilon \, U$, either $a \, \epsilon \, (A \cap B)$ or $(\bar{A} \cap B)$ or $(A \cap \bar{B})$ or $(\bar{A} \cap \bar{B})$. (Such a division of a universe set by two distinct sets is called a *classification*.) Give a concrete example of a classification of this sort.

5. In Prob. 4, which of the following are true?
   a. $A \cap B \subseteq A$
   b. $A \cap B \subseteq B$

c. $A \cap \bar{B} \subseteq A$

d. $A \cap \bar{B} \subseteq B$

e. $\bar{A} \cap B \subseteq A$

f. $\bar{A} \cap B \subseteq B$

g. $\bar{A} \cap \bar{B} \subseteq \bar{A}$

h. $\bar{A} \cap \bar{B} \subseteq A$

6. Let $U = \{x|x$ is a stock listed on the New York Stock Exchange$\}$. Let

$$I = \{x|(x \in U) \ \& \ (x \text{ is an industrial stock})\}$$
$$R = \{x|(x \in U) \ \& \ (x \text{ is a rail stock})\}$$
$$U = \{x|(x \in U) \ \& \ (x \text{ is a utility stock})\}$$

Form the classification of the stocks in U. (*Hint:* The subsets are $I \cap \bar{R} \cap \bar{U}$, $I \cap R \cap U$, etc.)   Which will be empty subsets?   If a stock is in one subset, can it be in any other?

7. In Prob. 6, form the union of the three sets, I, R, and U.

8. Let $S = \{x|x$ is an integer between 5 and 25$\}$ and $T = \{x|x$ is an integer between 7 and 15$\}$. Form $S \cap T$ and $S \cup T$.   If $U = \{x|x$ is a positive integer$\}$, find $\bar{S} \cup T$, $\bar{S} \cup \bar{T}$, $S \cup \bar{T}$.

9. The gross national product of a country is divided into the categories consumption, investment, and government.   What subsets would define the private (i.e., nongovernment) part of the gross national product?

10. Export industries include automobile, agriculture, and machines.   Domestic consumer industries include automobiles, agriculture, and clothing.   Domestic investment industries include steel, construction, and machinery.   Write each group of industries in set notation.   What is the universe set?   If E denotes the set of export industries, C the set of consumer industries, and I the set of investment industries, define

$$E \cap I, E \cup I, E \cup \bar{C}, \quad (E \cap I) \cup (\bar{E} \cap I)$$

2.4 VENN DIAGRAMS

Pictures often help visualize abstract concepts.   Venn diagrams are particularly helpful in the present discussion.   We use a rectangle to illustrate the universe set, and for each set under consideration we draw a circle inside the rectangle.   We make the circles overlap in order to achieve a classification.   In each case the points inside the rectangle or the circles represent the elements of the set.   We say that the set of points is equivalent to the given set.

The Venn diagram for a set P is shown in Fig. 2.1.   All points outside the circle P are in $\bar{P}$.

The Venn diagram for two sets P and Q is shown in Fig. 2.2.   Clearly two sets divide the universe into four regions, as indicated in the diagram. If we desire to indicate a particular region for special consideration we crosshatch that region.

Figure 2.3 shows the region $P \cap Q$ and Fig. 2.4 region $P \cup Q$.   Figure 2.5 is the Venn diagram for three sets P, Q, and R.

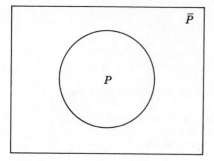

Fig. *2.1*

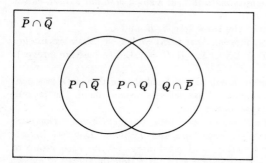

Fig. *2.2*

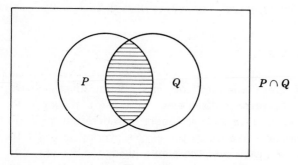

Fig. *2.3*

Example 2.20.   Draw a Venn diagram for the set denoted by $P \cap (Q \cup R)$, where P, Q, and R are sets.

Solution.   Draw a rectangle with three circles interlocking as in Fig. 2.5.   Crosshatch the area $(Q \cup R)$ first, since the parentheses indicate this to be a unit, using horizontal lines.   Now use vertical lines to crosshatch the intersection of $(Q \cup R)$ with P.   The resulting area shown in Fig. 2.6 contains both horizontal and vertical lines.   The areas so hatched are $(P \cap Q)$ and $(P \cap R)$.   Therefore we denote this area by $(P \cap Q) \cup (P \cap R)$ (Fig. 2.6).   This may be used as a demonstration that $P \cap$

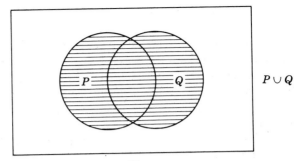

Fig. 2.4

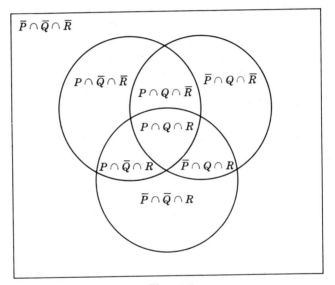

Fig. 2.5

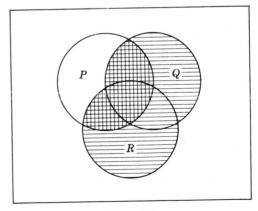

Fig. 2.6

$(Q \cup R) = (P \cap Q) \cup (P \cap R)$ since the two expressions denote the same region in the Venn diagram.

When we are concerned with sets, it is often necessary to designate specifically whether or not a set is empty. We adopt the following rules:

If a set is empty, we shall write the symbol $\emptyset$ in the region in the Venn diagram corresponding to the set.

If no mark is in a region, it is not known whether the set is empty or nonempty.

These conventions enable us to draw Venn diagrams for four very important types of statements:

1. All s is p (in set terminology $S \subseteq P$ or $S \cap \bar{P} = \emptyset$).
2. Some s is p (in set terminology $S \cap P \neq \emptyset$).
3. No s is p (in set terminology $S \cap \bar{P}$ or $S \cap P = \emptyset$).
4. Some s is not p (in set terminology $S \cap \bar{P} \neq \emptyset$).

We shall draw Venn diagrams for each type of statement (see Figs. 2.7, 2.8, 2.9, and 2.10, respectively).

Notice that the area $\bar{S} \cap P$ has no symbol in it since $S \subseteq P$ does not entail that $\bar{S} \cap P$ is either empty or nonempty.

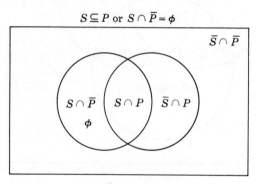

Fig. *2.7*

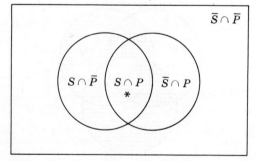

Fig. *2.8*

$$S \cap P = \phi$$

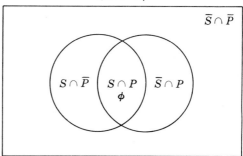

Fig. *2.9*

$$S \cap \bar{P} \neq \phi$$

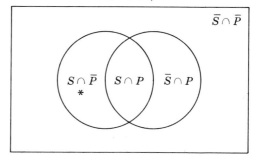

Fig. *2.10*

If a region has either Ø or an asterisk (*) in it, we omit the cross-hatching.

Example 2.21. Draw the Venn diagram representing the following two statements:

1. All stockholders vote.
2. Some officers are stockholders.

Solution. Let

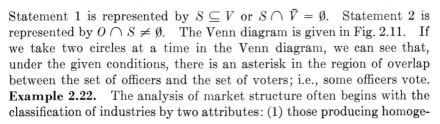

$$S = \{x|x \text{ is a stockholder}\}$$
$$V = \{x|x \text{ is a voter}\}$$
$$O = \{x|x \text{ is an officer}\}$$

Statement 1 is represented by $S \subseteq V$ or $S \cap \bar{V} = \emptyset$. Statement 2 is represented by $O \cap S \neq \emptyset$. The Venn diagram is given in Fig. 2.11. If we take two circles at a time in the Venn diagram, we can see that, under the given conditions, there is an asterisk in the region of overlap between the set of officers and the set of voters; i.e., some officers vote.

Example 2.22. The analysis of market structure often begins with the classification of industries by two attributes: (1) those producing homoge-

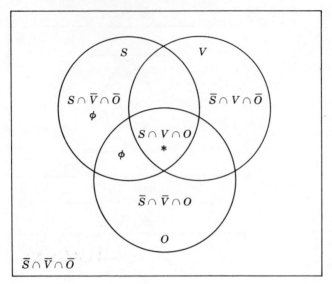

Fig. *2.11*

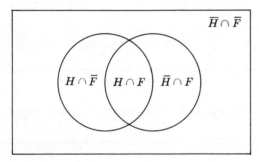

Fig. *2.12*

neous products, e.g., steel, as contrasted with those producing nonhomogeneous products, e.g., automobiles; and (2) those producing products manufactured by only a few companies, and those producing products made by many companies. Denote the set of industries producing homogeneous products by H and the set of industries in which there are a few producers by F. Draw a Venn diagram, and identify the regions.

Solution. See Fig. 2.12. Special names are given to the regions:

1. A pure oligopoly $\epsilon\ H \cap F$.
2. A differentiated oligopoly $\epsilon\ \bar{H} \cap F$.
3. A monopolistically competitive industry $\epsilon\ \bar{H} \cap \bar{F}$.
4. A perfectly competitive industry $\epsilon\ H \cap \bar{F}$.

(The student should translate each region into words.)

Example 2.23. A union has the following rules:

1. The financial committee shall be chosen from the executive committee.

2. Everyone who is on both the executive and the appropriations committee must be on the financial committee.

3. No member of the appropriations committee shall be on the financial committee.

Simplifying these rules,

$$F = \{x|x \text{ is a member of the financial committee}\}$$
$$E = \{x|x \text{ is a member of the executive committee}\}$$
$$A = \{x|x \text{ is a member of the appropriations committee}\}$$

Rule 1 states that $F \cap \bar{E} = \emptyset$.

Rule 2 states that $E \cap A \cap \bar{F} = \emptyset$.

Rule 3 states that $A \cap F = \emptyset$.

We put these rules on a Venn diagram (Fig. 2.13). All hatched-out areas are empty sets. We note that the three rules are equivalent to two.

Rule 1: $$F \cap \bar{E} = \emptyset$$

All members of the financial committee are on the executive committee.

Rule 2: $$E \cap A = \emptyset$$

No member of the executive committee is on the appropriations committee. Part of $F \cap E$ is empty. But the part of $F \cap E$ that is empty is also A.

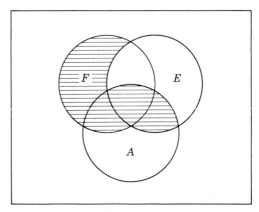

Fig. *2.13*

PROBLEM SET 2.4

1. Draw Venn diagrams for the following pairs of sets:
   a. $\bar{P} \cap \bar{Q}, P \cap Q$
   b. $\bar{P} \cap \bar{Q}, \overline{P \cup Q}$
   c. $\bar{P} \cup \bar{Q}, \overline{P \cap Q}$
   d. $P \subseteq Q, Q \subseteq P$
   e. $P \cup (Q \cup R), (P \cup Q) \cup R$
   f. $P \subseteq Q, Q \subseteq \bar{P}$
   g. $\overline{P \cap Q}, \bar{P} \cup Q$
   h. $(P \cap Q) \cup (P \cap R), P \cup (Q \cap R)$
   i. $P \cap \bar{P}, P \cup P$
   j. $P \cap U, P \cup U$
2. Draw Venn diagrams for
   a. Some businessmen are not lawyers.
   b. No member of the board is a member of the labor union.
3. Compare the Venn diagrams for "All s is p" and "Some s is not p." What can you conclude from this about statements of this form with the same subject and predicate?

2.5 FUNDAMENTAL LAWS OF SETS

We state some of the fundamental laws of set operation. Venn diagrams will illustrate that they are laws. The student should carefully compare these laws for set operations with the analogous tautologies in Problem Set 1.2. Wherever needed, Venn diagrams should be drawn. P, Q, and R will denote sets.

The commutative laws:

$$ (a) \qquad P \cap Q = Q \cap P $$
$$ (b) \qquad P \cup Q = Q \cup P \tag{2.1} $$

The associative laws:

$$ (a) \qquad P \cap (Q \cap R) = (P \cap Q) \cap R $$
$$ (b) \qquad P \cup (Q \cup R) = (P \cup Q) \cup R \tag{2.2} $$

The distributive laws:

$$ (a) \qquad P \cap (Q \cup R) = (P \cap Q) \cup (P \cap R) $$
$$ (b) \qquad P \cup (Q \cap R) = (P \cup Q) \cap (P \cup R) \tag{2.3} $$

The laws of tautology:

$$ (a) \qquad P \cap P = P $$
$$ (b) \qquad P \cup P = P \tag{2.4} $$

Laws of absorption:

(a)
$$P \cap (P \cup Q) = P$$
(b)
$$P \cup (P \cap Q) = P$$

(2.5)

Laws of complementation:

(a)
$$P \cap \bar{P} = \emptyset$$
(b)
$$P \cup \bar{P} = U$$

(2.6)

Law of double complementation:

$$(\bar{\bar{P}}) = P$$

(2.7)

De Morgan's laws:

(a)
$$\overline{(P \cap Q)} = \bar{P} \cup \bar{Q}$$
(b)
$$\overline{(P \cup Q)} = \bar{P} \cap \bar{Q}$$

(2.8)

Laws of $\emptyset$ and U:

(a)
$$\emptyset \cap P = \emptyset$$
(b)
$$U \cup P = U$$
(c)
$$U \cap P = P$$
(d)
$$\emptyset \cup P = P$$
(e)
$$\bar{\emptyset} = U$$
(f)
$$\bar{U} = \emptyset$$

(2.9)

The student should recognize that all these laws hold if we interpret P, Q, and R as statements rather than as sets and if we replace $\bar{P}$ by $-P$, $P \cup Q$ by $p \vee q$, $P \cap Q$ by $p \,\&\, q$, $\emptyset$ by contradiction.

These laws can be used to expand or simplify expressions, just as in ordinary algebra.

Example 2.24.   Expand $(P \cup Q) \cap (\bar{P} \cup R)$.

Solution.   If we let $P \cup Q$ be replaced by some letter (say, A), we know that A is a set since $P \cup Q$ is.   Then we have

$$A \cap (\bar{P} \cup R) = (A \cap \bar{P}) \cup (A \cap R)$$

by (2.3a).   Replacing A by $P \cup Q$ on the right, we obtain

$$[(P \cup Q) \cap \bar{P}] \cup [(P \cup Q) \cap R]$$
$$= [\bar{P} \cap (P \cup Q)] \cup [R \cap (P \cup Q)]$$
$$= [(\bar{P} \cap P) \cup (\bar{P} \cap Q)] \cup [(R \cap P) \cup (R \cap Q)]$$
$$= [\emptyset \cup (\bar{P} \cap Q)] \cup [(R \cap P) \cup (R \cap Q)]$$
$$= (\bar{P} \cap Q) \cup (R \cap P) \cup (R \cap Q)$$

Example 2.25.   Simplify $P \cup (\bar{P} \cap Q)$.

Solution. $P \cup (\bar{P} \cap Q) = (P \cup \bar{P}) \cap (P \cup Q)$ by (2.3b), but

$$P \cup \bar{P} = U$$

Therefore

$$P \cup (\bar{P} \cap Q) = U \cap (P \cup Q) \qquad \text{by (2.6b)}$$
$$= P \cup Q \qquad \text{by (2.9c)}$$

Example 2.26. Simplify (a) $\overline{A \cap B} \cup B$; (b) $\overline{A \cap \bar{B}} \cup B$.

(a) $\overline{A \cap B} \cup B = (\bar{A} \cup \bar{B}) \cup B = \bar{A} \cup (\bar{B} \cup B)$
$$= \bar{A} \cup U = U$$

(b) $\overline{A \cap \bar{B}} \cup B = (\bar{A} \cup B) \cup B = \bar{A} \cup (B \cup B)$
$$= \bar{A} \cup B$$

PROBLEM SET 2.5

1. Draw Venn diagrams for the laws of absorption.
2. Translate the distribution laws into the language of statements.
3. Show by Venn diagrams that

$$(\bar{A} \cap B) \cup (A \cap \bar{B}) = \emptyset \qquad \text{and} \qquad A = B$$

are equivalent expressions. [*Hint:* After indicating the condition $(\bar{A} \cap B) \cup (A \cap \bar{B}) = \emptyset$, what parts of A and B are left?]
4. Simplify:
    a. $(A \cap B) \cup (A \cap \bar{B})$
    b. $[A \cup (\bar{B} \cap A)] \cap [A \cup (B \cap C)]$
    c. $(A \cap C) \cup (A \cap B \cap C) \cup (A \cup C)$
    d. $(A \cup B) \cap (\bar{A} \cup B)$
5. Show by Venn diagrams that

$$(A \subseteq B) \, \& \, (B \subseteq C) \rightarrow (A \subseteq C)$$

(*Hint:* Indicate the two conditions on a Venn diagram, and then show that the resulting diagram $A \subseteq C$.)
6. Show by Venn diagrams that the conclusion of the following argument is valid (i.e., that, when the premises are true, the conclusions must be true).

> All stockholders vote.
> No one who is an officer votes.
> Therefore no stockholder is an officer.

(*Hint:* Change the statements to appropriate set-operation expressions, indicate the premises on the same Venn diagram, and see whether or not conclusion is true.)

2.6 A SET MODEL FOR A PROBLEM IN TRADE

An elementary example of how these concepts can be applied is now given. The student should study the example carefully.

Example 2.27. International trade or trade between regions of a country results when two or more countries or regions are differently endowed with the factors of production (viz., labor, land, and capital) and when they require the various commodities that result from the different combinations of these factors. For example, a country with large amounts of land and little labor and capital, producing wheat as a result, may need machinery produced by another country having the relatively little land and greater amount of labor and capital needed for the production of machinery.

Let us make the following assumptions:

1. A country C_1 will export commodities whose production requires its abundant factors.

2. A country C_2 will import commodities which it wants but which require factors of production it lacks.

3. Imports must be paid for by exports.

Write, using set notation, the conditions necessary for trade to occur.

Solution. Let

$A = \{x|x$ is a country with relatively large quantities of labor and capital and little of land$\}$

$B = \{x|x$ is a country with relatively little labor and capital and large quantities of land$\}$

$X = \{x|x$ is a country desiring commodities requiring little labor and much land$\}$

$Y = \{x|x$ is a country desiring commodities requiring much labor and capital and little land$\}$

Trade will therefore take place between the elements of $(A \cap \bar{B}) \cap (A \cap X)$ and the elements of $(B \cap \bar{A}) \cap (B \cap Y)$.

But

$$(A \cap \bar{B}) \cap (A \cap X) = A \cap \bar{B} \cap X \qquad (2.10)$$
$$(B \cap \bar{A}) \cap (B \cap Y) = B \cap \bar{A} \cap Y \qquad (2.11)$$

PROBLEM SET 2.6

1. Describe two countries between which trade will not take place.
2. Would there be any country in the intersection of Eqs. (2.10) and (2.11)?
3. Describe a country in
   a. $\bar{A} \cap B \cap Y$
   b. $A \cap \bar{B} \cap X$
4. Name a country that is an element of (a) and (b) above.
5. Can you construct an example like Example 2.27, indicating conditions under which one country might declare war on another?

2.7 PARTITIONS OF A SET

In later chapters it will be necessary to divide a given set into a number of subsets such that each and every element in the given set will belong to one and only one of the subsets. We therefore give the following definition.

Definition 2.28.   Given two sets

$$B = \{b_1, b_2, \ldots, b_r\} \quad \text{and} \quad A = \{A_1, A_2, \ldots, A_n\}$$

(note that A is a set of sets), A is a partition of B if and only if

(a) $A_i \subseteq B$ $i = 1, 2, \ldots, n$

(b) $A_i \cap A_j = \emptyset$ $i = 1, 2, \ldots, n;$
                                      $j = 1, 2, \ldots, n; i \neq j$

(c) $A_1 \cup A_2 \cup \cdots \cup A_n = B$

Thus, a partition of a set B is a set of subsets of B that are disjoint or mutually exclusive and exhaustive. Every element of B is a member of one and only one of the subsets of A.

Example 2.29.   List three partitions of the set B of 52 playing cards.

Solution.   Let A_1, A_2, A_3, and A_4 be the subsets which are, respectively, clubs, diamonds, hearts, and spades. Then

$$A = \{A_1, A_2, A_3, A_4\}$$

is a partition of the set of 52 playing cards.
Let

$$C_2, C_3, C_4, C_5, \ldots, C_{10}, C_J, C_Q, C_K, C_A$$

be the subsets which are, respectively, twos, threes, fours, fives, . . . , tens, jacks, queens, kings, and aces. Then

$$C = \{C_2, C_3, C_4, C_5, \ldots, C_{10}, C_J, C_Q, C_K, C_A\}$$

is a partition of B. Finally, let D_1, D_2, and D_3 be the subsets which have, respectively, a face value ≥ 2 but < 8, ≥ 8 but $<$ jack, and $\geq$ jack but $\leq$ ace. Then $D = \{D_1, D_2, D_3\}$ is a partition of B.

Example 2.30.   The set of products produced by company Z is given by

$$P = \{c_1, c_2, c_3, f_1, f_2, r_1, r_2, r_3, r_4\}$$

the products designated by the letter c being produced by the chemical division, f by the fibers division, and r by the rubber division. Last year the company made a profit on all products except c_1 and r_2. List two partitions of P.

Solution. Let C, F, and R be the subsets which are produced, respectively, by the chemical, fibers, and rubber divisions. Then $X_1 = \{C,F,R\}$ is a partition of P. Let M and N be the subsets which earned a profit and which did not earn a profit, respectively. Then $X_2 = \{M,N\}$ is a partition of P, with $M = \{c_2,c_3,f_1,f_2,r_1,r_3,r_4\}$ and $N = \{c_1,r_2\}$.

PROBLEM SET 2.7

1. A management consultant has constructed a sales-forecasting model for company Z. Applying this model to the past 48 months, the consultant is able to generate a set of 48 errors, each element of which is defined as the algebraic difference between actual sales and sales as forecast from his model. How many partitions of this set of errors can you list? (*Hint:* There are $+$, $-$, and 0 errors; errors associated with turning points; large, moderate, and negligible errors; errors which appear correlated with time and those which appear to be completely random, etc.)

2. If $A = \{A_1,A_2, \ldots ,A_m\}$ and $C = \{C_1,C_2, \ldots ,C_n\}$ are two partitions of the same set B, we can obtain a new partition, called a *cross partition* of A and C, by listing all subsets of B of the form $A_i \cap C_j$ ($i = 1, 2, \ldots , m; j = 1, 2, \ldots , n$). Cross partitions can be employed to classify elements and sets of elements. Consider Example 2.30. $X_1 = \{C,F,R\}$ and $X_2 = \{M,N\}$ are two partitions of P. The cross partition of X_1 and X_2 is $X_3 = \{C \cap M, C \cap N, F \cap M, F \cap N, R \cap M, R \cap N\}$. Verbally describe how X_3 gives a complete classification of company Z's products according to their source of production and to their profitability.

3. In Example 2.29, describe the cross partition $A_i \cap C_j$ ($i = 1, 2, 3, 4; j = 2, 3, \ldots , 10$, jack, queen, king, ace).

3 COUNTING—PERMUTATIONS AND COMBINATIONS

3.1 NUMBER OF SUBSETS OF A SET

We defined a subset S of a set T ($S \subset T$) as a set whose elements were elements of T. Is it possible to calculate how many distinct subsets can be formed from a set T if we know that T has n elements? Suppose that we try to calculate the number of subsets of a set of three elements, $T = \{a,b,c\}$. No subset can have more than three elements, although we can have subsets of zero, one, or two elements. Consider the element a. There are two possibilities for a. Either it can be in a given subset or not. The same thing is true of the element b: it can be in a subset or not. If a is in a subset, b can be in that subset or not; and if a is not in the subset, b can be in that subset or not.   Thus, for a and b, we have the following $2^2 = 4$ possibilities:

a in the subset, b not in the subset
a in the subset, b in the subset
a not in the subset, b not in the subset
a not in the subset, b in the subset

We still need to take c into account.   For each of the four possibilities there are two additional ones: c may be in the subset or not.   This gives a total of 2^3 subsets.

We will now prove the following theorem:

Theorem 3.1

If T is a set of n elements, then there are 2^n subsets of T.

Proof.   Let $T = \{a_1, a_2, a_3, \ldots, a_n\}$, where the subscripts are used only to identify the elements.   Consider any element a_i; if a_i is an element of a subset, we shall denote this by 1, if not by 0.

The numbers 1 and 0 are used to designate the fact that a given element is in a subset or not.   So if we have two elements, then the "number" 11 designates that both are in a given subset.   We have the following possible numbers:

$$00 \quad 01 \quad 10 \quad 11$$

For three elements we have the possibilities

$$000 \quad 001 \quad 010 \quad 011$$
$$100 \quad 101 \quad 110 \quad 111$$

Each number tells us which elements of the given set T are contained in each of the possible subsets.   So 101 denotes the subset containing the first and third elements of T, but not the second.   The number 000 represents the empty set, while 111 represents the set T itself.

For a set T of n elements, the number of n-place such numbers consisting of 0's and 1's will give us the number of subsets of T.   Since for each of the n places we have two possibilities, we have

$$2 \times 2 \times \cdots \times 2 = 2^n \text{ possibilities}$$

For example, the number $000 \cdots 0$ (to n places) designates the empty set, while the number $01000 \cdots 0$ (to n places) designates the subset containing one element of T, namely, the second one.

Example 3.2.   1. How many subsets does $T = \{a, b, c, d, e, f\}$ have?
2. What subset is denoted by 001001?
Solution.   (1) 2^6; (2) $\{c, f\}$.

Example 3.3. Suppose that a trucking company has a crew of four repairmen. How many different subsets of these four repairmen can be constructed?

Solution. The set consists of four elements. Hence there are $2^4 = 16$ subsets.

Example 3.4. A board of four men A, B, C, and D is appointed to decide for or against a given policy. When a vote is to be taken, A will have one vote as will B, C will have two votes, and D three. Five votes will be needed to approve the policy. List all combinations that will carry the policy.

Solution. Evidently neither A, B, C, nor D alone will win. So we eliminate all subsets containing a single element.

If C and D form a coalition (that is, $\{C,D\}$), then they will win. All subsets containing C and D will be winning coalitions,

$$\{C,D\} \qquad \{A,C,D\} \qquad \{B,C,D\} \qquad \{A,B,C,D\}$$

However, all coalitions in which $\{A,D\}$ is a proper subset will win also, as will coalitions in which $\{B,D\}$ is a proper subset. This gives $\{A,B,D\}$, $\{A,C,D\}$, $\{B,C,D\}$, $\{A,B,C,D\}$. We cross out repetitions. These sets may be denoted by 1101, 1011, 0111, 1111.

Notice that if D votes against the measure, no winning subset is possible.

Example 3.5. An automobile manufacturer has purchased a full page of advertising in a national magazine. The manufacturer produces six models and must make a decision as to how many of these models he should describe in his page of advertisement. He must also decide which models should be described. How many possibilities are there for him to consider?

Solution. Since the set consists of six elements, there are $2^6 = 64$ subsets. However, since he has already purchased the page of advertising, the empty set is not a realistic alternative. Therefore, the number of possibilities that he must consider is 63.

PROBLEM SET 3.1

1. A supermarket has allotted a soft-drink manufacturer 5 feet of floor space. The manufacturer produces four kinds of soft drinks and must therefore make a decision as to which kind (or kinds) he will display. Assuming that the manufacturer definitely wants to market his product in this supermarket, how many possibilities are there for him to consider? Assume, now, that he is relatively indifferent about marketing his product in this supermarket—how many possibilities are there for him to consider?

2. A manufacturer of four soap products has purchased 3 minutes of radio time.

A marketing consultant insists that no more than two products can be effectively advertised in this amount of time. What are the different possibilities that the manufacturer can consider? (*Hint:* How many four-place "numbers" of the kind described under Theorem 3.1 have two 1's and two 0's?)

3.2 NUMBER OF ELEMENTS IN COMBINATIONS OF SETS

We want to derive formulas for computing the number of elements in the union and intersection of two sets, knowing the number of elements in the given sets. Let $n(A)$ denote the number of elements in the set A. For example, if A has three elements, then $n(A) = 3$.

Theorem 3.6

If $A \cap B = \emptyset$, then $n(A \cap B) = 0$.

Proof. The theorem follows immediately.

Theorem 3.7

If A and B are any two sets, then

$$n(A \cup B) = n(A) + n(B) - n(A \cap B)$$

Proof. Since all the elements of A and all the elements of B are in $A \cup B$, then $n(A \cup B)$ must be at most as great as $n(A) + n(B)$. However, if $A \cap B \neq \emptyset$, then those elements both in A and in B will be counted twice. Hence we need to subtract $n(A \cap B)$. This gives the theorem.

Corollary 3.8. If $A \cap B = \emptyset$, then $n(A \cup B) = n(A) + n(B)$.

Example 3.9. Let A be a set containing 20 elements, and B be a set containing 30 elements. A and B have 10 elements in common. How many elements are there in $A \cup B$?

Solution

$$n(A) = 20$$
$$n(B) = 30$$
$$n(A \cap B) = 10$$
$$n(A \cup B) = 20 + 30 - 10 = 40$$

Example 3.10. A sales firm consists of 25 salesmen who sell parts, 45 who sell services, and 10 who sell both. How many salesmen are there in the firm?

Solution

$$P = \{x|x \text{ sell parts}\} \qquad S = \{x|x \text{ sells services}\}$$
$$n(P) = 25 \qquad n(S) = 45 \qquad n(S \cap P) = 10$$
$$n(S \cup P) = n(S) + n(P) - n(S \cap P) = 45 + 25 - 10 = 60$$

How many sell parts alone?

$$n(P) - n(S \cap P) = n(P \cap \bar{S}) \qquad 25 - 10 = 15$$

[Use Venn diagrams to show that $P - (S \cap P) = (P \cap \bar{S})$.]

PROBLEM SET 3.2

$C(5,1)$

1. A set S contains five elements. How many subsets can be formed containing at least one element? Indicate 16 of these subsets, using the digits 0 and 1.

2. A set S contains six elements. How many proper subsets can be formed? Indicate the set containing only the fifth and sixth elements.

3. A set T contains three elements. How many subsets, each containing exactly two elements, can be constructed?

4. A survey of 60 workers in a plant showed that 46 owned their own home, 25 owned a car, 27 owned a television set, 19 owned their home and a car, 8 owned their home and a television set, 10 owned a car and a television set, and 3 owned their home, a car, and a television set. Show that the report is inaccurate because the data are not consistent.

5. The following information was discovered in a survey of 100 workers in a factory: All men were more than 20 years old. There were 50 women in the group. Altogether 60 were over 20 years old. Twenty-five of the women were married, while 15 of the married workers were over 20 years old, and 10 of the married women were over 20 years old. Draw Venn diagrams, and find:

    a. How many married workers there are
    b. How many unmarried women are over 20
    c. How many of the unmarried men are under 20
    d. How many married men there are
    e. How many workers are under 20

3.3 CARTESIAN PRODUCTS

We have seen that we can have sets whose elements are themselves sets, as, for example, the set of all subsets of a set of n elements. We are now going to define a set whose elements are couples (i.e., sets containing two elements) of great importance. First we need the concept of an ordered couple.

Suppose that $S = \{a,b\}$ and $T = \{c,d\}$; then we know that $S = T$ if and only if $a = c$ and $b = d$ or $a = d$ and $b = c$, that is, if the elements are the same regardless of where they occur in the set. Now, if S and T

are viewed as *ordered* couples, then $S = T$ if (1) the elements are equal and (2) a equals c and b equals d. If S and T are ordered couples, then if $a = d$ and $b = c$, $S \neq T$. In other words, two ordered couples are equal if and only if the first and second elements in one set are equal, respectively, to the first and second elements of the other set. We shall denote an ordered couple by $\langle a,b \rangle$.

Example 3.11. $S = \{1,2\}$, $T = \{2,1\}$. If S and T are not considered ordered couples, then $S = T$; if they are considered to be ordered couples, $S \neq T$.

We now define the cartesian product of two sets S and T.

Definition 3.12. The cartesian product of a set S and a set T is denoted by $S \times T = \{\langle x,y \rangle | x \in S \ \& \ y \in T\}$; that is, the cartesian product of S and T is the set of all ordered couples $\langle x,y \rangle$ such that x is in S and y is in T.

Example 3.13. Let $S = \{x | x$ is an even number$\}$ and $T = \{x | x$ is an odd number$\}$. Then $S \times T = \{\langle x,y \rangle | x$ is even and y is odd$\}$. For example $\langle 2,1 \rangle \in S \times T$, $\langle -6,101 \rangle \in S \times T$, $\langle -6,1001 \rangle \in S \times T$, etc.

Example 3.14. Suppose that $S = \{1,3,5\}$ and $T = \{a,b\}$. Then

$$S \times T = \{\langle 1,a \rangle, \langle 1,b \rangle, \langle 3,a \rangle, \langle 3,b \rangle, \langle 5,a \rangle, \langle 5,b \rangle\}$$

Since nothing prevents T from being equal to S, we can find $S \times S$.

Example 3.15. $S = \{a,b,c\}$; then $S \times S = \{\langle a,a \rangle, \langle a,b \rangle, \langle a,c \rangle, \langle b,a \rangle, \langle b,b \rangle, \langle b,c \rangle, \langle c,a \rangle, \langle c,b \rangle, \langle c,c \rangle\}$.

A final example will serve to illustrate the practical applications of this concept.

Example 3.16. Let $S = \{$sedan, station wagon, truck$\}$, $T = \{$blue, black, red$\}$. The cartesian product $T \times S = \{\langle$blue, sedan$\rangle$, $\langle$blue, station wagon$\rangle$, $\langle$blue, truck$\rangle$, $\langle$black, sedan$\rangle$, $\langle$black, station wagon$\rangle$, $\langle$black, truck$\rangle$, $\langle$red, sedan$\rangle$, $\langle$red, station wagon$\rangle$, $\langle$red, truck$\rangle\}$.

Can we count the number of elements in the cartesian product of two sets if we know the number of elements in each set? We state the following theorem.

Theorem 3.17

If $n(S) = n_1$ and $n(T) = n_2$, then $n(S \times T) = n_1 \times n_2$.

The theorem should be intuitively evident, since each element in S can be paired with each element in T. If we take one element from S, this can be paired with n_2 elements of T; a second element from S can be paired with n_2 elements of T, and so on. So n_1 elements can be paired with the n_2 elements $n_1 \times n_2$ ways. Obviously, if $S = T$, $n(S \times S) = n^2$; also $n(S \times T) = n_1 \times n_2 = n_2 \times n_1 = n(T \times S)$.

Example 3.18. Let $S = \{a,b,c\}$, $T = \{r,s,t,u\}$; then $n(S) = 3$, $n(T) = 4$, $n(S \times T) = 3 \times 4 = 12$.

Example 3.19. Let $S = \{x|x \text{ is a factory outlet}\}$ and $T = \{x|x \text{ is a salesman}\}$. If company A has 20 factory outlets and 30 salesmen, in how many ways can the salesmen be assigned to the outlets? (We assume that all can be assigned to the same outlet and anyone to any number of outlets).

Solution. $n(S) = 20$, $n(T) = 30$. Since the salesmen are to be assigned to the factory outlets, let us take $n(T \times S) = 30 \times 20 = 600$.

Clearly in making such assignments an administrator would want to assign one salesman to one outlet. The solution of this type of problem will be considered later.

PROBLEM SET 3.3

1. The specifications for the assembly of an electronic device require two different tubes. If both these tubes are defective, the device will not function; however, if just one of the tubes is defective, it will function. The first tube is being selected from a box of five such tubes, and the second from a box of four tubes.

   a. How many different samples of two tubes, one from each box, can result?

   b. Assume that two of the tubes in the first box are defective and one of the tubes in the second is defective. How many of the possible samples will result in the failure of the electronic device to function? (*Hint:* Let $F = \{g_1, g_2, g_3, d_1, d_2\}$ and $S = (g_1, g_2, g_3, d_1\}$ represent the good and defective tubes in the first and second boxes, respectively.)

2. In the above problem, how many of the possible samples will have a good tube from the first box, followed by a defective tube from the second box?

3. The members of a local union are known to be either Democrats, Independents, or Socialists. The faculty of a local college are known to be either Democrats, Republicans, Independents, or Socialists. A committee of two is to be selected, one from each group. If a committee is distinguished by its political composition, how many different possible committees are there?

4. In Prob. 3, how many of the possible committee compositions will be made up of persons who belong to the same political party?

3.4 COUNTING ELEMENTS OF SUBSETS OF CARTESIAN PRODUCTS

We can easily compute $n(S \times S)$ from Theorem 3.17. If $n(S) = k$, then $n(S \times S) = k \times k = k^2$. So if $S = \{x|(x \text{ is an integer}) \,\&\, (1 \leq x \leq 12)\}$, then $n(S) = 12$ and $n(S \times S) = 12^2 = 144$.

In many cases we wish to count only those elements of $S \times S$ which contain different constituents; i.e., we wish the number of elements $\langle x, y \rangle$ of that subset of $S \times S$ for which $x \neq y$. So, in the set S consisting of integers 1 to 12 inclusive, we may want to count only those elements not of the form $\langle a,a \rangle$; for example, we would not count $\langle 1,1 \rangle$ or $\langle 2,2 \rangle$, etc. Evidently, if S has n elements, we can use as the first element in $\langle x,y \rangle \, \epsilon \, S \times S$ any one of the n elements of S, but as the second element in $\langle x,y \rangle \, \epsilon \, S \times S$ we can use only $n - 1$ elements of S, since we allow no repetitions. In this way we can form $n \times (n - 1)$ couples. We have therefore the following theorem.

Theorem 3.20

If S is a set such that $n(S) = k$, then the number of elements $\langle x,y \rangle$ in that subset of $S \times S$ for which $x \neq y$ is $k(k - 1)$.

Example 3.21. Let $S = \{1,2,3,4\}$. Count the number of elements in that subset of $S \times S$ which is made up of elements in which $x \neq y$.

    Solution. Since $n(S) = 4$, $n(S \times S) = 4^2 = 16$. If $x \neq y$, then we can use four elements for x and only three for y. The result is $4 \times 3 = 12$.

    This can be shown by the schema of Fig. 3.1. Each block contains an element of $S \times S$. To count the desired elements of $S \times S$, we count the blocks in which the numbers are distinct. Each row will contain only three such elements, and there are four rows. The total is therefore 12.

Example 3.22. A repair-service company has in its employ seven repairmen. In how many ways can a team of two men be sent out on a repair job?

    Solution. Evidently this is an application of Theorem 3.20. $7 \cdot 6$ With each of the seven men, the company can pair one of the six remaining men. The total number of possible teams would therefore be $7 \times 6 = 42$.

Example 3.23. In how many ways can a pair of dice fall so that the sum of the faces is 6?

    Solution. If $S = \{1,2,3,4,5,6\}$, then $n(S \times S) = 36$. But we want only that subset of $S \times S$ for which the sum of the faces is 6. Since $1 + 5 = 6$, $2 + 4 = 6$, $3 + 3 = 6$, $4 + 2 = 6$, $5 + 1 = 6$, the subset in which we are interested is $S' = \{\langle 1,5 \rangle, \langle 2,4 \rangle, \langle 3,3 \rangle, \langle 4,2 \rangle, \langle 5,1 \rangle\}$ or $n(S') = 5$.

	1	2	3	4
1	$\langle 1,1 \rangle$	$\langle 1,2 \rangle$	$\langle 1,3 \rangle$	$\langle 1,4 \rangle$
2	$\langle 2,1 \rangle$	$\langle 2,2 \rangle$	$\langle 2,3 \rangle$	$\langle 2,4 \rangle$
3	$\langle 3,1 \rangle$	$\langle 3,2 \rangle$	$\langle 3,3 \rangle$	$\langle 3,4 \rangle$
4	$\langle 4,1 \rangle$	$\langle 4,2 \rangle$	$\langle 4,3 \rangle$	$\langle 4,4 \rangle$

Fig. *3.1*

PROBLEM SET 3.4

1. Give two examples of cartesian products.
2. Ten men are being considered for promotion. Only two promotions will be made. In how many ways can the two promotions be made, if no man can hold two jobs?
3. Suppose that five men are being considered for two jobs. All five can fill one of the jobs, but only three can fill the second job. How many distinct pairs of appointments can be made? (*Hint:* Construct a table as in Example 3.21.)
4. A committee of six men is to vote on a proposal. Three of the men have three votes apiece, while the other three have one vote each. In how many ways can two of the members block the proposal?

3.5 COUNTING THE NUMBER OF ORDERED SETS WITH A FINITE NUMBER OF ELEMENTS (PERMUTATIONS)

In the case of ordered sets, for two sets to be equal their elements must be the same and in the same order. It is often important to discover how many distinct ordered sets can be formed from a set of n elements. The procedure is quite simple and is illustrated by the following example.

Example 3.24. How many distinct ordered sets can be made of the elements of the set $S = \{a,b,c\}$?

Solution. We can of course write out all the arrangements of the letters a, b, and c. This would give us the answer to the problem. But we can solve the problem by the following method, which also provides a general principle.

Let us imagine that we have three boxes into which we can put a letter. In box 1, we can obviously put any one of the three letters a, b, or c. Having put one of the three letters in box 1, we have but two left. So we can put one of these two in box 2; that is, we can fill box 2 in two ways. This means that together there are $3 \times 2 = 6$ ways of filling boxes 1 and 2. Since only one letter is left for box 3, altogether we have $3 \times 2 \times 1 = 6$ distinct ordered sets that can be made of the elements of the set $S = \{a,b,c\}$. These are

$$a, b, c \quad b, a, c \quad c, a, b$$
$$a, c, b \quad b, c, a \quad c, b, a$$

We shall call each arrangement of the three letters a permutation. There are six permutations of the elements of a set S for which $n(S) = 3$.

The above example can be generalized in the following principle.

Principle 3.25.   If S is a set and $n(S) = k$, then the number of permutations of the elements of S is $k(k - 1)(k - 2)(k - 3) \cdot \cdot \cdot 1$.

Example 3.26.   A salesman has five articles to display.   In how many ways can he arrange these five articles?

   Solution.   If each article is given a number, the salesman will have a set of five numbers $S = \{1,2,3,4,5\}$. $n(S) = 5$.   He can arrange these articles on a shelf $5 \times 4 \times 3 \times 2 \times 1 = 120$ ways.

   Our next problem concerns the number of ordered subsets of a given number of elements that can be formed from the n elements of a given set. We might want to know, for example, how many ordered subsets of two elements can be formed from a set of five elements.   We can solve this problem as follows.   Consider in this case that there are only two boxes into which an element can be placed.   Evidently in the first box we can place any one of the five elements and in the second any one of the four remaining elements.   So we have $5 \times 4 = 20$ possible ordered subsets containing two elements each.

   In solving this problem we used the following principle.

Principle 3.27.   If S is a set such that $n(S) = k$, then the number of ordered subsets of the elements of S each containing p elements is $k(k - 1)(k - 2) \cdot \cdot \cdot (k - p + 1)$.

Example 3.28.   Let S be a set containing seven elements.   How many ordered subsets of S each containing four elements can be formed from the seven elements?

   Solution.   As above, if we make believe we have four boxes each of which is to contain an element of S, we can put any one of the seven elements in the first box, then in the second box any one of six elements, in the third any one of the remaining five, and in the fourth any one of the remaining four.   This makes a total of $7 \times 6 \times 5 \times 4 = 840$ possible ordered subsets of four elements out of the elements of S.

   If we use Principle 3.27, then $k = 7$ and $p = 4$, so we obtain, since $k - p + 1 = 7 - 4 + 1 = 4, 7 \times 6 \times 5 \times 4 = 840$.

Example 3.29.   An engineering firm sends out teams of three men on certain types of repair jobs.   It has a total force of 10 men.   The first man selected for a given team is considered the foreman of the team, and the second is considered the assistant foreman.   How many teams can be formed if we assume that two teams with different foremen and/or different assistant foremen are different teams?

   Solution.   Upon applying Principle 3.27, $k = 10$, $p = 3$,

$$k - p + 1 = 10 - 3 + 1 = 8; 10 \times 9 \times 8 = 720$$

   The student should notice that the number of ordered subsets of a set S of n elements each containing two elements is really the number of elements in the cartesian product $S \times S$ (with $x \neq y$).

PROBLEM SET 3.5

1. How many subsets are there of the set $S = \{x | 1 \leq x \leq 5 \ \& \ x$ is an integer} such that the elements of the subsets add to 8?

2. In Prob. 1, how many ordered subsets are there containing exactly two elements? How many are different unordered subsets of two elements?

3. In Prob. 1, how many ordered subsets are there containing three elements? Containing four elements? How many different subsets are there of three elements? Of four elements?

4. In Prob. 1, how many different ordered sets can be formed containing all the elements of S?

5. In Prob. 1, how many ordered subsets are there of the elements of S? Add the results of the first part of Prob. 2, Prob. 3, and Prob. 4. What subsets are missing to make the total number of ordered subsets of S?

6. If a word is an arrangement of letters, how many words can be formed from the letters a, b, c, and d if no letters can occur twice? Suppose that repetitions are allowed, how many words can be formed?

7. How many three-letter words can be formed from the letters a, b, c, and d if the first letter is to be a and no letter can occur twice?

8. A florist has 10 distinct varieties of tulips. How many arrangements containing 3 distinct varieties can be made?

9. How many permutations can be made of the elements of the set $S = \{x | 0 \leq x \leq 9\}$, with x an integer and no digit used twice?

10. How many subsets containing 10 elements are there of the elements of S in Prob. 9?

11. A firm owns three factories, A, B, and C. Whether these operate or not depends on sales requirements in their areas. If a factory operates, it submits an operating report. How many sets of operating reports are possible? (Do not include the empty set.)

12. In Prob. 11, assume that factory A is always in operation regardless of conditions. How many sets of operating reports are now possible?

13. When a series of products are put on the market in sequence, products marketed later often have less appeal than those marketed earlier. Suppose that five products are to be marketed in sequence. In how many sequences can they be marketed? In how many ways can a given product be first?

14. A survey of tariff experts is conducted to determine which industries are most deserving of continued protection. Each expert is asked to rank four industries from a list of eight. How many different ranked ballots are possible from each expert?

3.6 THE FACTORIAL AND BINOMIAL NUMBERS

We need to introduce three symbols to facilitate our work. We have had occasion to multiply all the integers from a given one, say n, down to 1. This product will be denoted by $n!$ (read "n factorial"). But in order to be sure we know what $n!$ means for an appropriate n, we write the following definition.

Definition 3.30. If N is the set of all nonnegative integers, then, if $n \in N$,

(a)　　　　For $n = 0$, $0! = 1$

(b)　　　　For $n \neq 0$, $n! = n(n - 1)(n - 2) \cdots 1$

Example 3.31. If $n = 5$, then $5! = 5 \times 4 \times 3 \times 2 \times 1$.

Example 3.32. What is $(m - k)!$ where m and k are nonnegative integers?

　　Solution. Clearly, if $(m - k)!$ is to be meaningful, $m - k$ must be greater than or equal to 0. If $m - k = 0$, $(m - k)! = 1$; if $m - k > 0$,

$$(m - k)! = [(m - k)][(m - k) - 1][(m - k) - 2)] \cdots 1$$

Certain properties of $n!$ are important.

Theorem 3.33

$$n! = n(n - 1)! = n(n - 1)(n - 2)!$$

Proof. The proof follows immediately from the definition of $n!$

$$n! = n(n - 1)(n - 2)(n - 3) \cdots 1$$

We use the associative law and write

$$n! = n[(n - 1)(n - 2)(n - 3) \cdots 1]$$

But

$$(n - 1)(n - 2)(n - 3) \cdots 1 = (n - 1)!$$

by definition. Therefore

$$n! = n(n - 1)! \tag{3.1}$$

We leave the proof of the other part to the student.

Theorem 3.34

$$n(n - 1)(n - 2) \cdots (n - k + 1) = \frac{n!}{(n - k)!}$$

Proof. We shall reduce the right-hand side to the left.

$$\frac{n!}{(n - k)!} = \frac{n(n - 1) \cdots (n - k + 1)\{(n - k)[(n - k) - 1] \cdots 1\}}{(n - k)[(n - k) - 1][(n - k) - 2] \cdots 1}$$
$$= n(n - 1) \cdots (n - k + 1)$$

Example 3.35

$$6! = 6 \times 5 \times 4 \times 3 \times 2 \times 1$$
$$= 6(5 \times 4 \times 3 \times 2 \times 1)$$
$$= 6(5!)$$

Example 3.36. Show that

$$9 \times 8 \times 7 \times 6 \times 5 \times 4 = \frac{9!}{(9-6)!}$$

Since $n = 9$, $n - k + 1 = 4$, or $9 - k + 1 = 4$, or $-k = -6$, or $k = 6$

and $\dfrac{9!}{(9-6)!} = \dfrac{9 \times 8 \times 7 \times 6 \times 5 \times 4 \times 3 \times 2 \times 1}{3 \times 2 \times 1}$

We next define the binomial number $\dbinom{n}{k}$ as follows.

Definition 3.37

$$\binom{n}{k} = \frac{n!}{k!(n-k)!}$$

with n and k positive integers and $n \geq k$.

Example 3.38

$$\binom{8}{3} = \frac{8!}{3!(8-3)!} = \frac{8!}{3!5!} = \frac{8 \times 7 \times 6}{3 \times 2} = 56$$

Another symbol is given in the following definition.

Definition 3.39. If $n, k_1, k_2, \ldots, k_n$ are positive integers such that $k_1 + k_2 + \cdots + k_n = n$, then

$$\binom{n}{k_1, k_2, \ldots, k_n} = \frac{n!}{k_1! k_2! \cdots k_n!} \tag{3.2}$$

Example 3.40

$$\binom{7}{4,3,0} = \frac{7!}{4! 3! 0!}$$

$$= \frac{7 \times 6 \times 5 \times 4 \times 3 \times 2 \times 1}{(4 \times 3 \times 2 \times 1)(3 \times 2 \times 1)(1)}$$

$$= 35$$

Example 3.41

$$\binom{8}{7,0,1} = \frac{8!}{7! 0! 1!} = \frac{8 \times 7!}{7! \times 1 \times 1} = 8$$

PROBLEM SET 3.6

1. Compute

   a. $\dbinom{5}{3}$

   b. $\dbinom{5}{1,1,3}$

c. $\binom{5}{0}$

d. $\binom{5}{5}$

e. $\binom{5}{4}$

f. $\binom{5}{1}$

2. Prove that $\binom{n}{k} = \binom{n}{n-k}$. Give an example.

3. Prove that $\binom{n}{r} = \binom{n-1}{r-1} + \binom{n-1}{r}$. Give an example.

4. Prove that $\binom{n}{0} = \binom{n}{n}$. Give an example.

5. Compute $\binom{40}{5}\binom{10}{0} \div \binom{41}{35}$.

6. Compute $\binom{6}{0}, \binom{6}{1}, \binom{6}{2}, \binom{6}{3}$. Do you know $\binom{6}{4}, \binom{6}{5}, \binom{6}{6}$ without computing them?

7. Compute $\binom{5}{3,1,1}, \binom{8}{1,0,7}$, and $\binom{9}{2,3,3,1}$.

8. Show that the number of ordered subsets of 13 things taken three at a time is $13!/(13-3)!$. Generalize to show that the number of ordered subsets of n things r at a time is $n!/(n-r)!$. (*Hint:* Use Theorem 3.34.)

9. How many telephone numbers could be put on an exchange using five digits for each number? If three letters were also used before the digits, how many numbers could be put on the exchange?

3.7 COUNTING SUBSETS WITH DIFFERENT ELEMENTS (COMBINATIONS)

We know that, if A and B are sets, then $A = B$ if and only if they contain the same elements. The order does not count. Now, when a sales manager sends out sales crews, he may want to know how many different crews he can send out, not simply how many crews, and by "different" he means crews with at least one different salesman. In problems of quality control it is often necessary to know how many different subsets of (say) m elements can be formed from a set of n elements. We illustrate the problem as follows.

Example 3.42. A set of 10 electronic tubes is selected. How many samples (subsets) of 2 tubes can be obtained from the set of 10 tubes?

Solution. If we were concerned with the order in which these two were selected, the answer would be 10×9. But clearly a sample of two tubes is the same sample regardless of the order in which they are selected. Since we have each sample consisting of two elements, for each two there are $2! = 2$ arrangements. Hence we really want only

$(1/2!)(10 \times 9)$ of the subsets. We can rewrite

$$\frac{10 \times 9}{2!} = \frac{(10 \times 9)(8!)}{2!8!} = \frac{10!}{2!8!} = \binom{10}{2}$$

When a set of n is divided into two subsets such that (1) every element is in one of the subsets, and (2) no element is in both subsets, we call the division a *dichotomy*.

Example 3.42 can be generalized to the following theorem.

Theorem 3.43

The number of dichotomies (samples, combinations, nonordered subsets) each containing r elements that can be made from a set of n elements is

$$\binom{n}{r} = \frac{n!}{r!(n-r)!}$$

Example 3.44. There are five men available for a special assignment that will demand a team of three men. In how many ways can a group of three men be selected?

Solution. Clearly this is a case of forming dichotomies of three from a set of five. The result is therefore

$$\binom{5}{3} = \frac{5!}{3!2!} = \frac{5 \times 4 \times 3 \times 2 \times 1}{(3 \times 2 \times 1)(2 \times 1)} = 10$$

Example 3.45. A machine produces 500 units a month. It is expected that 497 of these will be perfect. How many possible combinations of 497 perfect units are there in a given month, each unit being distinguished according to whether it was the first, second, . . . , or five-hundredth produced?

Solution. By Theorem 3.43, the solution is

$$\binom{500}{497} = \binom{500}{3} = \frac{500!}{3!497!} = \frac{500 \times 499 \times 498}{3 \times 2}$$

$$\left[\text{Why is } \binom{500}{497} = \binom{500}{3}? \right]$$

Example 3.46. A manufacturer receives a lot of 600 metal parts, 10 per cent of which are defective. The following acceptance sampling plan is followed: (1) A sample of 20 parts is selected at random. (2) If more than 2 of the parts in the sample are defective, the entire lot is rejected; otherwise it is accepted. How many different samples of 20 are possible, and how many of these will lead to rejection of the entire lot in this case?

Solution. The total number of different samples possible is equal to the number of combinations of 20 objects selected from 600,

$$\binom{600}{20} = \frac{600!}{20!580!} = 10,910 \times 10^{33}$$

All those samples which contain more than 2 defective parts will cause rejection of the lot. The total number of such samples equals the total number of possible samples of size 20 (which was just shown to be $10,910 \times 10^{33}$) minus the number of samples which contain 0, 1, or 2 defective parts. The number of samples which contain 2 defective parts is calculated as the number of ways of selecting 18 good parts from the 90 per cent ($= 540$) good parts in the lot, multiplied by the number of ways of selecting 2 defective parts from the 60 such parts in the lot,

$$\binom{540}{18}\binom{60}{2} = \frac{540!}{18!522!} \cdot \frac{60!}{2!58!} = (1,788 \times 10^{30})(1,770) = 3,165 \times 10^{33}$$

This calculation shows that, for each of the $1,788 \times 10^{30}$ ways of selecting 18 good parts, there are 1,770 ways of selecting the 2 defective parts. The number of samples which will contain 1 or 0 defective parts is determined similarly,

$$\binom{540}{19}\binom{60}{1} = \frac{540!}{19!521!} \cdot \frac{60!}{1!59!} = 2,947 \times 10^{33}$$

$$\binom{540}{20}\binom{60}{0} = \frac{540!}{20!520!} \cdot \frac{60!}{0!60!} = 1,280 \times 10^{33}$$

Thus, the number of samples which will contain 0, 1, or 2 defective parts is $10^{33}(3,165 + 2,947 + 1,280) = 10^{33} \times 7,392$. The number of samples which will lead to rejection of the entire lot is therefore

$$10^{33}(10,910 - 7,392) = 10^{33} \times 3,518$$

Efficient methods for solving combinatorial formulas will be taken up in a later section.

More often than not, when a division of the elements of a set is to be made, the division will consist of more than two subsets. So the employees of a factory may be divided into subsets of operators, maintenance men, accounting personnel, and so on. If a set S of n elements is divided into subsets $A_1 A_2 \cdots A_k$ such that

1. Every element of the set is in one of the subsets,

2. No element of the set is in more than one subset, then, following Sec. 2.7, the k subsets are called a *partition* of the set. (Some of the subsets $A_1, \ldots, A_k$ may be empty.) Evidently

$$n(A_1) + n(A_2) + \cdots + n(A_k) = n$$

To count the number of partitions of a set of n elements into subsets of $n_1, n_2, \ldots, n_k$ elements, we reason as in the following example.

Example 3.47. A set containing 10 elements is to be partitioned into three subsets containing 5, 3, and 2 elements, respectively. How many such partitions can be made?

Solution. Let us assume that we have three boxes B_1, B_2, and B_3 and that B_1 has places for 5 elements, B_2 for 3, and B_3 for 2. We can fill B_1 in $10 \times 9 \times 8 \times 7 \times 6$ ways, but not all will be distinct. Indeed, since there are 5 elements in B_1, these can be arranged in 5! ways without changing the content of the box; so we want only $(10 \times 9 \times 8 \times 7 \times 6)/5!$ ways for B_1. Now B_2 can be filled in $5 \times 4 \times 3$ ways, and if these are to be distinct, we would again want only 1/3! of these ways, that is, $(5 \times 4 \times 3)/3!$. B_3 can be filled in 2×1 ways, and we want only 1/2! of these, that is, $(2 \times 1)/2!$. Since B_1, B_2, and B_3 can each be filled in a definite number of ways, all three can be filled in $[(10 \times 9 \times 8 \times 7 \times 6)/5!][(5 \times 4 \times 3)/3!][(2 \times 1)/2!]$ ways, or $10!/(5!3!2!)$ ways.

This can be generalized to the following theorem.

Theorem 3.48

The number of partitions of a set of n elements into r subsets of $n_1, n_2, \ldots, n_r$ elements is given by $\begin{pmatrix} n \\ n_1, n_2, \ldots, n_r \end{pmatrix}$.

Example 3.49. How many different "deals" are there in a bridge game?

Solution. In this case we have a set of 52 elements (the cards) to be partitioned into four subsets of 13 elements each. The result is therefore

$$\begin{pmatrix} 52 \\ 13,13,13,13 \end{pmatrix} = \frac{52!}{13!13!13!13!}$$

Example 3.50. How many "words" consisting of 11 letters can be made from the letters in "Mississippi"?

Solution. Although we are not exactly making a partition, the reasoning will show that the result is obtained as in the case of the partition problem.

Since there are 11 letters, there are 11! permutations. However, not all these are distinct. Because there are four i's, we can interchange the i's 4! times without changing the form of a given permutation. Thus, a given permutation will give rise to at least 4! nondistinct permutations. Moreover, for each of these 4! nondistinct permutations, the four s's will give rise to 4! more nondistinct permutations; for each of these 4!4! nondistinct permutations the two p's will give rise to 2! more nondistinct permutations; and for each of these 4!4!2! nondistinct permutations the one M will give rise to 1! permutation.   Thus each distinct permutation will give rise to 4!4!2!1! nondistinct permutations.   If we denote the number of distinct permutations by the letter D, then the total number of permutations (11!) will equal $D(4!4!2!1!)$, and

$$D = \frac{11!}{4!4!2!1!}$$

That is, the number of distinct words of 11 letters is $\begin{pmatrix} 11 \\ 4,4,2,1 \end{pmatrix}$.

We can reformulate Theorem 3.48 as follows.

Theorem 3.51

If a set S contains n elements, k_1 of one kind, k_2 of another kind, . . . , k_n of another kind, then the number of distinct arrangements that can be made of the n elements is $\begin{pmatrix} n \\ k_1, k_2, \ldots, k_n \end{pmatrix}$.

Example 3.52.   A foreman has a force of seven men at his disposal; two are plumbers, two are electricians, two are carpenters, and one is a heating engineer.   How many distinct teams can be formed consisting of these seven men?

Solution. $n = 7$, $k_1 = 2$, $k_2 = 2$, $k_3 = 2$, and $k_1 = 1$.   Therefore we obtain

$$\begin{pmatrix} 7 \\ 2,2,2,1 \end{pmatrix}$$

PROBLEM SET 3.7

1. Evaluate

a. $\begin{pmatrix} 10 \\ 7 \end{pmatrix}$

b. $\begin{pmatrix} 5 \\ 3,1,1 \end{pmatrix}$

c. $\begin{pmatrix} 20 \\ 5,10,5 \end{pmatrix}$

d. $\begin{pmatrix} 10 \\ 3 \end{pmatrix}$

2. How many dichotomies can be made, each containing 20 elements, from a set containing 50 elements?

3. How many partitions of a set containing 25 elements can be made if the partitions are to contain 15, 5, and 5 elements, respectively?

4. A book publisher buying rights to English novels has narrowed his choice to nine books.   He is authorized to purchase only four.   In how many ways can he select four books from the nine?

5. In Prob. 4, suppose that four books were paperbacks and five were cloth. How many ways could the publisher choose four books if two were to be paperbacks and two were to be cloth?

6. The director of the antitrust division has been given a list of 12 firms cited for monopolistic practices. Because of staff shortages, only one-third of these 12 can be brought to trial, another one-fourth can be referred for further study, and the rest must be filed for future action. How many different partitions of the 12 firms can be made?

7. A company is to submit bids on contract work every month. The accountant reports that the company must be low bidder four times, tied three times, and high bidder the rest of the time. Write an expression indicating in how many ways this minimum result can occur. (*Hint:* Let x = total number of bids a month.)

8. A sample of 5 items is selected at random from a lot of 20 items, 6 of which are defective. The entire lot will be rejected if 2 or more of the items in the sample are found to be defective. How many different samples of 5 could be selected? How many of these samples will lead to rejection?

9. Assume, in the above problem, that (*a*) if 0 or 1 item is found to be defective, the lot will be accepted; (*b*) if more than 2 are found to be defective, the lot will be rejected; (*c*) if exactly 2 are found, a second sample of 3 is selected, the lot now being accepted only if all 3 items in the second sample are good. How many different samples could result under (*c*), and how many of these would lead to rejection?

3.8 THE BINOMIAL THEOREM

We shall now apply some of the concepts we have learned to an old friend, the binomial expansion, and connect the binomial number with the binomial expansion. Any expression of the form $(x + y)^n$, where x and y represent terms and n is a nonnegative integer, will be called a *binomial*. The student has probably learned in secondary school that

$$(x + y)^n = x^n + nx^{n-1}y + \frac{n(n - 1)}{2!} x^{n-2}y^2 + \frac{n(n - 1)(n - 2)}{3!} x^{n-3}y^3$$
$$+ \cdots + y^n \quad (3.3)$$

For example, if $n = 3$,

$$(x + y)^3 = x^3 + 3x^2y + \frac{3 \times 2}{2 \times 1} xy^2 + y^3 = x^3 + 3x^2y + 3xy^2 + y^3$$

An examination of formula (3.3) reveals interesting features. If we call the sum of the exponents of the variables in each term the *degree* of each term, then we note that the degree of each term is equal to the exponent of the binomial, that is, n. Second, we note that the coefficients are as follows:

The coefficient of x^n is 1, but $\binom{n}{0} = 1$.

The coefficient of $x^{n-1}y$ is n, but $\binom{n}{1} = n$.

The coefficient of $x^{n-2}y^2$ is $\dfrac{n(n-1)}{2!}$, but $\dbinom{n}{2} = \dfrac{n(n-1)}{2!}$.

It would appear that the coefficient of the term $x^{n-r}y^r$ may be $\dbinom{n}{r}$. If this is so, then $(x + y)^n$ could be written in the following fashion:

$$(x + y)^n = \binom{n}{0} x^n + \binom{n}{1} x^{n-1}y + \binom{n}{2} x^{n-2}y^2 + \binom{n}{3} x^{n-3}y^3 + \cdots$$
$$+ \binom{n}{r} x^{n-r}y^r + \cdots + \binom{n}{n} y^n \quad (3.4)$$

Example 3.53.   Expand $(x + y)^5$.

Solution

$$(x + y)^5 = \binom{5}{0} x^5 + \binom{5}{1} x^4y + \binom{5}{2} x^3y^2 + \binom{5}{3} x^2y^3 + \binom{5}{4} xy^4$$
$$+ \binom{5}{5} y^5$$

Since $\dbinom{n}{r} = \dbinom{n}{n-r}$, we need compute only $\dbinom{5}{0}$, $\dbinom{5}{1}$, and $\dbinom{5}{2}$.

That (3.4) is true we can see by the following argument for the special case $(x + y)^4$: We write

$$(x + y)^4 = (x + y)(x + y)(x + y)(x + y)$$

In expanding we select one x or y from each factor. Let us assume that when we select an x from a factor we put that factor in a box labeled x and that when we select a y we put that factor in a box labeled y. Suppose then that we want the term x^4. This means that we need to select four x's, one from each factor $x + y$. We then have a dichotomy of the factors into two subsets 4 and 0. The number of ways this can be done is $\dbinom{4}{4} = \dbinom{4}{0} = 1$ (since there are no y's in this term, we can select no y's in one way). Suppose that we want the coefficient of the term x^3y. We now have a dichotomy of three factors in the x box and one in the y box. This can be done in $\dbinom{4}{3}$ ways. The coefficient of the term x^2y^2 is $\dbinom{4}{2}$. The coefficient of xy^3 is $\dbinom{4}{1} = \dbinom{4}{3}$ and of y^4 is $\dbinom{4}{4} = \dbinom{4}{0}$.

Example 3.54.   Find the coefficient of the term containing x^5y^7 in the expansion of $(x + y)^{12}$.

Solution.   The coefficient is $\dbinom{12}{5}$.

Example 3.55. Find the coefficient of the term containing x^3y^4 in the expansion of $(2x + 3y)^7$.

Solution. Let us write $(2x + 3y)^7 = [(2x) + (3y)]^7$. We obtain the coefficient of the term containing $(2x)^3 \cdot (3y)^4$, since that will contain x^3y^4. The coefficient of $(2x)^3(3y)^4$ is obtained as follows:

$$\binom{7}{3} = \binom{7}{4} = \frac{7!}{4!3!} = \frac{7 \times 6 \times 5 \times 4!}{4!3!} = \frac{7 \times 6 \times 5}{3 \times 2 \times 1} = 35$$

So we have

$$35(2x)^3(3y)^4 = 35 \times 2^3 \times 3^4 \times x^3y^4$$

The coefficient we seek is therefore $35 \times 8 \times 81$.

Note that this is the fifth term in the given expansion. The coefficient of the fourth term would be $2^4 \times 3^3 \times \binom{7}{4}$.

In general, the rth item of $(x + y)^n$ would be $\binom{n}{r-1} x^{n-(r-1)}y^{r-1}$.

So $\binom{n}{5} x^{n-5}y^5$ would be the sixth term in the expansion $(x + y)^n$. More specifically, the sixth term in the expansion $(x + y)^{10}$ would be $\binom{10}{5} x^5y^5$.

The following example illustrates an interesting and important application of the binomial expansion.

Example 3.56. Suppose that a coin is tossed six times. How many possible outcomes will there be of four tails and two heads?

Solution. Each set of six tosses is considered an outcome of the tosses. What we ask therefore is the number of ways a set of six tosses can result in four tails and two heads. Let us denote the possibilities of a single toss by $t + h$. Since there are to be six tosses, we can denote the set of possibilities by $(h + t)^6$. We seek, therefore, the coefficient of the term having t four times (that is, t^4) and h two times (that is, h^2). This is

$$\binom{6}{4} = 6!/4!2! = 15.$$

PROBLEM SET 3.8

1. Suppose that a coin is tossed 10 times. How many outcomes will there be with three heads and seven tails?

2. Show that the sum of the coefficients of $(a + b)^n$ is 2^n, the number of subsets of a set of n elements.

3. Find the coefficient of the term containing x^2y^5 in the expansion of $(x - y)^7$. Give two interpretations of this coefficient.

4. Expand the binomial $(x - 2y)^4$.

5. Find an approximation for $(1.02)^{10}$. [*Hint:* Write $(1 + .02)^{10}$, and use the first three terms of the expansion.]   Find the value of $(99)^3$.   [*Hint:* Use $(100 - 1)^3$.]

6. A set of 12 employees is divided into two groups in all possible ways, one group to work in a new building and one group in an old building.   In how many ways will the group in the new building have exactly 4 employees?   In how many ways will it have at most 4 employees?   (*Hint:* $n = 1, 2, 3,$ and 4.)

7. Show that the sum of the ratios of the coefficients of $(a + b)^n$ to 2^n is always 1.

8. In how many ways can three accepted objects appear in a sample of eight objects?   (Solve by following the reasoning of Example 3.56, using a for accepted and r for rejected, instead of h and t.)

9. An accounting firm needs 4 clerks.   If 10 people apply for the jobs, in how many ways can the firm select 4?

10. Nine objects are to be partitioned into three subsets S_1, S_2, S_3.   Find the number of ways we can put two objects in S_1, three in S_2, and four in S_3.   Show that this is the coefficient of the terms $x^2 y^3 z^4$ in the expansion of $(x + y + z)^9$.

11. A buyer purchases apples, oranges, and pears.   On six consecutive days he wishes to buy three boxes of apples, one box of oranges, and two boxes of pears.   In how many ways can he make his purchases?

12. Suppose that we have

$$(x_1 + x_2 + \cdots + x_s)^n =$$
$$\underbrace{(x_1 + x_2 + \cdots + x_s)(x_1 + x_2 + \cdots + x_s) \cdots (x_1 + x_2 + \cdots + x_s)}_{n \text{ factors}}$$

This product is expanded by selecting an $x_1, x_2, \ldots,$ or x_s from each factor, multiplying these terms together, doing this for all possible choices, and adding the results. A typical result will be of the form

$$x_1^{n_1}, x_2^{n_2}, \ldots, x_s^{n_s} \qquad n_1 + n_2 + \cdots + n_s = n$$

The number of times a given result will occur equals the number of partitions of a set of n elements into s subsets of $n_1, n_2, \ldots, n_s$ elements; from Theorem 3.48, this is

$$\binom{n}{n_1, n_2, \ldots, n_s}$$

a. Find the coefficient of the term containing x_1^2, x_2^3, x_3^4 in the expansion of $(x_1 + x_2 + x_3)^9$.

b. Expand $(x_1 + 2x_2 + 3x_3)^3$.

3.9 LOGARITHMS OF FACTORIALS

In practical work, efficient methods for solving expressions involving factorials of large numbers are required.   Such methods are aided by a table of logarithms of factorials, which can be employed by using the ordinary rules of logarithmic computation.

Example 3.57.   In Example 3.46, the number $\binom{600}{20} = 600!/(20!580!)$ was given as $10{,}910 \times 10^{33}$.   Show how this number is determined, using Appendix Table 1.

Solution. Looking up 600!, 20!, and 580!, in Appendix Table 1, and employing the ordinary rules for determining the quotient and product of numbers, we obtain

$$\frac{600!}{20!580!} = \log 600! - (\log 20! + \log 580!)$$

$$= (0.10229 + 1{,}408) - [(0.38612 + 18) + (0.67830 + 1{,}352)]$$
$$= (0.10229 + 1{,}408) - (0.06442 + 1{,}371)$$
$$= 0.03787 + 37$$

Looking up the antilog of this number in a table of common logarithms (Appendix Table 2), we find that

$$\frac{600!}{20!580!} = 10{,}910 \times 10^{33}$$

PROBLEM SET 3.9

1. Determine $\binom{540}{18}\binom{60}{2}$ (see Example 3.46).

2. Determine $\binom{540}{19}\binom{60}{1}$ (see Example 3.46).

3. Determine $\binom{540}{20}\binom{60}{0}$ (see Example 3.46).

4 PROBABILITY

4.1 PROBABILITY AS A MEASURE

In the preceding chapter we counted the elements of sets and their subsets. We can consider the number of elements in a finite set S to be a measure of the set, and we shall use the symbol $m(S)$ to denote that number. We also saw in the preceding chapter that, for a given fixed set S, subsets of various measures could be formed.

Now, suppose that we wish to find out what happens when a certain act is performed. We proceed to act in the way described *one or more times* and observe what happens. We can distinguish the various aspects of this process and assign names to each. Each performance will be called a *trial*, and the set of all trials will be named an *experiment*. The result of a trial will be an *outcome*, and the set of all possible outcomes, for the stated number of trials making up the experiment, will be called a *sample space*. The sample space will be a function of the experiment, and since experiments are sets of trials, different types and/or numbers of trials mean different experiments. The following examples will clarify the meaning of these terms.

Example 4.1. Suppose that we wish to see what happens when we toss a coin. We toss the coin. We have then performed an experiment consisting of a single trial. Since a coin has but two sides, a head (H) and a tail (T), the sample space S is

$$S = \{H, T\}$$

There are two elements in this sample space $[m(S) = 2]$, and if the coin is "fair," either H or T may be the outcome of a single toss.

An experiment is fair if all its outcomes are equally likely to occur. We shall not try to define "equally likely" but trust the reader to have an intuitive idea of this notion. For example, it could be said that the various outcomes of an experiment are equally likely if there is no physical reason, inherent in the nature of the experiment, which would cause one outcome to occur with a greater frequency than any of the others, if the experiment were performed an indefinitely large number of times under identical conditions.

Example 4.2. Suppose that we toss a single die. Again we have performed an experiment consisting of a single trial. The sample space is

$$S = \{1,2,3,4,5,6\}$$

There are six elements in this sample space $[m(S) = 6]$, and if the die is fair, each outcome is equally likely.

Example 4.3. Suppose that we now toss a coin twice. The experiment consists of two trials. The logical possibilities for the first toss are the set $\{H, T\}$ and for the second $\{H, T\}$. The sample space, composed of four equally likely outcomes, is the cartesian product of these two sets, namely,

$$S = \{\langle H,H \rangle, \langle H,T \rangle, \langle T,H \rangle, \langle T,T \rangle\} \qquad m(S) = 4$$

This sample space is the same sample space that would result if two coins were tossed once. (Why?) Unless otherwise stated, assume that, in all future experiments involving the tossing of coins or dice, fair coins and unbiased dice are being employed.

Example 4.4. A lot of 25 radios is received by a dealer. He wishes to select three from this lot for testing. Describe the sample space.

Solution. First we need a definition.

Definition 4.5. An item is selected *at random* from a group of items if the selection procedure is such that each item in the group is equally likely to be selected. If of two or more outcomes each is equally likely to occur, we say that each has an equal chance of occurring.

In all the sampling experiments to be described in this text, it is assumed, unless otherwise stated, that items are selected at random.

To return to Example 4.4, an experiment consisting of three trials is performed (each trial being the selection of one radio at random). Employing the results of the previous chapter, this experiment has $\binom{25}{3} = 25!/(3!22!) = 2{,}300$ possible outcomes. The sample space S_1 can therefore be said to have 2,300 equally likely elements.

In this case, the sample space can also be described in another way. If we denote a defective outcome by 0 and a nondefective outcome by 1, then the sample space is

$$S_2 = \{\langle 1,1,1\rangle, \langle 1,1,0\rangle, \langle 1,0,1\rangle, \langle 1,0,0\rangle, \langle 0,1,1\rangle, \langle 0,1,0\rangle, \langle 0,0,1\rangle, \langle 0,0,0\rangle\}$$

Carefully note, however, that the eight elements in this sample space are not necessarily equally likely. For example, assume that five of the radios are defective. Intuitively, because there are four times as many nondefective as defective radios, you would expect that the element $\langle 1,1,1\rangle$ would have a greater chance of occurring than the element $\langle 0,0,0\rangle$ and therefore would occur more frequently if the experiment were performed an indefinitely large number of times.

So far, we have been considering the entire sample space associated with a given experiment. Consider, now, subsets of the set of all possible outcomes of a given experiment. Such subsets, when defined by some specific condition, will be called *events* in the relevant sample space.

For example, in the sample space of Example 4.3, the event "the appearance of the two heads" is the subset E of S whose element is the outcome (HH); that is, $E = \{(\text{HH})\}$. Clearly, $m(E) = 1$. The event "at least two defective radios" in Example 4.4 is the subset E of S_2,

$$E = \{\langle 1,0,0\rangle, \langle 0,1,0\rangle, \langle 0,0,1\rangle \langle 0,0,0\rangle\}$$

Clearly, $m(E) = 4$

An event is said to have occurred if some one of its elements occurs.

The ratio of the measure of an event to the measure of the finite sample space in which it is a subset is of particular importance in making predictions. This ratio, under certain conditions, is called the "probability" of an event and is defined as follows:

Definition 4.6. The probability of an event, $P(E)$, is the ratio of $m(E)$ to $m(S)$, where S is a finite sample space containing elements which are equally likely and where $E \subseteq S$ $(S \neq \emptyset)$. Or $P(E) = m(E)/m(S)$ (under the stated conditions).

Example 4.7. Suppose that a single die is thrown once. What is the probability that the face that appears will be even?

Solution. The sample space here is

$$S = \{1,2,3,4,5,6\} \quad \text{and} \quad m(S) = 6$$

The event is the set of outcomes (elements of S) which are even numbers.

$$E = \{2,4,6\} \quad m(E) = 3$$

Therefore,
$$P(E) = \frac{m(E)}{m(S)} = \frac{3}{6} = \frac{1}{2}$$

Example 4.8. Two dice are thrown. What is the probability that the sum of the faces that appears will be 4?

Solution. Here the sample space consists of $6 \times 6 = 36$ couples.

$$S = \{\langle x,y \rangle | x \text{ is a face on die 1 and } y \text{ is a face on die 2}\}$$
$$m(S) = 36$$

The event in question is the subset of S such that $x + y = 4$. This will be

$$E = \{\langle 1,3 \rangle, \langle 2,2 \rangle, \langle 3,1 \rangle\} \quad m(E) = 3$$
$$P(E) = \tfrac{3}{36} = \tfrac{1}{12}$$

On the basis of our definition of probability, the student will note that probability may be interpreted as a measure of the relative frequency with which one can expect an event to happen.

Example 4.9. A television repairman has by accident mixed 3 bad tubes with 20 good ones. If he cannot tell by looking which tube is good, what is the probability that he will select a good tube when needed? What is the probability that he will select a bad one?

Solution. The sample space consists of the 23 tubes,

$$S = \{x | x \text{ is a tube}\} \quad m(S) = 23$$

The event $E = \{x | x \text{ is a good tube}\}$ has $m(E) = 20$. Therefore,

$$P(E) = \frac{m(E)}{m(S)} = \frac{20}{23}$$

The event $E' = \{x | x \text{ is a bad tube}\}$ has $m(E') = 3$. Therefore,

$$P(E') = \tfrac{3}{23}$$

[Note that $P(E) + P(E') = \tfrac{20}{23} + \tfrac{3}{23} = \tfrac{23}{23} = 1$.]

Example 4.10. In Example 4.9, suppose that two tubes were to be selected. What is the probability that both will be good?

Solution. We note that the sample space is no longer the set of tubes, but the set of 23 tubes taken 2 at a time.

$$m(S) = \binom{23}{2} = \frac{23 \times 22 \times 21!}{2!21!} = 23 \times 11 = 253$$

The event "Both tubes are good" is that subset of S containing the couples of tubes that are both good. Since there are 20 good tubes,

$$m(E) = \binom{20}{2} = \frac{20 \times 19}{2!} = 10 \times 19 = 190$$

$$P(E) = \frac{m(E)}{m(S)} = \frac{\binom{20}{2}}{\binom{23}{2}} = \frac{190}{253} \cong 0.75$$

Example 4.11. An employer wishes to fill two positions from a group of 13 employees, 5 male and 8 female. If he selects without knowing the identity of the employee (say, by assigning a number to each and picking two numbers from a hat), what is the probability that one will be male and the other female?

Solution. As in Example 4.10, the sample space will be the number of employees taken two at a time, that is $m(S) = \binom{13}{2}$.

The event E will be the set of couples of employees, one male and one female. The measure of E is then the number of ways we can select couples containing one male and one female. We can select one male from five in $\binom{5}{1}$ ways, and for each of these $\binom{5}{1}$ ways one female can be selected from eight in $\binom{8}{1}$ ways. $m(E) = \binom{5}{1}\binom{8}{1}$.

$$P(E) = \frac{\binom{5}{1}\binom{8}{1}}{\binom{13}{2}} = \frac{5 \times 4}{13 \times 3} = \frac{20}{39}$$

PROBLEM SET 4.1

1. A poll is taken among 50 employees in a plant on the question of affiliation with a union. The results of the poll are tabulated in Table 4.1 (the table is completely fictitious.)

TABLE 4.1

	Foremen	Piece-workers	Weekly salaried	Totals
Favor affiliation...........	1	25	4	30
Oppose affiliation..........	3	10	2	15
No opinions..............	1	0	4	5
Totals................	5	35	10	50

 a. What is the probability that an employee selected at random will oppose affiliation?

 b. What is the probability that an employee selected at random will be a pieceworker?

 c. What is the probability that an employee selected at random will be a foreman who favors affiliation?

 d. What is the probability that an employee selected at random will be weekly salaried and will have no opinion?

 2. An investment club is advised by its broker that its next purchases should be chosen from utilities or electronics and is offered a half-dozen equally attractive firms in each category. If the club selects two issues at random, what is the probability that both issues will be utilities? That there will be one of each?

 3. A firm buys three lots of material a month, choosing at random from four local and five out-of-state suppliers. What is the probability that the lots go to two local and one out-of-state?

 4. An oil company is sending a team prospecting for new reserves into an area one-half of which is known to contain oil. The region is divided into eight equal sections, three of which can be covered a month. What is the probability that exactly one reserve will be proved the first month? Two? Three?

 5. A firm has three research divisions, each carrying out four projects. For budget reasons, two projects are to be canceled by a random drawing. What is the chance that a particular division will lose two?

 6. A machine turns out 20 units an hour, 5 per cent of which are defective. If a sample of 10 is taken at the end of an hour, what is the probability that no defective will show up?

 7. The personnel of a company totals 100 and is made up of four-fifths wage workers and one-fifth salaried workers, one-half of each category being male. What is the probability that two randomly selected individuals would be female salaried workers?

 8. A firm sells three varieties of four products. What is the probability that an order for two items will be for a single product?

 9. In Prob. 1*b*, Problem Set 3.3, what is the probability that the electronic device will fail to function? What is the probability that a good tube from the first box will be followed by a defective tube from the second?

 10. In Prob. 4, Problem Set 3.3, what is the probability that a committee will be made up of persons who belong to the same political party?

 11. In Example 3.46, what is the probability that the sample selected will lead to a rejection of the entire lot? What is the probability in Prob. 8, Problem Set 3.7?

4.2 COMPLEMENTARY EVENTS

A very important theorem that frequently makes computation easier is the following.

Theorem 4.12

If E is an event in a sample space S and $\bar{E}$ is the event not E (that is, the complement event to E) in the sample space S, then

$$P(E) + P(\bar{E}) = 1$$

This theorem, and all those stated in Secs. 4.2 to 4.5, will be proved for those sample spaces in which all elements are equally likely. These theorems can be proved for other sample spaces as well.

Proof. It is evident that $E \cup \bar{E} = S$ (the universe set), while $E \cap \bar{E} = \emptyset$. Then

$$m(E) + m(\bar{E}) = m(S)$$

But

$$P(E) = \frac{m(E)}{m(S)}$$

$$P(\bar{E}) = \frac{m(\bar{E})}{m(S)}$$

$$P(E) + P(\bar{E}) = \frac{m(E)}{m(S)} + \frac{m(\bar{E})}{m(S)} = \frac{m(\bar{E}) + m(E)}{m(S)}$$

$$= \frac{m(S)}{m(S)} = 1$$

We can then use this to compute probabilities more simply.

Example 4.13. An employer wishes to hire two people from a set of 13 applicants, 5 women and 8 men. What is the probability that, if he selects two at random, at least one will be a man?

Solution. The set of outcomes, i.e., the sample space S, consists of the couples of 13 applicants taken two at a time,

$$m(S) = \binom{13}{2}$$

The event "At least one is a man" (M) is the complement of the event "None is a man" $(\bar{M})$. Therefore,

$$P(M) = 1 - p(\bar{M}) \qquad \text{Why?}$$

$$= 1 - \frac{m(\bar{M})}{m(S)}$$

But $$m(\bar{M}) = \binom{5}{2} \qquad \text{Why?}$$

Therefore, $$P(M) = 1 - \frac{\binom{5}{2}}{\binom{13}{2}} = \frac{34}{39}$$

Since E is a subset of S, $E \subseteq S$, it follows

(a) $$m(E) \leq m(S)$$

If in (a) we divide by $m(S)$, we get

$$\frac{m(E)}{m(S)} \leq \frac{m(S)}{m(S)} = 1$$

or $$P(E) \leq 1$$

Moreover E may be the empty set, in which case

$$\frac{m(E)}{m(S)} = \frac{0}{m(S)} = 0$$

(It is given that $S \neq \emptyset$.)

Therefore we have the following fundamental inequality.

Theorem 4.14

$$0 \leq P(E) \leq 1$$

PROBLEM SET 4.2

1. Prove that, if $E = S$ and $\bar{E}$ is the complement of E, then $P(E) \cdot P(\bar{E}) = 0$ [that is, $P(\emptyset)$].

2. Two coins are thrown. Write the sample space. What is the probability that at least one tail will appear?

3. Two dice are thrown. What is the probability of not getting a double? (*Hint:* First find the probability of getting a double.)

4. If the probability that a given stock will increase in price is 0.6, what is the probability that it will not rise in price?

5. A poll taker reports that the probability that candidate A will win an election is $\frac{3}{4}$, while the probability of his losing the election is $\frac{2}{3}$. Is this possible?

6. A firm has entered three of its products in an international competition with seven other products. If two are to be chosen and all can be considered of equal quality, what is the probability that at least one of the firm's products will be chosen?

7. In Prob. 6 of Problem Set 4.1, what is the probability that one or more defectives will show up?

8. In Prob. 4 of Problem Set 4.1, what is the probability that one or more reserves will be proved the first month?

9. In Prob. 5 of Problem Set 4.1, what is the probability that a particular division would lose one or two of its projects?

4.3 UNION OF EVENTS

Mutually Exclusive Events. In computing probabilities, the relation of events to each other must be taken into consideration. Clearly, if S is a sample space and E_1 and E_2 are events relative to S, we can have the following cases:

(a) $\qquad\qquad E_1 \cap E_2 = \emptyset$

(b) $\qquad\qquad E_1 \cap E_2 \neq \emptyset$

Definition 4.15. If S is a sample space and E_1 and E_2 are events in S such that $E_1 \cap E_2 = \emptyset$ (that is, E_1 and E_2 are disjoint), then E_1 and E_2 are said to be *mutually exclusive* events.

Evidently, if E_1 and E_2 are mutually exclusive, then

$$P(E_1 \cap E_2) = 0$$

If $\qquad\qquad E_1 \cap E_2 \neq 0$

then $\qquad\qquad P(E_1 \cap E_2) = \dfrac{m(E_1 \cap E_2)}{m(S)}$

Example 4.16. An experiment consists of two trials, namely, the tossing of a single die twice. The sample space S is accordingly made up of 36 elements—for each of the six outcomes possible on the first trial there are six outcomes possible on the second. Let E_1 represent the event "The sum of the two dice is greater than 8," and let E_2 represent the event "The sum of the two dice is an even number greater than 6." What is $P(E_1 \cap E_2)$?

Solution. We have

$$
\begin{aligned}
E_1 &= \{\langle x,y\rangle | (\langle x,y\rangle \in S) \,\&\, (x + y > 8)\} \\
&= \{\langle 3,6\rangle,\langle 4,5\rangle,\langle 4,6\rangle,\langle 5,4\rangle,\langle 5,5\rangle,\langle 5,6\rangle,\langle 6,3\rangle,\langle 6,4\rangle,\langle 6,5\rangle,\langle 6,6\rangle\} \\
E_2 &= \{\langle x,y\rangle | (\langle x,y\rangle \in S) \,\&\, (x + y) \text{ is an even number} > 6\} \\
&= \{\langle 2,6\rangle,\langle 3,5\rangle,\langle 4,4\rangle,\langle 4,6\rangle,\langle 5,3\rangle,\langle 5,5\rangle,\langle 6,2\rangle,\langle 6,4\rangle,\langle 6,6\rangle\} \\
(E_1 \cap E_2) &= \{\langle 4,6\rangle,\langle 5,5\rangle,\langle 6,4\rangle,\langle 6,6\rangle\} \\
m(S) &= 36 \quad m(E_1) = 10 \quad m(E_2) = 9 \quad m(E_1 \cap E_2) = 4
\end{aligned}
$$

Therefore, $\qquad P(E_1 \cap E_2) = \dfrac{m(E_1 \cap E_2)}{m(S)} = \dfrac{4}{36} = \dfrac{1}{9}$

Example 4.17. Let S be a set of 60 students studying at least one of the two languages French or German. Let $F = \{x | x \text{ studies French}\}$ and $m(F) = 30$. Let $G = \{x | x \text{ studies German}\}$, $m(G) = 50$, while $m(F \cap G) = 20$. What is the probability that a student selected at

$m(S) = 60$

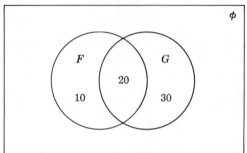

$P(F-G) = \frac{10}{60} = \frac{1}{6};$ $P(G-F) = \frac{30}{60} = \frac{1}{2};$ $P(F \cap G) = \frac{20}{60} = \frac{1}{3}$

Fig. 4.1

random (1) will study both German and French; (2) will study German but not French?

Solution. A Venn diagram (Fig. 4.1) will help. Since all 60 study at least one of the two languages, we need simply two intersecting circles. We find that

$$P(F - G) = \frac{10}{60} = \frac{1}{6} \qquad P(G - F) = \frac{30}{60} = \frac{1}{2} \qquad P(F \cap G) = \frac{20}{60} = \frac{1}{3}$$

Example 4.18. A firm sells 11 products abroad, 14 domestically, and 5 both at home and abroad. What is the probability that a product selected at random is sold both at home and abroad?

Solution. Let

$$F = \{x | x \text{ sold abroad}\}$$

and
$$H = \{x | x \text{ sold at home}\}$$

Then
$$m(S) = m(F) + m(H) - m(F \cap H)$$

(see Theorem 3.7)
$$= 11 + 14 - 5 = 20$$

and
$$P(F \cap H) = \frac{m(F \cap H)}{m(S)} = \frac{5}{20}$$

We now have a very important theorem.

Theorem 4.19

If S is a sample space and E_1 and E_2 are mutually exclusive events in S, then

$$P(E_1 \cup E_2) = P(E_1) + P(E_2)$$

Proof

$$P(E_1 \cup E_2) = \frac{m(E_1 \cup E_2)}{m(S)}$$
$$= \frac{m(E_1)}{m(S)} + \frac{m(E_2)}{m(S)}$$
$$= P(E_1) + P(E_2)$$

Note that Theorem 4.12 is a corollary of Theorem 4.19.

Example 4.20. In a lot of 500 bolts 10 per cent are usually too large and 5 per cent too small. The remainder are usually sufficiently correct to be acceptable. A prospective buyer selects a bolt at random. What is the probability that it will be acceptable?

Solution 1. Let S be the sample space. $m(S) = 500$. Let

$$E_1 = \{x | x \text{ is too large a bolt}\}$$

Ten per cent of $500 = 50$. Therefore

$$m(E_1) = 50$$

Let

$$E_2 = \{x | x \text{ is too small a bolt}\}$$

Five per cent of $500 = 25$. Therefore

$$m(E_2) = 25$$

Since E_1 and E_2 are mutually exclusive,

$$P(E_1 \cup E_2) = P(E_1) + P(E_2)$$
$$= \tfrac{50}{500} + \tfrac{25}{500} = \tfrac{1}{10} + \tfrac{1}{20} = \tfrac{3}{20}$$

Therefore the probability that the bolt will be acceptable is

$$1 - \tfrac{3}{20} = \tfrac{17}{20}$$

Solution 2. By our definition of probability we may interpret probability as a relative frequency. Therefore to say that 10 per cent are usually too large means that $P(E_1) = 10\% = \tfrac{1}{10}$; likewise to say that 5 per cent are too small means that $P(E_2) = 5\% = \tfrac{1}{20}$. Since E_1 and E_2 are mutually exclusive, $P(E_1 \cup E_2)$ (that is, probability of a defective bolt) $= 0.10 + 0.05 = 0.15$. Therefore the probability of an acceptable bolt will be $1 - 0.15 = 0.85 = \tfrac{17}{20}$.

Example 4.21. Consumer products are classified in the national income accounts as durable goods, nondurable goods, and services. Their proportions of all consumer products are 0.12, 0.48, and 0.40. What is the probability that a consumer good selected at random is a durable good? Is *not* a durable good?

Solution. Since the denominator in the calculation of the three proportions is the same, the proportion 12 per cent can be interpreted as

$$\frac{m(\text{durable goods})}{m(\text{all services and goods})} = 0.12$$

The probability that a consumer good is not a durable good will be $1 - 0.12 = 0.88$.

Overlapping Events. We consider now the case where the events are not mutually exclusive, i.e., where

$$E_1 \cap E_2 \neq \emptyset$$

Theorem 4.22

If S is a sample space and E_1 and E_2 are subsets of E such that $E_1 \cap E_2 \neq 0$, then

$$P(E_1 \cup E_2) = P(E_1) + P(E_2) - P(E_1 \cap E_2)$$

Proof. The theorem follows immediately from the fact that

$$m(E_1 \cup E_2) = m(E_1) + m(E_2) - m(E_1 \cap E_2)$$

which we proved in Theorem 3.7.

Example 4.23. What is the probability in Example 4.17 that a student studies either French or German?

Solution. Let F and G denote the sets of students who study French and German, respectively. We first note that we cannot write

$$P(F \cup G) = P(F - G) + P(G - F) = \tfrac{1}{6} + \tfrac{1}{2} = \tfrac{2}{3}$$

because we would have omitted taking into consideration the 20 students who study both French and German.

We also cannot write

$$P(F \cup G) = P(F) + P(G) = \tfrac{30}{60} + \tfrac{50}{60}$$

since that gives $\tfrac{80}{60} > 1$. This result follows because $F \cap G \neq \emptyset$.

Using the formula of Theorem 4.22, we get

$$P(F \cup G) = P(F) + P(G) - P(F \cap G) = \tfrac{30}{60} + \tfrac{50}{60} - \tfrac{20}{60} = \tfrac{60}{60} = 1$$

which is what we expect, since by assumption all the 60 students study French or German.

Example 4.24. Suppose in Example 4.17 that there were a total of 80 students, with the conditions as given. What is the probability that a student selected at random studies French or German?

Solution

$$P(F \cup G) = \tfrac{30}{80} + \tfrac{50}{80} - \tfrac{20}{80} = \tfrac{60}{80} = \tfrac{3}{4}$$

Example 4.25. An employer has three positions to fill. He decides to fill them by selecting three employees at random from among his top five assistants, A, B, C, D, and E. What is the probability that both A and B will be chosen, or that C and D will be chosen, or that C, D, and E will be chosen?

Solution. In this case the sample space is made up of triplets of the letters A, B, C, D, E. We know that there are ten such triplets

$$\binom{5}{3} = \frac{5 \times 4 \times 3!}{2!3!} = 10$$

$$S = \{(ABC),(ABD),(ABE),(ACD),(ACE),(ADE),(BCD),(BCE),$$
$$(BDE),(CDE)\}$$

$$m(S) = 10$$

Let E_1 be the event "A and B are chosen," E_2 the event "C and D are chosen," and E_3 the event "C, D, and E are chosen."

$$E_1 = \{(ABC),(ABD),(ABE)\} \qquad m(E_1) = 3$$
$$E_2 = \{(ACD),(BCD),(CDE)\} \qquad m(E_2) = 3$$
$$E_3 = \{(CDE)\} \qquad m(E_3) = 1$$

If we examine E_1 and E_2, we note that they have no elements in common but that E_2 and E_3 have one element in common.

We can solve this problem by combining the results of our previous discussions.

$$E_1 \cup E_2 \cup E_3 = E_1 \cup (E_2 \cup E_3)$$

because E_1, E_2, and E_3 are sets and the associative law holds. Therefore

$$P(E_1 \cup E_2 \cup E_3) = P[E_1 \cup (E_2 \cup E_3)]$$
Since $\quad E_1 \cap (E_2 \cup E_3) = (E_1 \cap E_2) \cup (E_1 \cap E_3)$
and $\qquad\qquad E_1 \cap E_2 = \emptyset \qquad E_1 \cap E_3 = \emptyset \qquad E_1 \cap (E_2 \cup E_3) = \emptyset$
then $\qquad P[E_1 \cup (E_2 \cup E_3)] = P(E_1) + P(E_2 \cup E_3)$
Now $\qquad\qquad\qquad E_2 \cap E_3 \neq \emptyset$
Therefore $\qquad P(E_2 \cup E_3) = P(E_2) + P(E_3) - P(E_2 \cap E_3)$

We finally get

$$P(E_1 \cup E_2 \cup E_3) = P(E_1) + P(E_2) + P(E_3) - P(E_2 \cap E_3)$$
$$P(E_1) = \tfrac{3}{10} \qquad\qquad P(E_3) = \tfrac{1}{10}$$
$$P(E_2) = \tfrac{3}{10} \qquad\quad P(E_2 \cap E_3) = \tfrac{1}{10}$$
Therefore $\qquad \tfrac{3}{10} + \tfrac{3}{10} + \tfrac{1}{10} - \tfrac{1}{10} = \tfrac{6}{10} = \tfrac{3}{5}$

PROBLEM SET 4.3

1. What is the probability of throwing a 2 or a 3 with a single die?

2. A die is thrown twice; what is the probability that the sum of the faces that appears will be at least 3? (*Hint:* Find the probability that the sum will be 2, and take the probability of the complementary event.)

3. A sample of three bulbs is to be drawn from a lot of six bulbs, one each of the following colors: red, green, blue, yellow, orange, and white. What is the probability that in a given sample neither the yellow nor the orange will appear?

4. It is known that 0.4 of the 1,000 persons who own stock in company *A* favor a new issue of stock, while 0.3 of those who own stock are opposed to the new issue. Of the 200 persons who do not own stock in the company but are entitled to vote on the matter, 0.2 favor and 0.1 oppose the issue. What is the probability that a voter selected at random favors the stock issue?

5. In Prob. 4 what is the probability that a voter selected at random favors the stock issue or owns stock?

6. An electrician has 25 fuses and knows that 5 are defective, while 10 are perfect but have too high an amperage. If he selects a fuse at random, what is the probability that he selects one that is either defective or has too high an amperage?

4.4 INTERSECTION OF EVENTS; INDEPENDENT EVENTS

Assume that two coins are tossed. Let S be the sample space, E_1 the event "heads on the first coin," and E_2 "Coins fall alike." Then

$$S = \{\langle H,H\rangle,\langle H,T\rangle,\langle T,H\rangle,\langle T,T\rangle\}$$
$$E_1 = \{\langle x,y\rangle | (\langle x,y\rangle \epsilon S) \& (x \text{ is a head})\} = \{\langle H,H\rangle,\langle H,T\rangle\}$$
$$E_2 = \{\langle x,y\rangle | (\langle x,y\rangle \epsilon S) \& (x = y)\} = \{\langle H,H\rangle,\langle T,T\rangle\}$$
$$E_1 \cap E_2 = \{\langle H,H\rangle\}$$
$$m(S) = 4 \quad m(E_1) = 2 \quad m(E_2) = 2 \quad m(E_1 \cap E_2) = 1$$

Thus
$$P(E_1 \cap E_2) = \frac{m(E_1 \cap E_2)}{m(S)} = \frac{1}{4}$$

Carefully note that $P(E_1 \cap E_2)$ is also equal to

$$P(E_1) \cdot P(E_2) = \frac{m(E_1)}{m(S)} \cdot \frac{m(E_2)}{m(S)} = \frac{2}{4} \cdot \frac{2}{4} = \frac{4}{16} = \frac{1}{4}$$

This result is no coincidence. In fact, it often occurs in situations in which interest centers in the probability that two events will occur together. Specifically, if E_1 and E_2 are two events, they may have no relation to each other or they may be so related that the occurrence of one influences the occurrence of the other. If they are not related, then the probability of E_1 should be independent of whether E_2 has occurred and that of E_2 independent of whether E_1 has occurred. Furthermore, the probability of E_1 and E_2 occurring together should depend only on these independent probabilities. This leads us to the following definition.

Definition 4.26. If E_1 and E_2 are events in a sample space S, then E_1 and E_2 are *independent* events if and only if

$$P(E_1 \cap E_2) = P(E_1) \cdot P(E_2)$$

As this implies, if E_1 and E_2 are independent events,

$$P(E_1 \cap E_2) = P(E_1) \cdot P(E_2)$$

The events defined in the coin-tossing example of this section are therefore independent.

Example 4.27. Are the events defined in Example 4.16 independent?
Solution. Since

$$m(S) = 36 \qquad m(E_1) = 10 \qquad m(E_2) = 9 \qquad m(E_1 \cap E_2) = 4$$

the relevant probabilities are

$$P(E_1 \cap E_2) = \tfrac{4}{36} = \tfrac{8}{72} \neq P(E_1) \cdot P(E_2) = \tfrac{10}{36} \cdot \tfrac{9}{36} = \tfrac{5}{72}$$

and the events are therefore not independent. That is, the probability of E_1 occurring does depend on whether E_2 has occurred. (Why?)

Example 4.28. A machine produces nails. If the machine is in good working order, only 0.2 per cent of the nails will be defective. It is known that the outcomes for successive nails are independent. What is the probability that two nails in a row are not defective?

Solution. Let $E_1 = \{x | x$ is a nondefective nail$\}$ and $E_2 = \{x | x$ is a second nail which is nondefective$\}$.

$$P(E_1) = P(E_2) = 1 - 0.002 = 0.998$$
$$P(E_1 \cap E_2) = 0.998 \times 0.998 = (1 - 0.002)^2$$

which is approximately

$$1^2 - 2 \times (0.002) = 1 - 0.004 = 0.996$$

Example 4.29. A firm discovers that a better basic material for its product is theoretically possible and that rival firms have already begun the search for it. If the probability is 0.9 that any one research group will hit on the formula in one year's time, and if the company is willing to accept a probability of failure of only 0.000001, how many separate research teams must be assigned the problem?

Solution.   Let

$$E_1 = \{x|x \text{ is unsuccessful year's work by team 1}\}$$
$$E_2 = \{x|x \text{ is unsuccessful year's work by team 2}\}$$
$$\cdots\cdots\cdots\cdots\cdots\cdots\cdots\cdots\cdots\cdots\cdots$$
$$E_n = \{x|x \text{ is unsuccessful year's work by team } n\}$$

Then
$$P(E_1) = P(E_2) = \cdots = P(E_n) = 0.1$$
$$P(E_1 \cap E_2 \cap \cdots \cap E_n) = 0.1 \times 0.1 \times \cdots \times 0.1 = 0.1^n$$

We know that 0.1^n must equal 0.000001, or $n = 6$.

PROBLEM SET 4.4

1.   Two coins are tossed.   If E_1 is the event "head on first coin," E_2 the event "head on second coin," and E_3 the event "The coins match," are the three events independent?   [*Hint:* We use the extended formula

$$P(E_1 \cap E_2 \cap E_3) = P(E_1) \cdot P(E_2) \cdot P(E_3)$$

if and only if E_1, E_2, and E_3 are independent.]

2.   Two dice, one red and the other blue, are tossed.   Are the events "The sum of the digits is 11" and "The red die falls with face different from 5" independent events?

3.   What is the probability that a machine producing 5 defective articles in every 1,000 will produce 3 defective articles in a row?

4.   Prove that, if E and F are independent events, then E and $\bar{F}$ are also ($\bar{F}$ is the complement of F.)

5.   A factory produces nuts, bolts, and rods to which the nuts and bolts are attached in random fashion.   It is known that 3 per cent of the nuts, 2 per cent of the bolts, and 1 per cent of the rods turn out defective.   What is the probability that an assembled unit will be nondefective?

6.   A stockbroker in the past has successfully predicted the action of the market, using his own method, 80 per cent of the time.   What is the probability that he will make 10 bad predictions in a row, if each prediction is made solely on the basis of his method and is independent of his other predictions?   Would you change brokers if he made 10 bad predictions in a row?

7.   Two brothers are in a group of six applicants for two positions.   If the personnel director simply draws first one, then another name at random, what is the probability that both brothers will be selected?

8.   A firm is test-marketing four different products.   The probabilities for product success have been accurately appraised at 0.8, 0.7, 0.6, and 0.5, respectively. What is the probability that all but the first will be successful?

9.   The chances are 99 out of 100 that at least one car will be sold each day on a used-car lot.   What is the probability of a 6-day business week without a sale?

10.   A stock clerk is away from his post 10 per cent of the time, and each of his assistants is busy elsewhere 20 per cent of the time.   What is the probability that the clerk will take a call and have no help in filling it?

11.   A speculator sold short in cotton (i.e., agreed to deliver in the future, at the current price, what he did not now own but would later buy) and simultaneously

contracted to buy future wheat. The probabilities that both commodities would rise in price are 0.1 and 0.8, respectively. What is the probability that he will lose in both markets?

4.5 INTERSECTION OF EVENTS; CONDITIONAL EVENTS

Often we need the probability of events with certain conditions attached. Similarly, we often require the probability of an event given that another event has occurred. Let us study the following example.

Example 4.30. Suppose that two dice are thrown. What is the probability that the sum of the two faces is 7, it being known that at least one face turned up 5?

Solution. The sample space obviously contains 6^2 outcomes. But for the probability in question we need, not these 36 outcomes, but only that subset E_2 containing the couples, at least one of whose elements is 5.

$$E_2 = \{\langle 5,1\rangle, \langle 5,2\rangle, \langle 5,3\rangle, \langle 5,4\rangle, \langle 5,5\rangle, \langle 5,6\rangle, \langle 1,5\rangle, \langle 2,5\rangle, \langle 3,5\rangle, \langle 4,5\rangle, \langle 5,5\rangle, \langle 6,5\rangle\}$$

Then $m(E_2) = 12$. Of these those which add to 7 are $E_1 = \{\langle 2,5\rangle, \langle 5,2\rangle\}$. $m(E_1) = 2$. The probability we are after is then $\frac{2}{12} = \frac{1}{6}$.

We can derive the general formula as follows:

Let S be a sample space and E_1 and $E_2 \neq \emptyset$ two events in S. Now we want the probability of E_1, given that E_2 has occurred. We call this the conditional probability of E_1 and write it as $P(E_1|E_2)$. Since we know that E_2 has occurred, all the elements in S cannot occur; i.e., only those elements in S which are also in E_2 can occur. Thus, the relevant space in this case is that defined by $E_2 \subseteq S$. As this implies, not all the elements in E_1 can now occur; i.e., only those elements which are also in E_2 can possibly occur. These elements are denoted by $E_1 \cap E_2$. The probability of E_1 occurring, given that E_2 has already occurred, is therefore given by

$$P(E_1|E_2) = \frac{m(E_1 \cap E_2)}{m(E_2)}$$

If on the right we divide numerator and denominator by $m(S)$, we get

$$P(E_1|E_2) = \frac{m(E_1 \cap E_2)/m(S)}{m(E_2)/m(S)}$$

But

$$\frac{m(E_1 \cap E_2)}{m(S)} = P(E_1 \cap E_2) \qquad \text{relative to } S$$

$$\frac{m(E_2)}{m(S)} = P(E_2) \qquad \text{relative to } S$$

Therefore we have the following theorem.

Theorem 4.31

$$P(E_1|E_2) = \frac{P(E_1 \cap E_2)}{P(E_2)}$$

Example 4.32. We solve Example 4.30 by means of this theorem. $E_1 \cap E_2$ is the set containing those elements of S which add to 7 and have one element 5.

$$m(E_1 \cap E_2) = 2 \qquad m(S) = 36$$
$$P(E_1 \cap E_2) = \tfrac{2}{36}$$

E_2 is the set containing the elements having at least one face 5.

$$m(E_2) = 12$$
$$P(E_2) = \tfrac{12}{36}$$
$$P(E_1|E_2) = \frac{\tfrac{2}{36}}{\tfrac{12}{36}} = \frac{2}{12} \qquad \text{as before}$$

Example 4.33. Given that 10 per cent of the light bulbs produced are blue and 2 per cent of all bulbs are blue and defective, what is the probability that a bulb selected at random is defective if we know that it is blue?

Solution. Let E_2 be the event "The light bulb is blue" and E_1 be the event "The light bulb is defective."

$$P(E_1|E_2) = \frac{P(E_1 \cap E_2)}{P(E_2)} = \frac{\tfrac{2}{100}}{\tfrac{10}{100}} = \frac{1}{5}$$

Example 4.34. In Prob. 1 of Problem Set 4.1, what is the probability that a salaried worker chosen at random will favor affiliation?

Solution. The problem is to find the probability of an employee who is a salaried worker favoring affiliation. By the table, the number of salaried workers is 10, while the number of salaried workers who favor affiliation is 4. The probability we seek is therefore

$$\frac{\tfrac{4}{50}}{\tfrac{10}{50}} = \frac{4}{10} = \frac{2}{5}$$

We can derive another important result if we multiply both sides of the equation of Theorem 4.31 by $P(E_2)$,

$$P(E_1 \cap E_2) = P(E_2) \cdot P(E_1|E_2) \tag{4.1}$$

This says that the probability of an event occurring which is both in E_1 and E_2 is the probability of E_2 occurring, multiplied by the probability that if E_2 occurred E_1 will also occur.

Definition 4.26 is really a special case of Eq. (4.1).   If E_1 and E_2 were independent, $P(E_1|E_2) = P(E_1)$ and Definition 4.26 and Eq. (4.1) would give identical results.   Definition 4.26 applies only to independent events, while Eq. (4.1) is more general, since it applies to independent and dependent events.

Example 4.35.   Sixty per cent of the bulbs in a box are blue.   Fifty per cent of the blue bulbs are defective.   What is the probability that if a bulb is selected at random it will be a blue bulb which is defective?

Solution.   Let S be the set of bulbs, E_2 the set of blue bulbs, and E_1 the set of defective bulbs.   Then

$$P(E_2) = 0.6 \qquad P(E_1|E_2) = 0.5$$

and, applying Eq. (4.1), we obtain

$$P(E_1 \cap E_2) = 0.6 \times 0.5 = 0.3$$

Example 4.36.   Assume that 2 cards are drawn at random from an ordinary deck of 52 playing cards.

1. If the first card is replaced before the second is drawn, what is the probability of drawing an ace followed by the king of spades?

2. If the first card is *not* replaced before the second is drawn, what is the probability of drawing an ace followed by the king of spades?

Solution.   There are two ways to solve this problem.

1a.   We can view the two draws as two trials which together make up a single experiment.   Then, the sample space S is the cartesian product of the set of 52 cards by itself.   The measure of the sample space is therefore 52^2.   We need the measure of the subset E of the sample space consisting of those ordered couples whose first element is an ace and whose second element is the king of spades.   Since there are four aces and only one king of spades, we have $4 \times 1 = 4$ such possible outcomes in the subset E; $m(E) = 4$.   By Definition 4.6,

$$P(E) = \frac{m(E)}{m(S)} = \frac{4}{52^2} = \frac{1}{13 \times 52}$$

1b.   Since we do not replace the first card when drawn, the sample space S is the cartesian product of the set of 52 cards and the set of 51 cards.   Therefore $m(S) = 52 \times 51$.   The outcomes of the subset of E of S are the possible ordered couples whose first element is an ace and second the king of spades.   As before, this subset has four elements, $m(E) = 4$.   Therefore,

$$P(E) = \frac{m(E)}{m(S)} = \frac{4}{52 \times 51} = \frac{1}{13 \times 51}$$

We can also solve Example 4.36 by giving a slight reinterpretation to Eq. (4.1), one which will enable us to use it in a wide variety of applications. Instead of thinking of $E_1 \cap E_2$ as the set of outcomes *in S* which is both in E_1 and in E_2 (as in Example 4.35), we shall think of $E_1 \cap E_2$ either as an outcome of E_2, a subset of a sample space S_2, *followed by* an outcome of E_1, a subset of another sample space S_1, or as an outcome of E_1 *in S_1 occurring together with* an outcome of E_2 *in S_2.* In other words, since different experiments may result in different sample spaces, we can view each draw as a separate experiment consisting of a single trial, each draw thereby generating its own sample space. This interpretation contrasts with that employed in solution 1, where the two draws were interpreted as a single experiment generating a single sample space. Of course, both interpretations lead to identical results. Thus, Eq. (4.1) can also be read as:

The probability that an outcome of E_1 in S_1 occurs together with an outcome of E_2 in S_2 is the probability of E_2 occurring, multiplied by the probability that if E_2 occurred E_1 will also occur.

2*a*. We take S_2 as the set of all the possible outcomes of drawing the first card *with replacement* from the deck, and we choose the subset E_2 as the event "An ace is drawn." We take S_1 as the set of all possible outcomes of drawing the second card, and we choose the subset E_1 as the event "A king of spades is drawn."

The measure of S_2 and, because of replacement, S_1 is 52, while $m(E_2) = 4$ and $m(E_1) = 1$.

Equation (4.1) applied to this problem means:

The probability that an element of E_1 in S_1 will occur, together with an outcome of E_2 in S_2 (that is, the probability of getting a king of spades along with an ace), is the probability of an outcome in E_2 (that is, the probability of getting an ace), multiplied by the probability of getting the king of spades, having drawn an ace.

$$P(E_2) = \tfrac{4}{52} \qquad P(E_1|E_2) = \tfrac{1}{52} \qquad \text{Why?}$$

Therefore $$P(E_2|E_1) = \frac{4}{52} \cdot \frac{1}{52} = \frac{1}{13 \times 52}$$

as before. Notice that Definition 4.26 also gives the same answer. Because the first card is replaced before the second is drawn, each experiment has a sample space which is in no way affected by the results of the other experiment, and as a result the two events are independent.

2*b*. Let E_1 and E_2 be defined as above. However, since there is no replacement, the sample space for the second experiment will depend on the outcome of the first experiment. As a result, the probability of E_1 will depend on whether E_2 occurred. Definition 4.26 cannot be used, but the more general equation (4.1) can be. The sample space for the first experiment, S_2, will have 52 elements, 4 of which are aces. Given that E_2 occurred, S_1 will have 51 elements, 1 of which must be the king of spades. (Why?) The probability of both E_1 and E_2 occurring is therefore

$$P(E_1 \cap E_2) = P(E_2) \cdot P(E_1|E_2) = \frac{4}{52} \cdot \frac{1}{51} = \frac{1}{13 \times 51}$$

This, of course, agrees with the answer derived by the first method.

Example 4.37. A manufacturer receives a lot of 20 steel rods. Unknown to him, 5 of these are defective. He picks 2 rods at random and tests them. What is the probability that the first will be satisfactory and the second defective?

Solution. Again two methods of solution are possible.

1. Using Definition 4.26, and letting E_1 represent the event "A satisfactory rod will be followed by a defective rod,"

$$P(E_1) = \frac{m(E_1)}{m(S)} = \frac{15 \times 5}{20 \times 19} = \frac{15}{76}$$

2. Using Eq. (4.1), and letting S_1 and S_2 represent, respectively, the sample spaces for the selection of the first and second rods, and letting E_1 and E_2 represent, respectively, the events "A satisfactory rod is selected first" and "A defective rod is selected second,"

$$P(E_2 \cap E_1) = P(E_1) \cdot P(E_2|E_1) = \tfrac{15}{20} \cdot \tfrac{5}{19} = \tfrac{15}{76}$$

Example 4.38. Show that

$$P(E_2) \cdot P(E_1|E_2) = P(E_1) \cdot P(E_2|E_1) \qquad (4.2)$$

Solution. From Theorem 4.31 we have

$$P(E_1|E_2) = \frac{P(E_1 \cap E_2)}{P(E_2)} \qquad P(E_1 \cap E_2) = P(E_2) \cdot P(E_1|E_2)$$

We also have

$$P(E_2|E_1) = \frac{P(E_2 \cap E_1)}{P(E_1)} \qquad P(E_2 \cap E_1) = P(E_1) \cdot P(E_2|E_1)$$

But from the commutative law for the intersection of two sets we have

$$(E_1 \cap E_2) = (E_2 \cap E_1)$$

so that
$$P(E_1 \cap E_2) = P(E_2 \cap E_1)$$

Therefore
$$P(E_2) \cdot P(E_1|E_2) = P(E_1) \cdot P(E_2|E_1)$$

Illustrate Eq. (4.2) using Examples 4.36 and 4.37.

PROBLEM SET 4.5

1. In Prob. 1, Problem Set 4.1, what is the probability that, if we select at random an employee who favors affiliation, he will be a pieceworker?

2. Suppose that a red and a white die are thrown simultaneously. Let E_1 denote the event "red die even," E_2 denote the event "White die shows 2." Construct the sample space and compute, by counting, $P(E_1 \cap E_2)$ and $P(E_1|E_2)$. Are they the same?

3. Prove that, if E_1 and E_2 are independent events, with probabilities nonzero, then $P(E_1|E_2) = P(E_1)$ and $P(E_2|E_1) = P(E_2)$. [*Hint:* Use the fact that, if E_1 and E_2 are independent, $P(E_1 \cap E_2) = P(E_1) \cdot P(E_2)$ and Theorem 4.31.]

4. Two dice, one red and one white, are thrown. Show that the event "Red die shows 4" is independent of the event "White die shows a number greater than 4." What is the probability, therefore, that the white die shows a number greater than 4, given that the red die shows 4?

5. Grocery stores usually stock special items to encourage sales. A given store advertises a special on bacon and eggs if purchased together. It is known that the probability of a customer buying both bacon and eggs is 0.07, while the probability of buying eggs alone is 0.20. What is the probability that a customer who has purchased eggs will buy bacon also?

6. The income earned by an individual generally varies directly with his age. If the probability that an individual both is over forty and makes more than \$10,000 is 0.1, and if the probability that an individual makes more than \$10,000 is 0.2, what is the probability that an individual is over forty if his income is known to be \$15,000?

7. A firm is considering a site for a new plant. The probability that the site is acceptable for both finished-product-market and raw-material-supply considerations is 0.6. It has been determined that the site is in fact acceptable from the supply viewpoint. Given that the probability of this latter is 0.8, what is the probability now that the site is acceptable for the product-market aspect?

8. The probability that a family has color TV is 0.2. What is the probability that any family would have two cars, if it were known that the probability of a family having both colored TV and two cars is 0.01, given that the family has color TV?

9. In Prob. 9, Problem Set 3.7, what is the probability that the lot will be rejected? (*Hint:* Theorems 4.19 and 4.31 are required.)

4.6 BAYES' THEOREM

Now we shall prove a theorem which is used repeatedly in decision theory.

Theorem 4.39

Let $E_1, E_2, \ldots, E_n$ be nonempty subsets of a set S such that $\{E_1, E_2, \ldots, E_n\}$ is a partition of S (see Sec. 2.7). Let A be any subset of S, not necessarily any E_i. Then, $B = \{A \cap E_1, A \cap E_2, \ldots, A \cap E_n\}$ is a partition of A.

Proof.   We shall show that B possesses the three properties required of a partition of A.

1. The subsets of B, $A \cap E_i$, are contained in A, that is,

$$A \cap E_i \subseteq A \qquad i = 1, 2, \ldots, n$$

2. Consider any two elements of B

$$A \cap E_i \qquad \text{and} \qquad A \cap E_j \qquad i \neq j$$

Then $(A \cap E_i) \cap (A \cap E_j) = (A \cap A) \cap (E_i \cap E_j)$

by the commutative and associative laws of sets.   Therefore

$$(A \cap E_i) \cap (A \cap E_j) = A \cap (E_i \cap E_j)$$

But since E is a partition, $E_i \cap E_j = \emptyset$, and

$$(A \cap E_i) \cap (A \cap E_j) = \emptyset$$

and the second property is met; the subsets of B are disjoint.

3. Because $E_1, E_2, \ldots, E_n$ is a partition of S, every element y in S belongs to some E_i. Because $A \subseteq S$, every element x in A, therefore, belongs to some E_i.   Therefore

$$B = \{x | x \in (A \cap E_i)\}$$

i.e., the subsets in B are exhaustive in that they contain all the elements in A.   Therefore

$$B = \{A \cap E_1, A \cap E_2, \ldots, A \cap E_n\}$$

possesses the three properties required of a partition of A.

Example 4.40.   Let S be the set of all Ford cars produced in September, 1964.   Let E_1, E_2, E_3, and E_4 be the subsets of red, green, blue, and black cars, respectively, and we shall assume that these are the only car colors used.   Then $\{E_1, E_2, E_3, E_4\}$ is a partition of S. Let $T = \{x | x \text{ is a Ford sedan}\}$.   Then $T \subseteq S$.   The set

$$B = \{T \cap E_1, T \cap E_2, T \cap E_3, T \cap E_4\}$$

is a partition of T.

Theorem 4.41

Let E_i and A be defined as in Theorem 4.39; then

$$P(A) = P(E_1)P(A|E_1) + P(E_2)P(A|E_2) + \cdots + P(E_n)P(A|E_n) \tag{4.3}$$

Proof. From Theorem 4.39 we know that $\{A \cap E_1, A \cap E_2,$
. . . $,A \cap E_n\}$ is a partition of A.

$$A = (A \cap E_1) \cup (A \cap E_2) \cup \cdots \cup (A \cap E_n)$$

expresses A as the union of n mutually exclusive events. Applying
Theorem 4.19, we obtain

$$P(A) = P(A \cap E_1) + P(A \cap E_2) + \cdots + P(A \cap E_n)$$

Substituting Eq. (4.1) for each term on the right, we get Eq. (4.3).

Example 4.42. Seventy per cent of the metal parts in a lot have been
graded "good," 20 per cent "fair," and 10 per cent "poor." Fifty per
cent of the good parts, 30 per cent of the fair parts, and 2 per cent of the
poor parts were manufactured by machine 1. If a part is selected at
random, what is the probability that it was manufactured by machine 1?

Solution. Let

$$A = \text{a part manufactured by machine 1}$$
$$E_1 = \text{a good part}$$
$$E_2 = \text{a fair part}$$
$$E_3 = \text{a poor part}$$

$\{E_1,E_2,E_3\}$ is a partition of the sample space S consisting of all parts in
the lot, and A is an event in S. We can therefore apply Eq. (4.3)
(with $n = 3$),

$$P(A) = 0.7 \times 0.5 + 0.2 \times 0.3 + 0.1 \times 0.02 = 0.412$$

We are now ready for Bayes' theorem.

Theorem 4.43

Let $\{E_1,E_2, \ldots ,E_n\}$ be a partition of the sample space S, and let $P(A)$
and $P(E_i) \neq 0$. Then for each integer k $(1 \le k \le n)$ we have

$$P(E_k|A) = \frac{P(E_k)P(A|E_k)}{P(E_1)P(A|E_1) + P(E_2)P(A|E_2) + \cdots + P(E_n)P(A|E_n)}$$

Proof. From Theorem 4.31 we have

$$P(E_k|A) = \frac{P(A \cap E_k)}{P(A)}$$

From Eq. (4.1) we have

$$P(A \cap E_k) = P(E_k)P(A|E_k)$$

so that

$$P(E_k|A) = \frac{P(E_k)P(A|E_k)}{P(A)}$$

Finally, from Eq. (4.3) we have

$$P(A) = P(E_1)P(A|E_1) + P(E_2)P(A|E_2) + \cdots + P(E_n)P(A|E_n)$$

so that

$$P(E_k|A) = \frac{P(E_k)P(A|E_k)}{P(E_1)P(A|E_1) + P(E_2)P(A|E_2) + \cdots + P(E_n)P(A|E_n)}$$

proving Theorem 4.43.

The importance of Bayes' theorem in statistical-decision theory lies in the fact that, under the stated conditions, it makes possible the revision of the probabilities of given events according to the results of additional or new information, which many times originates in samples. Thus the uncertainty associated with initial situations is reduced, and decisions, while still based on uncertainty, can be made with a smaller margin of error. The following examples will illustrate these principles.

Example 4.44. Colored balls are distributed in four boxes as shown in Table 4.2. A ball is selected at random from a box which has been selected at random. The color of the ball is black. What is the probability before the ball is selected that box 3 will be selected? What is the probability after the ball is selected that box 3 has been selected?

Solution. Let

$$A = \text{a black ball is selected}$$
$$E_1 = \text{box 1 is selected}$$
$$E_2 = \text{box 2 is selected}$$
$$E_3 = \text{box 3 is selected}$$
$$E_4 = \text{box 4 is selected.}$$

Thus, $P(E_3)$ is the first probability asked for, and $P(E_3|A)$ is the second. Because the box was chosen at random,

$$P(E_1) = P(E_2) = P(E_3) = P(E_4) = \tfrac{1}{4} = 0.25$$

[These probabilities are often called the *a priori probabilities* of event

TABLE 4.2

Box	Color			
	Black	White	Red	Blue
1	3	4	5	6
2	2	2	2	2
3	1	2	3	1
4	4	3	1	5

E_i, in contrast to $P(E_i|A)$, which are called the *a posteriori probabilities* of event E_i.] From the data given we can derive the following conditional probabilities:

$$P(A|E_1) = \tfrac{3}{18} \qquad P(A|E_2) = \tfrac{1}{4} \qquad P(A|E_3) = \tfrac{1}{7} \qquad P(A|E_4) = \tfrac{4}{13}$$

Since $\{E_1, E_2, E_3, E_4\}$ is a partition of the sample space made up of ordered couples, the first object of which identifies the number of the box and the second object the color of the ball, and since A is an event in this sample space, we can apply Bayes' theorem,

$$P(E_3|A) = \frac{\tfrac{1}{4} \cdot \tfrac{1}{7}}{\tfrac{1}{4} \cdot \tfrac{3}{18} + \tfrac{1}{4} \cdot \tfrac{1}{4} + \tfrac{1}{4} \cdot \tfrac{1}{7} + \tfrac{1}{4} \cdot \tfrac{4}{13}} = 0.165$$

Example 4.45. A box containing eight parts is received from a supplier. In the past, 70 per cent of all such boxes have had zero defective parts, 20 per cent have had one defective part, and 10 per cent have had two defective parts. Three parts are selected at random from this box, and one is found to be defective. Before the sample was taken, what was the probability of receiving a box with two defective parts? Given the sample result, what is the probability that the box originally contained two defective parts?

Solution. Obviously, the first probability asked for is 0.10. Now, let

$$A = 1 \text{ defective part in a sample of 3 parts}$$
$$E_1 = \text{a box with 0 defective parts}$$
$$E_2 = \text{a box with 1 defective part}$$
$$E_3 = \text{a box with 2 defective parts}$$

$\{E_1, E_2, E_3\}$ is a partition of that sample space consisting of all samples of three parts which could be selected from all boxes of parts produced, and A is an event in this sample space. This sample space can also be described as a set of ordered triplets, the first member of which indicates whether a given sample of three was taken from a box with zero, one, or two defectives; the second member of which designates the particular sample (for example, 1, 2, . . . , 9, . . .) out of the many possible from a given box; and the third member of which indicates the number of defective parts in the sample. $P(A|E_2)$ is calculated as follows: Because there are eight parts in each box, if we have a box with one defective part (E_2), there must be seven good parts. The probability of finding one defective part in a sample of three selected from this box is given by

$$P(A|E_2) = \frac{\dbinom{1}{1}\dbinom{7}{2}}{\dbinom{8}{3}} = \frac{3}{8} = 0.375$$

Similar calculations give

$$P(A|E_1) = 0 \qquad P(A|E_3) = \tfrac{15}{28} = 0.536$$

Applying Bayes' theorem, we therefore obtain

$$P(E_3|A) = \frac{0.1 \cdot 0.536}{0.7 \cdot 0 + 0.2 \cdot 0.375 + 0.1 \cdot 0.536} = 0.417$$

The added information derived from the sample has increased the probability of E_3 more than fourfold. What has it done to the probability of E_1?

PROBLEM SET 4.6

1. A questionnaire is submitted to a group of people, 30 per cent of whom are Republicans, 30 per cent Democrats, 35 per cent Independents, and 5 per cent other. Eighty per cent of the Republicans, 10 per cent of the Democrats, 45 per cent of the Independents, and 10 per cent of the others vote in favor of a given policy. What is the probability that if a person is selected at random he will vote in favor of this policy?

2. Fifty-five per cent of the sophomores, 30 per cent of the juniors, and 5 per cent of the seniors in a particular college are taking an economics course. Forty per cent of all upper-class students are sophomores, 30 per cent are juniors, and 30 per cent are seniors. If an upper-class student is selected at random, what is the probability that he takes an economics course?

3. Three boxes of metal parts, each from a different supplier, lie in a storeroom. In the past, 80 per cent of the parts of supplier 1 have been graded "excellent," 10 per cent "fair," and 10 per cent "poor"; the corresponding percentages for supplier 2 are 70, 20, and 10 per cent and for supplier 3 are 75, 20, and 5 per cent. A box is selected at random, and a part is selected from it, the part being "poor." Before the part was selected what was the probability of selecting the box of supplier 3? After the part is selected, what is the probability?

4. A box containing 12 parts is received from a supplier. In the past, 60 per cent of all such boxes have had no defective parts, 20 per cent have had one defective part, 15 per cent have had two defective parts, and 5 per cent have had three defective parts. Four parts are selected at random from this box, and two are found to be defective. Before the sample was taken, what was the probability of receiving a box which had three defective parts? After the sample has been taken, what is the probability that the box received has 3 defective parts?

4.7 REPEATED EVENTS (BINOMIAL PROBABILITIES)

The type of problem we shall now consider ties in directly with the binomial expansion. It is recalled that the general term of the binomial expansion $(p + q)^n$ involving p^r is $\binom{n}{r} p^r q^{n-r}$. It is also recalled that the expression $\binom{n}{r}$, denoting the coefficient of the term involving p^r, may be interpreted as the number of combinations of n things r at a time, or the number of subsets of r elements of a set of n elements. We shall now show by an example how this is related to a specific type of probability problem.

Example 4.46. Five awards are to be made to four people, A, B, C, and D, by selecting their names from a bag at random. After a name has been selected, it is to be replaced in the bag for the next drawing. It is agreed that five drawings are to be made. What is the probability that a given individual, say, A, will receive exactly three awards?

Solution. We can think of this example as an experiment consisting of five trials, each trial being the drawing of a name. Each *trial* has two possible outcomes: A's name is selected, or A's name is not selected. We denote these outcomes by A and $\bar{A}$, respectively. The outcome of an *experiment* can therefore be designated by a sequence of five A's and $\bar{A}$'s, as, for example, $\bar{A}\bar{A}AA\bar{A}$, $\bar{A}\bar{A}AA\bar{A}$, $AAAAA$, etc. The set of all possible outcomes of the experiment, i.e., the relevant sample space for the experiment, contains $2^5 = 32$ elements. (The first position in the sequence of A's and $\bar{A}$'s can be filled in either of $2^1 = 2$ ways; for each of these the second position can be filled in either of two ways, making $2^2 = 4$ possible ways for the first two positions; for each of these the third position can be filled in either of two ways, making $2^3 = 8$ possible ways for the first three positions; etc.) But the elements of this sample space are not equally likely. For example, we would intuitively expect the element $\bar{A}\bar{A}\bar{A}\bar{A}\bar{A}$ to occur more frequently, if the experiment were performed many times, than the element $AAAAA$. Below, we shall show this to be the case. In situations in which the elements of the relevant sample space are not equally likely, it is necessary to use Theorem 4.22 and/or Eq. (4.1) in conjunction with Definition 4.6.

This necessitates thinking of this example in a different fashion. Let each draw represent an experiment consisting of a single trial. Let S_1, S_2, S_3, S_4, and S_5 designate the sample spaces for these five experiments. There are four possible outcomes for each experiment, i.e., the relevant sample space contains four elements. These elements, which are equally likely, represent the drawing of A's, B's, C's, or D's name. Let A_1 represent the event "A's name is selected on the first draw," A_2 the event "A's name is selected on the second draw," and similarly for A_3, A_4, and A_5. Let $\bar{A}_1$ represent the event "A's name is not selected on the first draw," $\bar{A}_2$ the event "A's name is not selected on the second draw," and similarly for $\bar{A}_3$, $\bar{A}_4$, and $\bar{A}_5$. Then

$$P(A_i) = \frac{m(A_i)}{m(S_i)} = \frac{1}{4} = p \qquad i = 1, 2, \ldots, 5$$

$$P(\bar{A}_i) = \frac{m(\bar{A}_i)}{m(S_i)} = \frac{3}{4} = 1 - p = q \qquad i = 1, 2, \ldots, 5$$

As this implies, the different events are independent—the probability that a given event will occur in a given experiment in no way depends on the result of any other experiment. This important characteristic of this sequence of experiments results because each name is replaced immediately after each draw.

We are interested in the probability of A's name being selected exactly r times in n draws, $r = 3$ and $n = 5$. Let B_1 be the "compound" event represented by the following intersection of events:

$$B_1 = (A_1 \cap A_2 \cap A_3 \cap \bar{A}_4 \cap \bar{A}_5)$$

If B_1 occurs, A's name will be selected three times. Since B_1 is made up of independent events, Definition 4.26 is applicable and

$$P(B_1) = P(A_1) \cdot P(A_2) \cdot P(A_3) \cdot P(\bar{A}_4) \cdot P(\bar{A}_5)$$
$$= \tfrac{1}{4} \cdot \tfrac{1}{4} \cdot \tfrac{1}{4} \cdot \tfrac{3}{4} \cdot \tfrac{3}{4} = (\tfrac{1}{4})^3 \cdot (\tfrac{3}{4})^2 = p^r q^{n-r}$$

But B_1 is not the only intersection of events which will result in A's name being selected three times. Two other possibilities are

$$\bar{B}_2 = (A_1 \cap A_2 \cap \bar{A}_3 \cap \bar{A}_4 \cap A_5) \qquad P(B_2)$$
$$= \tfrac{1}{4} \cdot \tfrac{1}{4} \cdot \tfrac{3}{4} \cdot \tfrac{3}{4} \cdot \tfrac{1}{4} = (\tfrac{1}{4})^3 (\tfrac{3}{4})^2 = p^r q^{n-r}$$
$$B_3 = (A_1 \cap A_2 \cap \bar{A}_3 \cap A_4 \cap \bar{A}_5) \qquad P(B_3)$$
$$= \tfrac{1}{4} \cdot \tfrac{1}{4} \cdot \tfrac{3}{4} \cdot \tfrac{1}{4} \cdot \tfrac{3}{4} = (\tfrac{1}{4})^3 (\tfrac{3}{4})^2 = p^r q^{n-r}$$

Notice that each possibility represents a distinct arrangement of five objects, three of one kind (the A's) and two of another (the $\bar{A}$'s). Theorem 3.51 tells us that the total number of such arrangements is

$$\binom{n}{r} = \binom{5}{3} = 10$$

Notice that the probability of each arrangement (i.e., intersection or compound event) is the same and that they are mutually exclusive. Notice, finally, that A's name will be selected three times if the following event occurs:

$$C = (B_1 \cup B_2 \cup \cdots \cup B_{10})$$

Therefore, employing Theorem 4.19, we have the solution to this problem,

$$P(C) = P(B_1 \cup B_2 \cup \cdots \cup B_{10}) = P(B_1) + P(B_2) + \cdots + P(B_{10})$$
$$= (p^r q^{n-r})_1 + (p^r q^{n-r})_2 + \cdots + (p^r q^{n-r})_{10}$$
$$= \binom{n}{r} p^r q^{n-r}$$
$$= \binom{5}{3}\left(\frac{1}{4}\right)^3\left(\frac{3}{4}\right)^2$$
$$= 10(\tfrac{1}{4})^3(\tfrac{3}{4})^2 \qquad\qquad (4.4)$$

Note that Eq. (4.4) represents the term involving $(\frac{1}{4})^3$ in the expansion of $(\frac{1}{4} + \frac{3}{4})^5$. If we write the expansion

$$\left(\frac{1}{4} + \frac{3}{4}\right)^5 = \left(\frac{1}{4}\right)^5 + \binom{5}{4}\left(\frac{1}{4}\right)^4\left(\frac{3}{4}\right) + \binom{5}{3}\left(\frac{1}{4}\right)^3\left(\frac{3}{4}\right)^2 + \binom{5}{2}\left(\frac{1}{4}\right)^2\left(\frac{3}{4}\right)^3$$
$$+ \binom{5}{1}\left(\frac{1}{4}\right)\left(\frac{3}{4}\right)^4 + \left(\frac{3}{4}\right)^5$$

we can say

The probability that A's name is drawn all five times is $(\frac{1}{4})^5$

The probability that A's name is drawn exactly four times is $\binom{5}{4}\left(\frac{1}{4}\right)^4\left(\frac{3}{4}\right)$

and so on.

We can generalize this to the following theorem.

Theorem 4.47

If p is the probability that any one event will occur in a single experiment and $q = 1 - p$ is the probability that the event will not occur, then the probability that the event will occur exactly r times in n experiments is the term with p^r in the expansion of $(p + q)^n$—that is, the probability is $\binom{n}{r}p^r q^{n-r}$.

For this theorem to be strictly applicable, the following conditions must be satisfied:

1. We are interested in the probability of an event E occurring exactly r times in n experiments.

2. Only two events are defined for each experiment—E and $\bar{E}$, the complement of E. These events must therefore be mutually exclusive and exhaustive.

3. The outcome of a given experiment is not influenced by that of any other experiment; i.e., the outcomes of all experiments are independent.

4. $P(E)$ is the same for each experiment.

Example 4.48. A manufacturing plant turns out a continuous stream of product throughout the year. Under normal conditions, 5 per cent of the items turned out by the process are defective. One morning, 10 items are selected at random from the assembly line. What is the probability that exactly 3 of these are defective?

Solution. We can think of the selection of each item as a separate experiment, there being 10 experiments. Let E be the event "The item selected is defective." We seek the probability that E will occur $r = 3$ times in $n = 10$ experiments, with $P(E) = p = 0.05$ and $q = 0.95$. If we can assume that the outcomes of all experiments are independent (not unreasonable in this type of situation) and that the process percentage defective has not changed from 5 per cent, then Theorem 4.47 is applicable. The desired probability is therefore

$$\binom{10}{3} (0.05)^3 (0.95)^7 = 0.0105$$

Example 4.49. Five parts are selected at random from a lot of 500 parts, 50, or 10 per cent, of which are defective. What is the probability that 2 of these are defective?

Solution. Again we can think of the selection of each part as a separate experiment and calculate the required probability by using Theorem 4.47.

$$\binom{n}{r} p^r q^{n-r} = \binom{5}{2} (0.1)^2 (0.9)^3 = 0.0729$$

However, this theorem is not strictly applicable in this case, because the probability of a given event depends on the outcomes of previous experiments (condition 3 is violated). For example, if the first four parts selected happened to be defective, the probability of the fifth part being defective would be $\frac{46}{496}$, but if the first four parts were good, the probability of the fifth part being defective would be $\frac{50}{496}$. This situation results because, of course, each sampled part is not replaced before the next part is selected.

The method employed in the solution of Examples 4.10 and 4.11 is the theoretically precise one to apply in this case. The probability calculated by this method is called a *hypergeometric* probability, in contrast to the *binomial* probabilities discussed in this section. If we let N denote the total number of parts in the lot, R the number of defective items in the lot, n the number of parts in the sample, and r the number of defective parts in the sample, the required probability is calculated from the formula

$$\frac{\binom{R}{r} \binom{N-R}{n-r}}{\binom{N}{n}} = \frac{\binom{50}{2} \binom{450}{3}}{\binom{500}{5}} = \frac{50!}{2!48!} \cdot \frac{450!}{3!447!} \cdot \frac{5!495!}{500!} = 0.0724$$

An interesting fact is evident. The hypergeometric probability is not significantly different from the binomial probability, the difference occurring in the fourth decimal place. This will always be the case when the sample size is small relative to the size of the *population*, or *universe* (the italicized words are equivalently defined as all the items in the group under study). In the present case, the sample size is only 5, while the population size is 500. In summary, a binomial probability can be employed as a close approximation to a hypergeometric probability when the sample size is small relative to the population size. This relationship is extremely helpful in computational work, because extensive tables containing binomial probabilities for different n's, r's, and p's are readily available.

Example 4.50. The quality-control director in a manufacturing plant examines a lot of 20 parts selected at random from one machine's production of 1,200 parts. Under normal operating conditions, 5 per cent of the parts turned out are defective. If the sample contains 2 or more defective parts, the director will order a check of the machine producing these parts. What is the probability that a check will be ordered if the machine is operating normally?

Solution. Since the sample size is small relative to the population size, the binomial approximation can be used. Let E represent a defective item, and let C_1 be the event "E occurs $r = 0$ times in $n = 20$ experiments" and C_2 be the event "E occurs $r = 1$ times in $n = 20$ experiments." Then the probability that a machine check will be ordered is

$$1 - [P(C_1) + P(C_2)]$$
$$= 1 - \left[\binom{20}{0} (0.05)^0 (0.95)^{20} + \binom{20}{1} (0.05)^1 (0.95)^{19} \right]$$
$$= 1 - (0.3585 + 0.3774) = 0.2641$$

Example 4.51. Twenty per cent of a very large class of stock pays no dividends. What is the probability that out of a random sample of 10 stocks 7 or more will pay dividends?

Solution. Since the sample size is small relative to the population size, Theorem 4.47 can be used as an approximation. Let

$$p = 0.2 \text{ (no dividend payment)}$$
$$q = 0.8 \text{ (dividend payment)}$$

Seven or more paying dividends is the same as three or less not paying dividends. The probabilities for the latter are

None did not pay:	$\binom{10}{0} (0.2)^0 (0.8)^{10}$	$= 0.1074$
One did not pay:	$\binom{10}{1} (0.2)^1 (0.8)^9$	$= 0.2684$
Two did not pay:	$\binom{10}{2} (0.2)^2 (0.8)^8$	$= 0.3020$
Three did not pay:	$\binom{10}{3} (0.2)^3 (0.8)^7$	$= 0.2013$
Three or less did not pay		$= 0.8791$

Example 4.52.   A factory produces nuts and bolts, and also rods to which the nuts and bolts are attached in random fashion.   It is known that 3 per cent of the nuts, 2 per cent of the bolts, and 1 per cent of the rods turn out defective.   An assembled unit is nondefective as long as the nut and bolt are nondefective—i.e., a defective rod, by itself, does not make the assembled unit defective.   What is the probability that three out of five assembled units, selected at random, are nondefective?

Solution.   The solution proceeds in two stages.

1. Think of the selection of a nut, bolt, and rod for a single assembly as experiments 1, 2, and 3, respectively.   Let N_1 denote the event "The nut selected for a single assembly is not defective," B_2 the event "The bolt is not defective," R_3 the event "The rod is not defective," $\bar{N}_1$ the event "The nut is defective," $\bar{B}_2$ the event "The bolt is defective," and $\bar{R}_3$ the event "The rod is defective."   Then an assembled unit will be nondefective if either of the following two events occurs:

$$A_1 = (N_1 \cap B_2 \cap R_3)$$
$$A_2 = (N_1 \cap B_2 \cap \bar{R}_3)$$

Since it is reasonable to assume that the events N_1, $\bar{N}_1$, B_2, $\bar{B}_2$, R_3, and $\bar{R}_3$ are independent, Definition 4.26 can be employed to determine the probabilities of these two intersections of events,

$$P(A_1) = P(N_1) \cdot P(B_2) \cdot P(R_3) = 0.97 \cdot 0.98 \cdot 0.99 = 0.9411$$
$$P(A_2) = P(N_1) \cdot P(B_2) \cdot P(\bar{R}_3) = 0.97 \cdot 0.98 \cdot 0.01 = 0.0095$$

Since A_1 and A_2 are mutually exclusive, Theorem 4.19 can be employed to determine the probability that their union, C, will occur,

$$C = (A_1 \cup A_2)$$
$$P(C) = P(A_1) + P(A_2) = 0.9506$$

$P(C)$ is, of course, the probability that a given assembly will be non-defective.

2. Now, think of the selection of an assembled unit as a single experiment.   We have just determined that the probability of a nondefective unit is approximately 0.95.   If we call this probability p, Example 4.52 is reduced to the calculation of the following binomial probability:

$$\binom{5}{3} (0.95)^3 (0.05)^2 = 0.0214$$

Example 4.53.   Over a long period of time, a machinist has produced parts, 70 per cent of which are graded "excellent," 20 per cent "fair," and 10 per cent "poor."   What is the probability that, in a random sample of five parts, two will be excellent, two fair, and one poor?

Solution.   Review Prob. 12, Problem Set 3.8.   Think of the selection of each part as a single experiment.   We shall need the *multinomial probability theorem.*

Theorem 4.54

If p_1, p_2, . . . , p_s $(p_1 + p_2 + \cdot \cdot \cdot + p_s = 1)$ are the probabilities, respectively, that events E_1, E_2, . . . , E_s will occur in a single experiment, then the probability that E_1 will occur n_1 times, that E_2 will occur n_2 times, . . . , that E_s will occur n_s times in n experiments

$$(n_1 + n_2 + \cdot \cdot \cdot + n_s = n)$$

is the term written $p_1{}^{n_1} \cdot p_2{}^{n_2} \cdot \cdot \cdot p_s{}^{n_s}$ in the expansion of $(p_1 + p_2 + \cdot \cdot \cdot + p_s)^n$; that is, the probability is

$$\binom{n}{n_1, n_2, \ \cdot \ \cdot \ \cdot \ , n_s} p_1{}^{n_1} p_2{}^{n_2} \cdot \cdot \cdot p_s{}^{n_s}$$

The conditions necessary for this theorem to apply are:
1. The events E_1, E_2, . . . , E_s are mutually exclusive and exhaustive.
2. The outcomes of all experiments are independent.
3. $P(E_1) = p_1$, $P(E_2) = p_2$, . . . , $P(E_s) = p_s$ are the same for each experiment.

Therefore, for the problem at hand, the required probability is

$$\binom{5}{2, 2, 1} (0.7)^2 (0.2)^2 (0.1)^1 = 0.0588$$

PROBLEM SET 4.7

1.   A truck fleet has a trip accident probability of 0.01.   What is the probability that no trucks will have an accident if 2 are sent out?   If 10 are sent out?

2.   The chance of complete loss on a certain class of investments is 0.05.   Six investments are made.   What is the probability that exactly three will completely fail?

3.   Ten per cent of consumer products are imported.   What is the probability that a random sample of eight consumer products will have two or less foreign items?

4.   A machine process turns out 15 defectives in 100.   The inspection procedure is set up so that the probability of finding no more than 1 defective in the inspection lot is exactly 0.5995.   What sample size is being used?

5.   The probability of qualifying for a particular job is $\frac{1}{3}$.   A personnel director has two interviews scheduled for the morning and six for the afternoon.   What is the probability that he will hire both individuals in the morning?   All six in the afternoon?   All eight for the day?

6. A company has a 0.30 dropout rate in its training program. What is the probability that the company will get four or more dropouts from its current group of nine in training?

7. Prove Theorem 4.54, using Example 4.46 as a guide.

8. Thirty-five per cent of the population of a large city are Democrats, 30 per cent Republicans, 25 per cent Independents, and 10 per cent other. What is the probability that a random sample of 12 persons will contain exactly 5 Democrats, 5 Republicans, 1 Independent, and 1 other?

9. In the above problem, what is the probability that the sample will contain a majority of Democrats? (*Hint:* Let D represent the event "Democrat" and $\bar{D}$ the event "non-Democrat," and use binomial probabilities.)

4.8 RANDOM VARIABLES, PROBABILITY DISTRIBUTIONS, AND EXPECTED VALUES

We shall conclude this chapter by introducing several concepts which are fundamental in that area of applied mathematics known as statistical decision theory.

Definition 4.55. A random (or stochastic, or chance) variable is a set V of ordered couples,

$$V = \{\langle x,y\rangle | x \in S \ \& \ y \in R\}$$

with S the set of outcomes in a given sample space and R a subset of the set of real numbers.

The values of the random variable are the second elements in the ordered couples given by V.

Example 4.56. An experiment consists in tossing a single coin three times. The sample space S is

$$S = \{HHH,HHT,HTH,HTT,TTT,TTH,THH,THT\}$$

We let V denote the random variable whose value y for any element x of S is the number of heads obtained. Then

$$V = \{\langle HHH,3\rangle,\langle HHT,2\rangle,\langle HTH,2\rangle,\langle HTT,1\rangle,\langle TTT,0\rangle,$$
$$\langle TTH,1\rangle,\langle THH,2\rangle,\langle THT,1\rangle\}$$

Note that a given value of V may arise from several different outcomes. For example, $y = 2$ arises from HHT, HTH, and THH. Furthermore, more than one random variable may be defined on the same sample space. For example, we could define W as the random variable whose value is the number of heads obtained plus 2. Then

$$W = \{\langle HHH,5\rangle,\langle HHT,4\rangle, \ . \ . \ . \ ,\langle THT,3\rangle\}$$

Example 4.57. A retailer knows that he will sell one, two, three, four, or five units of a given product daily. He makes a profit of \$2 on each unit sold. If we let T denote the random variable "total profit," we have

$$T = \{\langle 1,2 \rangle, \langle 2,4 \rangle, \langle 3,6 \rangle, \langle 4,8 \rangle, \langle 5,10 \rangle\}$$

In this example, an experiment consists in finding out the number of units sold at the end of the day, the sample space for the experiment being $S = \{1,2,3,4,5\}$.

Definition 4.58. The probability distribution of a random variable is a set P of ordered couples

$$P = \{\langle y,p \rangle | y \, \epsilon \, B \, \& \, p \, \epsilon \, C\}$$

with B the set of possible values of the random variable and C the set of probabilities for these values.

Example 4.59. The reader should be able to verify that the probability distribution for the random variable V defined in Example 4.56 is

$$P = \{\langle 0,\tfrac{1}{8} \rangle, \langle 1,\tfrac{3}{8} \rangle, \langle 2,\tfrac{3}{8} \rangle, \langle 3,\tfrac{1}{8} \rangle\}$$

Example 4.60. The retailer of Example 4.57 believes that the probabilities of having one, two, three, four, and five units demanded daily are, respectively, 0.10, 0.15, 0.35, 0.25, and 0.15. The probability distribution for the random variable "total profit" is then

$$P = \{\langle 2,0.10 \rangle, \langle 4,0.15 \rangle, \langle 6,0.35 \rangle, \langle 8,0.25 \rangle, \langle 10,0.15 \rangle\}$$

Definition 4.61. If the values of a random variable are $y_1, y_2, \ldots, y_n$ and the respective probabilities are $p_1, p_2, \ldots, p_n$, then the expected value E of the random variable is

$$E = p_1 y_1 + p_2 y_2 + \cdots + p_n y_n$$

Thus E is the sum of n terms, each term being the product of the two elements of an ordered couple defined by the probability distribution of the random variable.

Example 4.62. The expected value of the random variable defined in Example 4.56 is

$$E = 0 \cdot \tfrac{1}{8} + 1 \cdot \tfrac{3}{8} + 2 \cdot \tfrac{3}{8} + 3 \cdot \tfrac{1}{8} = \tfrac{12}{8} = 1.5$$

Example 4.63. The expected value of the random variable "total profit" (Example 4.57), is

$$E = 2 \cdot 0.10 + 4 \cdot 0.15 + 6 \cdot 0.35 + 8 \cdot 0.25 + 10 \cdot 0.15 = 6.40$$

The expression "expected value" (sometimes referred to as "mathematical expectation") does not imply that the value of E is in any sense expected to occur in a single experiment. The expected value of a random variable will most often not equal any of the values in the set of possible values. It is better to view E as a mathematical expression which is a measure of the value of the variable.

E can also be interpreted as the value of the random variable *on the average in the long run.* For example, if the same experiment were performed many times, say, N times, then it would be expected that the value y_1 would occur p_1N times, that y_2 would occur p_2N times, . . . , and that y_n would occur p_nN times, so that the value per experiment *on the average* would be

$$\frac{y_1(p_1N) + y_2(p_2N) + \cdots + y_n(p_nN)}{N}$$

$$= \frac{N(y_1p_1 + y_2p_2 + \cdots + y_np_n)}{N} = E$$

The concepts introduced in this section will be applied to the area of decision theory as more mathematics is introduced (see, for instance, Example 7.42).

PROBLEM SET 4.8

1. On the basis of past experience it is estimated that there is a 10 per cent probability of selling zero units per day, a 20 per cent probability of selling one unit, a 20 per cent probability of selling two units, a 30 per cent chance of selling three units, and a 20 per cent probability of selling four units. If one or two units are sold, the profit on each unit is \$2; if three units are sold, the profit on each unit is \$3; and if four units are sold, the profit on each unit is \$4. What is the expected value of the random variable "total profit"?

2. Two dice are rolled. V denotes the random variable whose value is the sum of the numbers obtained from the roll of the two dice. What is the expected value of the random variable?

5 RELATIONS AND FUNCTIONS

5.1 SETS AND THEIR GRAPHS

It is often convenient to have geometric representations of sets. We have already studied Venn diagrams, which are representations of sets. A given set is associated with a circle. The union and intersection of sets as well as the complements of sets can then be easily recognized from these representations. When sets have real numbers as elements, these real numbers may be associated in a special way with the points in a plane. The resultant set of points in the plane is called the *graph* of the set.

5.2 RELATIONS AND FUNCTIONS

We first define the concept of relation.

Definition 5.1. Let S and T be sets. Then a relation of S to T is a set of ordered couples $\langle x,y \rangle$ such that $x \in S$ and $y \in T$, or

$$r = \{\langle x,y \rangle | (x \in S) \ \& \ (y \in T)\}$$

Evidently a relation is any subset of the cartesian product set $S \times T$. (Review Sec. 3.3.)

Example 5.2. Let $S = \{2,3\}$ and $T = \{3,4,5\}$. Then we can define a relation of S to T as follows:

$$r = \{\langle 2,3 \rangle, \langle 2,4 \rangle, \langle 2,5 \rangle, \langle 3,4 \rangle, \langle 3,5 \rangle\}$$

This relation of S to T can also be defined by

$$r = \{\langle x,y \rangle | (x \in S) \ \& \ (y \in T) \ \& \ (x < y)\}$$

Other relations of S to T can of course be defined, e.g.,

$$r = \{\langle x,y \rangle | (x \in S) \ \& \ (y \in T) \ \& \ (x = y)\} = \{\langle 3,3 \rangle\}$$

Example 5.3. Let $S = \{x | x$ is a positive integer$\}$ and $T = \{y | y$ is the square of any integer$\}$. We define a relation r as follows:

$$r = \{\langle x,y \rangle | (x \in S) \ \& \ (y \in T) \ \& \ (y = x^2) \ \& \ (x < 5)\}$$
that is, $\qquad r = \{\langle 1,1 \rangle, \langle 2,4 \rangle, \langle 3,9 \rangle, \langle 4,16 \rangle\}$

In Example 5.2, r is first described simply by listing the couples which are elements of r. In Example 5.3, the elements of r can be described by defining S and T and writing the general element of r, that is, $\langle x,x^2 \rangle$, or by writing $y = x^2$: $r = \{\langle x,y = x^2 \rangle | (x \in S) \ \& \ (y \in T)\}$.

The element y may be written also as $r(x)$, and in Example 5.3, $y = r(x) = x^2$. So $r(1) = 1$; $r(2) = 4$; $r(3) = 9$; $r(4) = 16$.

It should be carefully noted that, in Definition 5.1, the definition of r put the elements of S first in the couples. In other words, the *order* of the components of $\langle x,y \rangle \in r$ is important. From Sec. 3.3, we know that a couple in which the order of its components makes a difference is an *ordered* couple. For ordered couples, $\langle x,y \rangle \neq \langle y,x \rangle$. We shall refer to the set whose elements are the first components of a relation as the *domain* of the relation, while the set whose elements are the second components is called the *range* of r. In defining any relation, the domain and range should be carefully stated.

Example 5.4. Given the relation $r = \{\langle 2,4 \rangle, \langle 3,9 \rangle, \langle 4,16 \rangle\}$, define the domain D and range R of r.

Solution

$$D = \{2,3,4\}$$
$$R = \{4,9,16\}$$

Note that r may be defined by $y = x^2$ ($y \in R$ & $x \in D$)

Example 5.5.   Eight articles are purchased.   The first two articles cost \$10 each, and the price, because of quantity discounts, decreases \$1 with each additional article purchased.   Show the relation of articles to price.

Solution.   Let us denote the set A of articles purchased by

$$A = \{a_1, a_2, a_3, a_4, a_5, a_6, a_7, a_8\}$$

and the set P of possible prices by

$$P = \{12,11,10,9,8,7,6,5,4,3\}$$

The relation of A to P will be

$$r = \{\langle a_1,10\rangle, \langle a_2,10\rangle, \langle a_3,9\rangle, \langle a_4,8\rangle, \langle a_5,7\rangle, \langle a_6,6\rangle, \langle a_7,5\rangle, \langle a_8,4\rangle\}$$

the range being

$$R = \{10,9,8,7,6,5,4\}$$

In this case two elements of the domain A are related to the same element of the range R.   The relation may be described as follows:

$$r = \begin{cases} r(a_1) = 10 \\ r(a_2) = 10 \\ r(a_i) = 10 - (i - 2) \qquad \text{for } i = 3, 4, \ldots, 8 \end{cases}$$

Relations in which for each element in the domain there is only one element in the range are of special importance.

Definition 5.6.   If x is an element of the domain D and y and z are elements of the range R of a relation r, and if $\langle x,y\rangle \in r$ and $\langle x,z\rangle \in r$ imply $y = z$, then r will be called a *function* (or a *mapping* of D to R, sometimes designated by $D \to R$).

Suppose that we have a set S and a set T and form the cartesian product $S \times T$.   If we define a relation r from S to T such that (1) r is a function, (2) the domain of r is S and the range of r is a *proper* subset of T, then r will be said to be a mapping of S *into* T.   If the range of r is the set T, then r will be called a mapping of S *onto* T.

Example 5.7.   The relation f defined by $y = 2x$, with domain D the set of positive integers and range R the set of positive even integers, is a function.   This is true because for each $x \in \{x|x$ is a positive integer$\}$ there exists one and only one positive even integer.   Since the range of the relation is the set of positive even integers, D is mapped onto R.   The student should be aware that if in this example we change the domain, for example, to the set of positive integers between 1 and 10 the range will change, and therefore the mapping $y = 2x$ will be different. (What will the range be now?)

If we consider any set S such that the range $R \subset S$, then we may also view the function as a mapping of D *into* S. For example, if S is the set of all integers, the mapping is *into* S.

Example 5.8.   Given the sets

$S = \{x|x$ is a positive integer$\}$

$T = \{y|y$ is a real number, and y is the square root of any positive integer$\}$

we define

$$r = \{\langle x,y \rangle|(x \in S) \ \& \ (y \in T) \ \& \ y = \sqrt{x}\}$$

Is the relation r a function of S to T?

Solution.   Let x equal any positive integer a. Then there are two possible values for $y = r(a)$, namely, $+ \sqrt{a}$ and $- \sqrt{a}$. Since Definition 5.6 has been violated, r is not a function of S to T.

Example 5.9.   In the above example, assume that

$T' = \{y|y$ is a nonnegative real number, and y is the square root of any positive integer$\}$

Is the relation r a function of S to T'?

Solution.   In this case r is a function, since for any positive integer a there is a unique value for $y = r(a)$, namely, $+ \sqrt{a}$. In this case, S is mapped *onto* T'. If T' were the set of nonnegative real numbers, then the range of the relation would be the subset of T' consisting of the square roots of positive integers and S would be mapped *into* T'.

In general, to avoid the difficulties of Examples 5.8 and 5.9, we define $\sqrt{a}$ as the positive number which when squared gives a.

Example 5.10.   If the market price of a commodity such as automobiles is fixed by collusion or regulation and if a firm can market as much as it can produce at this price, the total revenue z from sales is the product of the fixed price p and the quantity q of goods sold ($z = p \cdot q$). z is a function f of q; that is, $z = f(q)$. (Why?)

The domain D of the function is the set of nonnegative integers 0 to capacity output c, while the range R is the set of rational numbers z, such that $0 \leq z \leq p \cdot c$. In this case

$$f = \{\langle q,z \rangle|(q \in D) \ \& \ (z \in R) \ \& \ z = p \cdot q\}$$

Definition 5.11.   A relation r of a set S to a set T is a 1-1—read "one-to-one"—correspondence if and only if for each element x of S in $\langle x,y \rangle \in r$

there is one and only one element y of T and for each element y of T there is one and only one element of S.

Example 5.12. Given $S = \{1,2,3\}$ and $T = \{a,b,c\}$. Let a relation f be defined as follows:

$$f(1) = a \quad f(2) = b \quad f(3) = c$$

that is,
$$f = \{\langle 1,a\rangle,\langle 2,b\rangle,\langle 3,c\rangle\}$$

Then f is a 1-1 correspondence between S and T. The range of f is T and the domain is S.

Suppose that we interchange range and domain and form the relation

$$f' = \{\langle a,1\rangle,\langle b,2\rangle,\langle c,3\rangle\}$$

Then f' is also a 1-1 correspondence. f' is called the *inverse* of f. Note that, in the inverse function f', the range and domain are interchanged. If f is a 1-1 correspondence, then f and its inverse f' are functions.

Example 5.13. The quantity of an article sold depends on such factors as the number of consumers, their tastes, their incomes, prices of all other goods, and its own price. If the first four factors are held constant, then the quantity bought, q, will be a function of its price p, that is, $q = f(p)$; specifically let us say that, for the good in question, if $p = \$11$, then $q = 0$, if $p = \$10$, $q = 1,000$, and if $p = \$9$, $q = 2,000$.

If we assume the inverse relation $p = f'(q)$, we may interpret this as indicating that the quantity of goods demanded determines the price. So if 2,000 units are demanded, the price will be $\$9$, etc. This assumption amounts to making the inverse relation f' also a function. Hence $q = f(p)$ is a 1-1 correspondence.

$$f = \{\langle 11,0\rangle,\langle 10,1,000\rangle,\langle 9,2,000\rangle\}$$
$$f' = \{\langle 0,11\rangle,\langle 1,000,10\rangle,\langle 2,000,9\rangle\}$$

Since f and f' consist of ordered couples and $\langle 11,0\rangle \neq \langle 0,11\rangle$, $f \neq f'$.

Although we shall define the notion "graph of a set" later in this chapter and show how to graph sets, we give the following definition here. **Definition 5.14.** A demand curve (in economics) is the graph of the relation from the quantity of a good demanded to its price, when all other factors (e.g., population, tastes, income, etc.) are held constant.

Example 5.15. Let

$$S = \{1,2,3\} \quad T = \{2,3,4\}$$
$$T' = \{2,3\} \quad T'' = \{2,3,4,5\}$$
$$r_1 = \{\langle x,y\rangle | (x \,\epsilon\, S) \ \& \ (y \,\epsilon\, T) \ \& \ (y = x + 1)\}$$
$$r_2 = \{\langle x,y\rangle | (x \,\epsilon\, S) \ \& \ (y \,\epsilon\, T') \ \& \ [(y = x) \text{ or } (y = x + 2)]\}$$
$$r_3 = \{\langle x,y\rangle | (x \,\epsilon\, S) \ \& \ (y \,\epsilon\, T'') \ \& \ (y = 3 \text{ for each and every } x)\}$$
$$r_4 = \{\langle x,y\rangle | (x \,\epsilon\, S) \ \& \ (y \,\epsilon\, T'') \ \& \ (y = x + 1)\}$$
$$r_5 = \{\langle x,y\rangle | (x \,\epsilon\, S) \ \& \ (y \,\epsilon\, T) \ \& \ (y > x)\}$$

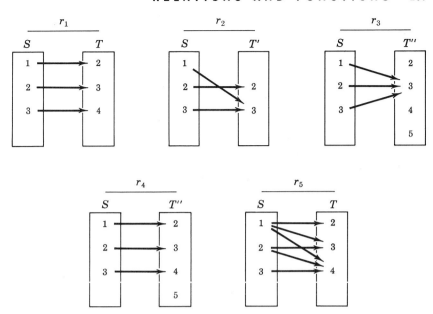

Fig. 5.1

Which of the five relations represents a 1-1 correspondence, which a mapping *onto*, which a mapping *into*, and which a relation which is not a function?

Solution. Let us study the box diagrams of Fig. 5.1 in relation to the required definition. We see that r_1 represents a 1-1 correspondence from S to T, r_2 a mapping from S onto T', r_3 and r_4 mappings from S into T'', and r_5 a relation which is not a function. (Why are the first four relations functions?) r_3 and r_4 demonstrate that distinct functions can be defined between two sets.

PROBLEM SET 5.1

1. Define a relation of the set

$$S = \{-4, -2, -1, 1, 2, 3, 4, 5\}$$

to the set $T = \{3, 2, 1, -5, 19, 20\}$

What are the range and what the domain of your relation? Define a function of S to T.

2. Define a function which will have as its domain the set N^2 of squares of negative integers and as its range the set P^2 of squares of positive integers. Define a 1-1 correspondence of N^2 to P^2.

3. Is the mapping defined by $y = 7 - x$ a 1-1 correspondence? Is it a function? What is the range, and what is the domain?

4. Is the relation defined by $y = \sqrt{x}$ a function? Explain. Describe the domain and range of the relation. Write a few elements of the relation.

5. For a fixed principal and interest rate, the value of a bank account is said to be a function of the time. Denote the function of time to interest.

6. Are all 1-1 correspondences functions? Are all functions 1-1 correspondences? If your answer is "no" in either case, give an example.

7. Is the inverse of a function always a function? Is the inverse of a 1-1 correspondence always a 1-1 correspondence? If your answer is "no" in either case, find an example.

8. Let the function $y = 1/x$ have the set of positive integers I as its domain and range. Is $y = 1/x$ a 1-1 correspondence of I into itself? (That is, is $y = 1/x$ defined for every value of x if its domain is the set of nonnegative integers?)

9. *a.* Assume that the aggregate consumption spending of an individual is a function of his income. Define the range and domain of the function.

   b. Assume that the total consumption spending of a country is a function of its national income. Define the range and domain of the function.

10. If corporate profits are no more than $25,000, they are taxed by the Federal government at 30 per cent; if they are over $25,000, they are taxed at 52 per cent. Express corporate tax collections as a function of corporate profits, and define the domain and range.

Hint: Let P_1 and P_2 denote the following sets:

$$P_1 = \{x|\$0 \le x \le \$25,000\}$$
$$P_2 = \{x|x > \$25,000\}$$

Then $r = \{\langle x,y \rangle|(x \ \& \ y \text{ are positive real numbers}) \ \& \ (y = 0.3x \text{ for } x \ \epsilon \ P_1)$
$\& \ [y = (0.3)(25,000) + 0.52(x - 25,000) \text{ for } x \ \epsilon \ P_2]\}$

Would the 1-1 correspondence defined by the function be affected by the tax law allowing corporations to carry losses forward in time and use them to offset the profits of other years?

5.3 THE REAL NUMBERS AND THE REAL LINE

In a preceding chapter we defined a rational number. The student knows how to add, subtract, multiply, and divide rational numbers. Moreover, if a rational number p/q is multiplied by itself, the result, designated by $(p/q)^2$ [for example, $(2/1)^2 = 2^2$], is also a rational number. We call this property of the rational numbers *closure with respect to multiplication.* However, the inverse relation is not closed; i.e., if p/q is a rational number, there does not necessarily exist a rational number r/s such that $(r/s)^2 = p/q$. For example, we know that, if 4 is given, there exists a rational number x such that $x^2 = 4$, namely, 2 (also -2). We write $x = \sqrt{4}$, and the solution set is $\{2, -2\}$. However, we can prove the following theorem.

Theorem 5.16

There exists no rational number p/q such that $(p/q)^2 = 2$. (That is, $\sqrt{2}$ is not a rational number.)

Proof. We prove this by the indirect method. We shall assume the theorem false and show that this leads to a contradiction and hence that the theorem must be true.

Suppose that a rational number p/q did exist such that $(p/q)^2 = 2$. We shall furthermore assume p and q to have no factors in common (that is, p and q are relatively prime). Although this is the crux of the proof, we can make this assumption since if p and q had factors in common we could divide them out.

$$\left(\frac{p}{q}\right)^2 = \frac{p^2}{q^2} = 2$$

Hence
$$p^2 = 2q^2$$

This of course means that p^2 is even. (Why?)

But if p^2 is even, p must be also and must have a factor 2. (Why?) Let us therefore write

$$p = 2m \qquad m \text{ a rational number}$$

Therefore
$$p^2 = 4m^2 = 2q^2$$
or
$$2m^2 = q^2$$

which proves that q^2 is even. It follows that q is also and therefore has a factor 2.

Consequently p and q both must have a factor 2. This contradicts the assumption that p and q are relatively prime.

Since this contradiction results from the assumption that the theorem is false, the theorem must be true.

It can be proved that many rational numbers have no rational square roots. In order to make such expressions as $\sqrt{2}$ meaningful, the number system is extended in such a way that we are justified in calling these expressions numbers. To distinguish them from the rational numbers, we call them *irrational numbers*, i.e., numbers that cannot be expressed as rational numbers. There are infinitely many of these. (The details of this extension are beyond the scope of this book.) The operations of addition, multiplication, subtraction, and division of irrational numbers can also be defined so that the rational numbers and the irrational numbers form a larger system of numbers called the *real-number system.*

Assuming that we know the positive numbers, we state the following definition.

Definition 5.17. If a and b are real numbers, then $a < b \leftrightarrow (b - a) > 0$.

We also state without proof the following theorem.

Theorem 5.18

If R is the set of all real numbers and C the set of points on a straight line L, then there exists a 1-1 correspondence between R and C.

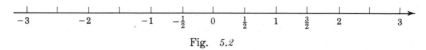

Fig. 5.2

The set of all points defined by this 1-1 correspondence is often referred to as the *real line*.

The set of points in this 1-1 correspondence is called the *graph* of *R*. A real number corresponding to a given point on the real line is called the *coordinate* of the point.

We can construct a representation of the graph of *R* in the following fashion (we shall speak of the representation of the graph and the graph interchangeably):

Select any point on the line *L*, and assign the real number 0 to it.

Denote the positive direction of the line by an arrow, as in Fig. 5.2.

Select any segment as a unit, and divide the line segment to the right and to the left of the 0 into intervals of unit length. Assign the positive numbers to the points to the right and negative numbers to the points to the left of the 0. We can now, in principle, divide the segments 0-1, 1-2, etc., into segments of ratio p/q, where p and q assume values taken from the set of positive integers and zero ($q \neq 0$) and p is less than q. To each point we assign a positive rational number $i + p/q$, where i denotes the first integer to the left of the point. We similarly divide the segments 0 to -1, -1 to -2, etc., and assign to each point the negative rational number $-(i + p/q)$. It is possible to discover geometrically the points to which irrational numbers are assigned.

Once we have the real line, we can relate any subset of the set of real numbers to a subset of the real line.

Definition 5.19. A 1-1 correspondence of a subset of real numbers to a subset of points of the real line will be called the *graph of the subset of real numbers*.

Example 5.20. Graph the set $f = \{x|x$ is an integer, and x is greater than 1 and less than 3\}.

Solution. Clearly, the set f consists only of the number 2, i.e., the intersection of the set of integers greater than 1 with the set of integers less than 3 (Fig. 5.3).

Example 5.21. Graph the subset *P* of real numbers x such that x is between -2 and 0.

Solution. We can define the relation by using $<$ and $>$ symbols, the domain being the subset *P* of real numbers which satisfies the stated

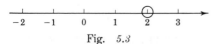

Fig. 5.3

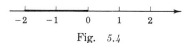

Fig. 5.4

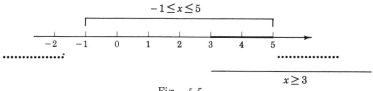

Fig. 5.5

relation,

$$P = \{x|x > -2 \,\&\, x < 0\}$$

The range is then the subset of points between -2 and 0. Note that, for real numbers 1, 2, etc., the relation is not defined. The heavy part of the real line in Fig. 5.4 is the representation of the graph of P.

Example 5.22. Graph the subset S of real numbers x which is the domain of the relation defined by $-1 \leq x \leq 5$ and $x \geq 3$,

$$S = \{x|(-1 \leq x \leq 5) \,\&\, (x \geq 3)\}$$

Solution. In this case we need to graph the intersection of the sets defined by $-1 \leq x \leq 5$ and $x \leq 3$, where the sign $\geq$ means "greater than or equal to" and the sign $\leq$ means "less than or equal to." The intersection is the set $3 \leq x \leq 5$, denoted by the shaded part of the line L (Fig. 5.5).

We shall give a precise definition of $<$ in the next chapter.

PROBLEM SET 5.2

1. Graph the set $S = \{x| -5 \leq x \leq -2\}$.
2. Is the relation of the set S in Prob. 1 into the real line defined if the domain is the set of positive integers?
3. Graph the set $S = \{x|\frac{1}{2} \leq x \leq \frac{3}{4}\}$ with domain the set of rational numbers.
4. Graph the set $S = \{-\frac{1}{2}, \frac{1}{2}, -1, 1, 0, 3, \frac{3}{2}\}$.
5. Graph the set $S = \{x|x < 0\}$.
6. Graph the set $S = \{x|(-1 \leq x \leq 0) \vee (1 \leq x \leq 2) \vee (x = 3)\}$ (*Hint:* We want the union of the three sets defining S.)

5.4 THE REAL PLANE

Let us now define a 1-1 correspondence of the cartesian product of the set of real numbers by itself with the set of all points in the plane. We shall denote the set of such points by E^2.

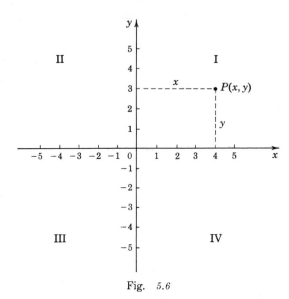

Fig. 5.6

We recall that

$$R \times R = \{\langle x,y \rangle | (x \text{ and } y \text{ are real numbers}) \text{ and } \langle x,y \rangle \text{ is an ordered couple}\}$$

Let us erect two real lines perpendicular to each other at the zero points of each line (Fig. 5.6). We shall call the two lines the coordinate axes. We shall denote the horizontal line as the x axis (axis of abscissas) and the vertical line the y axis (axis of ordinates). This will divide the plane into four *quadrants* indicated by I, II, III, and IV. The quadrants are always named in this counterclockwise manner. The point of intersection will be the *origin* and denoted by the couple $\langle 0,0 \rangle$. We shall identify any point P in the plane by an ordered couple $\langle x,y \rangle$ of real numbers as follows:

The first number x will denote the perpendicular distance of P from the y axis and will be called the *abscissa*. The second number y will be the perpendicular distance of P from the x axis and will be called the *ordinate*. If an abscissa is to the left of the y axis, we use negative numbers; if an ordinate is below the x axis, we use negative numbers. Each point P is therefore completely determined by the intersection of the perpendicular from P to the x axis with the perpendicular from P to the y axis. For example, the point $\langle -5,4 \rangle$ is the point in the second quadrant five units left of the y axis and four units above the x axis.

The point $P(-5, -3)$ is the point five units to the left of the y axis and three units below the x axis. It is therefore in the third quadrant. We assign any element $\langle x,y \rangle$ of $R \times R$ to one and only one point $\langle x,y \rangle$ of the plane. The plane together with the rectangular coordinate system described above will be called the *real plane*. We have therefore shown that there is a 1-1 correspondence between $R \times R$ and E^2.

5.5 GRAPH OF A FUNCTION

We recall that a function f from S to T is a subset of $S \times T$. We shall consider functions from R to R, that is, subsets of the cartesian product $R \times R$, which we shall call *real functions*.

Definition 5.23. The graph of a real function f is the subset of E^2 in 1-1 correspondence with f.

It is frequently convenient to connect the points of a graph and to refer to the resulting figure as the graph.

5.6 LINEAR FUNCTIONS AND THEIR GRAPHS

Definition 5.24. A linear function L is a set of ordered couples $\langle x,y \rangle$ of the following forms:

a. $\{\langle x,y \rangle | y = mx + b\}$, with domain the set of real numbers, range a subset of the set of real numbers, and m and b real numbers, or

b. $\{\langle x,y \rangle | x = c\}$, with range the set of real numbers and c a real number, or

c. $\{\langle x,y \rangle | y = c\}$, with domain the set of real numbers and c a real number

[Note that (*b*) is not technically a function but is by definition to be considered a *linear function*.]

We shall often refer to the expressions $y = mx + b$, $y = c$, and $x = c$ which define the function as the linear function itself. The student should remember, however, that these define the function f and are not the function.

Linear equations can be expressed as linear functions by appropriate arithmetical operations.

Example 5.25. The expression $y + 2 = 3x + 4$ can be written as a linear function $y = 3x + 2$, $m = 3$, $b = 2$.

Example 5.26. The expression $2y = 4x - 5$ can be written as a linear function in the form $y = \frac{4}{2}x - \frac{5}{2} = 2x - \frac{5}{2}$, $m = 2$, $b = -\frac{5}{2}$.

We state the following theorem without proof.

Theorem 5.27

The graph of a linear function f, described by $y = mx + b$, is a straight line which cuts the y axis at the point $(0,b)$. Moreover, every point on the line is the map of an element of f, and conversely.

Example 5.28. Graph the function defined by $x = 2$.

Solution. The set of all points with x coordinate 2 is the set of all points two units to the right of the y axis. The graph of this set f is the straight line parallel to the y axis, cutting the x axis at the point $(2,0)$ (Fig. 5.7). Since $x = 0$ leads to the contradictory statement $0 = 2$, there is no point $(0,b)$ and the line does not cut the y axis.

Example 5.29. Graph the function $y = -3$.

Solution. The graph is the set of all points whose ordinate is -3. This will be a straight line parallel to the x axis, three units below the x axis (Fig. 5.8).

Example 5.30. Graph the function which can be obtained from $4x + 2y = -1$.

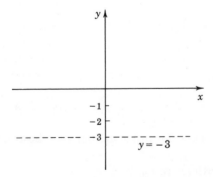

Fig. *5.7*

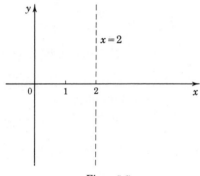

Fig. *5.8*

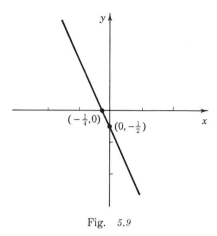

Fig. *5.9*

Solution. Writing this as a linear function, we obtain

$$2y = -4x - 1$$
or
$$y = -2x - \tfrac{1}{2}$$
$$f = \{\langle x,y \rangle | x \text{ and } y \text{ are real numbers } \& \ y = -2x - \tfrac{1}{2}\}$$

with domain and range the set of real numbers. The graph is a straight line cutting the y axis at $(0, -\tfrac{1}{2})$.

Since we know from elementary geometry that two points determine a straight line, all we need to determine the graph of a linear function are two points. The most convenient points to get are the points, if they exist, where the line cuts the x axis (x intercept) and the y axis (y intercept). The x intercept is the point where $y = 0$, that is, $(-\tfrac{1}{4},0)$, and the y intercept is the point where $x = 0$, that is, $(0, -\tfrac{1}{2})$ (Fig. 5.9).

Example 5.31. The cost function for a given product is defined as the mapping of some subset Q' of the set Q of possible outputs into some subset C' of the set C of possible dollar costs, where Q and C are sets of nonnegative real numbers; the function is therefore defined by the set of ordered couples

$$f = \{\langle x,y \rangle | (x \ \epsilon \ Q') \ \& \ (y \ \epsilon \ C')\}$$

where the domain and range of the function must be specified and, typically, will be different for different products and/or firms and/or points in time.

The unit of cloth output for company A is a running yard, so that fractional outputs, for example, 102.25 running yards, can be produced. The cost function is defined by the equation $y = 2x + 2$, with appropriate range and domain. Graph the function.

Solution. We need first to define the function completely, i.e., to determine its domain and range. Since at full capacity the firm can

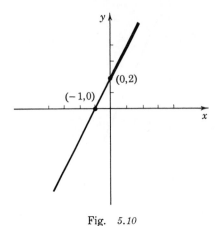

Fig. *5.10*

produce $c = 200$ running yards per day, the domain is the set Q' of non-negative real numbers less than or equal to 200, while the range is the set C' of nonnegative real numbers greater than or equal to 2 and less than or equal to 402. (Why?)

$$Q' = \{x|0 \leq x \leq 200 \,\&\, x \text{ is a real number}\}$$
$$C' = \{y|2 \leq y \leq 402 \,\&\, y \text{ is a real number}\}$$

We need to find two points of the graph. We take $x = 0$ and compute $y = 2$, giving the point (0,2) for the element $\langle 0,2 \rangle$ of

$$f = \{\langle x,y \rangle|(x \,\epsilon\, Q') \,\&\, (y \,\epsilon\, C') \,\&\, y = 2x + 2\}$$

and also the couple $\langle -1,0 \rangle \,\epsilon\, f$. We find the maps of these couples on the graph and connect them by a straight line [Fig. 5.10; note that the graph cuts the y axis at the point (0,2)].

The graph of the cost function f is the heavy part of the line in Fig. 5.10.

Example 5.32. In the preceding example, suppose that company A has a budgetary, as well as a capacity, constraint which limits the dollar costs that can be incurred to \$300 daily. What are the domain and range of the function now?

Solution. Since y must be less than or equal to 300, x must be less than or equal to 149; we can see this by solving the cost equation for x and substituting $y = 300$.

$$y = 2x + 2$$
$$x = \frac{y}{2} - 1 = 149 \qquad \text{when } y = 300$$

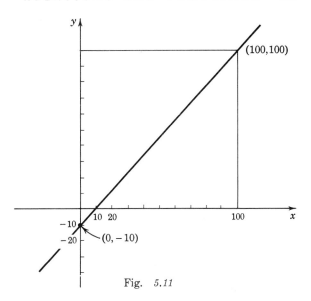

Fig. *5.11*

The domain Q' and range C' are now given by

$$Q' = \{x|0 \leq x \leq 149 \ \& \ x \text{ is a real number}\}$$
$$C' = \{y|2 \leq y \leq 300 \ \& \ y \text{ is a real number}\}$$

Example 5.33. Suppose that a factory manufacturing a certain item loses $10 an hour if it is idle, while if it is operating at capacity, which is 100 units an hour, it earns a profit of $100. Assume that the relation between profit and units produced is a linear function. Graph the function.

Solution. Let y = profit and x = number of units produced. Then, for $x = 0$, $y = -10$; that is, we have the point $(0, -10)$. For $x = 100$, $y = 100$; that is, we have the point $(100,100)$. Since a linear function graphs as a straight line and a straight line is determined by two points, the graph of the function is determined. Using units of 10 on the graph, we have Fig. 5.11. We shall learn later how to find the definition of the function.

PROBLEM SET 5.3

1. Graph the following linear functions:
   a. $x = 0$
   b. $y = 0$
   c. $y = -x$

2. Write as a function and graph, determining the domain and range first:

a. $2x + 3y = 1$

b. $x + 7y - 2 = 0$

c. $2x + 4y = 0$

3. Assume that the relation between the price of goods, p, and the quantity q of goods sold can be expressed as a linear function

$$p = 200 - 2q$$

and graph the function. Determine the range and domain of the function.

4. The total supply of land in a community is unalterably fixed at 100 units and is of no personal use to the owners. Graph the supply of land (on the x axis) as a function of price of land (on the y axis).

5. If all the resources of a country were devoted to military security, the total output of such goods would equal 20 units, while if all resources were alternatively devoted to civilian goods, 25 units could be produced. Assuming that the relation is a linear function, measure military goods on the y axis and civilian goods on the x axis, and graph the "transformation" curve for this country. In units of civilian goods sacrificed, what is the "cost" of a military good?

5.7 DISTANCE BETWEEN TWO POINTS

It is often useful to find the "distance" between two elements in a real function.

Definition 5.34. If f is a real function and $\langle x_1, y_1 \rangle$ and $\langle x_2, y_2 \rangle$ are elements of f, then the distance between $\langle x_1, y_1 \rangle$ and $\langle x_2, y_2 \rangle$ is

$$d = \sqrt{(y_2 - y_1)^2 + (x_2 - x_1)^2}$$

(d is always taken positive).

This has a natural geometric interpretation. Draw a rectangular coordinate system, and locate the points P_1 and P_2 whose coordinates are (x_1, y_1) and (x_2, y_2), respectively (Fig. 5.12). Connect P_1 and P_2.

Draw P_2Q perpendicular to the x axis and P_1R perpendicular to the y axis. Extend P_1R until it intersects P_2Q. Call the point of intersection P_3. The coordinates of P_3 are evidently (x_2, y_1). P_1P_3 and P_2P_3

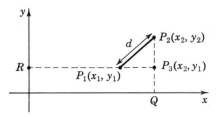

Fig. *5.12*

are perpendicular. (Why?)   We now have a right triangle $P_1P_3P_2$ and therefore, from the pythagorean theorem,

$$d^2 = (P_1P_2)^2 = (P_3P_2)^2 + (P_1P_3)^2$$

But

$$P_3P_2 = y_2 - y_1$$
$$P_1P_3 = x_2 - x_1$$

Therefore

$$d^2 = (y_2 - y_1)^2 + (x_2 - x_1)^2$$
$$d = \sqrt{(y_2 - y_1)^2 + (x_2 - x_1)^2}$$

Example 5.35.   Find the distance between the points $(2, -4)$ and $(-5,7)$.

Solution

$$d^2 = [7 - (-4)]^2 + (-5 - 2)^2$$
$$= 11^2 + (-7)^2$$
$$= 121 + 49$$
$$= 170$$
$$d = \sqrt{170}$$

Example 5.36.   Find the distance between the points $(2,5)$ and $(2,7)$.
   Solution.   Both points lie on the line $x = 2$.   Hence the distance is simply the difference of the y coordinates, namely, 2.

5.8 DIRECTED DISTANCE

It is often important not merely to know the distance between P_1 and P_2 but also to know whether we are measuring from P_1 to P_2 or from P_2 to P_1. We adopt the convention that conforms to the structure of the graph. If P_1 is to the left of P_2, then we denote the distance from P_1 to P_2 by $+d$ and the distance from P_2 to P_1 by $-d$.   Therefore

$$\overrightarrow{P_1P_2} = -\overrightarrow{P_2P_1} = \overleftarrow{P_2P_1}$$

If P_2 is directly above P_1, then the distance from P_1 to P_2 is $+d$ and from P_2 to P_1 is $-d$.
   From these conventions it follows that if P_1, P_2, and P_3 lie on the same straight line (Fig. 5.13), with P_3 between P_1 and P_2 and P_1 to the

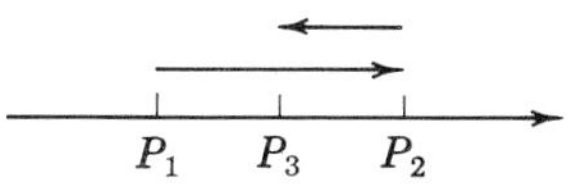

Fig. *5.13*

left of P_2 and P_3, then

$$\overrightarrow{P_1P_3} = \overrightarrow{P_1P_2} + \overrightarrow{P_2P_3} = \overrightarrow{P_1P_2} - \overrightarrow{P_3P_2} = \overrightarrow{P_1P_2} + \overleftarrow{P_3P_2}$$

The student should note carefully the directions of the arrows and the equivalence of the three expressions.

PROBLEM SET 5.4

1. Find the distance between the following points:
   a. $(-2,1)$ and $(-3,-2)$
   b. $(-3,-5)$ and $(-4,3)$
   c. $(2,1)$ and $(5,-4)$
   d. $(2,5)$ and $(2,-9)$
   e. $(-4,0)$ and $(-9,0)$
2. Find the directed distance from the points:
   a. $(-3,2)$ to $(-7,5)$
   b. $(3,-5)$ to $(-7,-5)$
3. The distance from $P_1(-3,5)$ to a point $P_2(-3,y)$ is 10. Find the ordinate of P_2.
4. If P_1P_2 and P_3 are on a straight line and the distance $\overrightarrow{P_1P_3}$ is 10 and $\overrightarrow{P_2P_1} = -3$, find the distance $\overrightarrow{P_3P_2}$.
5. A triangle has its vertices at $(0,0)$, $(10,-4)$, and $(2,5)$. Show that the triangle is a right triangle. (*Hint:* Use the pythagorean theorem.)

5.9 SLOPE OF A LINEAR FUNCTION

We are going to define a ratio related to a linear function that will have a very interesting and important geometric representation.

Definition 5.37. Given the linear function f described by $y = mx + b$, with domain and range the set of real numbers. Let $\langle x_1,y_1 \rangle$, $\langle x_2,y_2 \rangle$ be any two elements of f. The *slope* of f is the fraction

$$\frac{y_2 - y_1}{x_2 - x_1}$$

We shall now prove the following theorem.

Theorem 5.38

The slope of a linear function f is the same for any two elements of f, and this fraction is the m in $y = mx + b$.

Proof. Let $\langle x_1, y_1 \rangle$, $\langle x_2, y_2 \rangle$ and $\langle x_3, y_3 \rangle$ be elements of f.   Then

$$y_1 = mx_1 + b$$
$$y_2 = mx_2 + b$$
$$y_3 = mx_3 + b$$
$$y_2 - y_1 = mx_2 + b - mx_1 - b = m(x_2 - x_1)$$

or
$$m = \frac{y_2 - y_1}{x_2 - x_1}$$

Likewise
$$y_3 - y_2 = mx_3 + b - mx_2 - b = m(x_3 - x_2)$$

or
$$m = \frac{y_3 - y_2}{x_3 - x_2}$$

Therefore
$$\frac{y_2 - y_1}{x_2 - x_1} = \frac{y_3 - y_2}{x_3 - x_2} = m$$

Since $\langle x_1, y_1 \rangle$, $\langle x_2, y_2 \rangle$ and $\langle x_3, y_3 \rangle$ were *any* three elements in f, the theorem is proved.

Example 5.39. Given the linear function f described by $y = 2x + 5$, determine the slope m of the linear function by finding two elements in f and computing the fraction m.

Solution. If $x = 0$, $y = 5$, and $\langle 0,5 \rangle \; \epsilon f$, if $x = -1$, $y = 3$, and $\langle -1,3 \rangle \; \epsilon f$.

$$m = \frac{3 - 5}{-1 - 0} = \frac{-2}{-1} = 2$$

Example 5.40. Find the slope of the function defined by $2x + 3y = 1$.

Solution. We write this as a linear function $y = -\frac{2}{3}x + \frac{1}{3}$. The slope is therefore $-\frac{2}{3}$.

Example 5.41. If $(1,0)$ and $(0,4)$ are on a line L, find the function whose graph is L.

Solution

$$m = \frac{4 - 0}{0 - 1} = \frac{4}{-1} = -4$$

Take any other point (x,y) on L; then

$$\frac{y - 4}{x - 0} = -4$$

using the point $(0,4)$, or

$$y - 4 = -4x$$
$$= -4x + 4$$

5.10 GEOMETRIC INTERPRETATION OF m

We know that the graph of a linear function is a straight line and that any element $\langle x_1, y_1 \rangle$ of a linear function f maps to a point in the real plane which lies on the line and has coordinates (x_1, y_1).   Let L be the line and (x_1, y_1) and (x_2, y_2) two points on L (Fig. 5.14).   Through $P_2(x_2, y_2)$ draw a line perpendicular to the x axis, and through $P_1(x_1, y_1)$ draw a line perpendicular to the y axis.   These two lines will meet at P_3 with coordinates (x_2, y_1).   Now the fraction

$$m = \frac{y_2 - y_1}{x_2 - x_1}$$

defines the tangent of the angle $P_2 P_1 P_3$ in the right triangle $P_1 P_3 P_2$.   But the angle $P_2 P_1 P_3$ is equal to the angle α which the line L makes with the x axis, since from elementary geometry we know that if two parallel lines are cut by a transversal the corresponding angles are equal.   Therefore, the slope m, of a linear function $y = mx + b$, is also the value of the tangent of the angle the graph of $y = mx + b$ makes with the x axis. This may be used as a measure of the rise of the line going from left to right.   The angle is measured counterclockwise.

We note that if m is positive, α is acute; if m is negative, α is obtuse (why?) and the line is falling from left to right.   If $m = 0$, $\alpha = 0°$; if m is undefined, $\alpha = 90°$.

Example 5.42.   Given the linear function $y = -x + 1$, what is the slope of its graph?   What angles does the graph make with the x axis? Draw the graph.

Solution. $m = -1$; $\alpha = 135°$, since tan $-1 = 135°$.   Since the graph is a straight line, all we need are two points (Fig. 5.15).

Example 5.43.   Total production cost C is a function of output Q. We can express this as $C = f(Q)$.   We shall assume f to be linear and determine its nature more accurately.   Total costs are broken down into two kinds: (a) fixed costs C_F, which do not vary with output, and (b) variable costs C_V, which vary directly with the output.   We assume, further, that the fixed costs amount to \$5 and that the variable costs are 20 cents

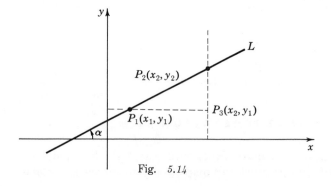

Fig. *5.14*

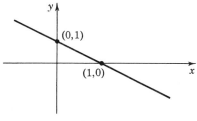

Fig. *5.15*

per unit. Therefore we have

$$C = 0.2x + 5$$

(where x = number of units produced). The graph (Fig. 5.16) is easily obtained, since we know that even if no units are produced the cost is $5. We have one point on the graph, and if five units are produced

$$C = (\tfrac{2}{10})(5) + 5 = 6$$

(Why is the graph terminated at the y axis?)

The slope of the graph is $\tfrac{1}{5}$.

We note that the fixed costs can be graphed as a line $C_F = 5$ and the variable costs as a line $C_V = 2x$, while the cost function C can be described by

$$C = C_F + C_V$$

and the ordinates of C can be obtained by adding the ordinates of C_F and C_V at each fixed x.

The slope of C_V will be the same as the slope of C.

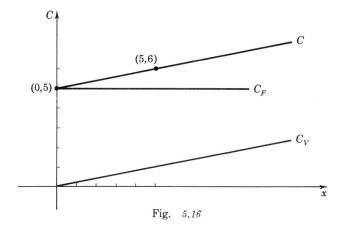

Fig. *5.16*

PROBLEM SET 5.5

1. In Probs. 1 and 2 of Problem Set 5.3 find the slope of each linear function. What angles do these lines make with the x axis? (Use tables if needed.) Decide whether the lines rise or fall.

2. Prove geometrically that the graphs of two linear functions having the same slope are either equal or parallel lines.

3. Which pairs of graphs of the following linear functions are parallel?

a. $y = 3x + 5$
   $y = 3x + 2$

b. $y = \quad 2x - 1$
   $y = -2x - 1$

c. $y = x$
   $y = x + 2$

d. $y = \quad \frac{2}{3}x$
   $y = -\frac{3}{2}x$

Draw the graphs.

4. Given the linear functions

$$y = \tfrac{1}{2}x + 2 \qquad \text{and} \qquad y = 2x - 4$$

Draw the graphs, and try to determine the relation of the lines to each other.

5. The points $(2,3)$ and $(-5,7)$ lie on a line L. Calculate the slope of L.

6. In Example 5.43, find the number of units that must be produced for fixed costs and variable costs to be equal.

7. A consumer can buy either of two products. His total income can buy 5 units of one product or 10 of the other. Assuming that the relation between his fixed income and the amounts of the two products he can buy is a linear function, graph the function. The resulting graph is called the *budget line*. Calculate the slope of the budget line.

8. In Prob. 7, find the equation of the budget line. [*Hint:* Since the slope is known, take any other point (x,y), and write the fraction for the slope.] Suppose that the consumer's income is doubled. Derive the resulting budget line. Can you find an interpretation of the slope of the budget line?

5.11 ABSOLUTE VALUES

We shall need the important concept of absolute value.

Definition 5.44. If a is a real number, then the absolute value of a, denoted by $|a|$, is

(*a*) $|0| = 0$
(*b*) $|a| = a$ when a is positive
(*c*) $|a| = -a$ when a is negative

Note, therefore, if we have an expression such as $|x + y|$ we do not know whether this is $(x + y)$ or $-(x + y)$ until we know whether $x + y$ is positive or negative.

Example 5.45

$$|7| = 7 \qquad |-7| = -(-7) = 7$$

We prove two important theorems.

Theorem 5.46

$$|a \times b| = |a| \times |b|$$

Proof. If either a or b is zero, the theorem follows at once. (Why?)
If a and b are both positive, $|a| = a$, $|b| = b$, $|a| \times |b| = a \times b$.
But $a \times b$ is also positive; $|a \times b| = a \times b$.
If a and b are both negative, $a \times b$ is positive and $|a \times b| = a \times b$,
while $|a| = -a$ and $|b| = -b$, so that $|a| \times |b| = (-a)(-b) = ab$.
If one, for example, a, is negative and the other positive, then $a \times b$
is negative, $|a \times b| = -(ab)$,

$$|a| = -a \qquad |b| = b \qquad |a| \times |b| = -(ab)$$

Theorem 5.47

$$|a + b| \le |a| + |b|$$

Proof. We prove this by separate cases.
Case 1. a or b is zero.
a. If both are zero, the proof is trivial.
b. If $a \ne 0$, $b = 0$.

$$|a + 0| = |a|$$
$$|a| + |0| = |a|$$

Case 2. $a \ne 0 \ne b$, a and b both positive.
$|a + b| = a + b$ by definition, since $a + b$ is positive if a and b are.
$|a| = a$, $|b| = b$, since both a and b are positive.

$$|a| + |b| = a + b$$

Case 3. $a \ne 0 \ne b$, a and b both negative. Let

$$a = -a_1$$
$$b = -b_1$$

where a_1 and b_1 are both positive. Then

$$a + b = -(a_1 + b_1)$$
$$|a + b| = |-(a_1 + b_1)|$$
$$= -[-(a_1 + b_1)] = a_1 + b_1$$
$$|a| = a_1$$
$$|b| = b_1 \qquad \text{Why?}$$

Hence $\qquad |a| + |b| = a_1 + b_1$

Case 4. $a \neq 0 \neq b$; one, say a, is negative, b is positive. $a + b$ is either positive or negative.   If $a + b$ is positive,

$$|a + b| = a + b$$

But if
$$|a| = -a$$
$$|b| = b$$

Therefore $|a| + |b| = b - a$

and $|a + b| = (a + b) < b - a$ Why?

If $a + b$ is negative

$$|a + b| = -(a + b) < b - a$$

Example 5.48.   Let $a = -7$, $b = 3$.

$$|a + b| = |-7 + 3| = |-4| = 4$$
$$|a| + |b| = |-7| + |3| = 7 + 3 = 10$$

$|a + b| < |a| + |b|$ in this case.

Example 5.49.   Graph the function $y = |x|$.

Solution.   We first note that $\langle 0,0 \rangle \, \epsilon \, f$.   We also see that the domain of x is the set of all real numbers but the range is the set of positive real numbers.   (Why?)   So no part of the graph lies below the x axis.

The graph of $y = |x|$ is equivalent to the union of the graph of $y = x$, with domain the nonnegative real numbers, and the graph of $y = -x$, with domain the set of negative real numbers, since $|x|$ is either x or $-x$.

$y = x$ has slope 1 and therefore makes an angle of 45° with the x axis.

$y = -x$ has slope -1 and makes an angle of 135° with the x axis. The graph is shown in Fig. 5.17.

Example 5.50.   Graph the set S described by $|x| = 5$.

Solution.   Evidently the set can be graphed either on the real line or in the real plane.   In the real line the solution set of $|x| = 5$ consists of two points, 5 and -5, that is, $S = \{5, -5\}$.   (Why?)   (See Fig. 5.18.)

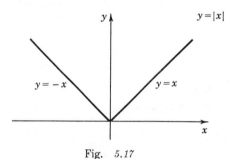

Fig. *5.17*

Fig. *5.18*

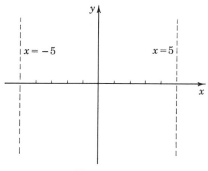

Fig. *5.19*

In the real plane $|x| = 5$ has as its solution set the set of all points with abscissa 5 or -5; so the set described by $|x| = 5$ consists of two lines each parallel to the y axis. (Why?) (See Fig. 5.19.)

Example 5.51. Graph $y = |x + 5|$ in E^2.

Solution. We note that this is equivalent to

$$y = |x + 5| = x + 5 \quad \text{if } x + 5 \text{ is positive}$$

and $$y = |x + 5| = -(x + 5) \quad \text{if } x + 5 \text{ is negative}$$

or $$y = x + 5 \quad \text{and} \quad y = -x - 5$$

The two functions are

$$f = \{\langle x,y\rangle | y = x + 5\}$$

and $$f' = \{\langle x,y\rangle | y = -x - 5\}$$

Since $|x + 5|$ is always positive in effect, the graph can never be negative. Hence the domain of f is the set of real numbers greater than -5, while its range is the set of nonnegative real numbers. The domain of f' is the set of real numbers less than or equal to -5, but its range is the set of nonnegative real numbers.

We leave the actual drawing of the graph to the student.

PROBLEM SET 5.6

1. Write the value of:
   a. $|5|$
   b. $|-5|$

    c. $|a|$
    d. $|-a|$
    e. $|x - y|$
    f. $|ab|$ if a is positive and b negative
    g. $|ab|$ if $a = 0$
2. Graph the following functions
    a. $y = |2|$
    b. $y = |-x|$
    c. $y = |x - 2|$
    d. $y = |-3|$
    e. $y = |-3x|$
    f. $y = -|3x|$
in the real plane.
3. Graph the following function on a real line:

$$x = |-5|$$

    4. Graph the function $y = |2x - 1|$. Determine its domain and range. What are the slopes of the functions?

5.12 BREAK-EVEN ANALYSIS: AN IMPORTANT BUSINESS APPLICATION

Break-even analysis is a type of economic analysis employed frequently in business. We treat the subject at this point because the underlying assumptions imply that all relevant relations are linear and because the graphing of these relations is an important part of the analysis. We shall begin by defining concepts, some of which have been introduced in earlier examples and which will also be utilized in later chapters.

    Production involves two types of costs: *variable costs*, such as labor and materials, which vary with quantity produced, and *fixed costs*, such as rent and insurance, which remain the same over all levels of output. Break-even analysis seeks to determine the output at which the producer will break even, i.e., where his costs will meet his revenue.

    In what follows we shall employ the symbols listed:

p, the price per unit of output sold, which is assumed constant for all
    possible outputs; $p > 0$
c, the maximum (full-capacity) output that the firm is capable of pro-
    ducing; $c > 0$
v, the variable cost per unit of output produced, which is assumed con-
    stant for all possible outputs; $v > 0$

We shall employ the following sets, whose definitions the student should carefully and completely learn:

$Q = \{q|q$ is a rational number ≥ 0 & q is an output$\}$

$V = \{\langle q,y \rangle | q \in Q$ & y is a rational number ≥ 0 & $y = vq$ & y is the total variable cost associated with $q\}$

$F = \{\langle q,y \rangle | q \in Q$ & y is a rational number > 0 & y is a constant k & y is the total fixed cost associated with $q\}$

$C = \{\langle q,y \rangle | q \in Q$ & y is a rational number > 0 & y is the total cost associated with $q\}$

$R = \{\langle q,y \rangle | q \in Q$ & y is a rational number ≥ 0 & y is the total revenue associated with q & $y = pq\}$

$P = \{\langle q,y \rangle | q \in Q$ & y is a rational number & y is the total profit associated with $q\}$

Note that the sets $V, F, C, R,$ and P show, respectively, total variable cost, total fixed cost, total cost, total revenue, and total profit as functions of q. The symbols $V(q), F(q), C(q), R(q),$ and $P(q)$ are used to denote the element in the range, of the respective function, corresponding to the specific domain value q.

Then, from the definitions of the relevant sets, we have

$$V(q) = vq$$
$$F(q) = k$$
$$R(q) = pq \tag{5.1}$$

Definition 5.52. For a given q,

$$C(q) = V(q) + F(q)$$
$$= vq + k \tag{5.2}$$

Therefore, since by definition $P(q) = R(q) - C(q)$,

$$P(q) = pq - (vq + k)$$
$$= q(p - v) - k$$

Note that, as a result of the typical break-even analysis assumptions, $V(q), F(q), R(q), C(q),$ and $P(q)$ are *linear* functions of q. Note, also, that if we were to graph Eq. (5.2), the y intercept would be $(0,k)$.

Definition 5.53. The element $\langle q^*,0 \rangle$ of P, if it exists, is called the *break-even point*.

Theorem 5.54

If $\langle q^*,0 \rangle$ of P is the break-even point for a given product, then $R(q^*) = C(q^*)$.

Proof. If $\langle q^*,0 \rangle$ is the break-even point, then $P(q^*) = 0$. But, by definition,

$$P(q) = R(q) - C(q)$$

Therefore $\qquad P(q^*) = R(q^*) - C(q^*) = 0$

and $\qquad R(q^*) = C(q^*)$

Consider now Eqs. (5.1) and (5.2). If we consider the graphs of the two functions, then the break-even point would be the point of intersection of the two lines defined by the equations. Evidently, if the lines are nonparallel, there would be one and only one break-even point.

The student should note carefully that if the slopes of the two functions are equal no break-even point will exist. We assert the following theorem.

Theorem 5.55

If $v = p$, no break-even point exists.

Since the break-even point is given when $C(q) = R(q)$, we have

$$C(q) = v \cdot q + k = R(q) = p \cdot q$$

or $\qquad pq - vq = k$

or $\qquad q^* = \dfrac{k}{p - v} \qquad\qquad (5.3)$

Note that we have designated the break-even output with an asterisk. The student should substitute Eq. (5.3) in Eqs. (5.1) and (5.2) to check the fact that $C(q) = R(q)$ when $q^* = k/(p - v)$. This proves the following theorem.

Theorem 5.56

$C(q) = R(q)$ if and only if $q^* = k/(p - v)$.

Example 5.57. A single product firm can market as many units as it is willing and able to produce at a price of \$1.50. Its plant and equipment can produce as many as 500 units a day. Total fixed cost is \$200 daily. Unit variable cost is 50 cents. What is the break-even point for this firm, i.e., how many units must be produced to at least cover all expenses?

Solution. Evidently $p = 1.50$, $R = 1.50q$, $c = 500$, $F = 200$, $V(q) = 0.50q$, and $C(q) = 0.50q + 200$.

Method 1. Since $C(q) = R(q)$ at the break-even point,

$$0.50q + 200 = 1.50q$$

or $\qquad q^* = 200$

Method 2. Using Eq. (5.3),

$$q^* = \dfrac{k}{p - v}$$

$$= \dfrac{200}{1.50 - 0.50} = 200$$

Method 3.   Graphing.   We erect two real lines perpendicular at the
origin.   We call the x axis the *output axis* and the y axis the *dollar axis*.
We graph

$$C(q) = 0.50q + 200$$

and $$R(q) = 1.50q$$

The graph is shown in Fig. 5.20.   It is possible to read from the
graph the profit or loss for any output $q = 0$ to $q =$ capacity (500).

Figure 5.20 clearly shows that the firm "loses money" (i.e., incurs a
loss or earns a negative profit) at outputs to the left of $q^* = 200$ [for
$q < 200$, $C(q) > R(q)$] and "makes money" at outputs to the right of
$q^* = 200$ [for $q > 200$, $C(q) < R(q)$].   At any q, the total profit is given
by the vertical distance between $C(q)$ and $R(q)$ at that q, the magnitude
being negative or positive depending, respectively, on whether $q < 200$
or $q > 200$.   Figure 5.20 also shows the profit function directly.

Example 5.58.   In one process the cost function, denoted by C_1, is

$$C_1 = 0.25q + 300$$

and in another, denoted by C_2, is

$$C_2 = 0.5q + 200$$

Which cost function increases more rapidly with increases in output?

Solution.   For C_1, $m = 0.25$, while for C_2, $m = 0.50$.   Evidently,
the rise in C_1 will be less than that in C_2.   The graph (left to the student)

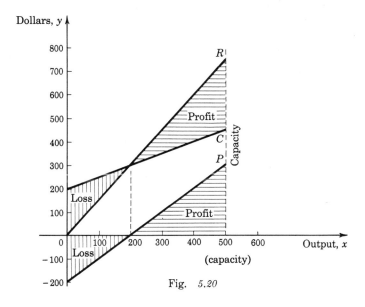

Fig. *5.20*

will show that, although C_2 starts lower on the y axis (since $200 < 300$), C_2 crosses the curve C_1 and rises more rapidly.

Associated with C_1 is a revenue function described by $R(q) = 0.25q$. Does a break-even point exist? Graphing $R(q) = 0.25q$ will give a line through the origin parallel to C_1. (Why?) Therefore no break-even point exists. At this price, therefore, the company can never make money.

Example 5.59. A firm decides to sell its present plant and to construct a new one. It can either install a manufacturing process identical with its present one or construct a new process. The present process has a cost function for $c = 500$,

$$C_1 = 0.5q + 200 \qquad (5.4)$$

The new process would have a cost function for $c = 500$,

$$C_2 = 0.25q + 300 \qquad (5.5)$$

For both processes the total revenue function is $R(q) = 1.5q$. Which process should be used?

Solution. The problem involves determining which process will be more profitable.

If we compare costs, we note that the fixed cost for Eq. (5.4) is $k_1 = 200$, while for Eq. (5.5) it is $k_2 = 300$. Hence, so far as fixed costs are concerned, $k_1 < k_2$. But the variable cost per unit for (5.4) is $v_1 = 0.5$, while for (5.5) it is $v_2 = 0.25$, and therefore $v_2 < v_1$.

If we compare break-even points, we find that the break-even point for (5.4) occurs when

$$q_1^* = \frac{200}{1.5 - 0.5} = 200$$

while for (5.5) it occurs when

$$q_2^* = \frac{300}{1.5 - 0.25} = \frac{300}{1.25} = 240$$

Therefore, $q_1^* < q_2^*$, and at $q = q_1^*$ the firm would be breaking even with the first process and losing with the second. But this apparent advantage could be offset by the slope of C_1, which is greater than that of C_2 (0.50 compared to 0.25).

It turns out that the answer to the problem depends upon the domain of $R(q)$ and the output at which the two cost curves cross. (We know that they will cross because $v_1 > v_2$ but $k_1 < k_2$; that is, at $q = 0$, $C_1 < C_2$, but as q increases, C_1 increases more rapidly than C_2.)

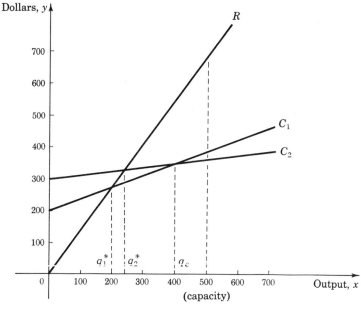

Fig. *5.21*

The two curves cross when

$$C_1 = C_2$$
$$0.5q + 200 = 0.25q + 300$$
$$q = 400$$

For output greater than 400, C_2 is below C_1. Our conclusion is therefore: If the output must (e.g., because of market limitations) be set between 0 and 400 (including $q = 0$ but not $q = 400$), the cost will be less and hence the profit greater if the process whose cost curve is C_1 is used.

If the output can be set above 400, the process whose cost curve is C_2 will yield the greater profit.

Figure 5.21 shows the graphs of all the functions involved (q_e denotes the output at which $C_1 = C_2$).

PROBLEM SET 5.7

1. Draw the graph appropriate in a situation in which $k_1 < k_2$, $v_1 > v_2$, and $q_1^* > q_2^*$. Clearly indicate the position of q_1^*, q_2^*, and the q where $C_1 = C_2$. Over what range of output is the process associated with C_1 more profitable (or less costly) than that associated with C_2?

2.   What is the maximum profit that can be obtained, and what is the corresponding q, with the cost function C_2 of Example 5.59, assuming that $R(q) = 1.50q$?   That $R(q) = 2.0q$?

3.   A single-product firm operates two plants which have, respectively, the following cost functions and capacities:

$$C_1 = 2q + 100 \qquad C_2 = \tfrac{5}{7}q + 200$$
$$c_1 = 100 \qquad\quad c_2 = 150$$

The price for the firm's product is fixed at \$5 for all relevant output levels.

a.   Which plant, 1 or 2, is more automated?   Why?

b.   Calculate the break-even point for each plant.

c.   Assuming that each plant is operated at the same absolute level of output, at what output do operations in plant 2 become more profitable than those in plant 1?

d.   If the capacity output of both plants can be marketed, what is the firm's total profit?

e.   If the firm divides output equally between the two plants, what is the minimum demand that the firm must achieve if both plants are at least to break even?

f.   Graph C_1, C_2 and $R(q)$, indicating q_1^*, q_2^*, the q where $C_1 = C_2$, c_1 and c_2.

6 INEQUALITIES AND INTRODUCTION TO LINEAR PROGRAMMING

6.1 MOTIVATION

Although we have used the concept of inequality in the preceding chapters, we now wish to define it more carefully and learn how to graph it. The last part of this chapter will show how inequalities are applied to that class of problems which comes under the heading of *linear programming*.

6.2 INEQUALITIES

The student knows that the expression $a = b$, where a and b are real numbers, means that a and b denote the same element. The expression $a \neq b$ will be used to denote the statement "It is false that $a = b$."

Logically it is clear that if a and b designate real numbers then either $a = b$ or $a \neq b$.   If $a \neq b$, we wish to express a precise relation between a and b.   The student of course knows that either a will be greater than b or b will be greater than a.   It is this relation of "greater than" (symbolized by $>$) that we wish to make precise.   The student also knows that a is greater than b if $a - b$ is greater than 0 (that is, is positive).   We shall first define the set of positive real numbers and then define the relation $>$ in terms of that set.

Definition 6.1.   Let R designate the set of real numbers.   If R^+ is a subset of R such that

1. R^+ is closed with respect to addition (i.e., the sum of any two or more elements of R^+ is also an element of R^+),

2. R^+ is closed with respect to multiplication (i.e., the product of any two or more elements of R^+ is also an element of R^+),

3. If $a \, \epsilon \, R$, then exactly one of the following holds: $a = 0$ or $a \, \epsilon \, R^+$ or $-a \, \epsilon \, R^+$ [where $-a$ is the additive inverse of a, that is, $a + (-a) = 0$], then R^+ is the set of *positive real numbers* and any element of R^+ is a positive real number.   We call the set of real numbers not in R^+ the negative numbers R^-.

We can now state the following definition.

Definition 6.2. $a > b$ (read "a is greater than b") if $a - b \, \epsilon \, R^+$.   From this follows a theorem.

Theorem 6.3

If $a, b \, \epsilon \, R$, then $a = b$ or $a < b$ or $b < a$.

   Proof. $a = b$ or $a \neq b$ follows from logic.

   Assume $a \neq b$.   Then $b - a$ is a real number, and by (3) of Definition 6.1

$$b - a \, \epsilon \, R^+ \qquad \text{or} \qquad -(b - a) \, \epsilon \, R^+$$

If $b - a \, \epsilon \, R^+$, then $b > a$.

   If $-(b - a) \, \epsilon \, R^+$, then $-b + a \, \epsilon \, R^+$ and therefore $a - b \, \epsilon \, R^+$, which implies $a > b$.

   By Definition 6.1, only one of $b - a \, \epsilon \, R^+$ or $-(b - a) \, \epsilon \, R^+$ is possible.

Example 6.4.   The numbers 7, 5 are real numbers.   Therefore $7 = 5$ or $7 - 5 \, \epsilon \, R^+$ or $5 - 7 \, \epsilon \, R^+$.

   But $7 \neq 5$, and $7 - 5 = 2 \, \epsilon \, R^+$.   Therefore $7 > 5$.

Corollary 6.5.   1. $a > 0$ means $a \, \epsilon \, R^+$.

   2. $-a > 0$ means $-a \, \epsilon \, R^+$.

   If $a \, \epsilon \, R^+$ and therefore $a > 0$, then $-a \, \not\epsilon \, R^+$, that is, $-a \, \epsilon \, R^-$.   If $-a \, \epsilon \, R^+$, then $a \, \epsilon \, R^-$.

Theorem 6.6

If $a > 0$, $b > 0$, then

(a) $\qquad\qquad a + b > 0$
(b) $\qquad\qquad a \cdot b > 0$

The proof is left as an exercise. (*Hint:* Use the principle of closure.)

In order to prove additional properties of the relation $>$, we need the following theorems about real numbers. We shall use the properties of real numbers which we assume the student knows. These theorems we shall call *lemmas*.

Lemma 6.7. If a, $b \in R$ and $-a$, $-b$ are the additive inverses of a and b, then $(-a) \cdot b = (-b) \cdot a = -(a \cdot b)$.

Proof. By an *additive inverse* of a real number r we mean a real number designated by $-r$, such that $r + (-r) = 0$.

We know then that $(a \cdot b) + [-(a \cdot b)] = 0$.

Also $a \cdot b + (-a) \cdot b = b[a + (-a)] = a \cdot 0 = 0$.

Therefore

$$a \cdot b + [-(a \cdot b)] = a \cdot b + (-a) \cdot b$$
or $\qquad\qquad -(a \cdot b) = (-a) \cdot b$

We leave the second part of the theorem to the student.

Lemma 6.8. If a, $b \in R$, then $(-a)(-b) = a \cdot b$.

Proof. As above, $(a \cdot b) + [-(a \cdot b)] = 0$.

$$(-a)(-b) + [-(a \cdot b)] = (-a)(-b) + [(-a) \cdot b]$$

by Lemma 6.7.

$$(-a)(-b) + [-(a \cdot b)] = -a(-b + b)$$
$$= a \cdot 0 = 0$$

Therefore $\quad (-a)(-b) + [-(a \cdot b)] = ab + [-(a \cdot b)]$
and $\qquad\qquad (-a)(-b) = ab$

Theorem 6.9

If $a < 0$, $b > 0$, then

$$0 > a \cdot b$$

Proof. $0 > a$ means $-a \in R^+$. $b > 0$ means $b \in R^+$.

$$(-a)(b) \in R^+ \text{ by closure}$$
$$(-a)(b) = -(a \cdot b) \in R^+$$

$[(-a)(b) = -(ab)$ is proved above]. Therefore

$$0 > a \cdot b$$

Theorem 6.10

If $a < 0$, $b < 0$, then

$$a \cdot b > 0$$

Proof. $a < 0$ means $-a \, \epsilon \, R^+$. $b < 0$ means $-b \, \epsilon \, R^+$. Therefore

$$(-a)(-b) \, \epsilon \, R^+$$

But $(-a)(-b) = a \cdot b$ Lemma 6.8

and

$$ab \, \epsilon \, R^+, \text{ that is, } ab > 0$$

Theorem 6.11

If $a < b$, then

$$a + c < b + c \quad \text{and} \quad a - c < b - c$$

Proof. Given $a < b$, then $b - a$ is a positive number.

$$b - a = b - a + (c - c) = (b + c) - (a + c)$$

Since a, b, and c are real numbers, $b + c$, $a + c$, and $(b + c) - (a + c)$ are also. (Why?) Therefore,

$$b + c > a + c \quad \text{or} \quad a + c < b + c$$

We leave the proof of the second half of the theorem as an exercise.

Theorem 6.12

If $a < b$ and $c > 0$, then $ac < bc$.

Proof. $a < b$ implies that $b - a$ is positive. Since c is positive also, $c(b - a)$ remains positive because the product of two positive numbers is positive. $c(b - a) = cb - ca = bc - ac$ is positive. Therefore $ac < bc$.

Theorem 6.13

If $a < b$ and $c < 0$, then $ac > bc$.

Proof. Since $a < b$, $b - a$ is positive.

$c(b - a)$ is negative, since the product of a positive number by a negative is negative.

$cb - ac$ is negative; therefore $ac - bc$ is positive, or $ac > bc$.

Example 6.14. $5 < 7$; therefore

$$10 < 14 \qquad \text{multiply by 2}$$

Therefore $-10 > -14$ multiply by -2
Therefore $5 + 2 < 7 + 2$ $5 - 2 < 7 - 2$

The expression $a \leq b$ (read "a is less than or equal to b") means "$b - a$ is positive or $b - a = 0$," which is logically equivalent to "$b - a$ is positive or $a = b$."

Theorem 6.15

If a is a real number $-a \leq |a| \geq a$ (that is, $|a| \geq a$ and $|a| \geq -a$).

   Proof.   If a is positive, then $|a| = a$; therefore

$$-a < |a| = a$$

If a is negative, then $|a| = -a$; therefore

$$-a = |a| > a$$

If $a = 0, 0 = |0| = 0$.
This proves the theorem.
Corollary 6.16. $|x| \leq a$, if and only if $-a \leq x \leq a$.

1. Write out the proof of Corollary 6.5 and Theorem 6.6.
2. Prove that, if $a < b$, $-b < -a$.
3. Given $-5 \leq x \leq 5$; write as an expression, using the absolute-value sign.
4. Given $|x| \leq 2a$; write as a set of inequalities, without the absolute value sign.
5. Prove: If $a < b$ and $b < c$, then $a < c$, given that a, b, and c are real numbers.
6. Prove: If a is a real number, then $a^2 \epsilon R^+$.

6.3 GRAPHING INEQUALITIES

Inequalities are not functions (why not?), but they are relations.   Hence we can find subsets of E^1 and E^2 which are the graphs of such relations.
Example 6.17.   Graph the inequality $x \leq 5$ on the real line.

   Solution.   The graph of $x \leq 5$ is the set of all points on the real line to the left of and including 5 (Fig. 6.1), since the coordinates of these points satisfy the given inequality.
Example 6.18.   Graph the conjunction of the inequalities $x \leq 2$ and $x > -3$.

Fig. *6.1*

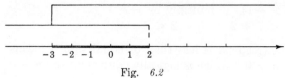

Fig. *6.2*

Solution. The graph of $(x \leq 2) \,\&\, (x > -3)$ or $-3 < x \leq 2$ is the intersection of the set of points on the real line to the left of and including 2 and the set of points on the real line to the right of -3 but not including -3. This is the set of all points on the real line from (but not including) -3 to 2 (Fig. 6.2). We call the resultant set the *interval* from -3 to 2, open at the lower end.

Example 6.19. Graph the inequality $|x| < 2$ on the real line.

Solution. $|x| < 2$ is logically equivalent to $(x < 2) \,\&\, (x > -2)$, that is, $-2 < x < 2$. (Why?) Hence the graph is the interval from -2 to 2 without the end points. We call this the open interval from -2 to $+2$.

6.4 ONE LINEAR INEQUALITY IN TWO VARIABLES

We now study linear inequalities of the form

$$ax + by < c$$

where $a \neq 0 \neq b$ and a, b, and c are real numbers.

Using the theorems on inequalities, we can write

$$by < c - ax$$

or for $b > 0$

$$y < \frac{c}{b} - \frac{a}{b} x \tag{6.1}$$

while for $b < 0$

$$y > \frac{c}{b} - \frac{a}{b} x \tag{6.2}$$

The solution set of (6.1) is the set of ordered couples $\langle x,y \rangle$ for which $y < c/b - (a/b)x$; and for (6.2) it is the set of couples $\langle x,y \rangle$ for which $y > c/b - (a/b)x$.

Example 6.20. Solve the linear inequality $2x + 4y < 8$.

Solution. Since 4 is positive, we obtain

$$4y < 8 - 2x$$

$$y < 2 - \frac{x}{2}$$

The solution set, that is, $\{\langle x,y \rangle | y < 2 - x/2\}$, contains $\langle 0,0 \rangle$, $\langle 0,1 \rangle$, $\langle 0,\frac{1}{2} \rangle$, etc.; for $x = 0$, $y < 2$; for $x = 2$, $y < 1$, etc.

Example 6.21.   Solve the linear inequality $2x - 4y < 8$.

Solution
$$-4y < 8 - 2x$$
$$y > -2 + \frac{x}{2} = \frac{x}{2} - 2$$

The solution set is
$$\{\langle x,y \rangle | y > \frac{x}{2} - 2\}$$

In order to graph a linear inequality on the real plane, we need to indicate the set of points to which the solution set is mapped, i.e., whose coordinates satisfy the inequality. We recall that, if a and b are any two numbers, $a = b$, $a < b$, or $a > b$. On the real plane, therefore, if we have the points (x,y) for which $y = x$, the points (x_i,y_i) for which $y_i < x_i$ will be below the line $y = x$ and all the points (x_i,y_i) for which $y_i > x_i$ will be above the line $y = x$. Using this idea, we shall graph a linear inequality in two variables by graphing the linear equality obtained by changing the inequality sign to an equality sign. The graph of the inequality will be the set of points above or below the line as defined by the equality.

Example 6.22.   Graph the linear inequality

$$2x + 4y < 8$$

Solution.   We write the equality $2x + 4y = 8$ or $x + 2y = 4$. The graph of $x + 2y = 4$ is the line whose slope is $-\frac{1}{2}$ and y intercept $y = 2$.

The shaded part of the graph (Fig. 6.3) denotes the set of points whose coordinates satisfy $2x + 4y < 8$. This does *not* include the set of points on the line. To indicate the set of points on the line and below it, we write

$$2x + 4y \le 8$$

The set of points above the line is defined by the inequality $2x + 4y > 8$.

Example 6.23.   Graph the relation $y \le x$.

Solution.   The graph is the union of the graphs of $y = x$ and $y < x$. The graph of $y = x$ is the set of points on the straight line through the origin making an angle of $45°$ with the x axis. The graph of $y < x$ is the set of points below and to the right of the line. We shade in the region of the plane in Fig. 6.4.

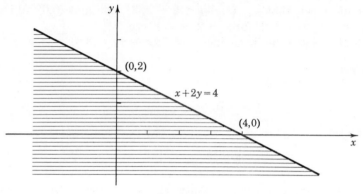

Fig. *6.3*

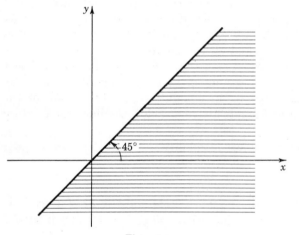

Fig. *6.4*

Example 6.24.   A firm produces two products, X and Y.   Each unit of product X produced requires 2 hours of work on a drilling machine, and each unit of product Y requires 5 hours of work on a drilling machine. The firm has a maximum of 40 drilling-machine hours available weekly. If the only constraint upon weekly production is the availability of drilling-machine hours, graph the relation which shows the combinations of the two products that the firm is capable of producing weekly.

   Solution.   Let x be the number of units of product X produced weekly, and let y be the number of units of product Y produced weekly. Since each unit of product X produced requires 2 drilling-machine hours, the product $2x$ will represent the number of drilling hours needed to produce the x units, and, similarly, $5y$ will be the number of drilling hours required to produce y units.   Since the total number of hours allocated to

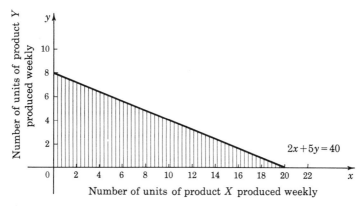

Fig. *6.5*

both products cannot exceed 40, we can write

$$2x + 5y \leq 40$$

We graph (Fig. 6.5) $2x + 5y = 40$.

The solution set for the inequality is defined as follows:

1. If only whole units are to be produced, then the solution set will be the set of all ordered couples $\langle x,y \rangle$, where x and y are nonnegative integers and $y \leq (40 - 2x)/5$. The graph will then be a set of points on or below the line defined by $2x + 5y = 40$ whose coordinates are integers, for example, $(4,2)$, $(8,2)$, etc.

2. If parts of units are included, then the solution set will contain all ordered couples $\langle x,y \rangle$ such that x and y are rational numbers and $y \leq (40 - 2x)/5$. The graph will then be the set of points on or below the line whose coordinates are rational numbers, for example, $(8,1.5)$, etc.

3. If we want a smooth curve, then the solution set will include all ordered couples $\langle x,y \rangle$ such that x and y are real numbers and $y \leq (40 - 2x)/5$. The graph will be the set of all points on and under the line $5y + 2x = 40$.

In no case will negative values of x and y be considered.   (Why?)

PROBLEM SET 6.2

1. Solve the following linear inequalities for y:

a. $2y + x > 5$

b. $-x - y < 0$

c. $\dfrac{x}{2} + \dfrac{y}{4} < 1$

d. $2x - 3y < -5$

e. $2x + 3y > 5$

2. Graph each of the linear inequalities in Prob. 1.

3. A manufacturer produces two products, X and Y. He has just one retail outlet, with which he has a contractual agreement such that the outlet will take up to six units of product X and up to three units of product Y daily. Graph the relation which shows the possible combinations of the two products that the manufacturer can ship daily. Assume that it is possible to ship fractional units of the two products. (*Hint:* X cannot be greater than 6, and Y cannot be greater than 3. Indicate this on the graph.)

4. A manufacturer has a contractual agreement that must be fulfilled, viz., that customer A must be supplied, daily, twice as many units of product X as product Y, the total number of units of both products combined being at least six. Graph the relation which shows the combinations of two products which legally can be shipped.

5. An animal feed is to be a mixture of two foodstuffs, X and Y. Foodstuff X contains 5 grams of protein per ounce, and foodstuff Y 3 grams. Each bag of the resulting mix is to contain at least 50 grams of protein. Graph the relation which shows the combinations of X and Y which will satisfy this requirement.

6.5 SIMULTANEOUS LINEAR INEQUALITIES

In solving simultaneous linear inequalities, we keep in mind that what we are seeking is the intersection of the solution sets of a system of two or more inequalities. This can most easily be achieved by graphing the inequalities and noting the intersection of their graphs. If the intersection is empty, there are no simultaneous solutions.

Example 6.25. Solve the system of linear inequalities by graphing

$$2x + 2y < 4$$
$$x - y < 0 \qquad \text{that is, } y > x$$

Solution. We graph $2x + 2y < 4$ or $x + y < 2$ by graphing $x + y = 2$ and $x - y < 0$ by $x = y$. The simultaneous solutions are in the crosshatched area in Fig. 6.6.

Example 6.26. Solve the system of linear inequalities

$$x - y < 0 \qquad \text{or} \qquad y > x$$
$$x + y > 2$$
$$x \leq 3$$
$$y \geq 0$$

Solution. The area (Fig. 6.7) enclosed in heavy lines contains the points whose coordinates will satisfy all four inequalities.

Example 6.27. The production of truck engines y requires twice as much time as the production of automobile engines x. A factory can produce either 50 automobile engines or 25 truck engines or some linear combination of automobile and truck engines. What is the equation of the

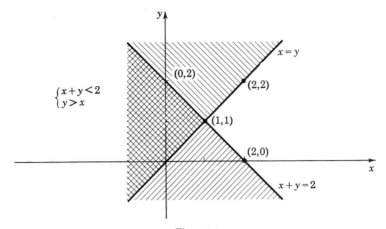

Fig. *6.6*

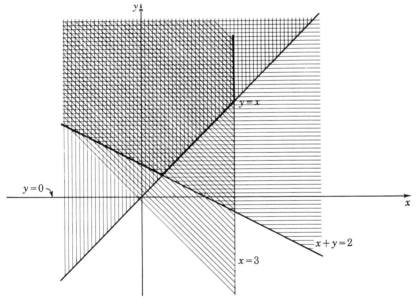

Fig. *6.7*

capacity relation between the two types of engines?   Graph the relation.
What are the domain and range?   Assuming that the full capacity is not
utilized, show on the graph the area representing the possible combinations of automobile and truck engines.

   Solution.   Since we assume a linear relation, we can obtain the
equation if we know the slope.   We know two points on the line, namely,

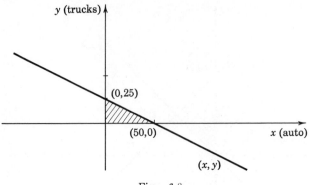

Fig. *6.8*

(0,25) and (50,0). Therefore the slope must be

$$m = \frac{25 - 0}{0 - 50} = -\frac{1}{2}$$

Taking any other point (x,y) on the line, we get

$$-\frac{1}{2} = \frac{y - 25}{x - 0} = \frac{y - 25}{x}$$
$$-x = 2y - 50$$
$$2y = -x + 50$$
$$y = -\tfrac{1}{2}x + 25$$

The domain is the set of integers from 0 to 50 and the range from 0 to 25. No negative numbers are possible in either the range or the domain. (Why?) The area representing the possible combination is shaded (Fig. 6.8) and is bounded by

$$x \geq 0$$
$$y \geq 0$$
$$y \leq -\tfrac{1}{2}x + 25$$

Example 6.28. A firm is planning production for the next week. It is making two products, X and Y, each of which requires certain foundry, machining, and finishing capacities as shown in Table 6.1. The following

TABLE 6.1

Product	Hours per unit		
	Foundry	Machining	Finishing
X	6	3	4
Y	6	6	2

number of hours is available in each area during the week planned:

Foundry, 110
Machining, 150
Finishing, 60

Graph the system of linear inequalities which shows the quantities of X and Y that can be produced.

Solution. Since products X and Y each require 6 hours of foundry time for each unit produced, and since there are 110 foundry hours available, the total amount of the available foundry time which is utilized must satisfy the relation

$$6x + 6y \leq 110$$

where x represents the number of units of product X processed and y the number of units of product Y. Similarly, the relations pertaining to machining and finishing capacity are, respectively,

$$3x + 6y \leq 150$$
$$4x + 2y \leq 60$$

In addition to the three production constraints indicated above, there are two additional conditions that any output combination must satisfy,

$$x \geq 0 \qquad y \geq 0$$

That is, production cannot be negative.

The shaded portion of Fig. 6.9 shows those output combinations which satisfy all restrictions. Note that in this problem machining capacity is not, in reality, a constraint at all; i.e., any output combination which satisfies the other two constraints will also satisfy machining capacity.

Example 6.29. An animal feed is to be a mixture of two foodstuffs, each unit of which contains protein, fat, and carbohydrate in the number of grams given in Table 6.2. Each bag of the resulting mixture is to

TABLE 6.2

	Foodstuff	
	1	2
Protein..........	10	5
Fat..............	0.1	0.9
Carbohydrate......	10	30

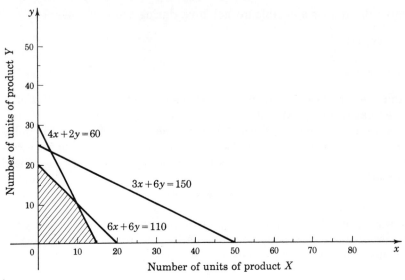

Fig. *6.9*

contain at least 40 grams of protein, 1.8 grams of fat, and 120 grams of carbohydrate. Graph the system of inequalities which shows the mixtures which meet these requirements.

Solution. Since each unit of foodstuff 1 contains 10 grams of protein and each unit of foodstuff 2 contains 5 grams of protein, and since each bag of the mixture must contain at least 40 grams of protein, one inequality which must be satisfied is

$$10x + 5y \geq 40$$

where x denotes the number of units of foodstuff 1 in the mixture and y the number of units of foodstuff 2. Similarly, the other relevant inequalities are

$$0.1x + 0.9y \geq 1.8 \quad \text{for fat}$$
$$10x + 30y \geq 120 \quad \text{for carbohydrate}$$

We also have, as in the preceding example, the nonnegativity constraints

$$x \geq 0 \quad y \geq 0$$

The portion of Fig. 6.10 which lies above and to the right of the heavy lines indicates those mixtures which meet these requirements.

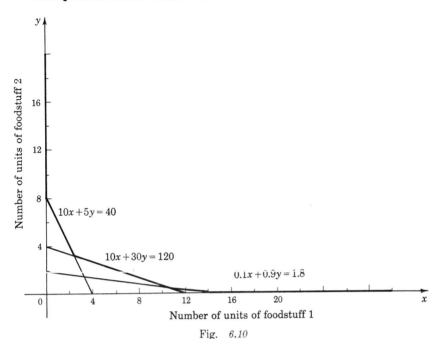

Fig. *6.10*

PROBLEM SET 6.3

1. Graph the following systems of linear inequalities:

    a. $x \leq 3$
       $y \geq 0$

    b. $x - y < 2$
       $2x - y < 3$
       $x - 4y < 5$

    c. $x > 0$
       $y > 0$
       $2x + 3y > 5$

    d. $x > 3$
       $y < 4$
       $x - y = -5$

2. In Prob. 5 of Problem Set 5.3, express the total possible output of military and civilian goods as a linear inequality.   Graph the inequality.

3. If a person must have at least 900 units of vitamins and 1,000 units of calories per day, express each condition as a linear inequality and determine what would constitute an acceptable diet.   Graph the inequalities.   (*Hint:* Let x be the number of units of vitamins needed and y the number of units of calories needed.)

4. To meet a budgetary limitation, an executive can hire not more than five secretaries and at least seven salesmen.   Write a system of inequalities expressing the permissible combinations he can hire.   If he must have at least one secretary, indicate the domain and range of the relation involved.   Graph the system of inequalities.

5. Determine directly from Fig. 6.10 (Example 6.29) which of the following combinations of foodstuffs meet all requirements. Indicate, for those combinations which do not meet these requirements, which of the constraints are being violated; if the figure is not sufficiently clear for this purpose, refer to the relevant equations.

a. $x = 2, y = 1$
b. $x = 2, y = 3$
c. $x = 2, y = 5$
d. $x = 10, y = 1$
e. $x = 1, y = 3$
f. $x = 3, y = 1$
g. $x = 14, y = 0.5$

6. A firm produces two different models of a product, model 1 and model 2. Each model must be processed by a drilling machine and a lathe. To complete one unit of model 1, the drilling machine must work 2 hours and the lathe must work 4 hours; to complete one unit of model 2, the drilling machine and the lathe must work 4 and 2 hours, respectively. A strong union enforces the rule that no machine may be operated more than 12 hours per day. Graph the system of linear inequalities which shows the combinations of the two models which can be produced daily.

7. A manufacturer is going out of business. However, he has two contractual agreements that must still be fulfilled. One agreement specifies that customer A must be supplied, daily, at least six units of products X and Y combined. The second agreement specifies that customer B must be supplied, daily, at least eight units of products X and Y combined. Graph the system of inequalities which shows which output combinations satisfy these requirements. Assume, now, that each unit of product X requires 1 man-hour, that each unit of product Y requires 2 man-hours, and that there are only 20 man-hours available daily. Show which output combinations satisfy the requirements. Finally, if a union rule prohibits the employment of less than 8 man-hours daily, show the feasible output combinations.

8. A manufacturer chemically processes bauxite ore into products X and Y. Each unit of product X contains 1 unit of ingredient A and 1 unit of ingredient B. Each unit of product Y contains 1 unit of ingredient A and 4 units of ingredient B. A customer desires at least 9 units of ingredient A and at least 18 units of ingredient B, and he does not care how many units of products X and Y he receives in order to obtain the specified amounts of the two ingredients. In order to process the two products, the manufacturer must bake product X for 4 hours and product Y for 1 hour. He has only 24 furnace-hours available each day. Graph the system of inequalities which show the combinations of X and Y which will satisfy the customer and still not exceed the available furnace capacity.

9. A bag of fertilizer requires at least six units of ingredient A and at least eight units of ingredient B. This fertilizer can be manufactured by mixing product X and product Y. The former product contains two units of ingredient A and one unit of ingredient B, while the latter contains one unit of ingredient A and three units of ingredient B. Graph the relevant system of inequalities, and shade the portion of the resulting figure which represents the feasible combinations of X and Y.

6.6 LINEAR PROGRAMMING—THE PROBLEM

In this section we shall describe the type of problem which the method of linear programming tries to solve. We shall then show how inequalities and their graphs can be used to arrive at a solution to the problem.

In the preceding sections we learned how to find the possible combinations of products that could be produced under certain conditions. Evidently, when one has a host of possible actions, he will want to choose that solution which is most to his advantage.   For example, in Example 6.28 we discovered that there was a whole set of combinations of the two products that could be produced under the given conditions, for example, 5 of each product, or 5 of X and 10 of Y, etc.   Now, if a profit of \$2 were made on each unit of product X and a profit of \$3 on each unit of product Y, then if 5 of X and 5 of Y were produced, the profit would be $5 \cdot 2 + 5 \cdot 3 = \$25$; but if 5 of X and 10 of Y were produced, the profit would be $5 \cdot 2 + 10 \cdot 3 = \$40$.

Evidently the set of profits is determined by the set of possible combinations of products that can be produced.   The manufacturer desires to maximize his profits, i.e., to find that combination of products which will give him the greatest element in the set of profits.

Under the conditions of Example 6.28, the elements of the set of profits are determined by the expression $2x + 3y$.   If we let P denote the set of profits, then

$$P = \{p | p = 2x + 3y\}$$

We shall assume that x and y can take on all real numbers in the set of possible combinations of products as given in Example 6.28.   The problem is to find the ordered couple $\langle x, y \rangle$ defined in Example 6.28 that will make p a maximum.

In Example 6.29, if each unit of foodstuff 1 costs \$1 and each unit of foodstuff 2 costs \$2, the total cost for each combination would be expressed by

$$x + 2y$$

Evidently the firm would want to find that combination (couple $\langle x, y \rangle$) for which the cost would be a minimum, i.e., the least element in the set,

$$C = \{c | c = x + 2y\}$$

The student will note that the set P and the set of ordered couples of Example 6.28 define a function f_p,

$$f_p = \{\langle \langle x, y \rangle, p \rangle | p = 2x + 3y\} \tag{6.3}$$

and the set C along with the set of ordered couples in Example 6.29 also define a function,

$$f_c = \{\langle \langle x, y \rangle, c \rangle | c = x + 2y\} \tag{6.4}$$

The problems are referred to as maximizing f_p and minimizing f_c, or, alternatively, as maximizing p or minimizing c.   Notice that the ordered couples $\langle x, y \rangle$ are elements of sets defined by specific conditions relevant to particular problems, that f_p and f_c are linear functions, and that x, y must be nonnegative.

In many situations, the specified conditions will involve linear equalities and/or inequalities. Examples 6.28 and 6.29 each involves, in addition to the nonnegativity restrictions, three linear inequalities. In the first example, the maximization problem requires the selection of the ordered couple(s) in the set,

$$\{\langle x,y \rangle | (x \ \& \ y \text{ are nonnegative real numbers}) \ \& \ (6x + 6y \leq 110)$$
$$\& \ (3x + 6y \leq 150) \ \& \ (4x + 2y \leq 60)\}$$

which maximizes relation (6.3). The latter example requires the selection of the ordered couple(s) in the set,

$$\{\langle x,y \rangle | (x \ \& \ y \text{ are nonnegative real numbers}) \ \& \ (10x + 5y \geq 40)$$
$$\& \ (0.1x + 0.9y \geq 1.8) \ \& \ (10x + 30y \geq 120)\}$$

which minimizes relation (6.4).

In the above examples, all functions and relations are linear (i.e., graph into lines). Linear programming is the mathematical technique which is employed to determine the required ordered couple(s) or, in general, the required ordered n-tuple(s) in problems of this sort. In the terminology of linear programming, the linear function to be maximized or minimized is the *objective function;* the nonnegativity requirements are the *nonnegativity constraints;* the linear relations peculiar to the specific problem are the *structural constraints;* any set of x, y, etc., which satisfies the structural constraints is a *solution* to the problem; any solution which satisfies the nonnegativity constraints is a *feasible solution;* and any feasible solution which optimizes, i.e., maximizes or minimizes, as the case may be, the objective function is an *optimal feasible solution.* Linear programming, then, is a technique by which optimal feasible solutions are obtained.

If we designate the variables x, y, etc., by the symbol x with a subscript, and if we let z denote the linear function to be optimized, we can formulate the above remarks symbolically. We can say that the purpose of linear programming is the determination of a set of nonnegative values of n variables,

$$x_j \geq 0 \qquad j = 1, 2, \ldots, n$$

which satisfies a set of m linear constraints (the structural constraints) in these n variables,

$$\sum_{j=1}^{n} a_{ij}x_j = a_{i1}x_1 + a_{i2}x_2 + \cdots + a_{in}x_n \leq b_i \qquad i = 1, 2, \ldots, m$$

(any of the $\leq$ signs may be replaced with $=$ or $\geq$ signs) and which also optimizes (i.e., maximizes or minimizes) a linear function (the objective function) of these n variables,

$$\sum_{i=1}^{n} c_i x_i = z = c_1 x_1 + c_2 x_2 + \cdots + c_n x_n$$

where a_i, b_i, and c_i are parameters, i.e., known constants, for the specific problem.

(More compactly, we can say that linear programming seeks to determine the following set of ordered n-tuples:

$$\big\{ \langle x_1, x_2, \ldots, x_n \rangle \,|\, (x_j \geq 0,\ j = 1, 2, \ldots, n)$$

$$\& \left[\left(\sum_{j=1}^{n} a_{ij} x_j \leq b_i \right) \veebar \left(\sum_{j=1}^{n} a_{ij} x_j = b_i \right) \right.$$

$$\left. \veebar \left(\sum_{j=1}^{n} a_{ij} x_j \geq b_i \right),\ i = 1, 2, \ldots, m \right] \& \left(z = \sum_{j=1}^{n} c_j x_j \text{ is optimized} \right) \big\}$$

For the definition of the summation symbol Σ, see Chap. 9.)

6.7 LINEAR PROGRAMMING: GRAPHICAL SOLUTIONS

Linear-programming problems involving more than three variables are generally solved by a method known as the *simplex method*. Since this method requires mathematical concepts we have not yet defined, e.g., vectors and matrices, it will be treated in Chap. 12. In this section we shall show how to solve graphically linear-programming problems involving two variables. We need an additional concept.

Definition 6.30. An *isoprofit* set is any subset I_p of P (the set of profits) such that the range of I_p is a constant p_1, that is,

$$I_p = \{ \langle \langle x, y \rangle, p \rangle \,|\, p = f(\langle x, y \rangle) \ \& \ p = p_1 \}$$

Note that any number of subsets I_p can be obtained from P.

Definition 6.31. The graph of an isoprofit set I_p is called the *isoprofit line*. An isoprofit line thus shows the different combinations of the two products which will yield the same total profit.

Since by assumption all relations and functions describing sets are linear, the graphs will be straight lines.

We obtain the function describing the isoprofit line from the objective function

$$p = c_1 x_1 + c_2 x_2$$

(we write x_2 for y) as follows. First we fix p equal to p_1. c_1 and c_2 are assumed known.   Then we solve for x_2,

$$c_2 x_2 = p_1 - c_1 x_1$$

$$x_2 = \frac{p_1 - c_1 x_1}{c_2} = \frac{p_1}{c_2} - \frac{c_1}{c_2} x_1$$

$$= -\frac{c_1}{c_2} x_1 + \frac{p_1}{c_2} \tag{6.5}$$

The slope of this line is $-c_1/c_2$, and it cuts the y axis at $(0, p_1/c_2)$.   For any given problem, an entire family of isoprofit lines can be generated by assigning different values to the profit constant p_1.   Since, in any given problem, c_1 and c_2 are fixed for all possible values of p_1, all isoprofit lines for a given problem will have the same slope $(= -c_1/c_2)$; however, the vertical-axis intercept $(= p_1/c_2)$ changes as p_1 changes, and changes in p_1 will therefore be associated with parallel shifts of the isoprofit line.

For Example 6.28,

$$p = 2x_1 + 3x_2$$

or

$$x_2 = -\frac{2x_1}{3} + \frac{p_1}{3}$$

For $p_1 = 15$,

$$x_2 = -\tfrac{2}{3}x_1 + 5$$

with slope $-\tfrac{2}{3}$ and y intercept 5.   •

Example 6.32.   The firm described in Example 6.28 seeks to determine the combination of products X and Y which is most profitable.   We denote the number of units of product X produced by x_1 and the number of units of product Y by x_2.   [The shift of notation to x_1, x_2 ($x_2 = y$) is for convenience of computation.]   As before, we assume that each unit of X produced results in a profit of \$2 and each unit of Y in a profit of \$3. What is the optimum combination of products to produce?

Solution.   The objective function to be maximized is defined by

$$p = 2x_1 + 3x_2$$

the nonnegativity constraints are

$$x_j \geq 0 \qquad j = 1, 2$$

and the structural constraints are

$$6x_1 + 6x_2 \leq 110$$
$$3x_1 + 6x_2 \leq 150$$
$$4x_1 + 2x_2 \leq 60$$

The structural constraints, which have already been graphed in Fig. 6.9, are graphed again in Fig. 6.11.   Also graphed in Fig. 6.11 are

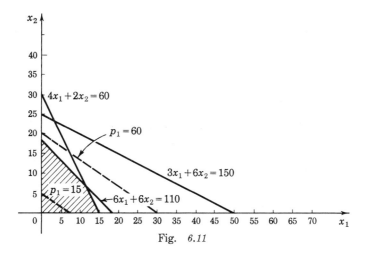

Fig. 6.11

the isoprofit lines for $p_1 = 15$ and $p_1 = 60$. Note that, at least in this problem, as p_1 is increased the vertical-axis intercept p_1/c_2 increases. As this implies, parallel shifts upward of the isoprofit line indicate a rising total profit p_1; the isoprofit line for $p_1 = 60$, for example, lies above the line for $p_1 = 15$ (Fig. 6.11). In general, since isoprofit lines may be positively or negatively sloped and they may shift up or down as p_1 increases, each problem must be analyzed separately in order to determine which movements of isoprofit lines are profitable.

To determine the optimum combination of products, we must first determine which combinations of the two products are capable of being produced, i.e., which combinations satisfy the nonnegativity and structural constraints. The dotted region, called the *technical feasibility polygon*, in Fig. 6.11 shows these combinations. For this problem, the most profitable of these combinations is the one which lies on the *highest* possible isoprofit line that can be drawn. As Fig. 6.11 illustrates, there are points in the polygon which lie on isoprofit lines higher than that corresponding to $p_1 = 15$, but none of the points in the polygon lie on an isoprofit line as high as that corresponding to $p_1 = 60$. The highest isoprofit line that will have at least one point in common with the feasibility polygon will therefore correspond to $\$15 < p_1 < \$60$.

By gradually shifting upward the line corresponding to $p_1 = 15$ (or gradually shifting downward that corresponding to $p_1 = 60$), the reader should be able to see that the desired isoprofit line is, in the present case, the one which cuts the vertical axis at the same point as the foundry-capacity constraint $6x_1 + 6x_2 = 110$. The only point which this isoprofit line has in common with the polygon is this vertical-axis intercept, and therefore the coordinates of this point represent the optimum combination of products.   To determine these coordinates, we solve for the vertical-axis intercept of the foundry-capacity constraint.   For $x_1 = 0$ we have

$$6x_1 + 6x_2 = 110$$
$$6x_2 = 110$$
$$x_2 = \frac{110}{6} = 18\tfrac{1}{3}$$

The optimum product mix is therefore $x_1 = 0$, $x_2 = 18\tfrac{1}{3}$.

Since we know the general equation [see Eq. (6.5)] for the desired isoprofit line as well as the values of c_1 and c_2 (2 and 3, respectively), we can determine the profit p_1 associated with it if we can locate one point on the line.   Since we know that the desired isoprofit line has the same vertical-axis intercept as the foundry-capacity constraint, one such point is $x_1 = 0$, $x_2 = 18\tfrac{1}{3}$.   The maximized profit is therefore

$$x_2 = -\frac{c_1}{c_2}x_1 + \frac{p_1}{c_2}$$
$$p_1 = c_1x_1 + c_2x_2$$
$$= (2)(0) + (3)(18\tfrac{1}{3})$$
$$= 55$$

As this calculation indicates, the maximized total profit can always be directly determined by substituting the optimum x_1 and x_2 values into the objective function.

From Fig. 6.11, the reader should be able to see that the optimum point is on the constraint relating to foundry capacity but beneath the constraints relating to machining and finishing capacity.   As this implies, foundry capacity is fully utilized, while machining and finishing capacity are underutilized.   The amount of idle capacity for each operation can be determined by substituting the optimum x_1 and x_2 values into the appropriate equation to determine the amount of capacity actually used and then subtracting this value from the capacity available.   Example 6.28 gives the relevant equations and capacities.   The amount of capacity (in hours) used is

$$6x_1 + 6x_2 = (6)(0) + (6)(18\tfrac{1}{3}) = 110 \qquad \text{foundry}$$
$$3x_1 + 6x_2 = (3)(0) + (6)(18\tfrac{1}{3}) = 110 \qquad \text{machining}$$
$$4x_1 + 2x_2 = (4)(0) + (2)(18\tfrac{1}{3}) = 36\tfrac{2}{3} \qquad \text{finishing}$$

The amount of capacity (in hours) available is

110	foundry
150	machining
60	finishing

and the amount of idle capacity (in hours) is

$$110 - 110 = 0 \qquad \text{foundry}$$
$$150 - 110 = 40 \qquad \text{machining}$$
$$60 - 36\tfrac{2}{3} = 23\tfrac{1}{3} \qquad \text{finishing}$$

Example 6.33.   Assume, now, that in the above example each unit of product X produced results in a profit of \$4 and each unit of product Y in a profit of \$3.   What is the optimum product mix?

Solution.   Now $c_1 = 4$ and $c_2 = 3$, the objective function is

$$p = 4x_1 + 3x_2$$

and the isoprofit equation [see Eq. (6.5)] is

$$x_2 = -\tfrac{4}{3}x_1 + \frac{p_1}{3}$$

The three structural constraints and the technical-feasibility polygon graphed in Figs. 6.9 and 6.11 are reproduced in Fig. 6.12, and three members—corresponding to $p_1 = 24$, $p_1 = 66\tfrac{2}{3}$, and $p_1 = 84$— of the new family of isoprofit lines are graphed.   We see that the highest isoprofit line which has at least one point in common with the polygon is now the one which passes through the intersection of the structural constraints for foundry and finishing capacity.

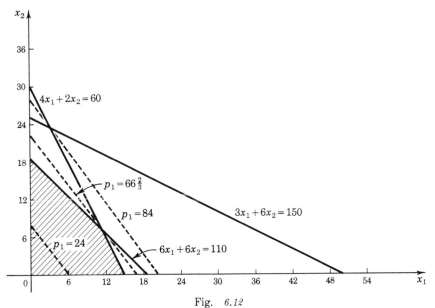

Fig. *6.12*

The only point on the line which is also in the polygon is this point of intersection. The optimum combination of products is therefore given by the coordinates of this point, which can be determined by simultaneously solving the equations for the two intersecting constraints:

$$4x_1 + 2x_2 = 60 \qquad x_1 = 15 - \tfrac{1}{2}x_2 \qquad \text{finishing}$$
$$6x_1 + 6x_2 = 110 \qquad x_1 = \tfrac{110}{6} - x_2 \qquad \text{foundry}$$
$$15 - \tfrac{1}{2}x_2 = \tfrac{110}{6} - x_2$$
$$x_2 = 6\tfrac{2}{3} \qquad x_1 = 11\tfrac{2}{3}$$

Thus, total profit will be maximized if $x_1 = 11\tfrac{2}{3}$ and $x_2 = 6\tfrac{2}{3}$. The maximized profit is

$$p_1 = c_1 x_1 + c_2 x_2$$
$$= (4)(11\tfrac{2}{3}) + (3)(6\tfrac{2}{3})$$
$$= 46\tfrac{2}{3} + 20$$
$$= 66\tfrac{2}{3}$$

Figure 6.12 shows that the desired point lies on the constraints for foundry and finishing capacity but beneath that for machining capacity; as this implies, idle capacity now exists only in the machining operation. Idle capacity is calculated below (assuming the optimum combination of $x_1 = 11\tfrac{2}{3}$, $x_2 = 6\tfrac{2}{3}$):

Hours available $-$	hours utilized	$=$	idle (excess) capacity
110	$- [(6)(11\tfrac{2}{3}) + (6)(6\tfrac{2}{3})] =$	0 hours	foundry
150	$- [(3)(11\tfrac{2}{3}) + (6)(6\tfrac{2}{3})] =$	75 hours	machining
60	$- [(4)(11\tfrac{2}{3}) + (2)(6\tfrac{2}{3})] =$	0 hours	finishing

The reader should note that, if the slope of the isoprofit line happens to equal that of any of the structural constraints, there is no unique optimum solution; on the contrary, there are an infinite number of optimum solutions. For example, if each unit of each product resulted in the same profit, say, $2, the objective function and isoprofit line would be, respectively,

$$p = 2x_1 + 2x_2$$

and

$$x_2 = \frac{p_1}{2} - 1x_1$$

The slope of this isoprofit line is the same as that of the constraint corresponding to foundry capacity, and as the reader can verify by shifting the isoprofit line in either Fig. 6.11 or Fig. 6.12, any output combination along this constraint between $x_1 = 0$ and $x_1 = 11\tfrac{2}{3}$, inclusive, will be equally profitable and no other combination will be more profitable.

The reader should now be able to verify Theorem 6.34, which we shall state without proof.

Theorem 6.34

If the slope of the family of isoprofit lines is different from that of any of the structural constraints, there will be a unique optimum solution and it will be represented by the coordinates of one of the vertices of the technical-feasibility polygon (note that the origin point is a possibility).

Example 6.35.   Determine the coordinates at each of the vertices of the polygon employed in the above examples, and, by substituting them into the relevant objective functions, verify the optimum product mixes obtained in Examples 6.32 and 6.33.

Example 6.36.   The manufacturer of animal feed described in Example 6.29 seeks to determine the combination of foodstuffs 1 and 2 which will satisfy the specified nutrient requirements at the lowest possible cost. Assume that each unit of foodstuff 1 costs 60 cents and each unit of foodstuff 2 costs 40 cents.   What is the optimum feed mix?

Solution.   We denote the number of units of foodstuff 1 employed in the mix by x_1 and the number of units of foodstuff 2 by x_2.   The objective function to be *minimized* is defined by

$$c = 0.6x_1 + 0.4x_2$$

The nonnegativity constraints are

$$x_j \geq 0 \qquad j = 1, 2$$

and the structural constraints are

$$10x_1 + 5x_2 \geq 40$$
$$10x_1 + 30x_2 \geq 120$$
$$0.1x_1 + 0.9x_2 \geq 1.8$$

We need, as in the preceding problem, two definitions.

Definition 6.37.   An *isocost* set is any subset I_c of C (the set of total costs) such that the range of I_c is a constant k, that is,

$$I_c = \{\langle\langle x,y\rangle,c\rangle | c = f(\langle x,y\rangle) \ \& \ c = k\}$$

Note that any number of subsets I_c can be obtained from C.

Definition 6.38.   The graph of an isocost set is called the *isocost line.* An isocost line thus shows the different combinations of the two foodstuffs which will result in the same total cost.

The analysis is now completely analogous to that employed in the preceding problem, except that now:

1. We want to *minimize* the objective function,

$$c = c_1 x_1 + c_2 x_2$$

2. We replace the isoprofit equation,

$$x_2 = -\frac{c_1}{c_2} x_1 + \frac{p_1}{c_2}$$

with the isocost equation

$$x_2 = -\frac{c_1}{c_2} x_1 + \frac{k}{c_2}$$

3. We employ inequalities of the type $\geq$ instead of $\leq$.

The structural constraints, which have already been graphed in Fig. 6.10, are graphed again in Fig. 6.13. Also graphed in Fig. 6.13 are the *isocost lines* for $k = \$2.40$ and $k = \$2.72$. In the present case, the isocost line is defined by

$$x_2 = \frac{k}{0.4} - \frac{0.6}{0.4} x_1 \tag{6.6}$$

The shaded region of Fig. 6.13 shows the technical-feasibility polygon for this problem. We seek that point (combination) in the polygon which corresponds to the lowest possible total cost. From Eq. (6.6) we see that all isocost lines, in a given problem, have the same slope (i.e., are parallel) and that, in the present problem, as the total cost k decreases the isocost line moves downward. Thus, the point we seek is the one which lies on the lowest possible isocost line that can be drawn and still have at least one point in common with the polygon.

As Fig. 6.13 shows, this will be the isocost line which just touches the intersection of the constraints corresponding to the protein and carbohydrate requirements. The feed mix at this intersection can be deter-

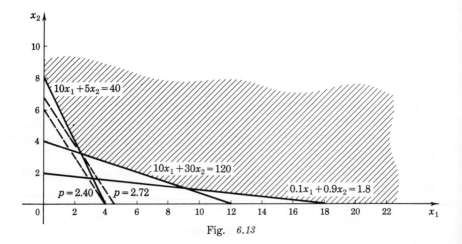

Fig. *6.13*

mined by simultaneously solving the two equations corresponding to the relevant constraints:

$$10x_1 + 5x_2 = 40 \qquad x_2 = 8 - 2x_1 \qquad \text{protein}$$
$$10x_1 + 30x_2 = 120 \qquad x_2 = 4 - \tfrac{1}{3}x_1 \qquad \text{carbohydrate}$$
$$8 - 2x_1 = 4 - \tfrac{1}{3}x_1$$
$$x_1 = 2\tfrac{2}{5}$$
$$x_2 = 3\tfrac{1}{5}$$

Since this point of intersection is the only one which is both on the specified isocost line and in the polygon, its coordinates, $x_1 = 2\tfrac{2}{5}$ and $x_2 = 3\tfrac{1}{5}$, represent the optimum feed mix. The minimum total cost is obtained from the objective function,

$$c = c_1x_1 + c_2x_2$$
$$= (\$0.60)(2\tfrac{2}{5}) + (\$0.40)(3\tfrac{1}{5}) = \$2.72$$

Note that this mix provides

$$(0.1)(2.4) + (0.9)(3.2) = 3.12$$

grams of fat, which is

$$3.12 - 1.8 = 1.32$$

grams more than is required.

PROBLEM SET 6.4

1. In Example 6.36, if each unit of foodstuff 1 costs 10 cents and each unit of foodstuff 2 costs 30 cents, what is the optimum mix? If each unit costs 10 cents and 60 cents, respectively?

2. In Prob. 6 of Problem Set 6.3, assume that the firm has no difficulty in selling all the units of both models that it chooses to produce. Its profit is $3 on each unit of model 1 and $5 on each unit of model 2. How many of each should it produce daily in order to maximize profit?

3. For each of the situations posed in Prob. 7 of Problem Set 6.3, determine the minimum-cost product mix and minimum total cost, assuming that each unit of product 1 costs $2 and each unit of product 2 costs $3.

4. In Prob. 8 of Problem Set 6.3, assume that each unit of product 1 produced results in a profit of $2 and that each unit of product 2 produced results in a loss of $2. What is the most profitable product mix, and what is the maximized profit?

5. In Prob. 9 of Problem Set 6.3, assume that each unit of product 1 costs $2 and that each unit of product 2 costs $3. What quantities of the two products should the firm purchase if it wants to minimize total cost, and what is this minimized cost?

6. A firm has two plants, A and B. Plant A has the capacity to produce 800 units daily, and plant B is able to produce as many as 400 units daily. The firm has three warehouses, $W1$, $W2$, and $W3$, which must receive, respectively, 300, 400, and 500 units daily. The cost per unit of transporting from the two plants to the three

TABLE 6.3

Plant	Warehouse		
	1	2	3
A	$4	$5	$8
B	6	3	5

warehouses is given in Table 6.3.   How much should each plant ship to each warehouse for total transportation costs to be a minimum?   What is this minimum cost?

7 LINEAR EQUATIONS, MATRICES, AND DETERMINANTS

7.1 LINEAR FUNCTIONS

Our discussion will be limited to functions whose ranges and domains are subsets of real numbers and whose coefficients are real numbers.

Definition 7.1. Any expression in two variables of the form $a_1x + a_2y + a_3 = 0$ will be called a *linear equation*.

For example, $2x + 3y + 5 = 0$ is a linear equation, with $a_1 = 2$, $a_2 = 3$, $a_3 = 5$. Any linear equation in which $a_2 \neq 0$ can be written as a linear function by "solving" for y.

$$a_1x + a_2y + a_3 = 0$$
$$a_2y = -a_1x - a_3$$
$$y = -\frac{a_1}{a_2}x - \frac{a_3}{a_2}$$

We can therefore graph a linear equation as a straight line and determine the slope m and y intercept of the line.

If $a_2 = 0$, but $a_1 \neq 0$, the equation is $a_1x + a_3 = 0$ or $x = -a_3/a_1$.

Example 7.2. Write the equation $2x - 6y + 4 = 0$ as a function.

$$-6y = -2x - 4$$
$$y = \frac{x}{3} + \frac{2}{3}$$

Therefore $$m = \tfrac{1}{3}$$

and the y intercept is $(0,\tfrac{2}{3})$.

Example 7.3. Every morning a supermarket purchases at a price of $2 four units of a product which it sells for a price of $4. Whenever the product is sold, a wrapping cost of 20 cents is incurred. Since the product is perishable, units remaining unsold at the end of the day are resold to the supplier for $1 for reprocessing. Express the relationship between the number of units demanded and total profit as a linear function. Graph the function.

Solution. Let Z denote the number of units demanded daily and Q the number of units stocked ($Q = 4$ in this example). Total profit can be calculated as total revenue minus total cost. For $0 \leq Z < Q = 4$, the profit function is defined by

$$\begin{aligned}
P &= R - C \\
&= [4Z + 1(Q - Z)] - (2Q + 0.20Z) \\
&= 4Z + 1Q - 1Z - 2Q - 0.20Z \\
&= 2.80Z - 1Q \qquad 0 \leq Z < Q
\end{aligned}$$

where $Q - Z$ represents the number of units stocked but not demanded. Since $Q = 4$, the above equation becomes

$$P = 2.80Z - 4 \qquad 0 \leq Z < 4$$

For $Z \geq Q = 4$, the profit function is defined by

$$\begin{aligned}
P &= 4Q - (2Q + 0.20Q) \qquad Z \geq Q \\
&= 1.80Q
\end{aligned}$$

which, since $Q = 4$, becomes

$$P = 7.20 \qquad Z \geq 4$$

Figure 7.1 graphs this profit function, which is referred to in the literature as a *broken-line conditional profit* function.

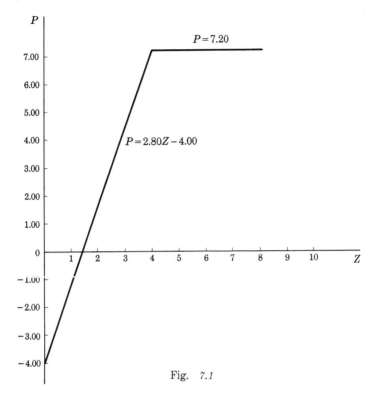

Fig. 7.1

Definition 7.4.   The solution set S of the linear equation is the set of all ordered couples $\langle x,y \rangle$ for which $a_1 x + a_2 y + a_3 = 0$ is true.

$$S = \{\langle x,y \rangle | a_1 x + a_2 y + a_3 = 0\}$$

If $\langle x_1, y_1 \rangle \; \epsilon \; S$, then $\langle x_1, y_1 \rangle$ is said to *satisfy* the equation.   Any element of the solution set will be called a solution of the equation.

Definition 7.5.   If $\langle x_1, 0 \rangle \; \epsilon \; S$, then x_1 is a root of the linear equation $a_1 x + a_2 y + a_3 = 0$ $(a_1 \neq 0)$.

The elements of a solution set of a linear equation are found by writing the equation as a linear function,

$$y = mx + b$$

and inserting real numbers for x.   In Example 7.2, elements of the solution set $y = x/3 + \frac{2}{3}$ are found by letting $x = 0, 1, -1, \frac{1}{2}, -\frac{1}{2}$, etc.

$$x = 0, y = \tfrac{2}{3} \qquad x = 1, y = 1 \qquad x = -1, y = \tfrac{1}{3} \qquad \text{etc.}$$
$$S = \{\langle 0, \tfrac{2}{3} \rangle, \langle 1, 1 \rangle, \langle -1, \tfrac{1}{3} \rangle, \langle -2, 0 \rangle, \; \ldots\}$$

or in general $S = \left\{ \langle x,y \rangle | y = \dfrac{x}{3} + \dfrac{2}{3} \right\}$

Theorem 7.6

The solution set of a linear function described by $y = mx + b$ $(m \neq 0)$ contains one and only one element $\langle x_1, 0 \rangle$ and one and only one element $\langle 0, y_1 \rangle$. (The first part shows that a linear function has one and only one root.)

Proof. Since $y = mx + b$,

$$mx = y - b$$
$$x = \frac{y - b}{m}$$

Since $m \neq 0$, x is defined. If $y = 0$, $x = -b/m$. Therefore $\langle -b/m, 0 \rangle$ exists.

Suppose that another couple $\langle x', 0 \rangle$ also existed as a solution. Then

$$x' = \frac{0 - b}{m}$$

or

$$x' = -\frac{b}{m}$$

Therefore $\qquad x' = x \qquad$ Q.E.D.

We leave the second part of the proof to the student. (What happens if $m = 0$?)

Definition 7.7 The zero of the function is the point on the graph, if it exists, denoted by $P(x, 0)$. From Theorem 7.6 and the graphing of a linear function, we can conclude that at most one zero exists for a linear function.

Certain facts are obvious. First, if $y = 0$, then $x = -a_3/a_1$ and the couple $\langle -a_3/a_1, 0 \rangle$ $(a_1 \neq 0)$ is a root of $a_1 x + a_2 y + a_3 = 0$. Second, the point $(-a_3/a_1, 0)$ lies on the graph and is the x intercept of the line. There is only one x intercept. Then, in Example 7.2, the root is -2, and the zero of the function is $(-2, 0)$.

7.2 TWO SIMULTANEOUS LINEAR EQUATIONS IN TWO VARIABLES

Our problem now is to find the intersection of the solution sets of two linear equations. Let

$$a_{11}x + a_{12}y = a_{13}$$
$$a_{21}x + a_{22}y = a_{23}$$

be a set of two linear equations asserted together. In the coefficient a_{ij}, the first subscript denotes the equation and the second the place of the coefficient in that equation.   For example, a_{12} occurs in the first equation as the second coefficient.

The intersection of the solution sets of these two equations will be the set of couples $\langle x,y \rangle$ which are common to the solution sets of each equation.   Since, from the preceding chapters, we know these two linear equations graph as straight lines, the intersection of the straight lines will be the graph of the intersection of the two solution sets.   But two straight lines intersect in at most one point.   Thus, if the slopes of two linear equations are unequal, the intersection of their solution sets will be a set containing a single couple $\langle x,y \rangle$.   (Why?)   If the graphs are parallel lines, the intersection of the two solution sets will be the empty set. That is, if the slopes are equal and their y intercepts are unequal, the intersection of the solution sets will be the empty set.   If their slopes are equal and their y intercepts are equal, the intersection of the two solution sets will be the same as the solution set of each equation.

Example 7.8.   Given the two linear equations

(a) $2x + 3y = 4$
(b) $x + y = 1$

The slope of (a) is $m_1 = -\frac{2}{3}$.   (Why?)
The slope of (b) is $m_2 = -1$.
Since the slopes are unequal, the intersection of the two solution sets will have one element.

(c) $2x + 4y = 5$
(d) $4x + 8y = 7$

The slope of (c) is $m_3 = -\frac{1}{2}$.
The slope of (d) is $m_4 = -\frac{1}{2}$.
Since the slopes are equal but the y intercepts unequal, there are no solutions in common.   The intersection of the solution sets is the empty set.

(e) $2x + 4y = 5$
(f) $4x + 8y = 10$

Equation (f) is logically equivalent to (e), and the graphs of (e) and (f) will be the same.   There are therefore an infinite number of solutions, namely, all couples in the solution set of (e) or (f).

Example 7.9.   The total revenue function of a given company is described by

$$R = 0.9Q$$

while its total cost function is described by

$$C = 10 + 0.5Q$$

In both cases Q = total output. Both functions are assumed to be linear.

Since the break-even point is the point where $R = C$, this will be the point where the two lines intersect. In this case, since the slope m_r of $R = 0.9$ and m_c of C is 0.5, there will be a break-even point.

7.3 SOLUTION SETS OF TWO LINEAR EQUATIONS IN TWO VARIABLES

Given the two linear equations

(a) $\qquad\qquad a_{11}x + a_{12}y = a_{13}$

(b) $\qquad\qquad a_{21}x + a_{22}y = a_{23}$

We seek a method of finding the intersection of the solution sets of (a) and (b); that is, we seek those couples $\langle x,y \rangle$ which will satisfy both (a) and (b) together. To accomplish this, we shall combine the two equations and seek the solution set of the resulting equation. All the operations we perform must result in logically equivalent expressions. We attempt to combine the two equations in such a way that one of the variables is eliminated.

Divide (a) by a_{11} so that the first coefficient will equal 1; replace (a) by an equivalent equation having the coefficient of x equal to 1.

(c) $\qquad\qquad x + \dfrac{a_{12}}{a_{11}} y = \dfrac{a_{13}}{a_{11}}$

If we multiply (c) by a_{21}, we get an equation whose first term is identical with that of (b).

Now subtract this new expression from (b),

$$a_{21}x + a_{22}y = a_{23}$$

$$-\left(a_{21}x + \frac{a_{21}a_{12}}{a_{11}} y = \frac{a_{13}a_{21}}{a_{11}} \right)$$

$$\overline{\left(a_{22} - \frac{a_{21}a_{12}}{a_{11}} \right) y = a_{23} - \frac{a_{13}a_{21}}{a_{11}}}$$

or dividing by the coefficient of y, we get

$$y = \frac{a_{23}a_{11} - a_{13}a_{21}}{a_{22}a_{11} - a_{21}a_{12}} \qquad\qquad (7.1)$$

In a similar fashion, to eliminate y we first divide (a) by a_{12} to get

(d)
$$\frac{a_{11}}{a_{12}} x + y = \frac{a_{13}}{a_{12}}$$

Now subtract a_{22} times (d) from (b),

$$a_{21}x + a_{22}y = a_{23}$$
$$- \left(\frac{a_{22}a_{11}}{a_{12}} x + a_{22}y = \frac{a_{22}a_{13}}{a_{12}} \right)$$
$$\overline{\left(a_{21} - \frac{a_{22}a_{11}}{a_{12}} \right) x = a_{23} - \frac{a_{22}a_{13}}{a_{12}}}$$

or
$$x = \frac{a_{23}a_{12} - a_{22}a_{13}}{a_{21}a_{12} - a_{22}a_{11}} = \frac{a_{22}a_{13} - a_{23}a_{12}}{a_{11}a_{22} - a_{21}a_{12}} \tag{7.2}$$

The expression $\Delta = a_{11}a_{22} - a_{21}a_{12}$ denotes a single number and is called the *determinant* of the coefficients. x and y are defined, and a common solution exists if and only if $\Delta \neq 0$. (Why?) Notice carefully that Δ is the denominator in the solution. The intersection of the solution sets will be given by (7.1) and (7.2). Equations for which $\Delta \neq 0$ we call consistent. Another way of denoting the determinant of the coefficients is

$$\Delta = \begin{vmatrix} a_{11} & a_{12} \\ a_{21} & a_{22} \end{vmatrix}$$

Therefore
$$\begin{vmatrix} a_{11} & a_{12} \\ a_{21} & a_{22} \end{vmatrix} = a_{11}a_{22} - a_{12}a_{21}$$

If in Δ we replace a_{11} by a_{13} and a_{21} by a_{23}, we can write

$$\begin{vmatrix} a_{13} & a_{12} \\ a_{23} & a_{22} \end{vmatrix} = a_{13}a_{22} - a_{12}a_{23}$$

the numerator for the value of x. And if in Δ we replace a_{12} by a_{13} and a_{22} by a_{23}, we get

$$\begin{vmatrix} a_{11} & a_{13} \\ a_{21} & a_{23} \end{vmatrix} = a_{11}a_{23} - a_{13}a_{21}$$

the numerator for y. The solutions can thus be written

$$x = \frac{\begin{vmatrix} a_{13} & a_{12} \\ a_{23} & a_{22} \end{vmatrix}}{\Delta} \qquad y = \frac{\begin{vmatrix} a_{11} & a_{13} \\ a_{21} & a_{23} \end{vmatrix}}{\Delta}$$

The element of the solution set is then the ordered couple

$$\left\langle \frac{\begin{vmatrix} a_{13} & a_{12} \\ a_{23} & a_{22} \end{vmatrix}}{\Delta}, \frac{\begin{vmatrix} a_{11} & a_{13} \\ a_{21} & a_{23} \end{vmatrix}}{\Delta} \right\rangle \qquad (7.3)$$

Example 7.10

(a) $\qquad\qquad\qquad\qquad 2x + 3y = 5$
(b) $\qquad\qquad\qquad\qquad x - y = 6$

Multiplying b by 2 and subtracting the result from a yields

$$\begin{aligned} 2x + 3y &= 5 \\ -(2x - 2y &= 12) \\ \hline 5y &= -7 \end{aligned}$$

or $\qquad\qquad\qquad\qquad y = -\tfrac{7}{5}$

Multiplying b by -3 and subtracting the result from a yields

$$\begin{aligned} 2x + 3y &= 5 \\ -\,(-3x + 3y &= -18) \\ \hline 5x &= 23 \\ x &= \tfrac{23}{5} \end{aligned}$$

Substituting the calculated x and y values into (a) and (b), we obtain

$$\tfrac{46}{5} - \tfrac{21}{5} = \tfrac{25}{5} = 5$$
$$\tfrac{23}{5} + \tfrac{7}{5} = 6$$

Substitution in Eqs. (7.1) and (7.2) gives

$$\begin{aligned} a_{11} &= 2 & a_{12} &= 3 & a_{13} &= 5 \\ a_{21} &= 1 & a_{22} &= -1 & a_{23} &= 6 \end{aligned}$$

$$y = \frac{(6)(2) - (5)(1)}{(2)(-1) - (1)(3)} = \frac{12 - 5}{-2 - 3} = \frac{-7}{5}$$

$$x = \frac{(-1)(5) - (6)(3)}{(2)(-1) - (1)(3)} = \frac{-5 - 18}{-2 - 3} = \frac{23}{5}$$

Example 7.11.   Solve the equations

(a) $\qquad\qquad\qquad\qquad 2x - 3y = 6$
(b) $\qquad\qquad\qquad\qquad 4x - 6y = 5$

Solution.   We first check to see whether or not these are consistent.

$$\Delta = \begin{vmatrix} 2 & -3 \\ 4 & -6 \end{vmatrix} = (2)(-)6 - (-3)(4) = -12 + 12 = 0$$

Therefore the two equations are not consistent, and there is no common solution. (Note that their slopes are equal.)

To illustrate the use of simultaneous linear equations, we need the following definitions.

Definition 7.12. The market-demand curve for a commodity is the graph of the function

$$f_d = \{\langle p,d \rangle | d \text{ is the number of units of the commodity demanded in the market per unit of time, and } p \text{ is the market price of the commodity}\}$$

The range and domain are subsets of the set of nonnegative real numbers.

Definition 7.13. The market-supply curve for a commodity is the graph of the function

$$f_s = \{\langle p,s \rangle | p \text{ is the market price of the commodity, and } s \text{ is the number of units of the commodity supplied in the market per unit of time}\}$$

In general, the slope of the demand curve is negative; i.e., increases in p are associated with decreases in d. In other words, p varies inversely as d.

Also, in general, the slope of the supply function is positive; i.e., increases in price p are associated with increases in quantity supplied. In other words, p varies directly as s.

Definition 7.14. If $\langle p,d \rangle \, \epsilon \, f_d$ and $\langle p',s \rangle \, \epsilon \, f_s$ such that $\langle p,d \rangle = \langle p',s \rangle$, that is, $p = p'$ and $d = s$, then p is the equilibrium market price.

This means that the equilibrium market price is the intersection of the solution sets of f_d and f_s.

Example 7.15. The weekly market demand for a commodity is expressed as a linear function

$$q_d = 16 - 3p$$

and the weekly market supply as a linear function

$$q_s = -4 + 2p$$

1. What is the equilibrium market price?

2. If excess demand is defined as the algebraic difference between the quantity demanded and supplied at a given market price, what is excess demand when $p = 3$?

3. If excess supply is defined as the algebraic difference between the quantity supplied and demanded at a given market price, what is excess supply when $p = 5$?

4. Graph the two functions, indicating the values requested above.

Solution

1. Employing Eq. (7.3), we determine the common element in the solution sets.

$$q = 16 - 3p \qquad 3p + q = 16$$
$$q = -4 + 2p \qquad -2p + q = -4$$
$$a_{11} = 3 \qquad a_{12} = 1 \qquad a_{13} = 16$$
$$a_{21} = -2 \qquad a_{22} = 1 \qquad a_{23} = -4$$

$$\left\langle \frac{\begin{vmatrix} a_{13} & a_{12} \\ a_{23} & a_{22} \end{vmatrix}}{\Delta}, \frac{\begin{vmatrix} a_{11} & a_{13} \\ a_{21} & a_{23} \end{vmatrix}}{\Delta} \right\rangle = \left\langle \frac{20}{5}, \frac{20}{5} \right\rangle = \langle 4, 4 \rangle$$

Thus, the equilibrium market price is $p = 4$, with the quantity demanded q_d and the quantity supplied q_s equal to 4; that is,

$$q_d = q_s = 4$$

2. When $p = 3$,

$$q_d = 16 - 3p = 16 - (3)(3) = 7$$
$$q_s = -4 + 2p = -4 + (2)(3) = 2$$

and excess demand is

$$q_d - q_s = 7 - 2 = 5$$

3. When $p = 5$,

$$q_d = 16 - (3)(5) = 1$$
$$q_s = -4 + (2)(5) = 6$$

and excess supply is

$$q_s - q_d = 6 - 1 = 5$$

4. Figure 7.2 is a graph of the relevant sets.

Example 7.16.   An electronics firm has two factories. Plant 1 produces exactly 6 amplifiers and 7 tuners a day, while plant 2 produces

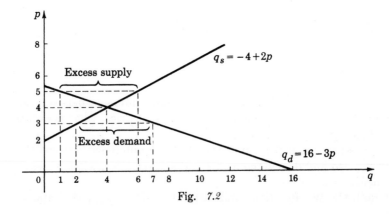

Fig. 7.2

exactly 4 amplifiers and 3 tuners a day. An order for 20 amplifiers and 20 tuners is received. How many days at each plant are required to produce the order?

Solution. If we let x represent the number of days required at plant 1 and y the number of days required at plant 2, then

$$6x + 4y = 20 \qquad \text{amplifiers}$$
$$7x + 3y = 20 \qquad \text{tuners}$$

Since
$$\Delta = \begin{vmatrix} 6 & 4 \\ 7 & 3 \end{vmatrix} = 18 - 28 = -10 \neq 0$$

there is a solution.

$$x = \frac{\begin{vmatrix} 20 & 4 \\ 20 & 3 \end{vmatrix}}{\Delta} = \frac{(20)(3) - (4)(20)}{-10} = \frac{60 - 80}{-10} = 2$$

$$y = \frac{\begin{vmatrix} 6 & 20 \\ 7 & 20 \end{vmatrix}}{\Delta} = \frac{(6)(20) - (7)(20)}{-10} = \frac{120 - 140}{-10} = 2$$

To fill the order, each plant must work 2 days.

PROBLEM SET 7.1

1. Write as a function $\frac{2}{3}x - \frac{4}{5}y = \frac{7}{2}$. Describe the solution set of the equation. What is the root of the equation? What is the zero of the function? What are the x and y intercepts of the graph of the function?

2. Do the same for $0.7x - 0.2y + 0.5 = 0$ as in Prob. 1.

3. In Example 7.9 find the break-even point. (*Hint:* Graph the two linear equations, using the y axis for both R and C.)

4. Modify the total revenue and total cost functions in Example 7.9 so that there will be no break-even point.

5. Justify the following statement: "If the intersection of the solution sets of two linear equations is empty, the equations are not consistent."

6. Solve the following systems of linear equations, using (a) the method summarized by Eq. (7.3); (b) Eqs. (7.1) and (7.2).

    a. $2x - 3y = 10$
         $2x - 3y = 5$
    b. $0.5x + 0.4y = 0.2$
         $0.2x - 0.3y = 0.1$
    c. $2x - 3y = 5$
         $x + y = 5$
    d. $2x - 3y = 10$
         $2x + 3y = 10$
    e. $2x - 3y = 10$
         $2 + y = 0$

Calculate the slopes of each line in (a), (d), and (e).

7.   The demand for an agricultural product is given by $p + 5q = 21$, and the supply schedule is $p - 2q = 7$. What are the equilibrium price and quantity? What is the lowest price at which no units will be sold? If the government will buy all offered to it at \$16, how much must it buy; i.e., how much will be supplied at that price, and how much will be demanded by consumers?

8.   Two products require, for each unit produced, the number and type of workers shown in the table.

Product	Male	Female
1	2	1
2	1	3

How many units of each product can be produced if the work force of 2,000 females and 3,000 males is to be fully employed?

7.4 THREE SIMULTANEOUS LINEAR EQUATIONS IN THREE VARIABLES. THE ECHELON METHOD

The intersection of the solution sets of a system of three linear equations in three variables can be discovered by a process similar to that of finding the common solution of a system of two linear equations in two variables. We shall try to get a system of equivalent equations from which the common solution will be evident. We shall first illustrate the method by an example.

Example 7.17.   Solve the system of equations

$$(a) \qquad 2x + y - z = 2$$
$$(b) \qquad 3x - 2y + z = 4$$
$$(c) \qquad x + 2y + 2z = 3$$

Solution

$$(d) \qquad 2x + y - z = 2 \leftrightarrow x + \tfrac{1}{2}y - \tfrac{1}{2}z = 1$$

Equation $(b) - [3$ times Eq. $(d)]$ is

$$3x - 2y + z = 4$$
$$-3x + \tfrac{3}{2}y - \tfrac{3}{2}z = 3$$
$$(e) \qquad \overline{\qquad - \tfrac{7}{2}y + \tfrac{5}{2}z = 1} \leftrightarrow 7y - 5z = -2$$

Equation $(c) -$ Eq. (d) is

$$x + 2y + 2z = 3$$
$$-x + \tfrac{1}{2}y - \tfrac{1}{2}z = 1$$
$$(f) \qquad \overline{\qquad \tfrac{3}{2}y + \tfrac{5}{2}z = 2} \leftrightarrow 3y + 5z = 4$$

So we have the system

(a) $2x + y - z = 2$

(e) $0x + 7y - 5z = -2$

(f) $0x + 3y + 5z = 4$

Evidently $(e) + (f)$ will give

(g) $10y = 2 \leftrightarrow y = 0.2$

So we have

(a) $2x + y - z = 2$

(e) $0x + 7y - 5z = -2$

(g) $0x + y + 0z = 0.2$

Putting $y = 0.2$ in (e), we get

$$(7)(0.2) - 5z = -2$$
$$1.4 - 5z = -2$$
$$-5z = -3.4$$
$$z = 0.68$$

Putting the values for z and y in (a), we get

$$x = 1.24$$

The common solution is the ordered triple $\langle 1.24, 0.2, 0.68 \rangle$; that is, $x = 1.24$, $y = 0.2$, $z = 0.68$.

To show that this is a solution, the reader can substitute the values in all three given equations to see whether or not the result is true for each.

Example 7.18. Solve the following system of equations:

(a) $x + y + z = -1$

(b) $2x - 3y - 2z = -4$

(c) $3x - 2y - z = -2$

Solution

Eq. $(b) - [2$ times Eq. $(a)]$ is

(d) $-5y - 4z = -2$

Eq. $(c) - [3$ times Eq. $(a)]$ is

(e) $-5y - 4z = 1$

Eq. $(e) -$ Eq. (d) is

$$0 + 0 = 3 \leftrightarrow 0 = 3$$

which is impossible.

Since the system leads to an absurdity, that is, $3 = 0$, the equations are inconsistent and there is no solution.

PROBLEM SET 7.2

1. Solve the system:
$$x - y + 5z = 2$$
$$2x + 2y + 4z = 10$$
$$x + 4y + 3z = -2$$

2. Solve the system:
$$x + 3y - 2z = 7$$
$$2x + 6y - 2z = 9$$
$$x + y + 8z = 10$$

3. Solve the system:
$$2x - y + 3z = 8$$
$$5x + 3y + 2z = 6$$
$$2x + 2y + 5z = 9$$

4. Solve the system:
$$4x - y - 2z = -4$$
$$6x + y + 4z = 15$$
$$2x + 4y - z = -2$$

7.5 n LINEAR EQUATIONS IN n VARIABLES. THE ECHELON METHOD FOR MACHINE PROGRAMMING[1]

The method described in the preceding sections for solving two equations in two variables and three equations in three variables can easily be generalized. We present a generalized method for solving n equations in n variables which lends itself easily to machine programming.

Eq. (1_1) $a_{11}x_1 + a_{12}x_2 + \cdots + a_{1n}x_n = b_1$

Eq. (2_1) $a_{21}x_1 + a_{22}x_2 + \cdots + a_{2n}x_n = b_2$

Eq. (3_1) $a_{31}x_1 + a_{32}x_2 + \cdots + a_{3n}x_n = b_3$ (7.4)

$$\cdots \cdots \cdots \cdots \cdots \cdots \cdots \cdots \cdots$$

Eq. (n_1) $a_{n1}x_1 + a_{n2}x_2 + \cdots + a_{nn}x_n = b_n$

These may be written as

Eq. (1_1) $\displaystyle\sum_{i=1}^{n} a_{1i}x_i = b_1$

Eq. (2_1) $\displaystyle\sum_{i=1}^{n} a_{2i}x_i = b_2$

$$\cdots \cdots \cdots \cdots$$

Eq. (n_1) $\displaystyle\sum_{i=1}^{n} a_{ni}x_i = b_n$

[1] This section may be omitted on first reading.

Later we shall learn to write all equations in (7.4) as a single equation. The a_{ij} and b_i are constants, and the x_j are variables, $i, j = 1, 2, \ldots, n$. Equation (6_1), for example, denotes Eq. (6) as it appears in the first set of equations; later we shall use Eq. (6_4), for instance, to denote this same equation as it appears, in an adjusted form, in the fourth set of equations.

By applying the echelon method illustrated in the preceding section, we can successively generate from (7.4) $n - 1$ additional *sets* of linear equations, each of these sets having one less equation and variable than the preceding set. The last (i.e., the nth) set in the series will contain one equation in one variable. Once the value of this variable is determined, it can be substituted into the $(n - 1)$st set, which contains two equations and two variables (one of which is the one determined from the nth set) and the value of a second variable can be determined. The two values thus determined can be substituted into the $(n - 2)$nd set, which contains three equations and three variables (two of which are the ones just determined), and the value of a third variable can be ascertained. This procedure is continued until all the n values of the variables are determined, the last value being determined from the first set, (7.4), which contains n equations and n variables. Note that the first variable determined is x_n, the second $x_{n-1}, \ldots$, the second to the last x_2, and the last x_1.

If the final equation is of the form $x = c$, there exists a nonempty solution set. If the final equation is $c_1 = c_2$, where $c_1 \neq c_2$, the set of equations is inconsistent and the solution set is empty.

The procedure for generating the $n - 1$ additional sets of equations can be concisely summarized as follows:

$$\text{Eq. } (i + j)_{j+1} = \text{Eq. } (i + j)_j - a_{(i+j,j)_j} \frac{\text{Eq. } (j_j)}{a_{(j,j)_j}} \tag{7.5}$$
$$i = 1, 2, \ldots, q = n - j; j = 1, 2, \ldots, n - 1$$

This says that Eq. $(i + j)$, as it appears in the $(j + 1)$st set of equations, is determined by taking the same equation, as it appears in the preceding —the jth—set, and subtracting from it the adjusted Eq. (j) taken from the preceding—the jth—set. This equation (j_j) is adjusted by setting the coefficient of its first nonzero term equal to the coefficient of the first nonzero term in Eq. $(i + j)$, as this equation appears in the jth set. The term $a_{(i+j,j)_j}$ denotes the coefficient of the x_j term in Eq. $(i + j)$ in the jth set; the term $a_{(j,j)_j}$ denotes the coefficient of the x_j term in Eq. (j) in the jth set. The expression Eq. $(j_j)/a_{(j,j)_j}$ means that every term in Eq. (j_j) is divided by $a_{(j,j)_j}$.

Note that we first fix $j = 1$ and then generate $n - 1$ equations for the second set by letting i vary from 1 to $q = n - j = n - 1$. We then fix $j = 2$ and generate $n - 2$ equations for the third set by letting i vary from 1 to $q = n - j = n - 2$. We follow this procedure, successively increasing j, until $j = n - 1$, in which case i varies from 1 to

$$q = n - j = n - (n - 1) = 1$$

Example 7.19. Use the method summarized by (7.5) to solve the following system of equation:

Eq. (1_1) $\qquad 2x_1 + 4x_2 + x_3 + 2x_4 = 4$
Eq. (2_1) $\qquad 3x_1 + 2x_2 + 2x_3 + x_4 = 6$
Eq. (3_1) $\qquad 2x_1 + 2x_2 - 4x_3 + 3x_4 = 1$
Eq. (4_1) $\qquad 4x_1 + x_2 + x_3 - x_4 = 2$

Solution. Since there are $n = 4$ equations and 4 variables, we shall have to generate $n - 1 = 3$ additional sets of equations from the initial set of $n = 4$ equations. The first of these new sets will have $n - 1 = 3$ equations [Eq. (2_2), Eq. (3_2), and Eq. (4_2)] and 3 variables (x_2, x_3, x_4). The second of these new sets (i.e., the third set of equations inclusive of the initial set) will have $n - 2 = 2$ equations [Eq. (3_3), Eq. (4_3)] and 2 variables (x_3, x_4), and the last set will have $n - 3 = 1$ equation [Eq. (4_4)], from which we can determine the value of x_4.

Following (7.5), we fix $j = 1$ and $i = 1$ and derive the first equation, Eq. $(i + j)_{j+1}$ = Eq. (2_2), in the second set,

$$\text{Eq. } (2_2) = \text{Eq. } (2_1) - a_{(2,1)_1} \frac{\text{Eq. } (1_1)}{a_{(1,1)_1}}$$

$$= (3x_1 + 2x_2 + 2x_3 + x_4 = 6) - 3 \frac{(2x_1 + 4x_2 + x_3 + 2x_4 = 4)}{2}$$

$$= -4x_2 + \tfrac{1}{2}x_3 - 2x_4 = 0$$

We then fix $i = 2$ (j still $= 1$) in order to derive the second equation, Eq. $(i + j)_{j+1}$ = Eq. (3_2), in the second set,

$$\text{Eq. } (3_2) = \text{Eq. } (3_1) - a_{(3,1)_1} \frac{\text{Eq. } (1_1)}{a_{(1,1)_1}}$$

$$= (2x_1 + 2x_2 - 4x_3 + 3x_4 = 1) - 2 \frac{(2x_1 + 4x_2 + x_3 + 2x_4 = 4)}{2}$$

$$= -2x_2 - 5x_3 + x_4 = -3$$

With $i = q = n - j = 3$ (j still $= 1$), the reader can verify that the third equation in the second set is

$$\text{Eq. } (4_2) = -7x_2 - x_3 - 5x_4 = -6$$

so that the completed second set of equations is

$$\text{Eq. } (2_2) = -4x_2 + \tfrac{1}{2}x_3 - 2x_4 = 0$$
$$\text{Eq. } (3_2) = -2x_2 - 5x_3 + x_4 = -3$$
$$\text{Eq. } (4_2) = -7x_2 - x_3 - 5x_4 = -6$$

We now fix $j = 2$ and $i = 1$ to obtain the first equation,

$$\text{Eq. } (i + j)_{j+1} = \text{Eq. } (3_3)$$

in the third set,

$$\text{Eq. } (3_3) = \text{Eq. } (3_2) - a_{(3,2)_2} \frac{\text{Eq. } (2_2)}{a_{(2,2)_2}}$$

$$= (-2x_2 - 5x_3 + x_4 = -3) - (-2)\frac{(-4x_2 + \tfrac{1}{2}x_3 - 2x_4 = 0)}{-4}$$

$$= \frac{-21}{4}x_3 + 2x_4 = -3$$

Since the next i value (j still $= 2$) is 2, and since $q = n - j = 2$, the next equation, Eq. $(i + j)_{j+1} = \text{Eq. } (4_3)$, will be the last in the second set. The reader can verify that it is

$$\text{Eq. } (4_3) = -\tfrac{15}{8}x_3 - \tfrac{3}{2}x_4 = -6$$

The completed third set of equations is

$$\text{Eq. } (3_3) = -\tfrac{21}{4}x_3 + 2x_4 = -3$$
$$\text{Eq. } (4_3) = -\tfrac{15}{8}x_3 - \tfrac{3}{2}x_4 = -6$$

We now fix $j = 3$ and $i = 1$ to obtain the single equation in the last set (notice that $i = q = n - j = 1$), which is

$$\text{Eq. } (4_4) = \text{Eq. } (4_3) - a_{(4,3)_3} \frac{\text{Eq. } (3_3)}{a_{(3,3)_3}}$$

$$= (-\tfrac{15}{8}x_3 - \tfrac{3}{2}x_4 = -6) - \left(-\frac{15}{8}\right)\frac{(-\tfrac{21}{4}x_3 + 2x_4 = -3)}{-\tfrac{21}{4}}$$

$$= x_4 = \tfrac{69}{31}$$

The student can verify that $x_3 = \tfrac{44}{31}$ by substituting the calculated value for x_4 into one of the equations of the third set, that $x_2 = -\tfrac{29}{31}$ by substituting the calculated values for x_4 and x_3 into one of the equations of the second set, and that $x_1 = \tfrac{29}{31}$ by substituting the calculated values for x_4, x_3, and x_2 into one of the equations of the initial set.

Example 7.20. In Example 7.19 replace the constants 4, 6, 1, 2 by 0, 0, 0, 0, and solve the resulting homogeneous equations.

Solution. The solution is left as an exercise.

PROBLEM SET 7.3

1. Do Probs. 1 and 3 of Problem Set 7.2, using the general method of this section.
2. In Probs. 1 and 3 of Problem Set 7.2 change the constants b_1, b_2, b_3 to zero, and solve the resulting homogeneous equations.

7.6 MATRICES

We introduce a very useful mathematical symbol called a *matrix* which will have application to the solution of systems of equations.

Definition 7.21. A matrix is a rectangular array of m rows and n columns of real numbers. When we use the term $m \times n$ to describe a matrix, the first value (m) always refers to the number of rows and the second value (n) to the number of columns in the matrix. If $m = n$, the matrix will be called a *square matrix*.

Example 7.22. The following are matrices:

$$(a) \qquad \begin{pmatrix} 2 \\ 0 \\ 1 \end{pmatrix} \qquad \text{a 3-row 1-column matrix}$$

$$(b) \qquad \begin{pmatrix} \tfrac{1}{2} & -7 & -2 & \tfrac{1}{5} \end{pmatrix} \qquad \text{a 1-row 4-column matrix}$$

$$(c) \qquad \begin{pmatrix} 1 & 2 & \tfrac{1}{2} \\ \pi & 5 & 0.3 \\ 2 & 0 & 0 \end{pmatrix} \qquad \text{a } 3 \times 3 \text{ square matrix}$$

$$(d) \qquad \begin{pmatrix} 1 & 2 & 2 & 1 & 1 & 5 \\ 0 & 0 & 2 & 1 & 2 & -1 \end{pmatrix} \qquad \text{a } 2 \times 6 \text{ matrix}$$

We shall call a $1 \times n$ matrix a *row vector*, and an $m \times 1$ matrix a *column vector*. The element in the ith row and jth column will be denoted by the symbol a_{ij}. The matrix itself will be named either by a capital letter, for example, A, B, etc., or by the symbol $(a_{ij})_{m \times n}$, which signifies a matrix having m rows and n columns. $A = (a_{ij})_{m \times n}$ (i takes on the values $1 \cdots m$ and j the values $1 \cdots n$). There are therefore m times n entries or elements.

We shall refer to the m rows and n columns of a matrix as its *shape*. Thus in Example 7.22, the matrix (a) has shape 3×1 and is a column vector, while the matrix (b) has shape 1×4 and is a row vector. Clearly, an $m \times n$ matrix will consist of m row vectors and n column vectors. So, in Example 7.22, matrix (c) has the shape 3×3 and contains three row and three column vectors, while in (d), of shape 2×6, there are 2 row and 6 column vectors.

Example 7.23.   Write out the matrix $A = (a_{ij})_{2 \times 3}$.   There are $2 \times 3 = 6$ entries, since the i can take on the values 1 and 2 and the j the values 1, 2, and 3.

Solution

$$A = \begin{pmatrix} a_{11} & a_{12} & a_{13} \\ a_{21} & a_{22} & a_{23} \end{pmatrix}$$

A has two row vectors, $(a_{11} \ \ a_{12} \ \ a_{13})$ and $(a_{22} \ \ a_{23} \ \ a_{24})$, and three column vectors

$$\begin{pmatrix} a_{11} \\ a_{21} \end{pmatrix} \quad \begin{pmatrix} a_{12} \\ a_{22} \end{pmatrix} \quad \begin{pmatrix} a_{13} \\ a_{23} \end{pmatrix}$$

Matrices may be used to summarize data in the following fashion:

Example 7.24.   An automobile producer manufactures trucks, passenger cars, and trailers in red, black, and blue.   His agency's sales may be represented as in the tabulation below.   This representation is a 3×3 matrix.   Note that each row vector shows how sales of a given color were

	Trucks	Passenger cars	Trailers
Red	15	20	5
Blue	25	25	10
Black	20	5	5

distributed among the different types of vehicles, while each column vector shows how sales of a given type of vehicle were distributed among the different colors.   If we want to know the number of black units sold, we add the components of the bottom row vector, that is,

$$20 + 5 + 5 = 30$$

Definition 7.25.   Two matrices are equal if and only if corresponding elements are equal.

Thus $(x \ y) = (2 \ 1)$ means $x = 2$ and $y = 1$ (compare this with the expressions of the solutions of two linear equations in two variables), and

$$A = B$$

where $A = \begin{pmatrix} a_{11} & a_{12} & a_{13} \\ a_{21} & a_{22} & a_{23} \end{pmatrix} \qquad B = \begin{pmatrix} b_{11} & b_{12} & b_{13} \\ b_{21} & b_{22} & b_{23} \end{pmatrix}$

means

$$a_{11} = b_{11} \qquad a_{12} = b_{12} \qquad a_{13} = b_{13} \qquad a_{21} = b_{21} \qquad a_{22} = b_{22}$$

$$a_{23} = b_{23}$$

7.7 ADDITION OF MATRICES

Two or more matrices can be added if and only if they are of the same shape.

Definition 7.26. Let $A = (a_{ij})_{m \times n}$ and $B = (b_{ij})_{m \times n}$ be two matrices of the same shape. Then

$$A + B = (a_{ij} + b_{ij})_{m \times n}$$

Example 7.27. Add the following matrices:

$$A = \begin{pmatrix} 0 & 1 & 2 \\ -5 & 6 & 3 \end{pmatrix}_{2 \times 3} \quad \text{and} \quad B = \begin{pmatrix} 1 & 1 & -2 \\ 4 & 0 & 0 \end{pmatrix}_{2 \times 3}$$

Solution. By definition $A + B$ is obtained by adding corresponding elements,

$$A + B = \begin{pmatrix} 0+1 & 1+1 & 2-2 \\ -5+4 & 6+0 & 3+0 \end{pmatrix} = \begin{pmatrix} 1 & 2 & 0 \\ -1 & 6 & 3 \end{pmatrix}_{2 \times 3}$$

Theorem 7.28

The commutative and associative laws hold for the addition of matrices.

Proof. 1. Let $A = (a_{ij})_{m \times n}$, $B = (b_{ij})_{m \times n}$; then

$$A + B = B + A$$
$$A + B = (a_{ij} + b_{ij}) = (b_{ij} + a_{ij}) = B + A$$

This follows since a_{ij} and b_{ij} are real numbers and we know that the commutative law holds for real numbers.

2. Let $A = (a_{ij})_{m \times n}$, $B = (b_{ij})_{m \times n}$, and $C = (c_{ij})_{m \times n}$; then

$$(A + B) + C = A + (B + C)$$
$$(A + B) + C = [(a_{ij} + b_{ij}) + c_{ij}] = [a_{ij} + (b_{ij} + c_{ij})] = A + (B + C)$$

Example 7.29. Let

$$A = \begin{pmatrix} 2 & 1 & 1 & 3 \\ 1 & 0 & 2 & -1 \\ 1 & 4 & 1 & 1 \end{pmatrix}$$

$$B = \begin{pmatrix} 1 & 0 & 1 & 0 \\ 2 & 0 & 2 & 0 \\ 3 & 1 & 2 & 1 \end{pmatrix}$$

$$C = \begin{pmatrix} -1 & 0 & 1 & 5 \\ 2 & 3 & 1 & 1 \\ 4 & 4 & 1 & 0 \end{pmatrix}$$

Show that

$$(A + B) + C = A + (B + C)$$

Solution

$$A + B = \begin{pmatrix} 3 & 1 & 2 & 3 \\ 3 & 0 & 4 & -1 \\ 4 & 5 & 3 & 2 \end{pmatrix} \qquad B + C = \begin{pmatrix} 0 & 0 & 2 & 5 \\ 4 & 3 & 3 & 1 \\ 7 & 5 & 3 & 1 \end{pmatrix}$$

$$(A + B) + C = \begin{pmatrix} 2 & 1 & 3 & 8 \\ 5 & 3 & 5 & 0 \\ 8 & 9 & 4 & 2 \end{pmatrix} \qquad A + (B + C) = \begin{pmatrix} 2 & 1 & 3 & 8 \\ 5 & 3 & 5 & 0 \\ 8 & 9 & 4 & 2 \end{pmatrix}$$

Example 7.30. A manufacturer has three factories, one in the East, one in the West, and one in a foreign country. Each factory produces clothing for boys and girls in three price styles, labeled 1, 2, and 3. The quantities produced by each factory are given in the matrices shown.

	East (E)				West (W)		
	1	2	3		1	2	3
Boys............	$\big(100$	50	$25\big)$	Boys............	$\big(70$	40	$20\big)$
Girls............	$\big(75$	60	$50\big)$	Girls............	$\big(50$	35	$15\big)$

	Foreign (F)		
	1	2	3
Boys..........	$\big(15$	10	$8\big)$
Girls..........	$\big(12$	9	$7\big)$

Express the total production as a single matrix T.

Solution $\qquad T = E + W + F$

$$T = \begin{pmatrix} 100 + 70 + 15 & 50 + 40 + 10 & 25 + 20 + 8 \\ 75 + 50 + 12 & 60 + 35 + 9 & 50 + 15 + 7 \end{pmatrix}$$

$$= \begin{pmatrix} 185 & 100 & 53 \\ 137 & 104 & 72 \end{pmatrix}$$

The total amount of boy's clothes is obtained from the vector $B = (185 \quad 100 \quad 53)$, while the total amount of clothes of price level 2 is obtained from the vector $C = \begin{pmatrix} 100 \\ 104 \end{pmatrix}$.

7.8 MULTIPLICATION OF MATRICES

In the interests of clarity we shall consider this topic in three stages: (a) the product of a matrix and a constant real number, (b) the product of a row vector and a column vector, (c) the product of two matrices.

Definition 7.31. If $A = (a_{ij})_{m \times n}$ is a matrix of shape $m \times n$ and c is a real number, then $cA = (ca_{ij})_{m \times n}$; that is, each and every element in A is multiplied by c.

Example 7.32

1. Let

$$A = \begin{pmatrix} 2 & 1 & 1 \\ 1 & 0 & 3 \end{pmatrix}$$

Then

$$5A = 5 \begin{pmatrix} 2 & 1 & 1 \\ 1 & 0 & 3 \end{pmatrix} = \begin{pmatrix} 10 & 5 & 5 \\ 5 & 0 & 15 \end{pmatrix}$$

2. Let

$$A = \begin{pmatrix} 6 \\ 8 \\ 10 \end{pmatrix}$$

Then

$$A = 2 \begin{pmatrix} 3 \\ 4 \\ 5 \end{pmatrix}$$

or

$$\tfrac{1}{2}A = \begin{pmatrix} 3 \\ 4 \\ 5 \end{pmatrix}$$

Definition 7.33. Let $A = (a_{ij})_{1 \times n}$ be a $1 \times n$ row vector and $B = (b_{ij})_{n \times 1}$ be an $n \times 1$ column vector; then $A \times B = C = (c_{ij})_{1 \times 1}$, where

$$c_{11} = a_{11}b_{11} + a_{12}b_{21} + a_{13}b_{31} + \cdots + a_{1n}b_{n1} = \sum_{i=1}^{n} a_{1i}b_{i1}$$

(Note that the number of columns in A is the same as the number of rows in B and that the product is a single number c_{11}.)

Example 7.34

$$A = (1 \quad 3 \quad 5 \quad 7) \qquad B = \begin{pmatrix} 2 \\ 1 \\ 3 \\ 4 \end{pmatrix}$$

Then $A \times B = C = (1 \times 2 + 3 \times 1 + 5 \times 3 + 7 \times 4)$
$$= 48$$

(Note that we defined $A \times B$ in that order!)

Example 7.35.   In Example 7.30, boy's clothes cost at level 1 is $20 per unit; at level 2, $25 per unit; and at level 3, $30 per unit.   Indicate the total cost of boy's clothes as a vector.

   Solution.   The vector for total production of boy's clothes is given as

$$B = (185 \quad 100 \quad 53)$$

The price vector is

$$P = \begin{pmatrix} 20 \\ 25 \\ 30 \end{pmatrix}$$

$$\text{Cost} = (185 \quad 100 \quad 53) \begin{pmatrix} 20 \\ 25 \\ 30 \end{pmatrix}$$

$$= (185 \times 20) + (100 \times 25) + (53 \times 30) = 7{,}790$$

Definition 7.36.   If $A = (a_{ij})_{m \times n}$ and $B = (b_{ij})_{n \times p}$, then

$$A \cdot B = C = (c_{ij})_{m \times p}$$

where c_{ij} is obtained by multiplying the ith row vector of A by the jth column vector of B, in that order.

Example 7.37.   Multiply

$$A = \begin{pmatrix} 1 & 3 & 2 & 4 \\ 2 & 1 & 0 & 5 \\ 1 & 1 & 2 & 1 \end{pmatrix} \quad \text{by} \quad B = \begin{pmatrix} 1 & 2 \\ 1 & 1 \\ 0 & 1 \\ 3 & 1 \end{pmatrix}$$

Since A has four columns and B four rows the product can be taken.   Let $A \times B = C = (c_{ij})_{3 \times 2}$.

$$c_{11} = (1 \quad 3 \quad 2 \quad 4) \begin{pmatrix} 1 \\ 1 \\ 0 \\ 3 \end{pmatrix} = 16 \qquad c_{12} = (1 \quad 3 \quad 2 \quad 4) \begin{pmatrix} 2 \\ 1 \\ 1 \\ 1 \end{pmatrix} = 11$$

$$c_{21} = (2 \quad 1 \quad 0 \quad 5) \begin{pmatrix} 1 \\ 1 \\ 0 \\ 3 \end{pmatrix} = 18 \qquad c_{22} = (2 \quad 1 \quad 0 \quad 5) \begin{pmatrix} 2 \\ 1 \\ 1 \\ 1 \end{pmatrix} = 10$$

$$c_{31} = (1 \quad 1 \quad 2 \quad 1) \begin{pmatrix} 1 \\ 1 \\ 0 \\ 3 \end{pmatrix} = 5 \qquad c_{32} = (1 \quad 1 \quad 2 \quad 1) \begin{pmatrix} 2 \\ 1 \\ 1 \\ 1 \end{pmatrix} = 6$$

Therefore

$$C = \begin{pmatrix} 16 & 11 \\ 18 & 10 \\ 5 & 6 \end{pmatrix}$$

Example 7.38. Multiply

$$A = \begin{pmatrix} 2 & 1 \\ 3 & 2 \\ 4 & 1 \end{pmatrix} \quad \text{by} \quad B = \begin{pmatrix} 4 \\ 2 \end{pmatrix}$$

$$\begin{pmatrix} 2 & 1 \\ 3 & 2 \\ 4 & 1 \end{pmatrix} \begin{pmatrix} 4 \\ 2 \end{pmatrix} = \begin{pmatrix} 8+2 \\ 12+4 \\ 16+2 \end{pmatrix} = \begin{pmatrix} 10 \\ 16 \\ 18 \end{pmatrix} = 2 \begin{pmatrix} 5 \\ 8 \\ 9 \end{pmatrix}$$

Example 7.39. The labor and capital requirements per unit for consumer and military goods are given in the matrix shown.

	Labor	Capital
Consumer goods...... Military goods.......	$\begin{pmatrix} 3 \\ 2 \end{pmatrix}$	$\begin{pmatrix} 3 \\ 5 \end{pmatrix} = R$

If labor costs are \$5 per unit and capital costs \$10 per unit, calculate the total cost of consumer and capital goods, using matrices.

Solution. Let $C = \begin{pmatrix} 5 \\ 10 \end{pmatrix}$ denote the matrix of the costs. Then

$$R \cdot C = \text{total costs}$$

$$\begin{pmatrix} 3 & 3 \\ 2 & 5 \end{pmatrix} \begin{pmatrix} 5 \\ 10 \end{pmatrix} = \begin{pmatrix} 3 \times 5 + 3 \times 10 \\ 2 \times 5 + 5 \times 10 \end{pmatrix} = \begin{pmatrix} 45 \\ 60 \end{pmatrix}$$

That is, total cost of consumer goods = 45, and total cost of military goods = 60. The total cost of all goods is 105. [Note that the matrix C was written as a column vector to make the product interpretable. If we had written $\begin{pmatrix} 10 \\ 5 \end{pmatrix}$, we would have multiplied the unit cost for capital by units of labor and the unit cost of labor by units of capital.]

In the case of multiplication, the commutative law does not hold in general, that is, $A \cdot B \neq B \cdot A$ always. This can be shown by multiplying

$$A = \begin{pmatrix} 2 & 1 \\ 3 & 2 \end{pmatrix} \quad \text{by} \quad B = \begin{pmatrix} 1 & 1 \\ 2 & 1 \end{pmatrix}$$

and then $B \cdot A$,

$$A \cdot B = \begin{pmatrix} 4 & 3 \\ 7 & 5 \end{pmatrix} \neq \begin{pmatrix} 5 & 3 \\ 7 & 4 \end{pmatrix} = B \cdot A$$

The associative law does hold, but the proof is too cumbersome to give. If $A = (a_{ij})_{m \times n}$, $B = (b_{ij})_{n \times p}$, and $C = (c_{ij})_{p \times q}$, then

$$A \cdot (B \cdot C) = (A \cdot B) \cdot C$$

and the result is a matrix of shape $m \times q$. Note carefully the shapes of A, B, and C.

Definition 7.40. The transpose of a matrix A is a matrix A' formed from A by interchanging rows and columns of A in such a way that row i of A becomes column i of A'. Thus, if

$$A = (a_{ij})_{m \times n}$$
then
$$A' = (a_{ji})_{n \times m}$$

Note that the shape of A' is the reverse of A if A is not a square matrix.

Example 7.41

1. If
$$A = \begin{pmatrix} a_{11} & a_{12} \\ a_{21} & a_{22} \\ a_{31} & a_{32} \end{pmatrix}$$
then
$$A' = \begin{pmatrix} a_{11} & a_{21} & a_{31} \\ a_{12} & a_{22} & a_{32} \end{pmatrix}$$

2. If
$$B = \begin{pmatrix} 2 \\ 3 \\ 4 \\ 5 \end{pmatrix}$$
then
$$B' = (2 \quad 3 \quad 4 \quad 5)$$

3. If
$$C = \begin{pmatrix} 2 & 1 \\ 4 & 5 \end{pmatrix}$$
then
$$C' = \begin{pmatrix} 2 & 4 \\ 1 & 5 \end{pmatrix}$$

Example 7.42. Every day a supermarket purchases for $2 a product which it sells for $4. Every unit sold entails a wrapping cost of 20 cents. Since the product is perishable, units remaining unsold at the end of the day are returned, without wrapping, to the supplier for reprocessing. The supplier pays $1 for returned units. The probability distribution for daily demand will be assumed to be as shown in the tabulation.

Number of units demanded daily Z	Probability that Z units will be demanded daily $P(Z)$
0	0.10
1	0.40
2	0.30
3	0.10
4	0.10

What is the optimum standing order that the supermarket should place?

   Solution. We shall base our answer on the expected-value analysis introduced in Sec. 4.8. Let Q denote the order quantity selected and Z

TABLE 7.1 PAYOFF TABLE FOR INVENTORY-CONTROL PROBLEM

Z	Conditional profit for Q				
	0	1	2	3	4
0	$0	$-1.00	$-2.00	$-3.00	$-3.00
1	0	1.80	0.80	-0.20	-1.20
2	0	1.80	3.60	2.60	1.60
3	0	1.80	3.60	5.40	4.40
4	0	1.80	3.60	5.40	7.20

the number of units demanded. Since Z never exceeds 4, the supermarket will never consider $Q > 4$. (Why?)   Total profit π, for demand less than the standing order ($Z < Q$), can be calculated as total revenue from direct sales to consumers ($4Z$) plus revenue from return sales to the supplier [$1(Q - Z)$, where $Q - Z$ denotes units ordered but not demanded], minus material cost ($2Q$) and minus wrapping cost ($0.20Z$). Total profit, for demand equal to or greater than the standing order ($Z \geq Q$), can be calculated as total revenue from direct sales to consumer of all that was ordered ($4Q$) minus material and wrapping costs on all that was ordered ($2Q + 0.20Q$).

Symbolically this becomes

$$\pi = [4Z + 1(Q - Z)] - (2Q + 0.20Z) \qquad Z < Q$$
$$= 2.80Z - Q \qquad\qquad\qquad\qquad Z < Q \qquad (7.6)$$
$$\pi = 4Q - (2Q + 0.20Q) \qquad\qquad Z \geq Q$$
$$= 1.80Q \qquad\qquad\qquad\qquad\quad Z \geq Q \qquad (7.7)$$

Table 7.1 (usually referred to as the *payoff* table) gives rise to a matrix (A) of *conditional profits;* i.e., a matrix of the profits associated with each act ($Q = 0, 1, \ldots , 4$) given that a specified event ($Z = 0, 1, \ldots , 4$) occurred.   Each element (i.e., conditional profit) was computed from (7.6) or (7.7), depending on which was appropriate given the particular Q/Z combination.   For example, $a_{23} = 0.80$ was computed from (7.6), since $Z = 1 < Q = 2$, while $a_{53} = 3.60$ was computed from (7.7), since $Z = 4 > Q = 2$.

$$A = \begin{pmatrix} 0 & -1.00 & -2.00 & -3.00 & -4.00 \\ 0 & 1.80 & 0.80 & -0.20 & -1.20 \\ 0 & 1.80 & 3.60 & 2.60 & 1.60 \\ 0 & 1.80 & 3.60 & 5.40 & 4.40 \\ 0 & 1.80 & 3.60 & 5.40 & 7.20 \end{pmatrix}$$

Matrix B gives the probabilities associated with each of the events $Z = 0, 1, \ldots, 4.$

$$B = \begin{pmatrix} 0.10 \\ 0.40 \\ 0.30 \\ 0.10 \\ 0.10 \end{pmatrix}$$

The expected value of each act (Q value) is determined by (1) multiplying each of the conditional profits associated with it by the probability of its occurrence and (2) summing these products. The optimum act is the one with the greatest expected value.

The calculation of the required expected values can be represented by matrix multiplication if we multiply the transpose of A by B.

$$\begin{array}{ccccc} & & A' & & \\ \begin{pmatrix} \hat{0} & \hat{0} & 0 & 0 & 0 \\ -1.00 & 1.80 & 1.80 & 1.80 & 1.80 \\ -2.00 & 0.80 & 3.60 & 3.60 & 3.60 \\ -3.00 & -0.20 & 2.60 & 5.40 & 5.40 \\ -4.00 & -1.20 & 1.60 & 4.40 & 7.20 \end{pmatrix} \end{array} \times \begin{array}{c} B \\ \begin{pmatrix} 0.10 \\ 0.40 \\ 0.30 \\ 0.10 \\ 0.10 \end{pmatrix} \end{array} = \begin{array}{c} C \\ \begin{pmatrix} 0 \\ 1.52 \\ 1.92 \\ 1.48 \\ 0.76 \end{pmatrix} \end{array}$$

We must use the transpose of A so that the summation of the products defined for each act in the preceding paragraph will be obtained from the matrix multiplication (what would be defined by $A \times B$?). Since the maximum value, $c_{31} = 1.92$, in the resulting matrix C of expected profits corresponds to $Q = 2$, the optimum standing order is for $Q = 2$ units.

PROBLEM SET 7.4

1. Perform the following operations:

a. $\begin{pmatrix} 2 & 3 & 5 \\ 1 & -1 & 0 \\ 2 & 1 & 1 \\ 3 & 3 & 3 \end{pmatrix} + \begin{pmatrix} 1 & 0 & 0 \\ 0 & 1 & 0 \\ 1 & 1 & 1 \\ 1 & 1 & 0 \end{pmatrix}$

b. $\begin{pmatrix} 2 & 3 & 5 & 3 \\ 1 & -2 & -3 & 2 \\ 6 & 5 & 4 & 1 \end{pmatrix} \times \begin{pmatrix} 1 & 0 \\ 0 & 1 \\ 1 & 1 \\ 0 & 0 \end{pmatrix}$

c. $\left\{ \begin{pmatrix} 2 & 0 & 1 \\ 3 & 2 & 1 \\ -1 & 5 & 2 \end{pmatrix} + \begin{pmatrix} -1 & 0 & 1 \\ 1 & 0 & 1 \\ 2 & 1 & 1 \end{pmatrix} \right\} \times \begin{pmatrix} 2 & 2 & 2 \\ 1 & 1 & 1 \\ 3 & 1 & 1 \end{pmatrix}$

$$d. \quad \begin{pmatrix} -1 & 0 & 1 & 2 \\ 2 & 1 & 3 & 4 \\ 5 & 1 & -1 & 0 \\ 2 & 1 & 3 & 1 \end{pmatrix} \times \begin{pmatrix} 1 & 0 & 0 & 0 \\ 0 & 1 & 0 & 0 \\ 0 & 0 & 1 & 0 \\ 0 & 0 & 0 & 1 \end{pmatrix}$$

$$e. \quad (3 \quad 2 \quad 1 \quad 5) \times \begin{pmatrix} 0 \\ 1 \\ 2 \\ 4 \end{pmatrix}$$

2. Prove: If $A = (a_{ij})_{m \times m}$ and $0 = (0_{ij})_{m \times m}$ (that is, every element $= 0$), then
   a. $A + 0 = A$
   b. $A \cdot 0 = 0$
3. Prove: If $-A = (-a_{ij})_{m \times n}$, then $A + (-A) = 0$.
4. If A, B, and C are 2×2 matrices, show that

$$A \times (B + C) = (A \times B) + (A \times C)$$

5. Let

$$A = \begin{pmatrix} 3 & 1 \\ 6 & 2 \end{pmatrix} \quad \text{and} \quad B = \begin{pmatrix} -1 & -1 \\ 3 & 3 \end{pmatrix}$$

Show that $A \times B = 0$ even though neither A nor B is zero.

6. If $A = \begin{pmatrix} 2 & 1 \\ 3 & 2 \end{pmatrix}$ and $B = \begin{pmatrix} 1 & 1 \\ 1 & 1 \end{pmatrix}$, find a matrix

$$X = \begin{pmatrix} x_{11} & x_{12} \\ x_{21} & x_{22} \end{pmatrix} \quad \text{for which } AX = B$$

(*Hint:* Form two sets of simultaneous linear equations in two variables.)

7. Matrix A shows the raw material requirements of four products produced by a single firm. Matrix B shows the number of units of each product scheduled for production in the coming week. Matrix C shows the unit raw material costs. Use matrix multiplication to derive the matrix of raw material requirements (*Hint:* $R = A' \times B$) and of total raw material costs [*Hint:* $K = (A' \times B)' \times C$].

Raw material			Product	Scheduled production	Product
1	2	3			

$$A = \begin{pmatrix} 2 & 1 & 4 \\ 1 & 0 & 1 \\ 4 & 3 & 2 \\ 4 & 1 & 2 \end{pmatrix} \begin{matrix} 1 \\ 2 \\ 3 \\ 4 \end{matrix} \qquad B = \begin{pmatrix} 4 \\ 5 \\ 6 \\ 2 \end{pmatrix} \begin{matrix} 1 \\ 2 \\ 3 \\ 4 \end{matrix}$$

	Cost	Raw material

$$C = \begin{pmatrix} 2 \\ 3 \\ 6 \end{pmatrix} \begin{matrix} 1 \\ 2 \\ 3 \end{matrix}$$

8. A firm operates four plants each of which produces three different products. Matrix A shows the number of units of each product scheduled for production in each plant over the next month. The assembly of each product requires a specified number of each of three types of parts. Matrix B shows the parts specifications for each product. Since the firm follows a policy of centralized purchasing, the purchasing agent must know the total number of units of each type of part required over the next month, as well as the requirements of specific plants for specific parts. Use matrix multiplication to solve the purchasing agent's problem. (*Hint:* $A' \times B = C$, where c_{ij} gives the requirements for part j in plant i.) If matrix D shows the cost of each part, use matrix multiplication to show the total parts cost at each plant. [*Hint:* $(A' \times B) \times D = K$.]

	Plant				Scheduled production of product		Part			Product
	1	2	3	4			1	2	3	

$$A = \begin{pmatrix} 1 & 2 & 4 & 0 \\ 2 & 3 & 0 & 0 \\ 4 & 2 & 1 & 5 \end{pmatrix} \quad \begin{matrix} 1 \\ 2 \\ 3 \end{matrix} \qquad B = \begin{pmatrix} 1 & 1 & 1 \\ 1 & 0 & 2 \\ 1 & 4 & 3 \end{pmatrix} \quad \begin{matrix} 1 \\ 2 \\ 3 \end{matrix}$$

	Unit cost	Part
$D = \begin{pmatrix} 2 \\ 3 \\ 5 \end{pmatrix}$		1 2 3

7.9 SQUARE MATRICES

We shall restrict our considerations to square matrices of shape $m \times m$.

Definition 7.43. If A is any $m \times m$ matrix, then the matrix $I = (a_{ij})_{m \times m}$ is the *identity* matrix if and only if $A \times I = I \times A = A$.

It is easily seen that $I = (a_{ij})_{m \times m}$ must be a matrix in which all elements are zero except those along the diagonal which are 1, that is, $a_{ij} = 0$ if $i \neq j$, $a_{ij} = 1$ if $i = j$. So $I = \begin{pmatrix} 1 & 0 \\ 0 & 1 \end{pmatrix}$ is the identity matrix for 2×2 matrices.

Definition 7.44 If $A = (a_{ij})$ is a matrix of shape $m \times m$, then the matrix B of order $m \times m$ is the *inverse* of A if and only if $A \times B = I$. We denote B by A^{-1}, so that $A \times A^{-1} = I$.

We can compute the inverse of any 2×2 in the following fashion: Let

$$A = \begin{pmatrix} a_{11} & a_{12} \\ a_{21} & a_{22} \end{pmatrix} \quad \text{and} \quad A^{-1} = \begin{pmatrix} x_{11} & x_{12} \\ x_{21} & x_{22} \end{pmatrix}$$

Then $$A \cdot A^{-1} = I$$

or $$\begin{pmatrix} a_{11} & a_{12} \\ a_{21} & a_{22} \end{pmatrix} \times \begin{pmatrix} x_{11} & x_{12} \\ x_{21} & x_{22} \end{pmatrix} = \begin{pmatrix} 1 & 0 \\ 0 & 1 \end{pmatrix}$$

or $$\begin{pmatrix} a_{11}x_{11} + a_{12}x_{21} & a_{11}x_{12} + a_{12}x_{22} \\ a_{21}x_{11} + a_{22}x_{21} & a_{21}x_{12} + a_{22}x_{22} \end{pmatrix} = \begin{pmatrix} 1 & 0 \\ 0 & 1 \end{pmatrix}$$

Because of the definition of equality of matrices we can write the following equations:

$$\begin{cases} a_{11}x_{11} + a_{12}x_{21} = 1 \\ a_{21}x_{11} + a_{22}x_{21} = 0 \end{cases} \quad \text{and} \quad \begin{cases} a_{11}x_{12} + a_{12}x_{22} = 0 \\ a_{21}x_{12} + a_{22}x_{22} = 1 \end{cases}$$

The solutions for each set of linear equations are

$$\Delta = \begin{vmatrix} a_{11} & a_{12} \\ a_{21} & a_{22} \end{vmatrix}$$

$$x_{11} = \frac{\begin{vmatrix} 1 & a_{12} \\ 0 & a_{22} \end{vmatrix}}{\Delta} = \frac{a_{22}}{\Delta}$$

and $$x_{21} = \frac{\begin{vmatrix} a_{11} & 1 \\ a_{21} & 0 \end{vmatrix}}{\Delta} = \frac{-a_{21}}{\Delta}$$

for the left-hand set of equations and

$$x_{12} = \frac{\begin{vmatrix} 0 & a_{12} \\ 1 & a_{22} \end{vmatrix}}{\Delta} = \frac{-a_{12}}{\Delta}$$

$$x_{22} = \frac{\begin{vmatrix} a_{11} & 0 \\ a_{21} & 1 \end{vmatrix}}{\Delta} = \frac{a_{11}}{\Delta}$$

for the right-hand set of equations.

Therefore the inverse of any 2×2 matrix, if it exists, is

$$A^{-1} = \begin{pmatrix} \dfrac{a_{22}}{\Delta} & \dfrac{-a_{12}}{\Delta} \\ \dfrac{-a_{21}}{\Delta} & \dfrac{a_{11}}{\Delta} \end{pmatrix}$$

The inverse clearly exists if and only if $\Delta \neq 0$. The student should multiply $A \times A^{-1}$ to see that the product is indeed I.

Example 7.45. Find the inverse of $A = \begin{pmatrix} 2 & 1 \\ 3 & 2 \end{pmatrix}$.

Solution

$$\Delta = (2 \times 2) - (3 \times 1) = 4 - 3 = 1 \neq 0$$

Therefore A has an inverse,

$$A^{-1} = \begin{pmatrix} \dfrac{2}{1} & \dfrac{-1}{1} \\ \dfrac{-3}{1} & \dfrac{2}{1} \end{pmatrix} = \begin{pmatrix} 2 & -1 \\ -3 & 2 \end{pmatrix}$$

For 3×3 matrices, the inverse will be approached in a different fashion, to avoid complications. We need first the concept of a determinant of a matrix.

7.10 MINORS AND COFACTORS

We define the *minor* of an element a_{ij} of a 3×3 matrix as follows.
Definition 7.46. The minor M_{ij} of an element a_{ij} of a 3×3 matrix is the determinant of the 2×2 matrix which results when the ith row and jth column are deleted from the 3×3 matrix. It will be recalled that the determinant of a 2×2 matrix was defined as

$$\Delta = \begin{vmatrix} a_{11} & a_{12} \\ a_{21} & a_{22} \end{vmatrix} = a_{11}a_{22} - a_{12}a_{21}$$

We define the *cofactor* of an element a_{ij} of a 3×3 matrix as follows.
Definition 7.47. The cofactor A_{ij} of an element a_{ij} of a 3×3 matrix is $A_{ij} = (-1)^{i+j}M_{ij}$.

When $i + j$ is an even number, the factor $(-1)^{i+j}$ will be $+1$, giving the minor a $+$ sign. If $i + j$ is odd, $(-1)^{i+j}$ will give the minor a negative sign. Since the factor $(-1)^{i+j}$ is simply a technique for generating $+$ and $-$ signs, we can think of a cofactor as a signed minor.
Example 7.48. Let

$$A = \begin{pmatrix} 1 & 2 & 1 \\ 3 & 1 & 2 \\ 1 & 1 & 1 \end{pmatrix}$$

then the cofactor of the element 2 $(= a_{23})$ is

$$A_{23} = (-1)^{2+3} \begin{vmatrix} 1 & 2 \\ 1 & 1 \end{vmatrix} = (-1)^5[(1 \times 1) - (2 \times 1)] = -1(1 - 2)$$
$$= (-1)(-1) = 1$$

and the cofactor of the element 3 $(= a_{21})$ is

$$A_{21} = (-1)^{2+1} \begin{vmatrix} 2 & 1 \\ 1 & 1 \end{vmatrix} = (-1)^3[(2 - 1)] = (-1)(1) = -1$$

7.11 DETERMINANT OF A 3X3 MATRIX

Definition 7.49. The determinant of a 3×3 matrix A (denoted by det A) is

$$\det A = a_{11}A_{11} + a_{12}A_{12} + a_{13}A_{13}$$

That is, the determinant of matrix A is the sum of the products of each element and its cofactor in row 1 (see Prob. 1 in Problem Set 7.5). We use the expression det A to indicate the fact that the abbreviation "det" denotes a function, i.e., a mapping of a square matrix A to a real number. We call the map of the function the *determinant*.

Example 7.50. The determinant of A in Example 7.48 is

$$\det A = (1)(-1)^{1+1}(-1) + (2)(-1)^{1+2}(1) + (1)(-1)^{1+3}(2)$$
$$= -1 - 2 + 2 = -1$$

7.12 ADJOINT AND INVERSE OF A 3X3 MATRIX

Definition 7.51. The *adjoint* of matrix A, denoted by A_{adj}, is the transpose of the matrix C consisting of the cofactors of each element a_{ij} in A.

Example 7.52. Given

$$A = \begin{pmatrix} a_{11} & a_{12} & a_{13} \\ a_{21} & a_{22} & a_{23} \\ a_{31} & a_{32} & a_{33} \end{pmatrix}$$

form A_{adj}.

 Solution. The matrix C of the cofactors of each element in A is

$$C = \begin{pmatrix} A_{11} & A_{12} & A_{13} \\ A_{21} & A_{22} & A_{23} \\ A_{31} & A_{32} & A_{33} \end{pmatrix}$$

so that

$$A_{adj} = C' = \begin{pmatrix} A_{11} & A_{21} & A_{31} \\ A_{12} & A_{22} & A_{32} \\ A_{13} & A_{23} & A_{33} \end{pmatrix}$$

Definition 7.53. If A is a 3×3 matrix, then

$$A^{-1} = \frac{A_{adj}}{\det A}$$

which exists if and only if det $A \neq 0$.

To express this in detail, we consider the following example.

Example 7.54.   Calculate the inverse A^{-1} of

$$A = \begin{pmatrix} 2 & 0 & 0 \\ 0 & 2 & 0 \\ 0 & 0 & 2 \end{pmatrix}$$

Solution.   det $A = 8 \neq 0$.   Therefore the inverse exists.

$$A^{-1} = \frac{1}{8}\begin{pmatrix} 4 & 0 & 0 \\ 0 & 4 & 0 \\ 0 & 0 & 4 \end{pmatrix} = \begin{pmatrix} \frac{1}{2} & 0 & 0 \\ 0 & \frac{1}{2} & 0 \\ 0 & 0 & \frac{1}{2} \end{pmatrix}$$

The calculations are left to the student.

PROBLEM SET 7.5

1.   Let A be a 3×3 matrix; show by calculation that

$$a_{11}A_{11} + a_{12}A_{12} + a_{13}A_{13} = a_{21}A_{21} + a_{22}A_{22} + a_{23}A_{23}$$
$$= a_{11}A_{11} + a_{21}A_{21} + a_{31}A_{31}$$

State the general theorem involved.

2.   Show in Prob. 1 that

$$a_{11}A_{21} + a_{12}A_{22} + a_{13}A_{23} = 0$$

State the general theorem involved.

3.   Calculate the inverse A^{-1} of

$$A = \begin{pmatrix} 2 & 0 & 1 \\ 3 & 1 & 1 \\ 2 & 1 & 2 \end{pmatrix}$$

and show that $A \times A^{-1} = I$.

4.   Can you write the inverse A^{-1} of a 4×4 matrix A?   (*Hint:* Generalize Definition 7.53.)

5.   Suppose that one row of a 3×3 matrix consists entirely of zeros.   What is the value of the determinant of the matrix?   Why?

6.   Suppose that two rows of a 3×3 matrix A are alike; prove that det $A = 0$.

7.   If A and B are two nonzero matrices of shape $m \times m$, such that $A \times B = 0$ (the zero matrix has all zeros), can either A or B have an inverse?

8.   Calculate the determinant of

$$A = \begin{pmatrix} 2 & 0 & 0 \\ 0 & 2 & 0 \\ 0 & 0 & 2 \end{pmatrix}$$

using the last row and its cofactors.

9.   Show that, if two rows or columns of a 3×3 matrix are interchanged, the value of the determinant is not changed except for the sign.

10.   Show that in a 3×3 matrix A, if a row is multiplied by a factor k, then the determinant of the resulting matrix is k det A.

11.   Show that in a 3×3 matrix A, if any row i is multiplied by a constant k and each element is added to the corresponding element of any other row j, then the

matrix B, which results when the jth row of A is replaced by the resulting elements, is such that det A = det B.

7.13 SOLUTION OF THREE LINEAR EQUATIONS IN THREE VARIABLES BY MATRICES

Matrices can be used to solve n linear equations in n variables. We illustrate the general procedure for the case of three equations in three variables.

Example 7.55. Let

$$a_{11}x_1 + a_{12}x_2 + a_{13}x_3 = b_1$$
$$a_{21}x_1 + a_{22}x_2 + a_{23}x_3 = b_2$$
$$a_{31}x_1 + a_{32}x_2 + a_{33}x_3 = b_3$$

be a set of three simultaneous linear equations in three variables, with b_1 or b_2 or $b_3 \neq 0$.

Suppose that we consider the 3×3 array of coefficients of the variables,

$$A = \begin{pmatrix} a_{11} & a_{12} & a_{13} \\ a_{21} & a_{22} & a_{23} \\ a_{31} & a_{32} & a_{33} \end{pmatrix}_{3 \times 3}$$

and the column vectors of the variables and of the constants

$$X = \begin{pmatrix} x_1 \\ x_2 \\ x_3 \end{pmatrix}_{3 \times 1} \qquad B = \begin{pmatrix} b_1 \\ b_2 \\ b_3 \end{pmatrix}_{3 \times 1}$$

Then the system of equations can be written as $AX = B$, which is a matrix equation. Evidently, if we multiply on the left by A^{-1}, we shall get

$$(A^{-1}A)X = A^{-1}B$$

or

$$X = A^{-1}B$$

We can therefore conclude that the system of three linear equations in three variables has a solution if the matrix of the coefficients has an inverse, and the 3×3 matrix of the coefficients has an inverse if the determinant of that matrix is not zero.

$$\begin{pmatrix} x_1 \\ x_2 \\ x_3 \end{pmatrix} = \frac{1}{\Delta} \begin{pmatrix} A_{11} & A_{21} & A_{31} \\ A_{12} & A_{22} & A_{32} \\ A_{13} & A_{23} & A_{33} \end{pmatrix} \begin{pmatrix} b_1 \\ b_2 \\ b_3 \end{pmatrix} \qquad (7.8)$$

where Δ = det A and A_{ij} is the cofactor of a_{ij}.

Therefore

$$x_1 = \frac{1}{\Delta}(b_1 A_{11} + b_2 A_{21} + b_3 A_{31})$$

$$x_2 = \frac{1}{\Delta}(b_1 A_{12} + b_2 A_{22} + b_3 A_{32})$$

$$x_3 = \frac{1}{\Delta}(b_1 A_{13} + b_2 A_{23} + b_3 A_{33})$$

But
$$b_1 A_{11} + b_2 A_{21} + b_3 A_{31} = \det\begin{pmatrix} b_1 & a_{12} & a_{13} \\ b_2 & a_{22} & a_{23} \\ b_3 & a_{32} & a_{33} \end{pmatrix} = \Delta_1$$

$$b_1 A_{12} + b_2 A_{22} + b_3 A_{32} = \det\begin{pmatrix} a_{11} & b_1 & a_{13} \\ a_{21} & b_2 & a_{23} \\ a_{31} & b_3 & a_{33} \end{pmatrix} = \Delta_2$$

$$b_1 A_{13} + b_2 A_{23} + b_3 A_{33} = \det\begin{pmatrix} a_{11} & a_{12} & b_1 \\ a_{21} & a_{22} & b_2 \\ a_{31} & a_{32} & b_3 \end{pmatrix} = \Delta_3$$

Note that the Δ_i's ($i = 1, 2, 3$) are formed by substituting the column vector of the constants b_i for the column vector corresponding to x_i ($i = 1, 2, 3$) in the A matrix. The solution is therefore stated as Cramer's rule,

$$x_1 = \frac{\Delta_1}{\Delta} \qquad x_2 = \frac{\Delta_2}{\Delta} \qquad x_3 = \frac{\Delta_3}{\Delta}$$

Evidently, if $\Delta \neq 0$ but $b_1 = b_2 = b_3 = 0$, the only solution is

$$x_1 = 0 \qquad x_2 = 0 \qquad x_3 = 0$$

Equations of the form $\sum_{i=1}^{n} a_i x_i = 0$ are called *homogeneous linear equations*.

Example 7.56. Solve the following system of equations by Cramer's rule:

$$3x_1 + 2x_2 - x_3 = 5$$
$$2x_2 + 3x_3 = 11$$
$$x_1 + x_2 + x_3 = 6$$

Solution. We first compute the determinant of the coefficients to see whether or not there is a solution and then compute Δ_1, Δ_2, and Δ_3.

$$\Delta = \det\begin{pmatrix} 3 & 2 & -1 \\ 0 & 2 & 3 \\ 1 & 1 & 1 \end{pmatrix} = 5 \qquad \Delta_2 = \det\begin{pmatrix} 3 & 5 & -1 \\ 0 & 11 & 3 \\ 1 & 6 & 1 \end{pmatrix} = 5$$

$$\Delta_1 = \det\begin{pmatrix} 5 & 2 & -1 \\ 11 & 2 & 3 \\ 6 & 1 & 1 \end{pmatrix} = 10 \qquad \Delta_3 = \det\begin{pmatrix} 3 & 2 & 5 \\ 0 & 2 & 11 \\ 1 & 1 & 6 \end{pmatrix} = 15$$

The solution is

$$x_1 = \tfrac{10}{5} = 2$$
$$x_2 = \tfrac{5}{5} = 1$$
$$x_3 = \tfrac{15}{5} = 3$$

or

$$\begin{pmatrix} x_1 \\ x_2 \\ x_3 \end{pmatrix} = \begin{pmatrix} 2 \\ 1 \\ 3 \end{pmatrix}$$

7.14 THE LEONTIEF MODEL

The use of simultaneous linear equations is illustrated in the Leontief model of an economic system.   The basic Leontief interindustry model of an economy assumes that the economy consists of n interacting industries, each of which produces a single product, and each of which purchases as intermediate goods the products of other industries.   For example, the wheat industry purchases tractors from the automotive industry and fertilizers from the chemical industry, while the automotive industry purchases steel from the steel industry and tires from the rubber industry. An industry, such as steel, can purchase some of its own product (one steel company selling to another steel company) as well as purchasing from an industry (such as the automotive industry) to which it also sells. Finally, in addition to selling its product to other industries as an intermediate product, a given industry, typically, will also sell its product to a final-demand category such as consumers, the government, or foreign countries.

Assume that in a given year each industry produces just enough to satisfy the intermediate product demand of other industries and final demand (i.e., there are no inventory changes).   Let x_i be the quantity of product i produced by industry i, r_{ij} be the number of units of product i demanded by industry j, and f_i the number of units of product i required by the final-demand categories.   Then

$$\begin{aligned} x_1 &= r_{11} + r_{12} + \cdots + r_{1n} + f_1 \\ x_2 &= r_{21} + r_{22} + \cdots + r_{2n} + f_2 \\ &\ \cdot\ \cdot\ \cdot\ \cdot\ \cdot\ \cdot\ \cdot\ \cdot\ \cdot\ \cdot\ \cdot\ \cdot\ \cdot\ \cdot\ \cdot\ \cdot\ \cdot\ \cdot \\ x_n &= r_{n1} + r_{n2} + \cdots + r_{nn} + f_n \end{aligned} \qquad (7.9)$$

In the more basic models, it is assumed that the amount of product i required to produce product j is directly proportional, the proportionality factor being denoted by a_{ij}, to the quantity of product j produced. Thus

$$r_{ij} = a_{ij}x_j \qquad (7.10)$$

the value of a_{ij} (generally called the *technical coefficient of production*) depending on the technology of industry j.

Substituting (7.10) in (7.9), we obtain

$$
\begin{aligned}
x_1 - a_{11}x_1 - a_{12}x_2 - \cdots - a_{1n}x_n &= f_1 \\
x_2 - a_{21}x_1 - a_{22}x_2 - \cdots - a_{2n}x_n &= f_2 \\
\cdots\cdots\cdots\cdots\cdots\cdots\cdots\cdots\cdots\cdots\cdots \\
x_n - a_{n1}x_1 - a_{n2}x_2 - \cdots - a_{nn}x_n &= f_n
\end{aligned}
$$

which is equivalent to

$$
\begin{aligned}
(1 - a_{11})x_1 - a_{12}x_2 - \cdots - a_{1n}x_n &= f_1 \\
-a_{21}x_1 + (1 - a_{22})x_2 - \cdots - a_{2n}x_n &= f_2 \\
\cdots\cdots\cdots\cdots\cdots\cdots\cdots\cdots\cdots\cdots\cdots \\
-a_{n1}x_1 - a_{n2}x_2 - \cdots + (1 - a_{nn})x_n &= f_n
\end{aligned}
\tag{7.11}
$$

If the final demands f_i are specified (e.g., in a yearly forecast) and if the a_{ij}'s are known, then (7.11) becomes a system of n linear equations in n variables and the system can be solved for the x_i's—that is, the amount that each industry in the economy should produce in order to satisfy both final and intermediate demands can be determined (see Probs. 8 and 9 in Problem Set 7.6). In matrix notation (7.11) becomes

$$
\begin{pmatrix}
1 - a_{11} & -a_{12} & \cdots & -a_{1n} \\
-a_{21} & 1 - a_{22} & \cdots & -a_{2n} \\
\cdots & \cdots & \cdots & \cdots \\
-a_{n1} & -a_{n2} & \cdots & 1 - a_{nn}
\end{pmatrix}
\times
\begin{pmatrix}
x_1 \\
x_2 \\
\cdots \\
x_n
\end{pmatrix}
=
\begin{pmatrix}
f_1 \\
f_2 \\
\cdots \\
f_n
\end{pmatrix}
$$

7.15 SOLUTION SETS OF TWO LINEAR EQUATIONS IN THREE VARIABLES

We now want to find the solution set of a system of two linear equations in three variables.

$$
\begin{aligned}
a_{11}x_1 + a_{12}x_2 + a_{13}x_3 &= b_1 \\
a_{21}x_1 + a_{22}x_2 + a_{23}x_3 &= b_2
\end{aligned}
\tag{7.12}
$$

where the a_{ij}'s and b_i's are constants and the x_i's variables.

The general procedure is to treat x_3 as if it were a constant and, by using Cramer's rule, solve for x_1 and x_2 in terms of x_3.

Theorem 7.57

The solution set of (7.12) for any specified x_3 consists of

$$\left\{ \langle x_1, x_2, x_3 \rangle \middle| x_1 = \frac{x_3 \begin{vmatrix} a_{12} & a_{13} \\ a_{22} & a_{23} \end{vmatrix} - \begin{vmatrix} a_{12} & b_1 \\ a_{22} & b_2 \end{vmatrix}}{\begin{vmatrix} a_{11} & a_{12} \\ a_{21} & a_{22} \end{vmatrix}} \ \& \right.$$

$$x_2 = \frac{-x_3 \begin{vmatrix} a_{11} & a_{13} \\ a_{21} & a_{23} \end{vmatrix} + \begin{vmatrix} a_{11} & b_1 \\ a_{21} & b_2 \end{vmatrix}}{\begin{vmatrix} a_{11} & a_{12} \\ a_{21} & a_{22} \end{vmatrix}}$$

$$\left. \& \ x_3 \text{ is a real number} \right\} \quad (7.13)$$

on the assumption that the determinant formed from the x_1 and x_2 coefficients is $\neq 0$.

Proof. The proof is obtained by inserting the values of x_1, x_2, and x_3 in (7.12).

The following should be noted:

1. The denominator in the formulas for both x_1 and x_2 is the determinant of the 2×2 matrix formed by deleting the x_3 column in the coefficient matrix of (7.12).

2. The first determinant in the numerator of each formula is the determinant of the 2×2 matrix formed by deleting the column in the coefficient matrix of (7.12) corresponding to the variable to which the formula applies.

3. The second determinant in the numerator of each formula is formed by replacing the x_3 column in the coefficient matrix of (7.12) with the constant column of (7.12) and taking the determinant of the 2×2 matrix formed by deleting the column in the new coefficient matrix corresponding to the variable to which the formula applies.

The student should realize that we can treat x_1 or x_2 or x_3 as the constant and solve for the other two in terms of it. In practice, we select any one of the three for which the determinant of the 2×2 matrix of the coefficients of the other two variables is not zero.

Example 7.58. Solve the following system of equations for x_1 and x_2 in terms of x_3.

$$\begin{aligned} x_1 + x_2 + \ x_3 &= 0 \\ 2x_1 + x_2 + 3x_3 &= 6 \end{aligned} \quad (7.14)$$

Solution. Employing (7.13), we have

$$x_1 = \frac{x_3\begin{vmatrix} 1 & 1 \\ 1 & 3 \end{vmatrix} - \begin{vmatrix} 1 & 0 \\ 1 & 6 \end{vmatrix}}{\begin{vmatrix} 1 & 1 \\ 2 & 1 \end{vmatrix}} = \frac{2x_3 - 6}{-1} = 6 - 2x_3$$

$$x_2 = \frac{-x_3\begin{vmatrix} 1 & 1 \\ 2 & 3 \end{vmatrix} + \begin{vmatrix} 1 & 0 \\ 2 & 6 \end{vmatrix}}{\begin{vmatrix} 1 & 1 \\ 2 & 1 \end{vmatrix}} = \frac{-x_3 + 6}{-1} = x_3 - 6$$

The solution set is $\{\langle x_1, x_2, x_3 \rangle | x_1 = 6 - 2x_3$ & $x_2 = x_3 - 6$ & x_3 is any real number$\}$. Thus, if x_3 were set equal to 1, x_1 and x_2 would be 4 and -5, respectively; for $x_3 = 2$, $x_1 = 2$ and $x_2 = -4$; etc. The reader should check these answers by substituting in (7.14).

Example 7.59. A firm has eight units of raw material 1, and six units of raw material 2 which it wants to use up. The firm produces three products, each unit of which requires the two raw materials in the amounts shown in the tabulation. What combinations of the three

Raw material	Product		
	1	2	3
1	1	1	3
2	1	2	1

products will completely exhaust the available supplies of the two materials?

Solution. If we denote the number of units of each product produced by x_1, x_2, and x_3, respectively, we can construct the following two linear equations in three variables,

$$x_1 + x_2 + 3x_3 = 8$$
$$x_1 + 2x_2 + x_3 = 6$$

which can be solved by using (7.13). Note that for this problem the relevant solution set S is a subset of the general solution set given by (7.13), that is,

$$S = \{\langle x_1, x_2, x_3 \rangle | \ x_1 \text{ and } x_2 \text{ are determined from (7.13) } \& \ x_1, x_2, x_3 \geq 0\}$$

The reader should realize, from the linear-programming principles introduced in the preceding chapter, that none of the 3-tuples in S need be optimum from the profit-maximization point of view.

PROBLEM SET 7.6

1. Solve the following system of equations,
    a. $2x + 3y - z = 4$
       $x + y - z = -2$
       $3x - y + z = 5$
    b. $x_1 + x_2 = 5$
       $4x_1 + 2x_2 + 3x_3 = 2$
       $x_2 - 5x_3 = -1$
    c. $\begin{pmatrix} 2 & -1 & 4 \\ 2 & 0 & 1 \\ 1 & 2 & 0 \end{pmatrix} \begin{pmatrix} x_1 \\ x_2 \\ x_3 \end{pmatrix} = \begin{pmatrix} 2 \\ 1 \\ 1 \end{pmatrix}$

by Cramer's rule.

2. Find the inverse of the following square matrices:
    a. $\begin{pmatrix} 1 & 0 & 0 \\ 0 & 1 & 0 \\ 0 & 0 & 1 \end{pmatrix}$
    b. $\begin{pmatrix} 1 & 1 & 1 \\ 1 & 1 & 1 \\ 1 & 1 & 1 \end{pmatrix}$
    c. $\begin{pmatrix} 1 & 1 & 1 \\ 0 & 2 & 1 \\ 0 & 0 & 2 \end{pmatrix}$
    d. $\begin{pmatrix} 2 & 2 & 2 \\ 1 & 1 & 1 \\ 0 & 0 & 0 \end{pmatrix}$
    e. $\begin{pmatrix} 3 & 4 & 5 \\ 6 & 8 & 10 \\ 1 & 2 & 1 \end{pmatrix}$

3. Does a 3×3 matrix, with one row a constant times another row, have an inverse? Why or why not?

4. Find the determinant of the matrix:
    a. $\begin{pmatrix} 2 & 0 & 0 \\ 0 & 2 & 0 \\ 0 & 0 & 2 \end{pmatrix}$
    b. $\begin{pmatrix} 1 & 2 & 1 \\ 1 & 2 & 1 \\ 3 & 2 & 1 \end{pmatrix}$
    c. $\begin{pmatrix} 0 & 0 & 2 \\ 0 & 2 & 0 \\ 2 & 0 & 0 \end{pmatrix}$

5. Show that

$$5^3 \times \det \begin{pmatrix} 1 & 0 & 0 \\ 0 & 1 & 0 \\ 0 & 0 & 1 \end{pmatrix} = \det \begin{pmatrix} 5 & 0 & 0 \\ 0 & 5 & 0 \\ 0 & 0 & 5 \end{pmatrix}$$

while

$$5 \times \begin{pmatrix} 1 & 0 & 0 \\ 0 & 1 & 0 \\ 0 & 0 & 1 \end{pmatrix} = \begin{pmatrix} 5 & 0 & 0 \\ 0 & 5 & 0 \\ 0 & 0 & 5 \end{pmatrix}$$

6.   Given

$$\begin{pmatrix} 1 & 2 & 1 \\ 2 & 3 & 0 \\ -1 & 2 & 1 \end{pmatrix}$$

Calculate the determinant of the matrix obtained by multiplying the last row by 2, adding corresponding elements to the second row, and using the results as the second row of a new matrix.

7.   Can two different matrices have the same determinant?   Why or why not?

8.   Assume that an economy is composed of three industries (see Sec. 7.14), that the technical coefficients of production are as shown in matrix A, and that the 1-year forecasts of final demand for each industry are as shown in matrix F_1.   How much must each industry produce in order to be able just to meet final demand and the intermediate demand of other industries?   Is this information, coming 1 year in advance, useful to the individual industry and the economy as a whole?   Upon what factors does the reliability of these forecasts depend?   Use Cramer's rule to solve the required equations.

	a_{ij}					f_i	i
	1	2	3	j / i			
$A =$	.3	.1	.2	1	$F_1 =$	3	1
	.1	.1	.1	2		4	2
	.4	.2	.6	3		1	3

9.   Use (7.8) to solve the necessary system in the above problem.   Assume, now, that the forecasts F_1 presented above are the most likely estimates, and that lower limits and upper limits of final demand requirements are forecast as shown in column vectors F_2 and F_3, respectively.   Determine the lower- and upper-limit forecasts for the x_i's, using (7.8).   Notice that only the column vector for the b_i [in (7.8)] changes as the system of linear equations is solved for different F_i's.

$$F_2 = \begin{pmatrix} 2 \\ 3 \\ 0.5 \end{pmatrix} \qquad F_3 = \begin{pmatrix} 4 \\ 5 \\ 2 \end{pmatrix}$$

10.   A biologist is attempting to develop a new food by chemically decomposing three other foods.   The table shows the number of units of protein and fat that can be obtained from the three foods.   If the new food is to have exactly 10 units of protein and 12 units of fat, which combinations of the three foods are satisfactory?

Number of units of	Food		
	1	2	3
Protein........	1	2	1
Fat..........	1	3	4

8 SOME NONLINEAR RELATIONS: QUADRATIC, EXPONENTIAL, AND LOGARITHMIC GRAPHS

8.1 MOTIVATION

In this chapter we shall study some nonlinear relations most of which will also be functions. In particular, we shall define the graphs of some very important relations. We recall that the graph of a linear relation is the subset of points of the real plane which are the maps of the elements of the relation. We also recall that a relation defined over a set S is a subset of the cartesian product of the set by itself. The relation is often defined by an equation. In what follows we restrict ourselves to the set of real numbers.

8.2 THE QUADRATIC FUNCTION

$f = \{\langle x,y \rangle | (y = ax^2 + bx + c) \ \& \ (a \neq 0)\}$

Our objective is to find solutions to the following problems:

1. To find the subset R of the solution set of the function whose elements are of the form $\langle x,0 \rangle$. If $R \neq \emptyset$, then the elements x of the domain of R will be called the *roots* of the equation $ax^2 + bx + c = 0$.

2. To find the maximum (or minimum) element of f.

3. To describe the graph of f.

To find the roots of the equation $ax^2 + bx + c = 0$, we shall use the expression defining the function,

$$y = ax^2 + bx + c$$

and transform it, by "completing the square," into a form from which we can readily derive the desired elements.   Since $(a + b)^2 = a^2 + 2ab + b^2$ is the square of a binomial, we know that an expression which is the expanded square of a binomial will contain three terms, the middle term being twice the product of the two terms in the unexpanded binomial and the first and third terms being, respectively, the squares of the first and second terms in the unexpanded binomial.

We use these observations as follows:

$$y = ax^2 + bx + c$$
$$= a\left(x^2 + \frac{b}{a}x\right) + c \tag{8.1}$$

If we treat the expression inside the parentheses as the sum of the first two terms of an expanded square of a binomial, then we know that the second term is equivalent to

$$\frac{b}{a}x = 2xq$$

where q is the second term in the unexpanded binomial.   Solving for q, we find

$$q = \frac{b}{2a}$$

so that the third term in the expanded binomial will be

$$q^2 = \frac{b^2}{4a^2}$$

Hence, to transform the expression inside the parentheses in (8.1) into the expanded square of a binomial, we must add $b^2/4a^2$ to the first two terms inside the parentheses.   To accomplish this, since the parentheses are multiplied by a, we must add $a(b^2/4a^2) = b^2/4a$ to (8.1), which means we must also subtract $b^2/4a$ from (8.1) to keep the original function $y = ax^2 + bx + c$ unchanged.   Thus

$$y = a\left(x^2 + \frac{b}{a}x\right) + c + a\frac{b^2}{4a^2} - \frac{b^2}{4a}$$

$$= a\left(x^2 + \frac{b}{a}x + \frac{b^2}{4a^2}\right) + \left(c - \frac{b^2}{4a}\right) \tag{8.2}$$

$$y = a\left(x + \frac{b}{2a}\right)^2 + \frac{4ac - b^2}{4a}$$

$$= a\left(x + \frac{b}{2a}\right)^2 - \frac{b^2 - 4ac}{4a} \tag{8.3}$$

To find the roots, we write

$$a\left(x + \frac{b}{2a}\right)^2 - \frac{b^2 - 4ac}{4a} = 0$$

or

$$a\left(x + \frac{b}{2a}\right)^2 = \frac{b^2 - 4ac}{4a}$$

$$\left(x + \frac{b}{2a}\right)^2 = \frac{b^2 - 4ac}{4a^2}$$

$$x + \frac{b}{2a} = \pm\frac{\sqrt{b^2 - 4ac}}{2a}$$

$$x = \frac{-b \pm \sqrt{b^2 - 4ac}}{2a} \tag{8.4}$$

This is known as the *quadratic formula*.   The roots of the quadratic equation are the elements of the domain of the solution set given in

$$\left\langle\frac{-b + \sqrt{b^2 - 4ac}}{2a}, 0\right\rangle, \left\langle\frac{-b - \sqrt{b^2 - 4ac}}{2a}, 0\right\rangle$$

We shall define the range and domain later.

Example 8.1.   Given the function described by

$$y = 2x^2 + 3x + 1$$

find the roots of

$$2x^2 + 3x + 1 = 0$$

Solution 1. $a = 2$, $b = 3$, $c = 1$.   Adding and subtracting $b^2/4a$ as in (8.2), we obtain

$$0 = 2(x^2 + \tfrac{3}{2}x + \tfrac{9}{16}) + (1 - \tfrac{9}{8})$$

$$= 2(x + \tfrac{3}{4})^2 - \tfrac{1}{8}$$

$$(x + \tfrac{3}{4})^2 = \tfrac{1}{16} \qquad x = -\tfrac{3}{4} \pm \tfrac{1}{4}$$

$$x_1 = -\tfrac{1}{2} \qquad x_2 = -1$$

The roots are $-\frac{1}{2}$ and -1, that is, the domain constituents of

$$\langle -\tfrac{1}{2}, 0 \rangle, \ \langle -1, 0 \rangle$$

Solution 2. $a = 2$, $b = 3$, $c = 1$.   Putting these into (8.4), we obtain

$$x = \frac{-3 \pm \sqrt{9 - 8}}{4}$$

or $\qquad x_1 = \dfrac{-3 + 1}{4} = -\dfrac{1}{2} \qquad x_2 = \dfrac{-3 - 1}{4} = -1$

The roots are $-\frac{1}{2}$ and -1, as in Solution 1.

Example 8.2.   The market-supply function for a government-supported farm commodity (such as wheat) is

$$q = 85 + 5p$$

where q denotes the quantity supplied and p denotes the market price. Each unit produced costs $c = \$1.60$.   The government feels that, if wheat farmers as a group are to achieve an adequate standard of living, total profit should be \$252.   What price would farmers have to receive in order to realize this profit?

Solution.   Total profit π equals total revenue $(R = pq)$ minus total cost $(c = cq)$, that is,

$$\pi = R - C = pq - cq = q(p - c)$$

The amount that farmers are willing to produce at different market prices is given by the supply function $q = 85 + 5p$.   To determine the price that farmers would have to receive in order to be willing to produce an amount sufficient to result in a \$252 profit, we substitute in the total-profit equation and solve for p.

$$\pi = q(p - c)$$
$$252 = (85 + 5p)(p - 1.6)$$
$$= 85p + 5p^2 - 136 - 8p$$
$$5p^2 + 77p - 388 = 0$$

Solving the above equation by (8.4), we obtain

$$p = \frac{-77 \pm \sqrt{5{,}929 - (-7{,}760)}}{10} = \frac{-77 \pm 117}{10} = -19.4, \ 4$$

Since negative prices have no economic meaning, the required price is $p = 4$.

Certain limitations on the roots are derived from the quadratic formula.

Theorem 8.3

If $b^2 < 4ac$ and the domain of (8.4) is the set of *real* numbers, then there are no roots.

Proof. The proof follows directly, since if $b^2 - 4ac < 0$, $\sqrt{b^2 - 4ac}$ is imaginary and therefore is not an element of the set of real numbers. No element in the range is defined.

Theorem 8.4

If $b^2 = 4ac$, the roots are real and equal; i.e.,

$$x = \frac{-b}{2a}$$

Theorem 8.5

If $b^2 > 4ac$, the roots are real and unequal; i.e., there are two distinct elements in the range defined by the quadratic formula. The proofs follow directly.

Example 8.6. Determine the nature of the roots of

$$5x^2 - 8x + 3 = 0$$

Solution. $a = 5$, $b = -8$, $c = 3$.

$$b^2 = 64 \qquad 4ac = 4 \times 5 \times 3 = 60$$
$$b^2 > 4ac$$

The roots are real and unequal.

From Theorems 8.3, 8.4, and 8.5 it follows that a quadratic function has at most two roots.

8.3 MAXIMUM OR MINIMUM OF THE QUADRATIC FUNCTION

We now seek to find an expression for that element of the solution set for which the function is a maximum or a minimum, i.e., that value of x for which y is a maximum or a minimum.

Consider the function described by (8.3),

$$y = a\left(x + \frac{b}{2a}\right)^2 - \frac{b^2 - 4ac}{4a}$$

Case 1. $a > 0$. In this case

$$a \left(x + \frac{b}{2a} \right)^2$$

is either positive or zero. (Why?)

$$- \frac{b^2 - 4ac}{4a}$$

will be positive, zero, or negative.

Now we must add to $-(b^2 - 4ac)/4a$ the first term $a(x + b/2a)^2$, which will give us a greater value except when $a(x + b/2a)^2 = 0$. Since $a(x + b/2a)^2 = 0$ when $x = -b/2a$, the *minimum* element is given by

$$\left(-\frac{b}{2a}, \ -\frac{b^2 - 4ac}{4a} \right)$$

Case 2. $a < 0$. This gives us the *maximum* element in the solution set. We leave the proof to the student.

We therefore have the following theorem.

Theorem 8.7

If $y = ax^2 + bx + c$ is given, then if $a > 0$, the function has a minimum, and if $a < 0$, the function has a maximum. Both are given by

$$\left(-\frac{b}{2a}, \ -\frac{b^2 - 4ac}{4a} \right)$$

(The point on the graph of this function which is the map of the maximum or minimum element of the solution set will be called the *vertex* of the graph.)

Example 8.8. Determine the maximum or minimum point of the function described by

$$y = -2x^2 - 3x + 7$$

Solution. $a = -2, b = -3, c = 7$. Since $a < 0$, there is a maximum at

$$x = -\frac{-3}{(2)(-2)} = -\frac{3}{4}$$

$$y = -\frac{9 - (4)(-2)(7)}{(4)(-2)} = -\frac{9 + 56}{-8} = \frac{65}{8}$$

Example 8.9. Determine the maximum or minimum of $y = 3x^2$.

Solution. $a = 3, b = c = 0$. Since $a > 0$, there is a minimum at

$$x = -\frac{b}{2a} = -\frac{0}{6} = 0$$

that is, $\qquad y = 0$

Example 8.10. The industry demand curve for wheat is given by

$$q = 100 - 2p$$

where q denotes the number of units demanded and p the price of each unit. Each unit sold costs $c = 3$ to produce. On the assumption that farmers are willing to produce and sell any output which consumers might demand, what price will maximize the total profit of wheat farmers, and what is this profit?

Solution. Total profit π equals total revenue R minus total cost C,

$$\pi = R - C = pq - cq = q(p - c) = q(p - 3)$$

The quantity that consumers will demand at different prices is given by the demand function $q = 100 - 2p$, which can be substituted into the above profit equation to give

$$\pi = (100 - 2p)(p - 3)$$
$$= -2p^2 + 106p - 300$$

This is a quadratic in which $a = -2$, $b = 106$, $c = -300$. Since $a = -2 < 0$, the function has a maximum at

$$p = -\frac{b}{2a} = -\frac{106}{-4} = 26.5$$

which is $\qquad \pi = -\frac{b^2 - 4ac}{4a} = -\frac{11{,}236 - 2{,}400}{-8} = 1{,}104.5$

Example 8.11. A firm produces a product each unit of which requires one-fourth unit of labor and one unit of a specific raw material. Each unit of labor costs $k_L = 2$. Since quantity discounts are allowed on all purchases of the raw material, its unit price k_m depends on the quantity m purchased, and is given by

$$f_m = \{\langle m, k_m \rangle | 0 < m \leq 35 \; \& \; k_m = 80 - 2m\}$$

The firm's average unit delivery cost increases the farther away it delivers, the area over which it delivers increasing as the quantity produced and sold increases. The relationship between average unit delivery cost and quantity q produced and sold is given by

$$f_d = \{\langle q, k_d \rangle | q > 0 \; \& \; k_d = 10 + 3q\}$$

Since the firm is just starting out and is the only supplier of its type of product in the area, and since the Federal government considers the product critical in time of war, the firm receives a government subsidy equal to $s = 100$ for each unit produced and sold. The firm's rent and other overhead is $K_o = 300$ per day. What level of daily output minimizes total cost?

Solution. If we consider the unit government subsidy as a negative cost (each unit sold results in cash flowing in and not out) $k_s = -s = -100$, total cost C becomes the sum of total labor cost K_L, total material cost K_m, total delivery cost K_d, total overhead cost K_o, and the negative total subsidy cost K_s,

$$C = K_L + K_m + K_d + K_o + K_s \tag{8.5}$$

Now

$$K_L = k_L L = 2L$$

(where L denotes the number of units of labor employed) and

$$K_m = k_m m = (80 - 2m)m = 80m - 2m^2$$

Since each unit of output requires one-fourth unit of labor and one unit of raw material, $L = q/4$ and $m = q$, which, when substituted into the preceding equations, give

$$K_L = \frac{q}{2}$$

$$K_m = 80q - 2q^2$$

We also have

$$K_d = k_d q = (10 + 3q)q = 10q + 3q^2$$
$$K_o = 300$$
$$K_s = k_s q = -100q$$

Note that total labor and delivery costs increase with q, that total material cost first rises and then falls with q, that subsidy cost decreases with q, and that total overhead cost is independent of q. Substituting the above relationships in (8.5), we obtain

$$C = \frac{q}{2} + (80q - 2q^2) + (10q + 3q^2) + 300 + (-100q)$$
$$= q^2 - \tfrac{19}{2}q + 300$$

This is a quadratic function with $a = 1$, $b = -\tfrac{19}{2}$, $c = 300$. Since $a = 1 > 0$, it will have a minimum value equal to

$$C = -\frac{b^2 - 4ac}{4a} \cong 277$$

at

$$q = -\frac{b}{2a} = 4\frac{3}{4}$$

8.4 GRAPH OF THE QUADRATIC FUNCTION

The graph of the quadratic function is called the *parabola*.

In sketching the graph of the quadratic function described by $y = ax^2 + bx + c$ we shall proceed as follows:

1. We determine whether or not the origin is on the graph.

2. We determine the vertex point of the graph.

3. We determine the zeros of the graph, if any exist (none exist if $b^2 < 4ac$).

4. We determine at least two other points.

5. We connect all these points by a smooth curve.

We can justify drawing a smooth curve through these few points which we selected, in the following manner: We can see by an examination of the expression $y = ax^2 + bx + c$ that the function is defined for every element in its domain. This means that there is a point in the plane for every element in the function. Let us make this specific. Let $y = x^2 + x + 1$. Then $\langle 1,3 \rangle$ and $\langle 2,7 \rangle$ are in the function, and the corresponding points are on the graph. If we take values of x between 1 and 2, we shall get values of y between 3 and 7. A little computation will make it intuitively evident that, as we let x get closer and closer to 2, the value of y will get closer and closer to 7. So, for every element in f with x between 1 and 2, we shall have a y between 3 and 7. Hence there will be points on the graph between (1,3) and (2,7). If we preassign a positive number, as small as we please, to be the difference between y and 7, we shall be able to determine another small positive number which will be the difference between x and 2. Hence we can draw a smooth curve from (1,3) to (2,7). And this can be done for any two points on the graph.

If a function has this property, we say that it is *continuous* at every element and the graph is continuous at every point.

Example 8.12. Graph the quadratic $y = x^2$.

Solution. 1. Since $\langle 0,0 \rangle$ is in the solution set, the origin is on the graph (Fig. 8.1).

2. Since $b = 0$, $a = 1$, $c = 0$, the point $(0,0)$ (that is, $x = -b/2a$) is either the maximum point or the minimum point. Since $a > 0$, namely, 1, $(0,0)$ is a minimum point.

3. The domain is the set of real numbers, and the range is the set of squares of real numbers. So the function has a value for every real number in the domain. Since $b^2 = 4ac = 0$, both roots are 0 and the zeros are at $(0,0)$.

4. The elements $\langle 1,1 \rangle$ and $\langle -1,1 \rangle$ are in the solution, and therefore the points are on the graph.

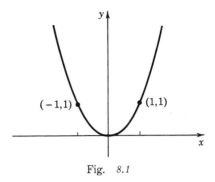

Fig. *8.1*

Example 8.13.   Graph the quadratic

$$y = -4x^2 + 2x - 3$$

Solution.   1. $\langle 0,0 \rangle$ is not in the solution set and therefore not on the graph (Fig. 8.2).

2. Since $a = -4 < 0$, the graph has a maximum. $b = 2, c = -3$. The maximum is at

$$x = -\frac{2}{(2)(-4)} = \frac{1}{4}$$

$$y = -\frac{4 - (4)(-4)(-3)}{(4)(-4)} = -\frac{4(1 - 12)}{(4)(-4)} = -\frac{-11}{-4} = -\frac{11}{4}$$

3. Since $b^2 < 4ac$, there are no zeros.

4. $(0, -3)$ is on the graph; $(1, -5)$ is on the graph.

Example 8.14.   In Example 8.10 we saw that the total-profit function for the wheat industry was given by

$$\pi = -2p^2 + 106p - 300$$

Show how total profit π varies with price p by graphing this function.

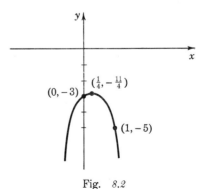

Fig. *8.2*

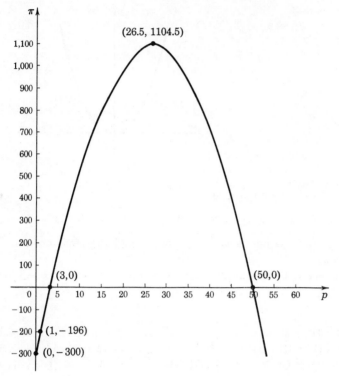

Fig. *8.3*

Solution.   1. $\langle 0,0 \rangle$ is not in the solution set and therefore not on the graph (Fig. 8.3).

2. Since $a = -2 < 0$, the graph has a maximum value of

$$\pi = -\frac{11,236 - 2,400}{-8} = 1,104.5$$

at

$$p = -\frac{106}{-4} = 26.5$$

That is, the maximum element in the solution set is $\langle 26.5,\ 1,104.5 \rangle$.

3. Since $b^2 > 4ac$, the graph has zeros which can be determined from (8.4),

$$x_1 = \frac{-106 + \sqrt{8,836}}{-4} = \frac{-106 + 94}{-4} = 3$$

$$x_2 = \frac{-106 - \sqrt{8,836}}{-4} = \frac{-106 - 94}{-4} = 50$$

The zeros of the graph are $\langle 3,0 \rangle$ and $\langle 50,0 \rangle$.

4. The elements $\langle 1, -196 \rangle$ and $\langle 0, -300 \rangle$ are in the solution set and are therefore points on the graph.

8.5 THE FUNCTION $f = \{\langle x,y \rangle | y = c/x$ & c is a constant not equal to $0\}$

From the equation describing the function $y = c/x$, we see that the domain and range are the set of real numbers excluding 0. $\langle 0,0 \rangle \notin f$. Therefore $(0,0)$ is not on the graph of the function, nor is any element of the form $\langle 0,r \rangle$ in f (r is a real number).

Likewise, if $y = 0$, we obtain $0 \cdot x = c$, or $c = 0$, which is impossible. Hence there are no roots to the equation, and therefore the graph does not cut the x axis; i.e., the graph has no zeros. Neither does the graph cut the y axis. (Why?) That is, no element of the form $\langle r,0 \rangle$ is in f.

If we consider the subset of the domain consisting of all positive real numbers and take $c > 0$, then, as x increases, y decreases without limit and gets closer and closer to 0. We denote this fact by the expression

$$\lim_{x \to \infty} \frac{1}{x} = 0$$

On the graph this means that, as x increases along the positive part of the x axis, the distance of each point from the x axis gets smaller and smaller but never quite reaches 0. When this happens, we call the x axis an *asymptote* to the graph.

Similarly the y axis is also an asymptote to the graph, since

$$\lim_{y \to \infty} \frac{1}{y} = 0$$

If $c > 0$, then both x and y must be positive or both must be negative. The graph will lie in the first or third quadrants.

The student should show that, if $c < 0$, the graph will lie in the second or fourth quadrants. We continue our discussion only for $c > 0$.

Evidently the graph is not continuous at $(0,0)$, since the function is undefined at $\langle 0,0 \rangle$.

For simplicity we show the graph of

$$f = \left\{ \langle x,y \rangle | y = \frac{1}{x} \right\} \ (x \neq 0)$$

$$\langle 1,1 \rangle \in f \quad \text{and} \quad \langle -1,-1 \rangle \in f$$

The curve is shown in Fig. 8.4 and is called a *rectangular hyperbola*.

The student should also notice that we may interpret $xy = c$ as follows:

$x \cdot y = c$ states that the product of the distances of any point on the graph from the x and y axes is constant.

The student should draw the graph of

$$f = \left\{ \langle x,y \rangle | y = \frac{-1}{x} \right\}$$

Example 8.15. In an earlier chapter, we pointed out that a firm has certain fixed-cost items during a given time interval. If a firm has total fixed cost equal to $c = \$100$ per day, show how average fixed costs (i.e., total fixed cost per unit of output) vary with output by graphing the relation.

Solution. We let y denote average fixed cost and x daily output. Then

$$y = \frac{100}{x}$$

We leave the actual graphing to the student. Note that, since only positive x values are meaningful in the context of this problem, only the portion of the curve in the first quadrant is relevant. The steady decline in average fixed cost as output increases is the phenomenon often referred to as "spreading the overhead."

Example 8.16. The demand function for cigarettes, let us assume, is given by

$$q_d = \frac{80}{p}$$

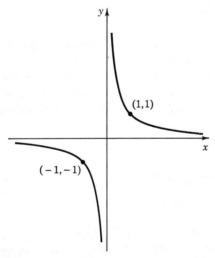

Fig. 8.4.

and the supply function by

$$q_s = 40p - 40$$

where q_d and q_s denote the number of units demanded and supplied, respectively, and p the price.

1. What is the equilibrium market price?

2. If the government now imposes an excise tax of $t = 2$ on each unit sold, will the equilibrium price change?

3. Are producers or consumers bearing the major burden of the tax?

4. Graph, on the same set of axes, the demand and supply functions both before and after the tax. What general characteristic of this type of problem can be observed?

Solution. 1. The equilibrium price is that price which equates the quantities demanded and supplied,

$$q_d = q_s$$
$$\frac{80}{p} = 40p - 40$$
$$40p^2 - 40p - 80 = 0$$
$$p^2 - p - 2 = 0$$

Applying (8.4),

$$p = \frac{1 \pm \sqrt{1 + 8}}{2} = 2, -1$$

Since negative prices have no economic meaning, the equilibrium market price is $p = 2$ and the equilibrium quantity, upon substituting $p = 2$ into either the demand or the supply function, is $q = 40$.

2. Before the tax is imposed, producers receive the full market price p and are willing to supply $q_s = 40p - 40$ units of output at a market price of p. After the tax is imposed, producers do not receive the full market price p; rather, they receive $p - t = p - 2$. Therefore, after the tax, the quantity that producers will be willing to supply at a market price of p is equivalent to what they would supply before the tax at a price of $p - 2$, that is,

$$q_s = 40(p - 2) - 40 = 40p - 120$$

The equilibrium price now will be

$$q_d = q_s$$
$$\frac{80}{p} = 40p - 120$$
$$40p^2 - 120p - 80 = 0$$
$$p^2 - 3p - 2 = 0$$
$$p = \frac{3 \pm \sqrt{17}}{2} \cong 3.6, -0.6$$

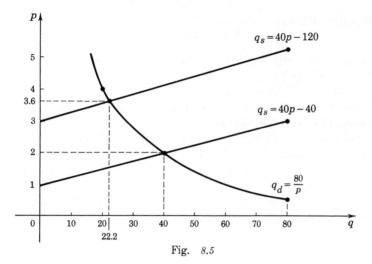

Fig. *8.5*

Since only positive p values have meaning in the context of the present problem, the equilibrium price is $p = 3.6$ and the quantity, upon substituting $p = 3.6$ into the demand or supply function, is $q \cong 22.2$.

3. The equilibrium market price paid by consumers has increased from $p = 2$ (before the tax) to $p = 3.6$ (after the tax). If we denote the before and after equilibrium market prices by p_b and p_a, respectively, we can say that the consumer pays $[(p_a - p_b)/t] \times 100 = [(3.6 - 2)/2] \times 100 = 80$ per cent of the tax. Since the producers' net price falls from $p_b = 2$ to $p_a - t = 3.6 - 2 = 1.6$, they are absorbing $[(2 - 1.6)/2] \times 100 = 20$ per cent of the tax. Note, also, that the tax has the effect of reducing the quantity produced and sold from $q = 40$ to $q = 22.2$, or $[(40 - 22.2)/40] \times 100 = 44.5$ per cent. In general, the relative burdens of a tax of this sort on producers and consumers depend on the shape, position, and slope of the demand and supply curves.

4. Following the convention employed by economists, we plot (Fig. 8.5) p on the vertical axis and q on the horizontal axis. Notice that the tax has had the effect of shifting the before-tax supply curve upward in a parallel fashion by an amount equal to $t = 2$.

PROBLEM SET 8.1

1. Given the quadratic $y = -2x^2 - 7x - 1$, find the zeros, if any, using the quadratic formula.
2. Find the maximum or minimum element of the function in Prob. 1.
3. Graph the function in Prob. 1.

4. Determine the nature of the zeros and the maximum value of the function

$$y = -2x^2 + 6x$$

5. Graph the function in Prob. 4.
6. Sketch the graph of:

   a. $y = \dfrac{-5}{x}$

   b. $-y = \dfrac{3}{x}$

   c. $y = \dfrac{3}{x}$

   d. $y = \dfrac{\frac{1}{2}}{x}$

7. Graph the function (a) $y = -2x^2$, (b) $y = 2x^2$, (c) $y = 4x^2$. What is the effect of the constant in $y = cx^2$ on the function?

8. The demand curve for a product is given by $q = 100 - 2p$. Graph the total revenue $(p \times q)$ curve.

9. The total revenue R and total cost C functions for a firm are, respectively,

$$R = \frac{-q^2}{2} + 10q$$
$$C = 5 + 3q$$

where q denotes output. Graph, on the same set of axes, the total revenue, cost, and profit $(\pi = R - C)$ functions.

10. In Prob. 9, determine the break-even points algebraically from the relevant equations. Check your answers by examining the intersections of the curves graphed in Prob. 9.

11. In Prob. 9, is the output at which dollar sales are at a maximum necessarily the best output for the firm?

12. The most "efficient" output for the firm is that output at which average cost (i.e., total cost per unit of output) is at a minimum. In the general case, economic theory holds that, as output increases over low levels, average cost falls, since the firm becomes more efficient, but that, as output increases over high levels and the plant capacity is approached, average cost rises, since the firm becomes less efficient. The average-cost curve is therefore taken to be U-shaped. If this curve, for a particular firm, is given by

$$C_a = 2q^2 - 8q + 10$$

what is the most efficient output? Graph C_a.

13. The demand curve for a commodity is given by

$$q_d = \frac{50}{p}$$

and the supply curve by

$$q_s = 25p - 25$$

where q_d and q_s denote quantity demanded and supplied, respectively, and p denotes price. What is the equilibrium market price (determine the answer graphically, plotting p on the vertical axis, and algebraically).

14. In the preceding problem, assume that the government now levies a $1 tax on each unit sold. Determine the new equilibrium price graphically and algebraically. Who bears the burden of this tax?

8.6 THE EXPONENTIAL FUNCTION $f = \{\langle x,y \rangle | y = ab^x\}$

We shall take as the domain of this function the set of real numbers and as its range a subset of the set of real numbers. Furthermore, we shall restrict the values of a to the set of real numbers excluding zero and those of b to the set of real numbers greater than 1 (that is, $a \neq 0$ and $b > 1$). We study the elements of f for two cases.

Case 1. $a > 0$.

1. If $x = 0$, $y = a \cdot b^0 = a \cdot 1 = a$; that is, there is only one element in f for $x = 0$, namely, $\langle 0,a \rangle$.

2. If $x > 0$, $y = a \cdot b^x$ is always positive. Moreover, as x increases, $a \cdot b^x$ increases, i.e.,

$$\lim_{x \to \infty} a \cdot b^x = \infty$$

This means that, if $\langle x_1,y_1 \rangle$ and $\langle x_2,y_2 \rangle$ are any two elements of f such that $0 < x_1 < x_2$, then $y_1 < y_2$.

3. If $x < 0$, let $x = -x_1$ where $x_1 < 0$. Then

$$y = ab^x = ab^{-x_1} = a\left(\frac{1}{b}\right)^{x_1}$$

We notice that, as x (<0) decreases, x_1 increases and $1/b^{x_1}$ must decrease, i.e.,

$$\lim_{x \to \infty} \frac{1}{b^{x_1}} = 0$$

It is intuitively evident that

$$a \frac{1}{b^{x_1}}$$

must also decrease to 0, since a is a constant and is repeatedly multiplied by something smaller. [We shall prove in Chap. 9 that $\lim_{x \to \infty} a(1/x) = a \lim_{x \to \infty} (1/x)$.] Therefore, if we start from very small values of x (x is negative!), we find that y increases with x. Again, if $\langle x_1,y_1 \rangle$ and $\langle x_2,y_2 \rangle$ are elements of f for which $x_1 < x_2 < 0$, then $y_1 < y_2$. The function is also increasing for values of $x < 0$.

A function in which the values of y increase always as x increases, no matter what values of x are considered, is called an *increasing function*.

For the case $a > 0$, the graph is easily constructed from (1), (2), and (3) above and is shown at the top of Fig. 8.6.

Case 2. $a < 0$. We leave the analysis of this case to the student. Notice that the effect of this case ($a < 0$) is to change the sign of $f(x)$.

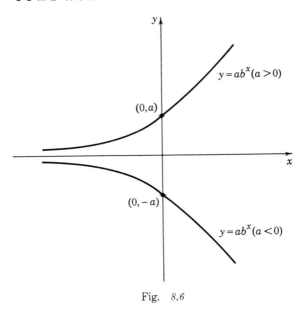

Fig. 8.6

The result is a decreasing function and is shown at the bottom of Fig. 8.6. Notice that the vertical-axis intercept is $-a$.

Example 8.17.   Graph the function $y = 10^x$.

Solution.   Since $y = 10^x$ is an exponential function of the general form $y = ab^x$ (with $a = 1$, $b = 10$), it must approach the negative portion of the x axis asymptotically. Furthermore, since $a = 1 > 0$, y will always be positive and will increase with x, so that the graph of the function will approach the x axis from above as we go from right to left. We know that the y-axis intercept will be $\langle 0,a \rangle = \langle 0,1 \rangle$. If we obtain at least four more points, we can thus graph the function. Substituting four arbitrary x values in $y = 10^x$, we obtain $\langle -2,0.01 \rangle$, $\langle -1,0.1 \rangle$, $\langle 1,10 \rangle$, $\langle 2, 100 \rangle$. Figure 8.7 shows these points connected by a smooth curve.

An interesting property of the exponential function is given by the following theorem. It turns out that equal arithmetic changes in x lead to equal proportionate changes in y. Furthermore, if c denotes the arithmetic change in x, $b^c - 1$ denotes the proportionate change in y.

Theorem 8.18

If x_1, x_2, x_3, and x_4 are any four elements in the domain of the exponential function such that $(x_2 - x_1) = (x_4 - x_3)$, then

$$\frac{f(x_2) - f(x_1)}{f(x_1)} = \frac{f(x_4) - f(x_3)}{f(x_3)}$$

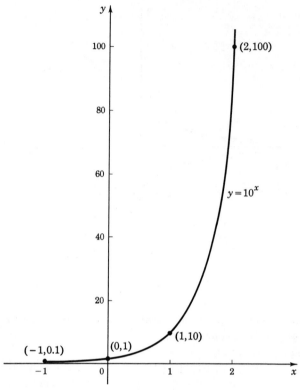

Fig. 8.7

Proof

$$y_2 = f(x_2) = ab^{x_2} \qquad y_4 = f(x_4) = ab^{x_4}$$
$$y_1 = f(x_1) = ab^{x_1} \qquad y_3 = f(x_3) = ab^{x_3}$$
$$\frac{f(x_2) - f(x_1)}{f(x_1)} = \frac{ab^{x_2} - ab^{x_1}}{ab^{x_1}} = \frac{ab^{x_2}}{ab^{x_1}} - \frac{ab^{x_1}}{ab^{x_1}} = \frac{b^{x_2}}{b^{x_1}} - 1$$
$$= b^{x_2 - x_1} - 1$$

Also $\qquad \dfrac{f(x_4) - f(x_3)}{f(x_3)} = \dfrac{ab^{x_4} - ab^{x_3}}{ab^{x_3}} = \dfrac{b^{x_4}}{b^{x_3}} - 1 = b^{x_4 - x_3} - 1$

But $\qquad x_2 - x_1 = x_4 - x_3$

Therefore $\qquad \dfrac{y_2 - y_1}{y_1} = \dfrac{y_4 - y_3}{y_3}$

Example 8.19. Let $y = 10^x$. Take as values of x,

$$x_1 = 2 \qquad x_2 = 7 \qquad x_3 = 4 \qquad x_4 = 9$$

Then $\qquad\qquad\qquad 7 - 2 = 9 - 4$

and therefore $\qquad \dfrac{10^7 - 10^2}{10^2} = \dfrac{10^9 - 10^4}{10^4}$

or $\qquad\qquad\qquad 10^5 - 1 = 10^5 - 1$

The proportional change in the function for an x difference of c is then $b^c - 1 = 10^c - 1$. For an x difference of 1, the proportional change in the function is $10^1 - 1 = 9$, or 900 per cent.

The exponential function has application in a number of fields, one of which is in time series, which can often be represented by exponential functions.

Definition 8.20. A time series is a function from the set of positive integers to a subset of the set of real numbers in which the set of positive integers designates measures of equal time intervals and the set of real numbers designates the values of a specific variable (such as sales, population, crime rate).

Example 8.21. Denote the time series for the data in the tabulation.

Month, 1965	*Sales*, $1,000
January	28
February	27
March	27
April	29

Solution. We designate January, 1965, by the number 1, February by the number 2, March by the number 3, and April by the number 4. The time series is then

$$T = \{\langle 1,28 \rangle, \langle 2,27 \rangle, \langle 3,27 \rangle, \langle 4,29 \rangle\}$$

Example 8.22. Company Z's sales trend over time (i.e., the time series for company Z's sales) is adequately described by the function

$$y = (2)(1.1)^x$$

where $x = 1$ in August, 1963, the time unit being 1 month. Forecast sales for March, 1965. Graph the function from January, 1955, to March, 1965. What is the monthly proportion of change in y?

Solution. Since $x = 1$ in August, 1963 (each x unit representing 1 month), March, 1965, which is 19 months (x units) later, corresponds to $x = 20$. Substituting $x = 20$ in $y = (2)(1.1)^x$, we obtain

$$y = (2)(1.1)^{20} = 13.5$$

as the forecast for March, 1965. Figure 8.8 shows the graph of this function, which, following the convention with respect to time-series analysis, shows time plotted on the horizontal axis. The specific elements of the set T graphed are $\langle 1,2.2 \rangle$, $\langle 2,2.4 \rangle$, $\langle 3,2.7 \rangle$, $\langle 10,5.2 \rangle$, $\langle 20,13.5 \rangle$. Since the x unit is 1 month, we can determine the monthly proportionate change in y directly from the function by subtracting 1 from the b value, that is, $b^c - 1 = (1.1)^1 - 1 = 1.1 - 1 = 0.1$, so that sales increase by 10 per cent each month.

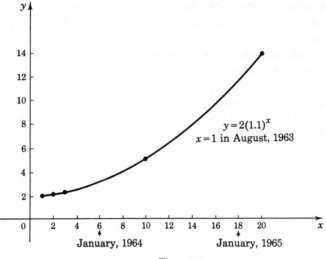

$$y = 2(1.1)^x$$
$$x = 1 \text{ in August, 1963}$$

January, 1964   January, 1965

Fig. *8.8*

8.7 THE EXPONENTIAL FUNCTION $f = \{\langle x,y \rangle | y = ae^{-cx^2}\}$

This is a particularly important function, since it has application in probability theory, growth and learning phenomena, and so on.

The symbol a designates a constant real number.

The symbol e designates the so-called *napierian base*, an irrational number whose value is approximately 2.71828. This constant has important properties and is used as a base for a system of logarithms. The so-called *normal distribution curve* (the bell-shaped curve) is the graph of an exponential function of this form. In this section we shall study only the special case of this function when $a = c = 1$, that is, $y = e^{-x^2}$.

Example 8.23. Discuss and graph the function

$$f = \{\langle x,y \rangle | y = e^{-x^2}\}$$

Solution. As usual, we shall discuss the statement describing the function, $y = e^{-x^2}$.

1. The domain of f is the set of real numbers.

2. Since $e^{-x^2} = 1/e^{x^2}$ and e and x^2 are both positive, the range is the set of positive real numbers without zero. ($e^0 = 1$; therefore y can never become 0.)

3. As x increases indefinitely, y decreases indefinitely; that is, y approaches 0. As x decreases indefinitely, y decreases indefinitely; that is, y again approaches 0.

4. When $x = 0$, we have the greatest value of y; that is,
$y = 1/e^{x^2} = 1/e^0 = \frac{1}{1} = 1$

5. Considerations similar to what we mentioned before make it plausible that the curve is smooth, with no breaks; i.e., it is continuous.

6. Evidently, for $x = k$ (some constant) and $x = -k$, we get the same element of the range; i.e., for any element $\langle k, 1/e^{k^2} \rangle$ we also have $\langle -k, 1/e^{k^2} \rangle$.

On the basis of items 1 to 6 we can sketch the graph as in Fig. 8.9. [The student should translate 1 to 6 into expressions about the graph. *Hint:* The x axis is an asymptote because of (3). (4) shows that the curve is symmetric about the y axis.   Why?]

$$f(0) = \frac{1}{e^0} = 1$$

$$f(-1) = f(1) = e^{-1} = \frac{1}{e} \cong \frac{1}{2.71828}$$

[this gives $(1, e^{-1})$ and $(-1, e^{-1})$]

$$f(-2) = f(2) = e^{-4} = \frac{1}{e^4} \cong \frac{1}{54.7}$$

[this gives $(2, e^{-4})$ and $(-2, e^{-4})$]

Example 8.24. On a particular college-board examination administered to high-school students throughout the United States, the most frequently occurring score was 500. The number of scores which were less than 500 by a specified number, say x, of points equaled the number of scores which were higher than 500 by the specified number x; that is, the relation between specific scores and the number of persons making these scores was symmetrical around the score 500. The greater the difference between a particular score and 500, the less frequent was the occurrence of this score. This particular relation was adequately described by the function $y = 4{,}000e^{-0.04x^2}$, where y represents the

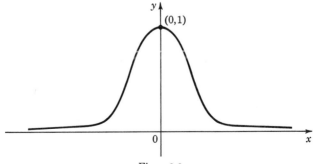

Fig. *8.9*

number of students receiving a score which differed from 500 by exactly
x points. How many students scored 500? 490? 510?

Solution. An x value of 0 corresponds to a score which differs
from 500 by 0, that is, a score of 500. Substituting 0 into

$$y = 4{,}000e^{-0.04x^2} = \frac{4{,}000}{e^{0.04x^2}}$$

indicates that 4,000 students scored 500. Scores of 490 and 510 represent
x values of -10 and $+10$, respectively, which when substituted in the
function yield

$$y(-10) = y(10) = \frac{4{,}000}{(2.718)^4} = \frac{4{,}000}{55} \cong 72$$

8.8 THE MODIFIED EXPONENTIAL FUNCTION
$f = \{\langle x,y \rangle | y = a - ae^{-cx}\}$. LEARNING CURVES

We place the following conditions on this function: $a > 0$, $c > 0$, and
a and c are constants. The domain of this function will be the set of
nonnegative real numbers. The range is the set of nonnegative real
numbers between 0 and a, that is, $0 \leq y < a$.

Example 8.25. Describe and graph the function $y = a - ae^{-cx}$.

Solution. 1. Evidently $\langle 0,0 \rangle \in f$ since, for $x = 0$, $1/e^{cx} = 1/e^0 = 1$,
so that $y = a - a(1/e^{cx}) = a - a(1) = 0$.

2. As x increases indefinitely, e^{cx} increases indefinitely, $1/e^{cx}$ approaches 0, and $a(1/e^{cx})$ also approaches zero. We express this as
follows:

$$\lim_{x \to \infty} a\,\frac{1}{e^{cx}} = a \lim_{x \to \infty} \frac{1}{e^{cx}}$$

Therefore at the limit

$$a \lim_{x \to \infty} \frac{1}{e^{cx}} = 0$$

Since $y = a - a(1/e^{cx})$, as x increases indefinitely y approaches but never
reaches a.

The graph of the function can now be drawn easily (Fig. 8.10).
(2) shows the line $y = a$ to be an asymptote. The modified exponential
function and its graph are often referred to as *learning curves*.

Learning curves have applications in psychology, education, and
management. In most, but not all, cases these curves show how learning, as measured by performance of the task being learned, progresses
over time or as the number of opportunities for performing the task
increases. Observation has shown that many learning situations have

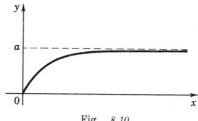

Fig. *8.10*

in common the following pattern: Learning increases quite rapidly at first as the more obvious errors are corrected and the basic intricacies of the task are mastered, but after a certain interval of time learning tapers off and an upper limit, or asymptote, representing the maximum performance physically achievable in the particular situation, is approached. Some learning situations which have been studied are:

1. The number of minutes it takes a rat to find its way out of a maze, related to the number of times it has been placed in the same maze

2. The number of correctly typed words per minute, or the number of words translated per hour, or the number of nonsense syllables memorized, related to the number of hours of instruction received

3. The number of products assembled per day, related to the number of days since production was started

Example 8.26.   The daily output y of assembled products x days after the beginning of the assembly operation is given by $y = 50 - 50e^{-0.1x}$. What is the maximum performance the firm expects to achieve, and what per cent of this maximum will be attained after 20 days?

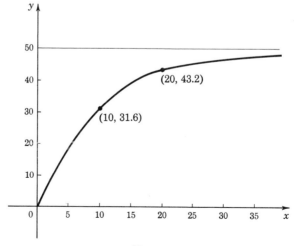

Fig. *8.11*

Solution. The maximum performance is given by $a = 50$. Substituting $x = 20$ into $y = 50 - 50e^{-0.1x}$, we obtain

$$y \cong 50 - \frac{50}{(2.718)^2} \cong 50 - 6.8 \cong 43.2$$

That is, 20 days after production starts, daily output should be 43.2, or $43.2/50 = 86$ per cent of the maximum attainable. The function is graphed in Fig. 8.11 by determining two points and connecting them with a smooth curve, it being remembered that the function starts at 0 and approaches $a = 50$. The two points are $(10, 31.6)$ and $(20, 43.2)$.

PROBLEM SET 8.2

1. The time series for company Q's sales is given in the tabulation. Graph the series, measuring time on the x axis and letting $x = 1$ in January, 1965. On the same set of axes, graph the function $y = (3)(1.2)^x$ for $x = 1, 2, \ldots, 13$. Do you think this function adequately describes the basic trend of company Q's sales? Extend this trend with a broken line to March, 1965, and use the ordinate at the end of the broken line as the forecast for March, 1965. Check your answer by direct substitution into the function. What is the monthly proportionate change in sales?

Month, 1965	Sales, $1,000	Month, 1965	Sales, $1,000
January................	6	August................	13
February..............	3	September.............	14
March.................	7	October...............	16
April..................	6	November.............	24
May...................	7	December.............	31
June..................	12	January, 1966..........	27
July...................	14		

2. Graph the function:
   a. $y = e^x$
   b. $y = e^{-x}$
   c. $y = e^{x^2}$
   d. $y = e^{-2x^2}$
   e. $y = e^{2x^2}$

3. Graph the function $y = 2e^{-x^2}$ and $y = 5e^{-x^2}$ on the same set of axes. Note that the center, or peak, of the curve is at a different position along the y axis in each case. What do you conclude, therefore, about the property associated with the constant a in the function $y = ab^{-cx^2}$?

4. The dispersion of the items in a distribution refers to the spread of the individual x values around the peak of the curve. Now graph the functions $y = 2e^{-x^2}$ and $y = 2e^{-2x^2}$ on the same set of axes. Note that each curve is at the same position along the y axis (why?) but that the dispersion of the two distributions is different. What do you conclude, therefore, about the property associated with the constant c in the function $y = ab^{-cx^2}$?

5. In the mass production of items in industry, chance factors usually prevent the production of a batch of items each of which is identical in every dimension. Many times a given quality dimension, say length, of the product being manufactured will exhibit a most frequently occurring value, other values being symmetrically distributed about it, those values which are further away occurring less frequently. Assume that the distribution of the length of mass-produced product Q is given by $y = 1,000e^{-\frac{1}{2}x^2}$ where y denotes the number of items in the last production lot which differed from the most frequently occurring value by x inches. Assume that the most frequently produced length measured 100 inches. How many of the items in the last lot were 100 inches? 98 inches? 102 inches? Graph the function.

6. The number y of nonsense syllables the typical person can memorize after x minutes of studying is given by $y = 26 - 26e^{-x}$. What per cent of the maximum will be attained after 3 minutes? Graph the function.

7. The monthly sales y of company Q after x dollars per month have been expended on advertising is given by $y = 22,000 + (10,000 - 10,000e^{-0.001x})$. What will sales be after \$3,000 has been spent on advertising? Will it pay the firm to spend an extra \$1,000 (a total of \$4,000) on advertising? Graph the function.

8. A child psychologist finds that the names and faces that a five-year-old can correctly associate x minutes after first being introduced is given by $y = 12 - 12e^{-x}$. How many names and faces will be correctly associated after 5 minutes? Graph the function.

9. The stock-room supervisor in a plant knows that the new production process being initiated requires three units of part Z for every unit of final product produced. The weekly output y of the final product x weeks after the start of production is given by $y = 500 - 500e^{-0.2x}$. How many units of part Z should the supervisor plan to have on hand for the fifth week? Graph the function.

8.9 THE INVERSE FUNCTION

Suppose that we have a function f defined by $y = f(x)$, with given domain and range. It is often desirable to find a function $y = f^{-1}(x)$ which is defined as follows.

Definition 8.27. A function f^{-1}, described by $y = f^{-1}(x)$, is the inverse of the function f, described by $y = f(x)$, if the domain of f^{-1} is the range of f and the range of f^{-1} is the domain of f [that is, if $\langle a,b \rangle \, \epsilon \, f$ then $\langle b,a \rangle \, \epsilon \, f^{-1}$].

In many cases, f^{-1} can be obtained by switching the variables in f and solving the resulting expression for y.

Example 8.28. Given the function described by $y = f(x) = 2x$, with domain and range the set of real numbers,

$$
\begin{aligned}
f &= \{\langle x,y \rangle | y = 2x\} \\
&= \{\langle 0,0 \rangle, \langle \tfrac{1}{4},\tfrac{1}{2} \rangle, \langle \tfrac{1}{2},1 \rangle, \langle 1,2 \rangle, \langle -1,-2 \rangle, \ldots\}
\end{aligned}
$$

The inverse is obtained by switching variables in f, so that $x = 2y$, and then solving for y, so that $y = f^{-1}(x) = \tfrac{1}{2}x$, with domain and range the set of real numbers,

$$f^{-1} = \{\langle x,y \rangle | y = \tfrac{1}{2}x\}$$
$$= \{\langle 0,0 \rangle, \langle \tfrac{1}{2}, \tfrac{1}{4} \rangle, \langle 1, \tfrac{1}{2} \rangle, \langle 2, 1 \rangle, \langle -2, -1 \rangle, \; \ldots \}$$

We note that in a particular case there may be no inverse.

Example 8.29. Find the inverse of $y = x^2$, with domain and range the set of real numbers.

Solution. $f = \{\langle x,y \rangle | y = x^2\}$ is given. To find the inverse of the function described by $y = x^2$, we interchange the variables obtaining $x = y^2$ and solve for y, that is, $y = \sqrt{x}$. However, since the domain is the set of real numbers, we can get, for example, $y = \sqrt{-5}$, which is undefined in the set of real numbers. Also, if $x = 4$, $y = \sqrt{4}$ gives $y = 2$ and $y = -2$. So $y = \sqrt{x}$ is not a function if the domain is the set of real numbers. If we change our problem and ask for the inverse function to f described by $y = x^2$, with domain and range the set of positive real numbers, then $y = \sqrt{x}$ is defined and a function. In this case

$$f^{-1} = \{\langle x,y \rangle | y = \sqrt{x}\}$$

Every function is a relation, but the converse is not true.

Theorem 8.30

If $y = f(x)$ is a function which has an inverse $y = f^{-1}(x)$, then the inverse of f^{-1}, denoted by $(f^{-1})^{-1}$, is f.

Proof. We have given that $y = f(x)$ and $y = f^{-1}(x)$, so that

$$f = \{\langle a_1, b_1 \rangle, \langle a_2, b_2 \rangle, \; \ldots \}$$
and
$$f^{-1} = \{\langle b_1, a_1 \rangle, \langle b_2, a_2 \rangle, \; \ldots \}$$

By Definition 8.27, $y = f^{-1}[f^{-1}(x)]$ is given by

$$(f^{-1})^{-1} = \{\langle a_1, b_1 \rangle, \langle a_2, b_2 \rangle, \; \ldots \}$$

But $(f^{-1})^{-1} = f$. *Q.E.D.*

8.10 THE LOGARITHMIC FUNCTION $L = \{\langle x,y \rangle | y = \log_{10} x\}$

The student probably already knows what is stated in the following definition.

Definition 8.31. If $y = 10^x$, then $x = \log_{10} y$.

For example, if $100 = 10^2$, then $2 = \log_{10} 100$. We shall use Definition 8.31 to find the inverse of the exponential function $y = b^x$, which we studied earlier in this chapter.

When the student has the integral calculus at his command, the logarithmic function can be defined somewhat differently.

Given the function $E = \{\langle x,y \rangle | y = b^x\}$, b is a nonnegative constant (most commonly to the base 10 or to the napierian base e), with domain the set of real numbers and range the set of nonnegative real numbers. This function was studied earlier, and the student should examine its graph again.

To find the inverse $E^{-1} = L$, we switch variables, obtaining $x = b^y$, and use Definition 8.31 to write $y = \log_b x$.

The domain of L is obtained from $x = b^y$. Clearly x can never be either negative or zero. Hence the domain of $y = \log_b x$ is the set of positive real numbers, and its range the set of real numbers. So with this

$$L = \{\langle x,y \rangle | y = \log_b x\}$$

We call this the *logarithmic function*.

We can study the graph of $y = \log_{10} x$ as follows: We use $y = 10^x$, giving

$$E = \{\langle 1,10 \rangle, \langle 0,1 \rangle, \langle -1,\tfrac{1}{10} \rangle, \ldots\}$$

As x increases, y increases; and as x gets smaller and smaller, y gets smaller and smaller but always remains positive; i.e., the negative x axis is asymptotic to $y = 10^x$.

For the graph of the function L, we repeat the conditions for E, interchanging the variables.

$$L = \{\langle 10,1 \rangle, \langle 1,0 \rangle, \langle \tfrac{1}{10},-1 \rangle, \ldots\}$$

As y increases, x increases; and as y gets smaller and smaller, x gets smaller and smaller but always remains positive so that the negative y axis is asymptotic to $y = \log_{10} x$. Note that $(1,0)$ is on the graph. We show the graph in Fig. 8.12.

If $y = \log_b x$, $b > 1$, then b is called the *base* of the logarithm. Two bases are in common use, 10 and e. Logarithms to the base 10 are called

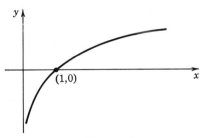

Fig. *8.12*

common logarithms; those to the base *e* are called *natural logarithms.* Tables for each are easily available. When no base is indicated, we are using common logarithms.

Using the laws proved in Probs. 3, 4, and 6, of Problem Set 8.3, we can write equations in logarithmic form.

Example 8.32. Write a logarithmic equation equivalent to $y^2 = \sqrt[3]{2}/\sqrt[3]{101}$. Use base 10.

Solution. We "take the logarithm" of both sides,

$$\log y^2 = \log \sqrt[3]{2} - \log \sqrt[3]{101}$$

$$2 \log y = \tfrac{1}{3} \log 2 - \tfrac{1}{3} \log 101 = \frac{\log 2 - \log 101}{3}$$

$$\log y = \frac{\log 2 - \log 101}{6}$$

The power of the logarithmic concept is shown in the following example.

Example 8.33. We define the geometric mean of a set of *n* values as

$$M_G = \sqrt[n]{\prod_{i=1}^{n} x_i}$$

where $\prod_{i=1}^{n} x_i = x_1 \cdot x_2 \cdot x_3 \cdots x_n$. Find M_G for $x_1 = 10$, $x_2 = 10^2$. $x_3 = 10^3$.

Solution

$$\prod_{i=1}^{3} x_i = 10 \cdot 10^2 \cdot 10^3 = 10^6$$

$$M_G = \sqrt[3]{10^6} = 10^2$$

Using logarithms, we solve as follows:

$$\log M_G = \frac{1}{n} \sum_{i=1}^{n} \log x_i \qquad \text{Why?}$$

$$\log 10 = 1 \qquad \log 10^2 = 2 \qquad \log 10^3 = 3$$

$$\log M_G = \tfrac{1}{3}(1 + 2 + 3) = 2$$

Therefore
$$M_G = 10^2 = 100$$

Example 8.34. The geometric mean is useful when we want to determine the "average" ratio of change in a variable over a period of time.

Assume that the population in a particular region in 1963 were $x_1 = 100$, in 1964 were $x_2 = 2,000$, and in 1965 were $x_3 = 10,000$. What is the average annual ratio of change over this period?

Solution. The population ratio from 1964 to 1963 is

$$\frac{x_2}{x_1} = \frac{2,000}{100} = 20$$

and from 1965 to 1964 is $x_3/x_2 = 10,000/2,000 = 5$. If we compute the geometric mean of these two ratios, we obtain

$$M_G = \sqrt{\frac{x_2}{x_1} \cdot \frac{x_3}{x_2}} = \sqrt{\frac{x_3}{x_1}} = \left(\frac{x_3}{x_1}\right)^{\frac{1}{2}}$$

$$\log M_G = \frac{1}{2} \log\left(\frac{x_3}{x_1}\right) = \frac{1}{2}(\log x_3 - \log x_1) = \frac{1}{2}(\log 10,000 - \log 100)$$

$$= \tfrac{1}{2}(4 - 2) = 1$$
$$M_G = 10^1 = 10$$

That is, the average, or typical, ratio of 1 year's population to the preceding year's is 10, indicating a yearly proportionate change of 900 per cent on the average. We can check this by applying the average ratio to the initial value $x_1 = 100$: if $x_1 = 100$ increased by 900 per cent, then x_2 should be $x_1 \times 10 = 100 \times 10 = 1,000$; and if $x_2 = 1,000$, x_3 should be $x_2 \times 10 = 1,000 \times 10 = 10,000$, which agrees with the actual x_3 which corresponds to the 1965 figure. Note that if the average ratio were determined from an arithmetic mean, denoted by M_A and defined as the sum of n values (which in this case are ratios) divided by n, we would have

$$\left(\frac{x_2}{x_1} + \frac{x_3}{x_2}\right) \div n = \left(\frac{2,000}{100} + \frac{10,000}{2,000}\right) \div 2 = 12.5$$

The average ratio of change would then be 1,150 per cent, and if this were applied to x_1 and cumulated to x_3, the computed and actual x_3 values would not be the same, indicating that M_A is not the proper average to employ in problems of this sort.

PROBLEM SET 8.3

1. In general $y = \log_a x \leftrightarrow a^y = x$ $(a > 1)$. Graph $y = \log_2 x$. What is the inverse of $y = \log_2 x$? Graph the inverse.
2. Graph the function and the inverse relation to the function:
   a. $y = 2x$
   b. $y = x^2$
In which cases, if any, is the inverse relation also the inverse function?

3. If $x = \log_a y \leftrightarrow a^x = y\ (a > 1)$, prove that $\log_a (y_1 \times y_2) = \log_a y_1 + \log_a y_2$ $(y_1$ and $y_2 > 0)$. (*Hint:* $y_1 = a^{x_1}$ and $y_2 = a^{x_2}$. Multiply and use the definition of a logarithm.)

4. If $x = \log_a y \leftrightarrow a^x = y\ (a > 1, y > 0)$, prove $\log_a y^k = k \log_a y$.

5. *a.* What is $\log_2 x$ if $x = 8$? If $x = 16$? If $x = 2$?

b. What are $\log_e e$ and $\log_{10} 10$?

6. Prove

$$\log_a \frac{y_1}{y_2} = \log_a y_1 - \log_a y_2 \qquad a > 1,\ y_1 \text{ and } y_2 > 0$$

7. Write the logarithmic equations equivalent to

a. $y = \sqrt{a^2 + x^2}$

b. $\sqrt[3]{y} = \sqrt[2]{x^3}$

c. $x^2 + y^2 = 25$

8. Is $\log (2 + 3) = \log 2 + \log 3$? Why or why not?

9. Compute M_G for the values 2, 4, 8, 16, 32. (*Hint:* Use logarithms to the base 2.)

10. The market price of a common stock at the end of the year for the period 1961 to 1965 is given in the table. Calculate the average annual rate of appreciation, using M_G. Can you derive a general formula for determining the average rate of growth of a variable over a period of time? Show that M_A is inappropriate in this type of problem.

Year	Stock price
1961	2
1962	3
1963	10
1964	20
1965	32

11. Company Z's annual sales for the period 1960 to 1965 are given in the table. Use M_G to determine the average annual rate of growth of sales (use logarithms to the base 3). Check your answer by applying this rate to $x_1 = 3$ in 1960 and cumulating to 1965 (the calculated and actual x_6 should be 729).

Year	Sales
1960	3
1961	6
1962	12
1963	50
1964	300
1965	729

12. We want to determine the average ratio of change in the yearly prices of two agricultural products in such a way that equal weights are assigned to equal ratios of change. That is, we want a doubling of one price exactly to offset a halving in price of the other, a tripling in the price of one to offset a price for the other which is just one-third of what it was initially, and similarly for any other two ratios whose product is 1. Compute this average, for the following data, using M_G. Show that, if the average ratio were determined from M_A, the desired offsets would not occur.

(Remember that, if the average ratio of actual prices in one year to prices in another is 1, the average ratio of *change* in prices is $1 - 1 = 0$ per cent.)

Commodity	Price		Ratio $\dfrac{1965}{1964}$
	1964	1965	
1	4	16	4
2	8	2	$\frac{1}{4}$

9 SEQUENCES, LIMITS, AND SUMMATION

9.1 SEQUENCES AND FUNCTIONS

We recall that a function f is a set of ordered couples. Let us consider a function f with domain the set of positive integers (denoted by I^+) and range a subset of the set of real numbers.

We define the range of the function as follows:

$$f(1) = a_1 \qquad f(2) = a_2 \qquad \ldots \qquad f(n) = a_n$$

where $a_1, a_2, \ldots, a_n$ are real numbers. We define

$$f = \{\langle 1, a_1 \rangle, \langle 2, a_2 \rangle, \ldots, \langle n, a_n \rangle, \ldots\}$$

The set $S = \{a_1, a_2, a_3, \ldots\}$, with elements *in this order*, is called a *sequence*.

Example 9.1.   Consider the function described by $f(n) = n + 1$, with domain I^+ and range the real numbers $f(n) = n + 1$; then

$$f(1) = 2 \qquad f(2) = 3 \qquad f(3) = 4 \qquad \text{etc.}$$
$$f = \{\langle 1,2 \rangle, \langle 2,3 \rangle, \langle 3,4 \rangle \ . \ . \ .\}$$

and the sequence is
$$S = \{2,3,4, \ . \ . \ .\}$$

Example 9.2.   Let $f(n) = 2n^2$, with domain I^+ and range a subset of real numbers determined from $f(n) = 2n^2$.

$$f = \{\langle 1,2 \rangle, \langle 2,8 \rangle, \langle 3,18 \rangle, \langle 4,32 \rangle, \ . \ . \ . , \langle n,2n^2 \rangle, \ . \ . \ .\}$$

and the sequence is

$$S = \{2,8,18,32, \ . \ . \ . , 2n^2, \ . \ . \ .\}$$

The fifteenth term in S is $f(15) = (2)(15)^2 = 450$.

Notice that any term in S may be obtained from the function with domain I^+ and range a subset of the set of real numbers.

We see that, if the elements of I^+ are arranged in natural order, the elements of the sequence are also arranged in order of the index of the term, that is, $f(1) = a_1, f(2) = a_2, \ . \ . \ .$.   Nothing, of course, prevents all a_i's being equal; e.g., we may have the sequence $\{1,1,1, \ . \ . \ .\}$, resulting from the function described by $f(n) = 1$.   In such a case the $1 - 1$ correspondence is between the position of the term in question in the sequence and the term.   There is then a $1 - 1$ correspondence between any element n of I^+ and the element of the sequence in the nth position in the sequence.

In what follows, we shall often discuss sequences without describing the function which gives rise to it.

Example 9.3.   Suppose that we have a sequence defined by the function $f(n) = 2n^2 + n$.   Write the nth term of the sequence and the ninth, tenth, and eleventh terms.

Solution

$$a_n = 2n^2 + n$$
$$a_9 = (2)(9)^2 + 9 = 162 + 9 = 171$$
$$a_{10} = (2)(10^2) + 10 = 200 + 10 = 210$$
$$a_{11} = (2)(11^2) + 11 = 242 + 11 = 253$$

Example 9.4.   A firm's total cost function is given by $C = 10 + 2q$ and its total revenue function by $R = 3q$, where q denotes the number of units produced and sold.   The firm manufactures radios, one unit of output being defined as one radio.   What is the total profit earned when $q = 16$ radios are sold?

Solution. Total profit π is given by

$$\begin{aligned}
\pi(q) &= R(q) - C(q) \\
&= 3q - (10 + 2q) \\
&= q - 10
\end{aligned}$$

In this problem fractional (as well as negative) q values have no economic meaning, and so the domain of the π function is I^+ and 0. The sequence defined by the function $\pi = q - 10$ then gives the total profit associated with unit sales of 1, 2, ... The sixteenth term in this sequence, therefore, corresponds to the total profit when $q = 16$,

$$\begin{aligned}
a_n &= n - 10 \\
a_{16} &= 16 - 10 = 6
\end{aligned}$$

9.2 ARITHMETIC SEQUENCE

Certain sequences are of particular importance. Consider a sequence $S = \{a_1, a_2, a_3, \ . \ . \ . \ , a_n, \ . \ . \ .\}$ such that

$$a_n = a_{n-1} + d$$

where d is a constant for every $n > 1$. Such a sequence is called an *arithmetic* sequence.

Example 9.5. The sequence $S = \{1, 2, 3, \ . \ . \ .\}$ is an arithmetic sequence because $a_n = a_{n-1} + 1$. For example,

$$\begin{aligned}
a_2 &= a_1 + 1 = 2 \\
a_3 &= a_2 + 1 = 2 + 1 = 3, \text{ etc.}
\end{aligned}$$

Example 9.6. The sequence

$$S = \{20, 25, 30, 35, \ . \ . \ .\}$$

is an arithmetic sequence, since $a_n = a_{n-1} + 5$.

Example 9.7. Each unit of product Z produced requires three units of raw material M. Write the raw-material requirements for integral outputs q as an arithmetic sequence.

Solution. The first element in each ordered couple of the following set R represents the output of product Z and the second element the raw-material requirements for the specified output,

$$R = \{\langle 1,3 \rangle, \langle 2,6 \rangle, \langle 3,9 \rangle, \ . \ . \ . \ , \langle q,3q \rangle, \ . \ . \ .\}$$

We can remove, in order, the second element in each couple and form the sequence S of raw-material requirements,

$$S = \{3,6,9, \ldots ,3n \ldots \}$$

Since $a_n = a_{n-1} + 3$, S is an arithmetic sequence.

9.3 GEOMETRIC SEQUENCE

We define a function

$$f = \{\langle 1,a_1\rangle, \langle 2,a_2\rangle, \langle 3,a_3\rangle, \ldots ,\langle n,a_n\rangle, \ldots \}$$

where a_n is a real number.   The sequence

$$S = \{a_1, a_2, a_3, \ldots ,a_n, \ldots \}$$

is called a *geometric sequence* if $a_n = a_{n-1} \cdot r$, where r is a constant and the same for every $n > 1$.

Example 9.8.   Given the function described by $f(n) = (5)(\frac{1}{2})^{n-1}$, where $n \in I^+$; then

$$f = \{\langle 1,(5)(\tfrac{1}{2})^0\rangle, \langle 2,(5)(\tfrac{1}{2})\rangle, \langle 3,(5)(\tfrac{1}{2})^2\rangle, \ldots ,\langle n,(5)(\tfrac{1}{2})^{n-1}\rangle, \ldots \}$$

and the sequence is

$$S = \left\{5, \frac{5}{2}, \frac{5}{4}, \frac{5}{8}, \ldots , \frac{5}{2^{n-1}}, \ldots \right\}$$

Since each term is obtained from the preceding term by multiplying by the constant $r = \frac{1}{2}$, S is a geometric sequence.

Example 9.9.   We define the *marginal propensity to consume* as the proportion of *additional* income received by consumers which is spent on goods and services.   Let us assume that the marginal propensity to consume, r, is 0.8 for a particular economy.   Because of increased government contracts, a firm works one of its employees overtime and pays him $100 more at the end of the month than it has paid him in the past. Trace the effect of this initial $100 increment in spending on total spending throughout the economy.

   Solution.   Total spending will increase, first by the initial increment of $100.   Second, the worker who receives this $100 will spend 80 per cent, or $80, of it; next the person or persons who receive the $80 will spend 80 per cent, or $64, of it; etc.   We have thus generated the sequence

$$S = \{100,80,64, \ldots ,(100)(0.8)^{n-1}, \ldots \}$$

This is a geometric sequence, $a_n = a_{n-1}(0.80)$.

9.4 THE nth TERM OF THE SEQUENCE

The Arithmetic Sequence

If we let d = the difference between any two terms of an arithmetic sequence, we can rewrite the sequence as

$$S = \{a_1, a_1 + d, a_1 + 2d, \ldots, a_1 + (n-1)d, \ldots\}$$

The nth term $L(n)$ of an arithmetic sequence is therefore

$$L(n) = a_1 + (n-1)d$$

Evidently if we know the nth term of an arithmetic sequence and the value of either d or a_1, we know the sequence.

Example 9.10.   If an arithmetic sequence has as its tenth term 25 and $d = 2$, write the sequence.

Solution

$$L(n) = a_1 + (n-1)d = a_n$$
$$L(10) = 25 = a_1 + (9)(2) = a_{10}$$
$$25 - 18 = a_1$$

or

$$a_1 = 7$$
$$S = \{7,9,11,13,15,17,19,21,23,25,27, \ldots\}$$

Example 9.11.   In Example 9.7, what are the raw-material requirements for $q = 118$?

Solution.   We want the one-hundred-eighteenth term in the sequence

$$S = \{3,6,9, \ldots, 3n, \ldots\}$$

Since $a_1 = 3$ and $d = 3$, the solution is

$$L(n) = a_1 + (n-1)d$$
$$L(118) = 3 + (117)(3)$$
$$a_{118} = 354$$

The Geometric Sequence

By definition, the nth term in a geometric sequence is

$$L(n) = a_{n-1} \cdot r \qquad (n = 2, 3, \ldots)$$

This means that the sequence can be written

$$S = \{a_1, a_1r, (a_1r)r, (a_1r^2)r, (a_1r^3)r, \ldots, (a_1r^{n-2})r, \ldots\}$$
$$= \{a_1, a_1r, a_1r^2, a_1r^3, a_1r^4, \ldots, a_1r^{n-1}, \ldots\}$$

with the nth term $L(n) = a_1r^{n-1}$.

Example 9.12.   A geometric sequence has as its first term $a_1 = 100$ and as its ratio $r = 0.02$.   Find the tenth term.

   Solution.   The nth term is $L(n) = a_1 r^{n-1}$.   Then

$$a_{10} = (100)(0.02)^{10-1} = (100)(0.02)^9$$

Example 9.13.   A geometric sequence has as its tenth term $L(10) = 125$ and as its ratio $r = 5$.   Find the first two terms.

   Solution

$$a_{10} = a_1 r^{n-1}$$
$$125 = a_1 5^9$$

or $\qquad a_1 = \dfrac{5^3}{5^9} = \dfrac{1}{5^6} = 5^{-6} \qquad a_2 = 5^{-6} \times 5 = 5^{-5}$

Example 9.14.   In Example 9.9, what is the increment to the total spending in the seventeenth round of spending?

   Solution.   We want the seventeenth term in the sequence

$$S = \{100, 80, 64, \ldots\}$$

It is given by $a_{17} = (100)(0.8)^{16}$.

PROBLEM SET 9.1

   1.   Indicate the sequence defined by the function (a) $f(n) = 1/n$; (b) $f(n) = n$; (c) $f(n) = 1$ if n is odd and $f(n) = -1$ if n is even; (d) $f(n) = 1/n!$; (e) $f(n) = (1 + 1/n)^n$; (f) $f(n) = 1/2^n$; (g) $f(n) = 2 - 1/2^{n-1}$; (h) $f(n) = 3/10^n$; (i) $f(n) = 2^n$. Which are arithmetic and which are geometric sequences?   Determine the difference for the arithmetic sequence and the ratio for the geometric sequence.
   2.   Write the fifth term of each of the sequences in Prob. 1.
   3.   A sequence whose terms are such that

$$a_1 \leq a_2 \leq a_3 \leq \cdots \leq a_{n-1} \leq a_n \cdots$$

is said to be *monotonically increasing*.   Which sequences in Prob. 1 are monotonically increasing?
   4.   A sequence whose terms are such that

$$a_1 \geq a_2 \geq a_3 \geq a_4 \cdots \geq a_{n-1} \geq a_n \cdots$$

is said to be *monotonically decreasing*.   Which sequences in Prob. 1 are monotonically decreasing?
   5.   The graph of a function defining a sequence is a set of unconnected points. Graph the functions defining the following sequences:

   a. $S = \{1, 2, 3, 4, \ldots\}$

   b. $S = \left\{\dfrac{1}{2}, \dfrac{1}{2^2}, \dfrac{1}{2^3}, \dfrac{1}{2^4}, \cdots\right\}$

   c. $S = \left\{x \,\middle|\, x = \left(1 + \dfrac{1}{n}\right)^n\right\}$

d. $s = \left\{ x \middle| x = 2 - \dfrac{1}{2^{n-1}} \right\}$

e. $S = \{ x | x = (2)(2)^n \}$

f. $S = \{ x | (x = 1 \text{ if } n \text{ is odd}) \,\&\, (x = -1 \text{ if } n \text{ is even}) \}$

(*Hint:* First define the function $\{ \langle x,y \rangle | x \, \epsilon \, I^+ \,\&\, y = a_n \}$.)

6. The marginal propensity to consume for an economy is 0.9. The government decides to increase its spending for *one* period (stage) by 200. Write the first three and the tenth increment to total spending as terms in a geometric sequence.

7. Show intuitively that an amount of money P deposited in a bank, paying a compound interest rate i, for n periods of time will grow to a value $a_n = P(1 + i)^n$. (*Hint:* a_n is the nth term in a geometric sequence. Write down a number of terms of this sequence.)

If the compound interest rate is $i = 0.25$ per cent and is paid quarterly, what is the value of a sum of \$1,000 at the end of 2 years? (*Hint:* Determine n first.) If the interest rate is 1 per cent and is paid annually, what is the value of \$1,000 at the end of 2 years?

8. Suppose that you wished to know how much to deposit now at a given compound interest rate i, so that you will receive a stated amount at the end of n periods of time. Using the formula in Prob. 7, show that the result is given by a geometric sequence with last term

$$P = a_n(1 + i)^{-n}$$

where P now designates the "present value" of the desired sum a_n to be received at the end of n periods of time.

Suppose that you wanted to receive \$1,000 at the end of 4 years. How much should you deposit if the compound interest rate is 2 per cent?

9. You know that you can earn $i = 0.10$ compounded annually on a given investment. Someone offers you an alternative investment opportunity, which, for an initial outlay of \$100, can be sold 5 years from now for \$170. Should you take this investment? Use the formula derived in Prob. 7 to answer the question; then show that the same answer is obtained if the formula derived in Prob. 8 is employed.

9.5 THE LIMIT OF A SEQUENCE

The notion of a limit is one of the most important in mathematics. It enables us to give meaning to sums when an unlimited number of terms is involved; it often enables us to evaluate a function at a point where ordinary arithmetic processes lead to undefined values; it enables us to calculate such concepts as instantaneous rates of change, and so on. Before giving a precise definition, we shall illustrate the concept.

Consider the sequence $S = \{ x | x = 1/2^n \}$. The first five terms of the sequence are

$$S = \left\{ \frac{1}{2}, \frac{1}{2^2}, \frac{1}{2^3}, \frac{1}{2^4}, \frac{1}{2^5}, \, \cdots \right\}$$

Evidently each term is getting smaller, since as n increases, the denominator increases and the fraction gets smaller. Of course, the fraction never can become zero, but as we go out in the sequence, the difference between any term we take and zero gets smaller and smaller. In fact, no matter what small positive number ϵ we take, we can go out in the sequence far enough and find a term a_m (call it the mth term) such that, for any term a_n after this $(n > m)$, $|a_n - 0|$ becomes and remains less than this ϵ. We say therefore that the limit of the sequence $\{x|x = 1/2^n\}$ as n increases indefinitely is zero. We write this as

$$\lim_{n \to \infty} \frac{1}{2^n} = 0$$

We now state the following definition.

Definition 9.15.   A number L is the limit of a sequence $\{a_1, a_2, \ldots, a_n, \ldots\}$ if, for any positive ϵ, no matter how small, there exists a number N such that, for every $n > N$, $|a_n - L| < \epsilon$.

This means that if we go out in the sequence far enough, the terms will be as close to L as we please. We write

$$\lim_{n \to \infty} \{a_n\} = L$$

We know that

$$|a_n - L| < \epsilon \qquad n > N$$

is equivalent to

$$-\epsilon < a_n - L < \epsilon \qquad n > N$$

or

$$L - \epsilon < a_n < L + \epsilon \qquad n > N$$

Example 9.16.   Does the sequence $S = \{x|x = 1 + 1/n\}$ have a limit?

Solution.   First we shall write a few terms of the sequence

$$\{1 + \tfrac{1}{1}, 1 + \tfrac{1}{2}, 1 + \tfrac{1}{3}, 1 + \tfrac{1}{4}, \ldots\}$$

Evidently this is a monotonically decreasing sequence. (Why?) If there is a limit L, then we can find an N such that, for every $n > N$,

$$\left| 1 + \frac{1}{n} - L \right| < \epsilon$$

regardless of the value (positive) of ϵ.

Suppose that we let

$$\epsilon = 0.001$$

Then

$$\left| 1 + \frac{1}{n} - L \right| < 0.001 \qquad n > N$$

or

$$-0.001 < 1 + \frac{1}{n} - L < 0.001$$

$$L - 0.001 - 1 < \frac{1}{n} < L + 0.001 - 1$$

$$L - 1.001 < \frac{1}{n} < L - 0.999$$

Let us try $L = 1$.

$$1 - 1.001 < \frac{1}{n} < 1 - 0.999 \qquad n > N$$

$$-0.001 < \frac{1}{n} < 0.001$$

$$n > 1,000$$

By taking $n > N = 1,000$, this inequality will hold.

By placing $L = 1$ in $|1 + 1/n - L| < \epsilon$, we get $|1/n| < \epsilon$, or $n > 1/\epsilon$, which can be satisfied no matter what $\epsilon > 0$ is.

Notice that if $L = 2$

$$\left| 1 + \frac{1}{n} - 2 \right| = \left| -1 + \frac{1}{n} \right| = \left| \frac{1 - n}{n} \right|$$

and if $\epsilon = \frac{1}{4}$, then, for $n > 1$, the inequality is not satisfied.   Therefore, 2 cannot be the limit.

Notice that the ϵ decides what the n is to be.   If two distinct ϵ's are taken, then in general the n's determined will differ.   What n is depends on what ϵ is chosen.   In any event

$$\lim_{n \to \infty} \left\{ 1 + \frac{1}{n} \right\} = 1$$

PROBLEM SET 9.2

1. Find the limit, if it exists, of the sequence:
   a. $S = \{1,1,1,1, \ldots, 1, \ldots\}$
   b. $S = \{1, -1, 1, -1, 1, -1, \ldots\}$ $\qquad f = \begin{cases} a_n = 1, \text{ if } n \text{ is odd} \\ a_n = -1, \text{ if } n \text{ is even} \end{cases}$
   c. $\{1, 3, 5, 7, \ldots, 2n - 1, \ldots\}$
   d. $S = \{a_n | a_n = 2 - 1/2^{n-1}\}$
   e. $S = \{1,2,1,2,1,2, \ldots\}$
   f. $S = \{1, \frac{1}{2}, \frac{1}{4}, \ldots, 1/2^{n-1}, \ldots\}$
   g. $S = \{a_n | a_n = 1/(1 + 0.05)^n\}$
   h. $S = \{a_n | a_n = (1 + 0.05)^n\}$

2. A sequence which has a limit is said to be *convergent*.   If no limit exists, the sequence is said to be *nonconvergent*.   Which of the sequences in Prob. 1 are convergent?

3. Prove: If C is a constant, then $\lim_{n \to \infty} C = C$.   (*Hint:* Use the definition and the fact that $C - C = 0 < \epsilon$.)

4. Prove: If we have a sequence with general term ka_n (k a constant), then

$$\lim_{n \to \infty} ka_n = k \lim_{n \to \infty} a_n$$

(Assume that $\lim_{n \to \infty} a_n$ exists.)

5.   If $a_n + b_n$ is the nth term of a sequence, prove that

$$\lim_{n \to \infty} (a_n + b_n) = \lim_{n \to \infty} a_n + \lim_{n \to \infty} b_n$$

(Assume that $\lim_{n \to \infty} a_n$, $\lim_{n \to \infty} b_n$ exist.)

6.   Prove that

$$\lim_{n \to \infty} \frac{1}{C^n} = 0 \qquad C > 1$$

9.6 THE SUMMATION SYMBOL

We now study a symbol which we have used before and which will aid in shortening some operations.   Let us suppose that we have a sequence

$$S = \{a_1, a_2, \ldots, a_n, \ldots\}$$

and wish to denote the sum of n elements of the sequence.   We can write

$$S_n = a_1 + a_2 + a_3 + \cdots + a_n$$

We can abbreviate this expression by writing

$$S_n = \sum_{i=1}^{n} a_i$$

Example 9.17.   Given the sequence

$$S = \{1, 2, 3, 4, \ldots, n, \ldots\}$$

denote the sum of the first 50 elements.

Solution

$$S_{50} = \sum_{i=1}^{50} i = 1 + 2 + 3 + \cdots + 49 + 50$$

Example 9.18.   Given the sequence

$$S = \{x \mid x = (5)(3)^n\}$$

denote the sum of the first five elements.

Solution

$$S_5 = \sum_{i=1}^{5} [(5)(3^i)] = 5 \cdot 3^1 + 5 \cdot 3^2 + 5 \cdot 3^3 + 5 \cdot 3^4 + 5 \cdot 3^5$$

Example 9.19.   Given the sequence

$$\left\{a_n \middle| a_n = \left(1 + \frac{1}{n}\right)^n\right\}$$

denote the sum of the first four elements.

Solution

$$S_4 = \sum_{i=1}^{4} \left(1 + \frac{1}{i}\right)^i = \left(1 + \frac{1}{1}\right)^1 + \left(1 + \frac{1}{2}\right)^2 + \left(1 + \frac{1}{3}\right)^3 + \left(1 + \frac{1}{4}\right)^4$$

Example 9.20.   The sum of elements 5 through 9 in the sequence

$$\{a_n | a_n = n\}$$

is

$$\sum_{i=5}^{9} i = 5 + 6 + 7 + 8 + 9$$

We prove the following theorem.

Theorem 9.21

$$\sum_{i=1}^{n} (a_i + b_i) = \sum_{i=1}^{n} a_i + \sum_{i=1}^{n} b_i$$

Proof

$$\sum_{i=1}^{n} (a_i + b_i) = (a_1 + b_1) + (a_2 + b_2) + \cdots + (a_n + b_n)$$

$$= (a_1 + a_2 + \cdots + a_n) + (b_1 + b_2 + \cdots + b_n) \qquad \text{Why?}$$

$$= \sum_{i=1}^{n} a_i + \sum_{i=1}^{n} b_i$$

Example 9.22

$$\sum_{i=1}^{4} \left(i + \frac{1}{i}\right) = \sum_{i=1}^{4} i + \sum_{i=1}^{4} \frac{1}{i}$$

That is,

$$(1 + \tfrac{1}{1}) + (2 + \tfrac{1}{2}) + (3 + \tfrac{1}{3}) + (4 + \tfrac{1}{4}) = (1 + 2 + 3 + 4)$$
$$+ (1 + \tfrac{1}{2} + \tfrac{1}{3} + \tfrac{1}{4}) = 10 + 2\tfrac{1}{12} = 12\tfrac{1}{12}$$

Theorem 9.23

$$\sum_{i=1}^{n} ca_i = c \sum_{i=1}^{n} a_i$$

where c is a constant.

TABLE 9.1

	Trucks	Sedans	Wagons	Compacts	Σ
A	2	5	3	5	15
B	1	10	2	5	18

$\boxed{33}$

Σ of all A's sales $= 15$

Σ of all B's sales $= 18$

Σ of all sales $= \Sigma$ of A's $+ \Sigma$ of B's $= 15 + 18 = 33$

Proof.   The proof is left as an exercise.

Definition 9.24

$$\sum_{i=1}^{n} c = nc$$

Example 9.25

$$\sum_{i=1}^{4} 5 = (4) \times (5) = 20$$

Theorem 9.26

$$\sum_{i=1}^{n} a_i = \sum_{i=1}^{m} a_i + \sum_{i=m+1}^{n} a_i \qquad m < n$$

Proof

$$\sum_{i=1}^{n} a_i = a_1 + a_2 + \cdots + a_{m-1} + a_m + a_{m+1} + \cdots + a_n$$

$$= (a_1 + a_2 + \cdots + a_{m-1} + a_m) + (a_{m+1} + \cdots + a_n)$$

$$= \sum_{i=1}^{m} a_i + \sum_{i=m+1}^{n} a_i$$

Example 9.27.   Table 9.1 shows the number of sales of trucks, sedans, station wagons, and compact cars sold by salesmen A and B.

If A earned \$100 for each sedan sold, then the total A earned on the sedans is

$$\sum_{1}^{5} 100 = (5)(100) = 500$$

9.7 PARTIAL SUMS

We often need to find the sum of some finite number of terms of a given sequence.   If $S = \{a_1, a_2, \ldots, a_n, \ldots\}$ is any sequence, then the sum of n terms, denoted by S_n or $\sum\limits_{i=1}^{n} a_i$, will be called a *partial sum* of the sequence. Evidently we can have a sequence of partial sums of a sequence.

Example 9.28.   Given the arithmetic sequence $S = \{2,4,6,8,10, \ldots\}$, then $S_3 = 2 + 4 + 6$, or $\sum\limits_{i=1}^{n} 2i$ is a partial sum of S.

$$S_1 = 2 \qquad\qquad S_3 = 2 + 4 + 6$$
$$S_2 = 2 + 4 \qquad\quad S_4 = 2 + 4 + 6 + 8 \qquad \text{etc.}$$

form a sequence

$$S' = \{S_1,S_2,S_3, \ldots ,S_n, \ldots\}$$

Evidently $S_n = S_{n-1} + a_n$

9.8 ARITHMETIC PROGRESSION

We define an arithmetic progression as a sequence of partial sums of an arithmetic sequence, and we prove the following theorem.

Theorem 9.29

If S' is an arithmetic progression, then the nth term is

$$S_n = \frac{n}{2}(a_1 + a_n)$$

Proof.   Since $a_n = a_1 + (n-1)d$, we can write

$$S_n = a_1 + (a_1 + d) + (a_1 + 2d) + \cdots + [a_1 + (n-1)d] \quad (9.1)$$

Taking the sum in reverse order (that is, $a_n + a_{n-1} + \cdots + a_1$), and in terms of a_n, we get

$$S_n = a_n + (a_n - d) + (a_n - 2d) + \cdots + [a_n - (n-1)d] \quad (9.2)$$

If we add (9.1) and (9.2), we get

$$2S_n = n(a_1 + a_n)$$

since all the d's cancel out.   Thus

$$S_n = \frac{n}{2}(a_1 + a_n) = \frac{n}{2}\{a_1 + [a_1 + (n-1)d]\} = \frac{n}{2}[2a_1 + (n-1)d]$$

Example 9.30.   The last term of an arithmetic sequence of 10 terms is 50, and the difference is 3.   Find the first 4 terms of the arithmetic sequence and the tenth term of the arithmetic progression.

$$a_n = a_1 + (n-1)d$$
$$50 = a_1 + (9)(3) = a_1 + 27$$
$$a_1 = 50 - 27 = 23 \qquad a_2 = 23 + 3 = 26$$
$$a_3 = 26 + 3 = 29 \qquad a_4 = 29 + 3 = 32 \qquad \text{etc.}$$
$$S_{10} = \tfrac{10}{2}(23 + 50) = (5)(73) = 365$$

Example 9.31. Find the first three elements of the sequence of partial sums of the progression in Example 9.30.

$$S_1 = 23$$
$$S_2 = 23 + 26 = 49$$
$$S_3 = \tfrac{3}{2}(23 + 29) = (3)(26) = 78 = 23 + 26 + 29$$
$$S' = \{23,49,78\}$$

Example 9.32. A firm follows a policy of increasing each employee's salary by $300 per year. Mr. X starts work at a salary of $6,000. How much money will he have received by the end of 16 years?

Solution. At the end of the first year his income for the first year is $a_1 = 6,000$; at the end of the second year his income for the second year is $a_2 = 6,000 + (300)(1) = 6,300$. At the end of the sixteenth year his income for the sixteenth year will be $a_{16} = 6,000 + (300)(15) = 10,500$. His total income over the 16 years is therefore

$$S_n = \frac{n}{2}(a_1 + a_n) = (8)(16,500) = \$132,000$$

or $\qquad S_n = \frac{n}{2}[2a_1 + (n-1)d] = 8(12,000 + 4,500) = \$132,000$

Example 9.33. A company's sales were $20,000 seven years ago and are $50,000 today. If sales increased by the same amount each year, what was this amount and what were total sales over this period?

Solution

$$a_1 = 20,000 \qquad a_8 = 50,000 \qquad n = 8$$

so that $\qquad S_8 = \frac{n}{2}(a_1 + a_8) = (4)(70,000) = 280,000$

We can determine the amount of increase from

$$S_8 = \frac{n}{2}[2a_1 + (n-1)d]$$
$$280,000 = 4(40,000 + 7d) = 160,000 + 28d$$
$$d = \frac{120,000}{28} = 4,285\frac{5}{7}$$

9.9 GEOMETRIC PROGRESSION

Theorem 9.34

We define a geometric progression as a sequence of partial sums of a geometric sequence. If S' is a geometric progression, then the nth term is

$$S_n = \frac{a_1 - a_1 r^n}{1 - r} = \frac{a_1(1 - r^n)}{1 - r} \qquad (9.3)$$

Proof

$$S_n = a_1 + a_1 r + a_1 r^2 + \cdots + a_1 r^{n-1}$$
$$r S_n = a_1 r + a_1 r^2 + a_1 r^3 + \cdots + a_1 r^n$$
$$S_n - r S_n = (1 - r) S_n = a_1 - a_1 r^n$$

Therefore
$$S_n = \frac{a_1 - a_1 r^n}{1 - r}$$

Example 9.35. The last term of a geometric sequence of five terms is 100, and the ratio is 2. Find the first four terms. Find the sum of the progression formed of these four terms.

Solution

$$a_n = a_1 r^{n-1}$$
$$100 = a_1 (2)^4$$
$$a_1 = \frac{100}{2^4} = \frac{25}{4}$$
$$a_2 = \left(\tfrac{25}{4}\right)(2) = \tfrac{25}{2} \qquad a_3 = \left(\tfrac{25}{4}\right)(2^2) = 25$$
$$a_4 = (25)(2) = 50$$
$$S_4 = \frac{\tfrac{25}{4} - \tfrac{25}{4} \cdot 2^4}{1 - 2}$$
$$= \frac{\tfrac{25}{4}(1 - 16)}{-1} = \frac{\tfrac{25}{4} \cdot (-15)}{-1}$$
$$= \frac{(25)(15)}{4} = 93\tfrac{3}{4}$$

Example 9.36. Calculate the first four elements of the sequence of partial sums of the progression in Example 9.35.

Solution

$$S_1 = \tfrac{25}{4}$$
$$S_2 = \tfrac{25}{4} + \tfrac{25}{2} = \tfrac{25}{4} + \tfrac{50}{4} = \tfrac{75}{4}$$
$$S_3 = \tfrac{75}{4} + 25 = \tfrac{75}{4} + \tfrac{100}{4} = \tfrac{175}{4}$$
$$S_4 = \tfrac{175}{4} + 50 = \tfrac{175}{4} + \tfrac{200}{4} = \tfrac{375}{4}$$

By formula (9.3)

$$S_4 = \frac{\frac{25}{4} - \left(\frac{25}{4}\right)(2^4)}{1 - 2} = \frac{\frac{25}{4} - \frac{400}{4}}{-1} = \frac{375}{4}$$

$$S' = \left\{\frac{25}{4}, \frac{75}{4}, \frac{175}{4}, \frac{375}{4}\right\}$$

Theorem 9.37

If S' is a geometric progression with $0 < r < 1$, then

$$\lim_{n \to \infty} S_n = \frac{a_1}{1 - r}$$

Proof

$$\frac{a_1 - a_1 r^n}{1 - r} = \frac{a_1}{1 - r} - \frac{a_1 r^n}{1 - r}$$

We use the fact that

$$\lim_{n \to \infty} \frac{a_1 - a_1 r^n}{1 - r} = \lim_{n \to \infty} \frac{a_1}{1 - r} - \lim_{n \to \infty} \frac{a_1 r^n}{1 - r} \qquad \text{(Prob. 5, Problem Set 9.2)}$$

Since $a_1/(1 - r)$ does not involve n, we can say that

$$\lim_{n \to \infty} \frac{a_1}{1 - r} = \frac{a_1}{1 - r} \qquad \text{(Prob. 3, Problem Set 9.2)}$$

For $a_1 r^n/(1 - r)$, we argue as follows:

1. If $r > 1$, r^n increases indefinitely and $\lim_{n \to \infty} a_1 r^n/(1 - r)$ would not exist. There is no limit to the expression $(a_1 - a_1 r^n)/(1 - r)$, and the progression of partial sums is nonconvergent.

2. If $0 < r < 1$, let us take $r = 1/c$, $c > 1$. Then

$$\frac{a_1 r^n}{1 - r} = \frac{a_1(1/c^n)}{1 - 1/c} = \frac{a_1/c^n}{(c - 1)/c}$$

$$= \frac{a_1}{c^n} \cdot \frac{c}{c - 1} = \frac{a_1}{c^{n-1}} \cdot \frac{1}{c - 1} = \frac{1}{c^{n-1}} \cdot \frac{a_1}{c - 1}$$

We now use

$$\lim_{n \to \infty} k \frac{1}{c^{n-1}} = k \lim_{n \to \infty} \frac{1}{c^{n-1}}$$

where $\qquad k = \frac{a_1}{c - 1} \qquad$ (Prob. 4, Problem Set 9.2)

Evidently

$$\lim_{n \to \infty} \frac{1}{c^{n-1}} = 0 \qquad \text{since } c \text{ is a constant} > 1 \qquad \text{(Prob. 6, Problem Set 9.2)}$$

Hence $\qquad \qquad \displaystyle \lim_{n \to \infty} \frac{a_1 - a_1 r^n}{1 - r} = \frac{a_1}{1 - r}$

The sequence of partial sums S_n of a geometric progression with $0 < r < 1$ converges as n increases indefinitely.

Example 9.38.   Find $\lim\limits_{n \to \infty} S_n$ for

$$S = \left\{ 1, \frac{1}{2}, \frac{1}{2^2}, \frac{1}{2^3}, \cdots, \frac{1}{2^n}, \cdots \right\}$$

Solution.   Since $0 < r < 1$,

$$\lim_{n \to \infty} S_n = \frac{a_1}{1 - r} = \frac{1}{1 - \frac{1}{2}} = \frac{1}{\frac{1}{2}} = 2$$

Example 9.39.   In Example 8.9, by how much will total spending throughout the economy have increased by the end of n $(n \to \infty)$ stages of spending?

Solution.   We want the sum of a geometric progression where $a_1 = 100$, $r = 0.8$, and $n \to \infty$.   Employing Theorem 9.37, we have

$$S_n = \frac{100}{0.2} = (100) \times (5) = 500$$

Thus an initial increment of \$100 in spending has resulted in a total change in spending of \$500; that is, the initial purchase of \$100 of goods and/or services has resulted in the purchase of \$500 of goods and services.

Note that Theorem 9.34 can be employed to determine the total change in spending by the end of any n $(n = 1, 2, \ldots)$ periods.

PROBLEM SET 9.3

1. Find:

  a. $\displaystyle\sum_{i=1}^{3} i$

  b. $\displaystyle\sum_{i=3}^{5} i$

  c. $\displaystyle\sum_{2}^{5} (i^2 + 1)$

  d. $\displaystyle\sum_{1}^{3} 2$

  e. $\displaystyle\sum_{1}^{3} 2i + \sum_{0}^{3} (i - 2)$

2. Show:

a. $\sum_{i=0}^{n} i = \sum_{i=1}^{n} i$

b. $\sum_{i=1}^{n} 2^i \neq \sum_{i=0}^{n} 2^i$

c. $\sum_{i=1}^{n} (ca_i + cb_i) = c \sum_{i=1}^{n} a_i + c \sum_{i=1}^{n} b_i$

3. Write S_1, S_2, S_3 for the sequence $S = \{x | x = (1 + 1/n)^n\}$.
4. Find S_n for $n = 1, 2, 3$ for each of the sequences in Prob. 1, Problem Set 9.2.
5. Using Theorem 9.37, find $\lim_{n \to \infty} S_n$ of (a) the sequence

$$S = \{0.3, 0.03, 0.003, \ldots\}$$

What is r? (b) The sequence $\{0.6, 0.06, 0.006, 0.0006, \ldots\}$.

6. If a sum of \$1 is invested at a rate of 0.03 per year compounded annually, the amount a_n at the end of n years is $a_n = (1 + 0.03)^n$. Find $\sum_{n=1}^{3} (1 + 0.03)^n$.

Find S_n for $n = 4$.

7. Given that S is an arithmetic sequence. Suppose that the fifth term is 10 and the tenth is 50. Find the difference, and write the partial sums S_n for $n = 1, 2, 3$. Also insert the sixth, seventh, and eighth terms. (*Hint:* Treat the fifth term as the first, the tenth term as the sixth in a new sequence.)

8. Suppose that S in Prob. 7 were a geometric sequence. Find r and S_n for $n = 1, 2, 3$.

9. A sequence is defined by the function $f(n) = 2 - 3n$. Write the first five terms in the sequence. Find the sum of the first n term of the sequence. (*Hint:*

$S_n = \sum_{i=1}^{n} 2 - 3i$, and use Theorem 9.21.)

10. Given $S = \{x | x = 5 + (n - 1)3\}$, find the smallest value of n such that $S_n > 100$.

11. Company Z's sales increased by \$500 a year over the past 10 years, starting at \$10,000 in the first year. What were total sales over this period? What were sales in the tenth year?

12. In Prob. 6 of Problem Set 9.1, what is the total change in spending throughout the economy by the end of $n = 6$ and $n \to \infty$ periods?

13. What would be the solution to the preceding problem if the marginal propensity to consume were 0.7?

9.10 PARTIAL SUMS OF SOME ADDITIONAL SEQUENCES

Theorem 9.40

$$\sum_{i=1}^{n} i = \frac{n + n^2}{2} = \frac{n(1 + n)}{2}$$

Proof

$$\sum_{n=1}^{n} i = 1 + 2 + 3 + \cdots + n$$

Since the difference between any two terms is 1, this is an arithmetic progression. Hence

$$S_n = \frac{n(1+n)}{2} = \frac{n+n^2}{2}$$

We prove this in another way, chiefly to become acquainted with a method. We note that.

$$\sum_{i=1}^{n} [i^2 - (i-1)^2] = \sum_{i=1}^{n} i^2 - \sum_{i=1}^{n} i^2 + 2\sum_{i=1}^{n} i - \sum_{i=1}^{n} 1$$

$$= 2\sum_{i=1}^{n} i - n$$

Let us write out the sum of the left-hand side, replacing i by 1, 2, . . . , n.

$$\sum_{i=1}^{n} [i^2 - (i-1)^2] = (1^2 - 0^2) + (2^2 - 1^2) + (3^2 - 2^2) + \cdots$$

$$+ [(n-1)^2 - (n-2)^2] + [n^2 - (n-1)^2]$$

By collecting terms we get

$$\sum_{i=1}^{n} [i^2 - (i-1)^2] = n^2$$

Therefore

$$2\sum_{i=1}^{n} i - n = n^2$$

or

$$\sum_{i=1}^{n} i = \frac{n^2 + n}{2}$$

Example 9.41.   Find

$$\sum_{i=1}^{n} (i+3)$$

Solution

$$\sum_{i=1}^{n} (i+3) = \sum_{i=1}^{n} i + \sum_{i=1}^{n} 3 = \frac{n^2 + n}{2} + 3n = \frac{n^2 + 7n}{2}$$

Theorem 9.42

$$\sum_{i=1}^{n} (2i - 1) = n^2$$

Proof. This theorem tells us that the sum of the first n odd numbers ($2i - 1$ is odd) is the square of the number of terms.

$$\sum_{i=1}^{n} (2i - 1) = \sum_{i=1}^{n} 2i - \sum_{i=1}^{n} 1 = 2 \sum_{i=1}^{n} i - n = (n^2 + n) - n = n^2$$

Example 9.43. Find

$$\sum_{i=1}^{5} (2i - 1)$$

Solution. $n = 5$. Therefore

$$\sum_{i=1}^{5} (2i - 1) = 25$$

PROBLEM SET 9.4

1. Find $\sum_{i=1}^{n} (2i + 1)$. Since $2i - 1$ and $2i + 1$ are both expressions for odd numbers, why the difference in the resultant formulas?

2. Find $\sum_{i=1}^{n} 2i$.

3. Prove that $S = \{x | x = 2n - 1\}$ and $T = \{x | x = 2n + 1\}$ are both arithmetic progressions, and obtain the sums for n terms by the formula for the sum of n terms of an arithmetic progression.

4. Using the expression

$$i^3 - (i - 1)^3$$

find

$$\sum_{i=1}^{n} i^2$$

9.11 CAPITAL THEORY AND INVESTMENT MANAGEMENT

In Prob. 7 of Problem Set 9.1 we showed that an initial deposit of P dollars which receives compound interest at the rate i for n periods will be worth $P(1 + i)^n$ by the end of n periods. We shall use this result to derive a theorem which is of fundamental importance in the field of capital theory and investment management.

Theorem 9.44

If interest is compounded each period at the rate i, then the value (denoted by $S_{\overline{n}|i}$) at the end of n equal periods of time, of a *sum* of n equal payments, each of which is received at the end of a period, is

$$S_{\overline{n}|i} = P\left[\frac{(1+i)^n - 1}{i}\right]$$

where P denotes the payment received at the end of each period.

Proof. The payment received at the end of the first period will draw interest only for $n - 1$ periods of time. Therefore, if P is the amount received at the end of the first period, it will be worth

$v_1 = P(1 + i)^{n-1}$ at the end of n periods. The payment P received at the end of the second period will draw interest for $n - 2$ periods; thus at the end of the n periods it will be worth

$v_2 = P(1 + i)^{n-2}$. This can be continued so that the payment P received at the end of the nth period will be worth

$$v_n = P(1 + i)^{n-n}$$

Now $\qquad S_{\overline{n}|i} = \sum_{j=1}^{n} v_j = \sum_{j=1}^{n} P(1 + i)^{n-j} = P \sum_{j=1}^{n} (1 + i)^{n-j}$

Since $\qquad\qquad\qquad \sum_{j=1}^{n} (1 + i)^{n-j}$

is a geometric progression, with $a_1 = 1$ and $r = 1 + i$,

$$S_{\overline{n}|i} = \frac{P[1 - (1 + i)^n]}{1 - (1 + i)} = \frac{P[1 - (1 + i)^n]}{-i} = \frac{P[(1 + i)^n - 1]}{i}$$

Theorem 9.44 is essential in the development of other theorems which are employed to determine whether a given investment opportunity should be undertaken. We shall state and prove one of these "capital-budgeting" criteria.

Example 9.45. Assume that a firm is able to invest as much money as it chooses at a compound interest rate i. A new investment opportunity now appears which will require an initial cash outlay of I dollars, which will yield P dollars of profit at the end of each of n periods, and which will be completely used up (worthless) at the end of n periods. Should the firm undertake this investment?

Solution. If the I dollars were not committed to this investment, they could be earning the compound interest rate i for n periods, so that at the end of n periods the firm would have $I(1 + i)^n$ dollars. By committing I dollars now to this investment, the firm foregoes the $I(1 + i)^n$ dollars so that the cost (denoted by $C_{\overline{n}|i}$) to the firm of the investment is $C_{\overline{n}|i} = I(1 + i)^n$ dollars. However, by undertaking this investment, the firm will receive P dollars at the end of each of n periods, so that by the end of n periods it will have $S_{\overline{n}|i} = P[(1 + i)^n - 1]/i$ dollars. On the assumption that the risks are identical in either commitment of funds, the firm should choose the new investment if $S_{\overline{n}|i} > C_{\overline{n}|i}$.

We can develop a criterion which the firm can employ to determine immediately whether this, or any other investment opportunity, should be undertaken. We need a definition and a theorem.

Definition 9.46. The *capital-recovery period* $\bar{n}$ is the value of n such that $S_{\overline{n}|i} = C_{\overline{n}|i}$, for a given interest rate i.

Theorem 9.47

The capital-recovery period is given by

$$\bar{n} = \frac{\log [P/(P - Ii)]}{\log (1 + i)}$$

Proof. Set $S_{\overline{n}|i} = C_{\overline{n}|i}$ (i fixed), and solve for n, denoting this value by $\bar{n}$.

$$S_{\overline{n}|i} = C_{\overline{n}|i}$$
$$\frac{P[(1 + i)^{\bar{n}} - 1]}{i} = I(1 + i)^{\bar{n}}$$
$$P(1 + i)^{\bar{n}} - P = iI(1 + i)^{\bar{n}} \qquad (9.4)$$
$$(1 + i)^{\bar{n}}(P - iI) = P$$
$$(1 + i)^{\bar{n}} = \frac{P}{P - iI}$$

Using logarithms,

$$\bar{n} \log (1 + i) = \log \frac{P}{P - iI}$$
$$\bar{n} = \frac{\log [P/(P - iI)]}{\log (1 + i)}$$

$S_{\overline{n}|i}$ and $C_{\overline{n}|i}$ are both monotonically increasing, since each succeeding term must be greater than its predecessor. (Why?) Therefore the two progressions increase without limit as n increases without limit.

If, as in the typical case, $I > P$, at the end of the first period receipts will be less than costs, since

$$S_{\overline{1}|i} = \frac{P[(1 + i)^1 - 1]}{i} = P < C_{\overline{1}|i} = I(1 + i)^1 = I + iI$$

This means that $S_{\overline{n}|i}$ increases faster than $C_{\overline{n}|i}$ as n increases, since when $n = \bar{n}$, $S_{\overline{n}|i} = C_{\overline{n}|i}$. So if n, the number of periods over which payments will be made, is greater than $\bar{n}$, the capital-recovery period, it is advisable to make the investment which is being considered.

PROBLEM SET 9.5

1. If we define the minimum periodic receipt $\bar{P}$ as the value of P for which $S_{\overline{n}|i} = C_{\overline{n}|i}$, show that

$$\bar{P} = \frac{iI(1 + i)^n}{(1 + i)^n - 1}$$

where n is the number of periods over which equal payments will be received. State a capital-budgeting criterion based on $\bar{P}$.

2. If we define the rate of return $\bar{i}$ as the value of i for which $S_{\overline{n}|i} = C_{\overline{n}|i}$, show that

$$\bar{i} = \frac{P}{I} - \frac{P}{I} \frac{1}{(1 + \bar{i})^n} \rightarrow \frac{P}{I} \qquad \text{as } n \rightarrow \infty$$

where P is the equal periodic receipt from the investment and n is the number of periods over which payments will be received. State a capital-budgeting criterion based on $\bar{i}$.

3. In Prob. 8 of Problem Set 9.1, we examined the concept of present value. Use the method of proof of Theorem 9.44 to show that, if interest is compounded each period at the rate i, then the present value of a sum of n equal payments, each of which is received at the end of a period, is given by

$$Q_{\overline{n}|i} = P \frac{1 - (1 + i)^{-n}}{i}$$

State a capital-budgeting criterion based on $Q_{\overline{n}|i}$. (*Hint:* What if $Q_{\overline{n}|i} > I$?)

4. A firm can invest as much money as it chooses at a compound rate of interest $i = 0.10$ per year. An investment opportunity appears which will (*a*) require an initial cash outlay of $I = \$10,000$; (*b*) yield a profit of \$3,100 at the end of each year for 5 years; (*c*) be worthless at the end of 5 years. Decide whether or not the firm should undertake the investment, employing each of the criteria developed in this section and in Probs. 1 to 3.

5. When a person takes out a mortgage on a house, he has borrowed a sum of money Z which he agrees to repay in $n = n'$ equal installments of P dollars each. Each installment is supposed to cover interest i on the principal outstanding for that period, plus a certain amount of principal reduction. What should the periodic payment P be? (*Hint:* The present value of each payment is $V_n(1 + i)^{-n}$ dollars, since the money is being lent at the rate i. The present value of the sum of payments over $n = n'$ periods is given by $Q_{\overline{n'}|i} = P\{[1 - (1 + i)^{-n'}]/i\}$ (see Prob. 3). But by the end of $n = n'$ periods $Q_{\overline{n'}|i}$ must equal Z, the amount of the original loan.)

9.12 PRODUCT FAILURE: A PROBABILITY APPLICATION OF LIMITS AND THE EXPONENTIAL FUNCTION[1]

In the preceding chapter, we introduced the constant $e \cong 2.71828$ (the napierian base). The study of this constant involves techniques beyond the scope of the present volume. However, we shall assume that e can be calculated from the following expression:

$$\lim_{n \to \infty} \left(1 + \frac{1}{n}\right)^n = e$$

We shall now provide an illustration of the way in which the exponential function $y = e^{-cx}$ can be used in a production problem.

A firm manufactures electronic parts which are used in the assembly of missiles. In the last k (k large) parts studied, the number of the time unit (a time unit could be 1 hour, 10 minutes, 1 minute, 1 second, etc.) in which the first, second, . . . , kth part failed is denoted by x_1, x_2, . . . , x_k. Table 9.2 summarizes these data, the symbols S denoting the fact that the part was functioning throughout the stated time unit and F that it failed during that time unit. For example, we see that the first part was functioning when examined at the end of each of the first three time units but not when examined at the end of the fourth time unit; it failed, therefore, sometime during the fourth time unit, so that $x_1 = 4$.

The physical properties of each part are such that the firm believes that the probability of a part failing during any one time unit is completely independent of the number of time units during which it has already been

[1] This section may be omitted on first reading.

TABLE 9.2

Part i	Time unit							Number of time unit in which part failed, x_i
	1	2	3	4	5	6	· · ·	
1	S	S	S	F				4
2	S	S	S	S	S	F		6
3	S	S	F					3
4	S	S	S	S	S	S	· · ·	· · ·
5	S	S	F					3
6	S	S	S	S	S	S	· · ·	· · ·
· · ·	· · ·	· · ·	· · ·	· · ·	· · ·	· · ·	· · ·	· · ·
k	·	·	·	·	·	·	· · ·	· · ·

successfully operating; i.e., the probability of failure during the yth time unit is the same as that during the $(y + j)$th $(j = \ldots, -2, -1, 0, 1, 2, \ldots)$ time unit. Using Definition 4.6, we can therefore say that the probability $P(E)$ of the event "a failure" occurring during any specified (e.g., the second, fourteenth, etc.) time unit is the ratio of the number of times k the event occurred to the number of opportunities $q = \sum\limits_{i=1}^{k} x_i$ it had to occur; that is, $P(E) = k/q$ (the time unit is defined so that q is large and greater than the number of failures k). Alternatively, we could define $P(E)$ as the ratio of the total number of F's in Table 9.2 to the total number of F's and S's in Table 9.2. (Why?)

If the reader finds the above probability calculation difficult to justify, he can think of the following analogous situation: Assume that a single unbiased die is tossed repeatedly until a 6 is obtained. Each toss corresponds to the examination of a single part during a single time unit, the examination of the given part being continued until an F is obtained. If a 6 turns up, we denote this outcome by A, and if some other number comes up, we denote this by B. If, in a sequence of n tosses we obtain n B's, this in no way affects the probability of our obtaining an A on the $(n + 1)$st toss; similarly, if in a sequence of n time units we have obtained n S's, this in no way affects the probability of our obtaining an F in the $(n + 1)$st time unit (since we are assuming independence). Each sequence of n B's and 1 A corresponds to the life pattern of a single part in Table 9.2. Finally, if we wanted to determine the probability of obtaining a 6 on any single toss (or the probability of a failure in any one time unit), we could closely approximate it, if the number of sequences of n B's and 1 A (or the number of parts examined) were large, by taking the ratio of the number of B's (or F's) to the total number of B's and A's (or F's and S's). In the die example, we would expect this ratio to be 1:6.

Example 9.48. The operating life of the missile in which these parts are to be used is x time units. What is the probability that a part will function for the full life (that is, x time units) of the missile?

Solution. We have the probability $P(E) = k/q$ that a part will fail during a single time unit. However, a part could fail at the beginning or end or in the middle of the time unit. We can more closely delimit the precise time in which the part fails if we define a new time unit equal to $1/n$ $(n = 1, 2, \ldots, \infty)$ of the original time unit. The probability of a failure during any one of these new (smaller) time units will be $1/n$ of what it was during the original time unit, that is, $(1/n)(k/q)$. If we let $\theta = q/k$ and $\Delta x = 1/n$, the probability of failure during a time unit equal to $1/n$ of the original time unit is $(1/\theta) \, \Delta x$.

The interval from 0 to x original time units has thus been divided into new time units, each of which is $1/n$ of the original time unit, so that the number of time units associated with the operating life of the missile has been increased by a factor of n; that is, it is now nx time units.

The probability of *no* failure in any one of these new time units is $1 - (1/\theta)\,\Delta x$. There will be no failure during the first nx *new* time units (that is, x original time units) if there is no failure during each of these nx time units. If the probability of failure is independent from time period to time period, the probability (Definition 4.26) is

$$\left(1 - \frac{1}{\theta}\Delta x\right)^{nx} = \left(1 - \frac{1}{\theta}\Delta x\right)^{x/\Delta x} = \left[\left(1 - \frac{\Delta x}{\theta}\right)^{-(\theta/\Delta x)}\right]^{-(x/\theta)} \quad (9.5)$$

Now let $\Delta x \to 0$ (that is, $\Delta x = 1/n \to 0$ as $n \to \infty$). The expression we have still indicates the probability of the part lasting x original time units, but the number of subintervals in the 0-x original time interval increases (each subinterval becoming smaller) and the probability of failure within them decreases. We can show that the expression inside the brackets in (9.5) approaches e.

Let $m = \theta/\Delta x$; then the expression inside the brackets in (9.5) becomes

$$\left(1 - \frac{\Delta x}{\theta}\right)^{-(\theta/\Delta x)} = \left(1 - \frac{1}{m}\right)^{-m} = \left(1 + \frac{1}{-m}\right)^{-m} = \left(\frac{-m+1}{-m}\right)^{-m}$$

$$= \left(\frac{m-1}{m}\right)^{-m} = \frac{1}{[(m-1)/m]^m}$$

$$= \frac{1}{(m-1)^m/m^m} = \frac{m^m}{(m-1)^m} \quad (9.6)$$

Assign any number > 1 to m in (9.6), and note that the next number in the sequence as m increases is

$$\left(\frac{m+1}{m}\right)^{m+1}$$

That is, if we let $f(m) = m^m/(m-1)^m$, then

$$f(m+1) = \frac{(m+1)^{m+1}}{[(m+1)-1]^{m+1}} = \frac{(m+1)^{m+1}}{m^{m+1}} = \left(\frac{m+1}{m}\right)^{m+1}$$

The next number in the sequence can therefore be obtained from

$$\left(\frac{m+1}{m}\right)^{m+1} = \left(1 + \frac{1}{m}\right)^{m+1} = \left(1 + \frac{1}{m}\right)^m\left(1 + \frac{1}{m}\right) \quad (9.7)$$

As $n \to \infty$, $\Delta x \to 0$, $m = \theta/\Delta x \to \infty$, and (9.7) equals e so that (9.5) becomes

$$\left(1 - \frac{1}{\theta}\Delta x\right)^{nx} = e^{-(x/\theta)}$$

That is, the probability $P(x)$ that the part will function successfully for x original time units is $P(x) = e^{-(x/\theta)}$.

PROBLEM SET 9.6

1. Table 9.3 shows the distribution of failure time for a part similar to the one described above.   If the missile's operating time is 3 hours, what is the probability that a missile failure will not be caused by a part failure?

2. Solve the above problem, assuming that the missile's operating time is 6 hours.

3. What is the probability, in general, of a part lasting x *or more* time units? *Hint:* Let f denote the probability that a part will fail during a single time unit and s the probability that it will not fail.   Then a part will last x or more time units if it does not fail until the $(x + 1)$st, or the $(x + 2)$d, . . . time unit.   But this probability is $s^x f + s^{x+1} f + \cdots = s^x f(1 + s + s^2 + \cdots)$.   Alternatively, we can determine the probability that the part will fail before or during the xth time unit and subtract this from 1; this probability is

$$1 - (f + sf + s^2 f + \cdots + s^{x-1} f) = 1 - f(1 + s + s^2 + \cdots + s^{x-1})$$

T A B L E   9 . 3

Number of the hour in which part failed a	Number of parts which failed in specified hour b	ab
1	100	100
2	200	400
3	400	1,200
4	200	800
5	100	500
Total..............	1,000	3,000

10 MATRICES, VECTOR SPACES, LINEAR DEPENDENCE, AND BASES[1]

10.1 MOTIVATION

In this chapter we shall introduce those additional concepts from the theory of matrices which are essential in the development of the simplex method of linear programming. This method will be treated in Chaps. 12 and 13. The concepts introduced in this chapter are also widely applicable in areas of management and social science other than linear programming.

We shall begin by generalizing some of the definitions given in Chap. 7, particularly those of Secs. 7.11 to 7.13. In what follows all matrices and vectors will be taken over the set of real numbers unless otherwise stated.

---

[1] It is recommended that the student reread Chap. 7 before proceeding with this chapter.

10.2 DETERMINANTS

We shall give a general definition of a determinant which will lead to general proofs. First, however, a few preliminary considerations are in order. We have learned that any arrangement of the n elements of the set $\{1,2, \ldots ,n\}$ is called a permutation. Suppose that we had a set of three numbers $\{1,2,3\}$; consider the permutation 3, 2, 1. If we restrict ourselves to interchanging only neighboring (i.e., adjacent) elements, how many interchanges do we need to put the elements in natural order? Evidently,

3	2	1	gives	3	1	2
3	1	2	gives	1	3	2
1	3	2	gives	1	2	3

i.e., three interchanges are needed.

Definition 10.1. If i_1, i_2, $\ldots$, i_n is a permutation of n different integers (for example, $i_1 = 4$, $i_2 = 8$, $\ldots$, $i_n = 3$) which requires an odd number of adjacent interchanges to bring them into natural order, we call it an *odd* permutation; if it requires an even number of such interchanges, we call it an *even* permutation. It can be proved that a given permutation is always odd or always even, no matter how we perform the interchanges. If α designates the number of interchanges needed to change a permutation of n numbers to the natural order, then if α is even, $(-1)^\alpha = 1$; if α is odd, $(-1)^\alpha = -1$.

We can now define the determinant function.

Definition 10.2

$$\det = \{\langle A,y\rangle | A \text{ is an } n \times n \text{ matrix } \& y = \sum_{i=1}^{n!} (-1)^\alpha a_{1i_1}a_{2i_2}a_{3i_3} \cdots a_{ni_n}\}$$

We write the determinant of the matrix A as

$$\det A = \sum_{i=1}^{n!} (-1)^\alpha a_{1i_1}a_{2i_2} \cdots a_{ni_n} \tag{10.1}$$

i_1, i_2, $\ldots$, i_n denotes a permutation of the second subscripts. There are $n!$ such permutations. α denotes the number of adjacent interchanges needed to convert any given i_1, i_2, $\ldots$, i_n to natural order. Each a_{ci_c} $(c = 1, 2, \ldots , n; i = 1, 2, \ldots , n!)$ denotes one of the n^2 elements from A.

Example 10.3. Let A be any 3×3 matrix. Find $\det A$.

Solution

$$A = \begin{pmatrix} a_{11} & a_{12} & a_{13} \\ a_{21} & a_{22} & a_{23} \\ a_{31} & a_{32} & a_{33} \end{pmatrix}$$

We form all products of form $a_{1i_1} \cdot a_{2i_2} \cdot a_{3i_3}$, where the i_1, i_2, i_3's are all possible permutations of the second subscripts. We first write these permutations,

$$
\begin{array}{ccccccccc}
1 & 2 & 3 & \quad & 2 & 1 & 3 & \quad & 3 & 1 & 2 \\
1 & 3 & 2 & \quad & 2 & 3 & 1 & \quad & 3 & 2 & 1
\end{array}
$$

Then, using Definition 10.2, we can write

$$
\begin{aligned}
\det A = &(-1)^{\alpha}(a_{11} \cdot a_{22} \cdot a_{33}) + (-1)^{\alpha}(a_{11} \cdot a_{23} \cdot a_{32}) \\
&+ (-1)^{\alpha}(a_{12} \cdot a_{21} \cdot a_{33}) + (-1)^{\alpha}(a_{12} \cdot a_{23} \cdot a_{31}) \\
&+ (-1)^{\alpha}(a_{13} \cdot a_{21} \cdot a_{32}) + (-1)^{\alpha}(a_{13} \cdot a_{22} \cdot a_{31})
\end{aligned}
$$

We need to determine the values of $(-1)^{\alpha}$ for each term. Since the permutation is on the column subscript, α is odd or even according to whether i_1, i_2, i_3 is an odd or even permutation.

For the first term $(-1)^{\alpha} = (-1)^0 = 1$.
For the second term $(-1)^{\alpha} = (-1)^1 = -1$.
For the third term $(-1)^{\alpha} = (-1)^1 = -1$.
For the fourth term $(-1)^{\alpha} = (-1)^2 = 1$.
For the fifth term $(-1)^{\alpha} = (-1)^2 = 1$.
For the sixth term $(-1)^{\alpha} = (-1)^3 = -1$.

Hence,

$$
\begin{aligned}
\det A = &a_{11} \cdot a_{22} \cdot a_{33} - a_{11} \cdot a_{23} \cdot a_{32} - a_{12} \cdot a_{21} \cdot a_{33} \\
&+ a_{12} \cdot a_{23} \cdot a_{31} + a_{13} \cdot a_{21} \cdot a_{32} - a_{13} \cdot a_{22} \cdot a_{31}
\end{aligned}
$$

Notice that the definition of a determinant really tells us to form all possible products of n factors taking one and only one element from each row and column.

From Definition 10.2, we see that, if the matrix is of shape $n \times n$, we shall have $n!$ terms to add in computing the determinant, since n elements (the second subscripts) give rise to $n!$ permutations. It can be proved, but we shall not do so, that half the terms to be added will have a plus sign and half a minus sign.

We now prove the following useful theorem.

Theorem 10.4

If A' is the transpose of an $n \times n$ matrix A, then det $A' = $ det A.

Proof. Let $A = (a_{kj})$ and $A' = (b_{kj})$. Then $b_{kj} = a_{jk}$, so that a typical term in det A' is

$$b_{1i_1} \cdot b_{2i_2} \cdots b_{ni_n} = a_{i_1 1} \cdot a_{i_2 2} \cdots a_{i_n n} \qquad (10.2)$$

From (10.2) we see that the absolute values of the terms in det A' are the same as those in det A, since the terms in det A' also give all possible products of n factors, one, and only one, from each row and column in A. Assume that $\alpha = r$ adjacent interchanges are required to place i_1, i_2, . . . , i_n in natural order. Then the typical term in det A' [left-hand side of (10.2)] has sign $(-1)^r$. We can convert the term in det A' to a typical term in det A by first rearranging the factors so as to restore the row subscripts of the right-hand side of (10.2) to natural order. Since this rearrangement of *factors* exactly parallels the rearrangement of *column subscripts* on the left-hand side of (10.2) (it represents the same permutation), r adjacent interchanges are required. We denote the result by

$$a_{1j_1} a_{2j_n} \cdots a_{nj_n} \qquad (10.3)$$

Since the permutation

$$j_1, j_2, \cdots, j_n \qquad (10.4)$$

has been obtained from the natural ordering 1, . . . , n by r adjacent interchanges, the same r interchanges performed in reverse order will restore (10.4) to natural order. Thus $\alpha = r$, and (10.3) has the same sign $(-1)^r$ as (10.2), proving the theorem.

An immediate corollary is as follows,

Corollary 10.5

$$\det A = \sum_{i=1}^{n!} (-1)^{\alpha} a_{1i_1} \cdot a_{2i_2} \cdots a_{ni_n} = \sum_{i=1}^{n!} (-1)^{\alpha} a_{i_1 1} \cdot a_{i_2 2} \cdots a_{i_n n}$$

The student can easily prove the following theorem from (10.1).

Theorem 10.6

If any row (or column) in a square matrix A is replaced by a row (or column) each element of which is c times the corresponding element of the row (or column) being replaced, then the determinant of the resulting matrix B is

$$\det B = c(\det A)$$

To prove the next important theorem, we need two lemmas.

Lemma 10.7. An adjacent interchange of two numbers in a given permutation makes the permutation even if it was originally odd and odd if it was originally even.

Proof. After the interchange, the two numbers will bear the same relationship to (i.e., they will still exceed or be less than) the other numbers in the permutation. The total number of adjacent interchanges required to form a natural ordering will therefore have been increased by exactly 1 or decreased by exactly 1, and the theorem follows.

Example 10.8. The permutation 2 1 4 3 is even, since it requires two adjacent interchanges:

$$1 \quad 2 \quad 4 \quad 3 \qquad 1 \quad 2 \quad 3 \quad 4$$

If the last two numbers in the original permutation are interchanged, the permutation becomes odd, since it then would require one adjacent interchange to be placed in natural order. If the second and third numbers in the original permutation are interchanged, the permutation still becomes odd, since now three adjacent interchanges would be required to place it in natural order.

Lemma 10.9. An interchange of any two numbers in a given permutation makes the permutation even if it was originally odd and odd if it was originally even.

Proof. Given the permutation

$$i_1, i_2, \ldots, i_{r-1}, i_r, i_{r+1}, \ldots, i_{s-1}, i_s, i_{s+1}, \ldots, i_n$$

assume that we interchange the numbers i_r and i_s. i_s must pass over $i_{s-1}, i_{s-2}, \ldots, i_{r+1}, i_r$; that is, the journey of i_s requires $s - r$ adjacent interchanges. Similarly, i_r must pass over $i_{r+1}, i_{r+2}, \ldots, i_{s-1}$; that is, $s - r - 1$ adjacent interchanges are required to place i_r in its new position. Therefore, $(s - r) + (s - r - 1) = 2(s - r) - 1$ adjacent interchanges are required to interchange r and s. This is an odd number. From Lemma 10.7, we know that each adjacent interchange changes the preceding permutation from odd (even) to even (odd). Since an odd number of adjacent interchanges are necessarily made when two numbers are interchanged, the theorem follows.

Example 10.10. When the first and last numbers of the even permutation 2 1 4 3 are interchanged, the permutation becomes odd, since three adjacent interchanges are now required to place the permutation in natural order: 3 1 4 2 → 1 3 4 2, 1 3 2 4, 1 2 3 4.

We now state the following theorem.

Theorem 10.11

If $A = (a_{ij})$ is a matrix of shape $n \times n$ and $B = (b_{ij})$ is obtained from A by interchanging two rows (or columns), then

$$\det A = -\det B$$

Proof. We obtain B by interchanging rows r and s ($s > r$) in A. Evidently A and B have the same shape, with $b_{ij} = a_{ij}$ ($i \neq r, s$) and otherwise $b_{rj} = a_{sj}$, $b_{sj} = a_{rj}$. From Definition 10.2 we have

$$\det B = \sum_{i=1}^{n!} (-1)^{\alpha_i} b_{1i_1} b_{2i_2} \cdots b_{ri_r} \cdots b_{si_s} \cdots b_{ni_n}$$

which, upon substituting the a_{ij}'s, becomes

$$\det B = \sum_{i=1}^{n!} (-1)^{\alpha_i} a_{1i_1} a_{2i_2} \cdots a_{si_r} \cdots a_{ri_s} \cdots a_{ni_n} \quad (10.5)$$

We can interchange the rth and sth factors of each term in (10.5) without changing its absolute value; neglecting signs for the moment, such an interchange in a typical term would give

$$a_{1i_1} a_{2i_2} \cdots a_{ri_s} \cdots a_{si_r} \cdots a_{ni_n} \quad (10.6)$$

This interchange puts the first subscripts in their natural order, and (10.6) acquires the appearance of a typical term in det A, there being the same number of terms in det A and det B. The absolute value of each term in det B is therefore equal to the absolute value of a term in det A. However, in obtaining (10.6) from (10.5), two column subscripts were interchanged. From Lemma 10.9, we then know that, if a given term in det B requires an odd (even) number of permutations to be placed in natural order, when this term is written as a term of det A having the same absolute value it will require an even (odd) number of permutations. Each term in det A is therefore -1 times the corresponding term in det B. The theorem follows. The same method of proof can be used to prove the theorem for the interchange of two columns.

From this, we can obtain immediately the following corollary.

Corollary 10.12. If A is a matrix of order $n \times n$ with two rows (or columns) equal, then det $A = 0$.

Proof. Interchanging the two rows gives a matrix B such that det $B = \det A = - \det A$. The only real number for which this holds is det $A = 0$.

Corollary 10.13. If A is a matrix of order $n \times n$ such that one row (or column), say r, is equal to a constant k times another row (or column), say s, then

$$\det A = 0$$

Proof. It is given that $a_{rj} = ka_{sj}$. Form the matrix $B = (b_{ij})$, where $b_{ij} = a_{ij}$ ($i \neq r$) and otherwise $b_{rj} = a_{sj}$. Since A differs from B only in that row r in A is a multiple k of row r in B, we can use Theorem 10.6 to show that $\det A = k \,(\det B)$. But B has two rows alike, namely, $b_{rj} = a_{sj} = b_{sj}$, so that, from Corollary 10.12, $\det B = 0$. Therefore $\det A = k \,(\det B) = 0$, proving Corollary 10.13.

PROBLEM SET 10.1

1. A matrix A may be considered as made up of a set of row (or column) vectors. State Theorems 10.6, 10.11, and Corollaries 10.12 and 10.13 in terms of vectors.
2. Show that the definition of the determinant of 2×2 and 3×3 matrices given in Chap. 7 follow from the definition given in this chapter.
3. Find $\det A$ if
   a. $A = (a_{ij})_{4 \times 4}$, where $a_{ij} = c$ if $i = j$, $a_{ij} = 0$ if $i \neq j$. In particular if $c = 1$, $\det A = 1$ (A is a scalar matrix).
   b.
   $$A = \begin{pmatrix} 2 & 3 & 4 & -1 \\ 1 & 0 & 2 & 1 \\ -1 & 0 & 2 & -1 \\ 4 & 6 & 8 & -2 \end{pmatrix}$$
   Solve by the definition and also by the theorems proved.
   c. Prove from the definition of det that, if one row (or column) of an $n \times n$ matrix A is zero, $\det A = 0$.
   d. $A = B + C$, where $B = \begin{pmatrix} 2 & 3 \\ 1 & 4 \end{pmatrix}$, $C = \begin{pmatrix} 0 & 1 \\ 2 & 1 \end{pmatrix}$. Find $\det A$ by adding $B + C$ and finding $\det (B + C)$; then find $\det B$ and $\det C$ and $\det B + \det C$.
   e. $A = B \times C$. Find $\det A$ in two ways analogous to (d).
4. Can you generalize either (d) or (e) of Prob. 3?
5. If $A = (ca_{ij})$ is an $n \times n$ matrix such that $ca_{ij} = 0$ ($i \neq j$) and $ca_{ij} = ck_i$ ($i = j$), use the definition of a determinant to show that $\det A = c^n(k_1 \cdot k_2 \cdots k_n)$.
6. Prove that, if in a matrix A of order $n \times n$, we replace the rth row by a multiple of the kth row added to the corresponding element of the rth row, obtaining a matrix B, then

$$\det B = \det A$$

(*Hint:* Use the definition of a determinant, and Corollary 10.13.)

10.3 MINORS AND COFACTORS

The following considerations enable us to discuss methods of evaluating determinants that do not involve the definition directly.

Definition 10.14. A submatrix A of a matrix B of order $m \times n$ is a matrix obtained from B by deleting r rows and s columns of B ($r < m$; $s < n$). A will then be of shape $(m - r) \times (n - s)$.

Definition 10.15. If A is a square matrix of order $n \times n$ and a_{ij} is an element in A, then

$$\text{Minor} = \{\langle x,y \rangle | x = a_{ij} \ \& \ y = \det M(a_{ij})\}$$

where $M(a_{ij})$ denotes the submatrix of A obtained by deleting the ith row and jth column of A. We write $\det M(a_{ij}) = M_{ij}$ (read "minor M_{ij} of a_{ij}").

Definition 10.16. If A is a square matrix of order n and a_{ij} is an element in A, then

$$\text{cof} = \{\langle x,y \rangle | x = a_{ij} \ \& \ y = (-1)^{i+j} M_{ij}\}$$

with domain the set of $n \times n$ matrices and range the set of real numbers. We write $(-1)^{i+j} M_{ij} = \text{cof} \ (a_{ij}) = A_{ij}$ (read "cofactor A_{ij} of a_{ij}").

Example 10.17. $A = (a_{ij})_{3 \times 3}$.   Then

$$\det M(a_{32}) = M_{32} = \det \begin{pmatrix} a_{11} & a_{13} \\ a_{21} & a_{23} \end{pmatrix} = a_{11}a_{23} - a_{13}a_{21}$$

$$\text{cof} \ (a_{32}) = A_{32} = (-1)^{3+2} M_{32}$$
$$= (-1)(a_{11}a_{23} - a_{13}a_{21})$$

We shall now prove a very important theorem.

Theorem 10.18

If $A = (a_{ij})$ is a square matrix of order n, then for each value of $i = 1$, $2, \ldots, n$

$$\det A = \sum_{j=1}^{n} a_{ij} A_{ij}$$

$$= \sum_{j=1}^{n} a_{ji} A_{ji}$$

Proof. We proceed in three steps.

1. First, we shall show that the sum of all the terms in det A which contain a_{11} is $a_{11}A_{11}$. If we gather all the terms in det A which contain a_{11} and factor out a_{11}, we obtain

$$a_{11} \sum_{i=1}^{(n-1)!} a_{2i_2} a_{3i_3} \cdots a_{ni_n} \tag{10.7}$$

where $i_2, i_3, \ldots, i_n$ is some permutation of the numbers $2, 3, \ldots, n$, there being $(n - 1)!$ such permutations. Each term in the sum of (10.7) is the product of $n - 1$ factors representing every row in A except row 1 and every column in A except column 1. Thus, the absolute values of the terms in the summation of (10.7) are the same as those in M_{11} (the minor of a_{ij}). To determine the signs of these terms, observe that, when each term in the sum of (10.7) is considered as a term in M_{11}, its sign is $(-1)^\alpha$, where α is the number of adjacent interchanges required to place the permutation $i_2, i_3, \ldots, i_n$ in natural order. Since the sign of the corresponding term in det A, that is, the term $a_{11}a_{2i_2} \cdots a_{ni_n}$, is derived, in effect, from the same permutation (since a_{11} is already in natural order), the sign of each term in the sum of (10.7) is the same as the sign of the corresponding term in M_{11}. Thus we can write

$$a_{11} \sum_{i=1}^{(n-1)!} a_{2i_2} \cdots a_{ni_n} = a_{11}M_{11} = a_{11}(-1)^{1+1}M_{11} = a_{11}A_{11}$$

2. We shall now show that the sum of all the terms in det A which contain the arbitrary but fixed element a_{ij} $(i, j = 1, \ldots, n)$ is $a_{ij}A_{ij}$. We are given the matrix

$$A = \begin{pmatrix} a_{11} & a_{12} & \cdots & a_{1j} & \cdots & a_{1n} \\ a_{21} & a_{22} & \cdots & a_{2j} & \cdots & a_{2n} \\ \cdots & \cdots & \cdots & \cdots & \cdots & \cdots \\ a_{i1} & a_{i2} & \cdots & a_{ij} & \cdots & a_{in} \\ \cdots & \cdots & \cdots & \cdots & \cdots & \cdots \\ a_{n1} & a_{n2} & \cdots & a_{nj} & \cdots & a_{nn} \end{pmatrix} \qquad (10.8)$$

Interchange row i of A with the row above it, repeating this process until after $i - 1$ interchanges row i appears in the top position. In the same fashion, move column j, one column at a time, until after $j - 1$ interchanges column j appears in the leftmost position. We use B to denote the resulting matrix,

$$B = \begin{pmatrix} a_{ij} & a_{i1} & a_{i2} & \cdots & a_{in} \\ a_{1j} & a_{11} & a_{12} & \cdots & a_{1n} \\ a_{2j} & a_{21} & a_{22} & \cdots & a_{2n} \\ \cdots & \cdots & \cdots & \cdots & \cdots \\ a_{nj} & a_{n1} & a_{n2} & \cdots & a_{nn} \end{pmatrix} \qquad (10.9)$$

Since B was obtained by making $(i - 1) + (j - 1) = i + j - 2$ row and column interchanges in A, we can use Theorem 10.11 and state that

$$\det B = (-1)^{i+j-2} \det A = (-1)^{i+j} \det A \qquad (10.10)$$

[since $(i + j) - 2$ is odd or even according to whether $i + j$ is odd or even]. From part 1 of this proof, we know that the sum of all terms in det B containing b_{11} as a factor is $b_{11}N_{11}$ (where N_{11} denotes the minor of

b_{11}). But a comparison of (10.8) and (10.9) shows that $b_{11} = a_{ij}$ and $N_{11} = M_{ij}$ (the submatrix formed by deleting row i and column j in A is the same formed by deleting row 1 and column 1 of B). Thus the sum of all terms in det B containing $b_{11} = a_{ij}$ as a factor is $a_{ij}M_{ij}$. We can use (10.10) to convert terms in det B to terms in det A, so that the sum of all the terms in det A which contain a_{ij} is $(-1)^{i+j}a_{ij}M_{ij} = a_{ij}A_{ij}$.

3. Since every term in det A contains exactly one element from the fixed row i, we can group all terms containing a_{ij} (i fixed; $j = 1, \ldots, n$), obtaining

$$\det A = a_{i1} \sum_{j=1}^{(n-1)!} a_{k_1 j_1} \cdots a_{k_{n-1} j_{n-1}} + a_{i2} \sum_{1=1}^{(n-1)!} a_{k_1 l_1} \cdots$$

$$a_{k_{n-1} l_{n-1}} + \cdots + a_{in} \sum_{m=1}^{(n-1)!} a_{k_1 m_1} \cdots a_{k_{n-1} m_{n-1}} \quad (10.11)$$

where $k_1, \ldots, k_{n-1}$ is a natural ordering of $n-1$ numbers $\neq i$ and $j_1, \ldots, j_{n-1}$ is some permutation of $n-1$ numbers $\neq 1; l_1, \ldots, l_{n-1}$ is some permutation of $n-1$ numbers $\neq 2; \ldots; m_1, \ldots, m_{n-1}$ is some permutation of $n-1$ numbers $\neq n$. From (2) we know that (10.11) can be written

$$\det A = a_{i1}A_{i1} + a_{i2}A_{i2} + \cdots + a_{in}A_{in}$$

Since this last expression holds for any fixed row i ($i = 1, \ldots, n$), and since the same argument can be applied to any fixed column j, the theorem is proved.

Example 10.19. Find

$$\det \begin{pmatrix} 2 & 1 & 3 \\ 4 & 1 & 2 \\ 1 & 1 & 0 \end{pmatrix}.$$

Solution. Using the last row, since it contains a zero, we obtain

$$A_{31} = (-1)^{3+1} \det \begin{pmatrix} 1 & 3 \\ 1 & 2 \end{pmatrix} = 2 - 3 = -1$$

$$A_{32} = (-1)^{3+2} \det \begin{pmatrix} 2 & 3 \\ 4 & 2 \end{pmatrix} = -1(4 - 12) = 8$$

$$A_{33} = (-1)^{3+3} \det \begin{pmatrix} 2 & 1 \\ 4 & 1 \end{pmatrix} = 2 - 4 = -2$$

$$\det A = (1)(-1) + (1)(8) + (0)(-2) = 7$$

If we use the elements of a row, we speak of the *row expansion* of a determinant; if we use the elements of a column, we speak of the *column expansion* of the determinant.

What happens if we take the sum of the products of the elements of one row and the cofactors of another row? We get at this as follows:

Suppose that in a square matrix A of order $n \times n$ we delete the sth row and replace it by the rth row $(r \neq s)$, obtaining matrix B. We then have $b_{ij} = a_{ij}$ $(i \neq s)$ and otherwise $b_{sj} = a_{rj}$. From Corollary 10.12, we know that det $B = 0$. Then, using Theorem 10.18, we have

$$\det B = \sum_{j=1}^{n} b_{sj}B_{sj} = 0 \qquad (10.12)$$

Since the submatrix formed by deleting row s and column j of B is the same as that formed by deleting row s and column j of A, we have $B_{sj} = A_{sj}$ and (10.12) becomes

$$\det B = \sum_{j=1}^{n} a_{rj}A_{sj} = 0 \qquad r \neq s \qquad (10.13)$$

Since we can form a matrix B satisfying (10.12) and (10.13) for any r and s $(r \neq s)$ in matrix A, we have proved the following theorem.

Theorem 10.19.1

If $A = (a_{ij})$ is a square matrix of order $n \times n$, then, if $r \neq s$,

$$\sum_{j=1}^{n} a_{rj}A_{sj} = 0.$$

A similar theorem holds for the column expansion.

PROBLEM SET 10.2

1. Illustrate Theorem 10.18, using the elements of the third row.
2. In Example 10.19, calculate the determinant of the given matrix by expanding over the elements of the second column.
3. Calculate the determinant of the matrix $I = (a_{ij})$, $a_{ij} = 0$ if $i \neq j$ and $a_{ij} = 1$ if $i = j$, using cofactors of the third row.
4. Evaluate

$$\det \begin{pmatrix} 1 & 0 & 0 & 0 \\ 2 & 3 & 0 & 0 \\ 1 & 1 & 3 & 0 \\ -5 & 7 & 4 & 2 \end{pmatrix}$$

(an upper triangular matrix).

Can you prove that the determinant of an upper triangular matrix is the product $a_{11} \cdot a_{22} \cdots a_{nn}$, that is, the product of the elements along the diagonal?

5. Expand the left side of the following expression, and write as an equation:

$$\det \begin{pmatrix} x & y & 1 \\ 2 & 1 & 1 \\ 3 & 1 & 1 \end{pmatrix} = 0$$

Evaluate

$$\det \begin{pmatrix} 1 - i & 2 \\ i & 1 + i \end{pmatrix}$$

10.4 TRANSPOSE, ADJOINT, AND INVERSE

We shall now redefine certain terms, using the concept of function.

Definition 10.20. If $A = (a_{ij})$ is a matrix of order $m \times n$, then

$$Tr = \{\langle x, y \rangle | x = A \;\&\; y = A^T\}$$

with domain the set of $m \times n$ matrices and range the set of $n \times m$ matrices, A^T denoting the matrix formed from A by interchanging rows and columns so that row i of A becomes column i of A^T,

$$A = \begin{pmatrix} a_{11} & a_{12} & \cdots & a_{1n} \\ a_{21} & a_{22} & \cdots & a_{2n} \\ \cdot & \cdot & \cdots & \cdot \\ a_{m1} & a_{m2} & \cdots & a_{mn} \end{pmatrix} \qquad A^T = \begin{pmatrix} a_{11} & a_{21} & \cdots & a_{m1} \\ a_{12} & a_{22} & \cdots & a_{m2} \\ \cdot & \cdot & \cdots & \cdot \\ a_{1n} & a_{2n} & \cdots & a_{mn} \end{pmatrix}$$

We call the matrix A^T the *transpose* of the matrix A.

Definition 10.21. As before, we denote the cofactors of a_{ij} in a matrix $A = (a_{ij})$ of order $n \times n$ by A_{ij} and define

$$\text{adj} = \{\langle x, y \rangle | x = (a_{ij}) \;\&\; y = (A_{ij})^T\}$$

with domain the set of $n \times n$ matrices (a_{ij}) and range the set of transposes of the matrices formed by the cofactors of the elements of (a_{ij}). We shall write $A_{adj} = (A_{ij})^T$ and call the matrix A_{adj} the *adjoint* of matrix A.

The following theorem will enable us to obtain an expression for the inverse of a matrix A of order $n \times n$.

Theorem 10.22

If A is a square matrix of order $n \times n$ and A_{adj} is the adjoint matrix, then

$$A \cdot A_{adj} = A_{adj} \cdot A = (\det A) I_n$$

where I_n is the identity matrix (a_{ij}) $(a_{ij} = 0, i \neq j; a_{ij} = 1, i = j)$.

Proof

$$A \cdot A_{adj} = \begin{pmatrix} a_{11} & a_{12} & \cdots & a_{1n} \\ a_{21} & a_{22} & \cdots & a_{2n} \\ \cdot & \cdot & \cdots & \cdot \\ a_{1n} & a_{2n} & \cdots & a_{nn} \end{pmatrix} \cdot \begin{pmatrix} A_{11} & A_{21} & \cdots & A_{n1} \\ A_{12} & A_{22} & \cdots & A_{n2} \\ \cdot & \cdot & \cdots & \cdot \\ A_{1n} & A_{2n} & \cdots & A_{nn} \end{pmatrix}$$

By definition of the multiplication of matrices and Theorems 10.18 and

10.19.1, we obtain

$$A \cdot A_{adj} = \begin{pmatrix} \det A & 0 & 0 & \cdots & 0 \\ 0 & \det A & 0 & \cdots & 0 \\ \multicolumn{5}{c}{\dotfill} \\ 0 & 0 & 0 & \cdots & \det A \end{pmatrix} = A_{adj} \cdot A = (\det A)I_n$$

Corollary 10.23. If $\det A \neq 0$, $\det A_{adj} = (\det A)^{n-1}$.

    Proof. From the proof to the above theorem we have

$$A \cdot A_{adj} = \begin{pmatrix} \det A & 0 & \cdots & 0 \\ 0 & \det A & \cdots & 0 \\ \multicolumn{4}{c}{\dotfill} \\ 0 & 0 & \cdots & \det A \end{pmatrix}$$

so that, by Definition 10.2, we obtain

$$\det (A \cdot A_{adj}) = (\det A)^n$$

[the only term in (10.1) which does not vanish is the term composed of the diagonal elements]. From Probs. 3e and 4, Problem Set 10.1, we can write

$$\det (A \cdot A_{adj}) = \det A \cdot \det A_{adj} = (\det A)^n$$

so that $\det A_{adj} = (\det A)^{n-1}$ (if $\det A \neq 0$).

    We are now in a position to define the inverse for a given matrix A of order $n \times n$ and determine the conditions under which such an inverse exists.

Definition 10.24. Given that A and B are square matrices of order n, then

$$\text{inv} = \{\langle x,y \rangle | x = A \ \& \ y = B \ \& \ yx = xy = I_n\}$$

with domain and range the sets of $n \times n$ matrices. B is the matrix which, when used to pre- or postmultiply A, yields I_n. We call B the inverse matrix to matrix A, and we denote B by A^{-1}.

Theorem 10.25

If A is an $n \times n$ matrix, then $A^{-1} = (1/\det A) \ A_{adj}$, provided that $\det A \neq 0$.

    Proof. The proof follows directly from Theorem 10.22.

    Theorem 10.25 also provides us with a method of forming the inverse to any square matrix A.

    We now need a new term.

Definition 10.26. A square matrix A of order n is nonsingular if $\det A \neq 0$. If $\det A = 0$ the matrix is singular.

Corollary 10.27. A square matrix A of order n has an inverse if and only if det $A \neq 0$ (that is, if A is nonsingular).

Theorem 10.28

If A is nonsingular, it is square.
    Proof. A is nonsingular implies that det $A \neq 0$. But only square matrices have determinants. This proves the theorem.

Theorem 10.29

If A^{-1} is the inverse of the $n \times n$ matrix A, then A^{-1} is $n \times n$.
    Proof. By definition $A \cdot A^{-1} = I = A^{-1} \cdot A$. Since I is of shape $n \times n$, then A^{-1} must be also, because of the definition of multiplication.

Theorem 10.30

If A is nonsingular, then A^{-1} is unique.
    Proof. If A_1^{-1} and A_2^{-1} were both inverses of A,

$$A_2^{-1}(A \cdot A_1^{-1}) = A_2^{-1}$$
$$A_1^{-1}(A \cdot A_2^{-1}) = A_1^{-1}$$

Then $A_2^{-1}(A \cdot A_1^{-1}) = A_1^{-1}(A \cdot A_2^{-1})$ by associativity. Hence

$$A_2^{-1} = A_1^{-1}$$

10.5 CRAMER'S RULE

By using matrices we can write a set of n equations in n variables as a single matrix equation and then solve it by using the inverse of a matrix, if there is a solution.
    Consider the set of equations

$$\sum_{j=1}^{n} a_{1j}x_j = b_1$$
$$\cdots \cdots \cdots$$
$$\sum_{j=1}^{n} a_{nj}x_j = b_n$$

(10.14)

We shall assume that at least one of the $b_i \neq 0$.

Suppose that we form the matrix of the coefficients,

$$A = \begin{pmatrix} a_{11} & a_{12} & \cdots & a_{1n} \\ \cdot & \cdot & \cdots & \cdots \\ a_{n1} & a_{n2} & \cdots & a_{nn} \end{pmatrix}_{n \times n}$$

also the matrix (row vector) $(x_1\ x_2\ \cdots\ x_n)$ and its transpose

$$X = \begin{pmatrix} x_1 \\ x_2 \\ \cdot \\ \cdot \\ \cdot \\ x_n \end{pmatrix}$$

and finally the column vector

$$B = \begin{pmatrix} b_1 \\ b_2 \\ \cdot \\ \cdot \\ \cdot \\ b_n \end{pmatrix}$$

Using the concepts of matrix multiplication and equality, (10.14) can be written as

$$AX = B \tag{10.15}$$

Evidently if A has an inverse, i.e., if det $A \neq 0$, we obtain

$$(A^{-1}A)X = A^{-1}B \quad \text{or} \quad X = A^{-1}B$$

That is,

$$\begin{pmatrix} x_1 \\ x_2 \\ x_3 \\ \cdot \\ \cdot \\ \cdot \\ x_n \end{pmatrix} = \frac{1}{\det A} \begin{pmatrix} A_{11} & A_{21} & \cdots & A_{n1} \\ A_{12} & A_{22} & \cdots & A_{n2} \\ \cdot & \cdot & \cdots & \cdot \\ A_{1n} & A_{2n} & \cdots & A_{nn} \end{pmatrix} \begin{pmatrix} b_1 \\ b_2 \\ b_3 \\ \cdot \\ \cdot \\ b_n \end{pmatrix}$$

Again from matrices, we have

$$x_1 = \frac{1}{\det A} (A_{11}b_1 + A_{21}b_2 + \cdots + A_{n1}b_n)$$

$$\cdots \cdots \cdots \cdots \cdots \cdots \cdots \cdots \cdots$$

$$x_n = \frac{1}{\det A} (A_{1n}b_1 + A_{2n}b_2 + \cdots + A_{nn}b_n)$$

In general

$$x_i = \frac{1}{\det A} \sum_{j=1}^{n} A_{ji}b_j \qquad i = 1, 2, \ldots, n$$

If in A we replace the ith column by the b's and designate the b's as b_{ji}, we obtain

$$x_i = \frac{1}{\det A} \sum_{j=1}^{n} A_{ji}b_{ji} \qquad i = 1, 2, \ldots, n$$

which is Cramer's rule.

PROBLEM SET 10.3

1. Solve the following set of equations (a) using Cramer's rule; (b) calculating the inverse of the coefficient matrix:

$$2x_1 - 3x_2 + x_3 = 5$$
$$x_1 + 2x_2 - 4x_3 = -2$$
$$3x_1 - x_2 + 3x_3 = 4$$

2. What is the inverse of a 3×3 scalar matrix, $a_{ii} = c$?
3. What is the inverse of a 3×3 upper triangular matrix?

10.6 THE VECTOR SPACE OVER THE REAL NUMBERS

We shall define a mathematical structure known as a *vector space* which will provide a set of concepts quite useful in mathematics and having wide interpretations in the physical and social sciences. The student should not be misled by the word space to think that these are geometric concepts. They are algebraic notions, with a major interpretation in geometry. These concepts will be used for the study of linear programming.

As before, all definitions are relative to the set of real numbers unless otherwise noted.

Definition 10.31.   Let V be a set of elements for which two operations, $+$ and $\cdot$, are defined. Then V is a vector space if the following conditions are satisfied:

1. If $a, b \epsilon V$, then $a + b \epsilon V$.
2. If $a, b \epsilon V$, then $a + b = b + a$.
3. There exists an element 0 in V such that, for every element a of V, $a + 0 = 0 + a = a$ (0 is called the *additive identity*).
4. If $a \epsilon V$, then there exists an element denoted by $-a$ in V such that $a + (-a) = 0$.

5. If c is a real number and a, $b \in V$, then $c \cdot (a + b) = c \cdot a + c \cdot b$.

6. If c and d are real numbers and $a \in V$, then $(c + d)a = c \cdot a + d \cdot a$.

7. If c, d are real numbers and $a \in V$, then $c \cdot (d \cdot a) = (c \cdot d) \cdot a$.

8. If $a \in V$, then $1 \cdot a = a$.

The following remarks are important. The operations of $+$ and $\cdot$ need to be defined for each set V. Different sets may have distinct definitions of their operations. The examples below will illustrate this.

Any set V with one operation which satisfies parts 1 to 5 is called an *Abelian group* (or commutative group).

The elements of V are called *vectors;* the elements of the set of real numbers are called *scalars*.

The type of multiplication defined is multiplication of a vector by a scalar and is called *scalar multiplication.*

Example 10.32. Let $V = \{x | x$ is an integer$\}$. We define $+$ and $\cdot$ as the usual addition and multiplication. The resulting structure is a vector space. The student should verify the fact that all conditions are satisfied. In this case the element 2 of V (for example) is a vector, but if considered a real number it is a scalar.

Example 10.33. Let $V(n) = \{x | x$ is a row vector of n components$\}$. We define $+$ as follows:

If $a = (a_1 \, a_2 \, \cdots \, a_n)$, $b = (b_1 \, b_2 \, \cdots \, b_n)$, then

$$a + b = (a_1 \, a_2 \, \cdots \, a_n) + (b_1 \, b_2 \, \cdots \, b_n)$$
$$= (a_1 + b_1 \, a_2 + b_2 \, \cdots \, a_n + b_n)$$

where a_i and b_i are real numbers.

We define $\cdot$ as follows:

If c is a real number and $a = (a_1 \, a_2 \, \cdots \, a_n) \in V$, then

$$c \cdot a = c(a_1 \, a_2 \, a_3 \, \cdots \, a_n) = (ca_1 \, ca_2 \, ca_3 \, \cdots \, ca_n)$$

The student should verify the fact that the system of V, with $+$ and $\cdot$ as defined, is a vector space. [*Hint:* The additive identity is n-components $(0 \quad 0 \quad \cdots \quad 0)$; also, if a, $b \in V$, then $a = b$ if a_i (of a) $= b_i$ (of b).]

Let U be any subset of V. Then U is *closed under addition* if U contains $c = a + b$ for every a and b in U, and U is *closed under scalar multiplication* if the presence of a in U implies the presence of ka in U for every scalar k. We now prove the following theorem.

Theorem 10.34

Let V be a vector space and $U \subseteq V$, $U \neq \emptyset$; then U is also a vector space (called a *subspace*) if and only if U is closed with respect to addition and scalar multiplication.

Proof. Since U is closed with respect to addition, it must satisfy (1) and (2).

Since U is closed with respect to scalar multiplication, if $a \epsilon U$ then $(-1)a \epsilon U$. But

$$(-1)a = (-1)(a_1\, a_2 \cdots a_n) = (-a_1\, -a_2 \cdots -a_n) = -a$$

and $-a \epsilon U$. But if $-a \epsilon U$ and $a \epsilon U$, $0 = (0 \cdots 0_n)$ also ϵU. This proves the theorem.

Definition 10.35. If V is a vector space over the set of real numbers, then $V(n)$ denotes the fact that the elements of V have n components.

For example, $V(3) = \{(x_1\, x_2\, x_3)|x_1, x_2, x_3 \text{ are real numbers } \& \ V(3) \text{ is a}$ vector space$\}$.

Since the set of all $1 \times n$ matrices (row vectors) with $+$ and scalar multiplication is a vector space, we denote it by $V(n)$.

PROBLEM SET 10.4

Prove the following theorems.
1. If $a \epsilon V$ and c is a real number, then $(-c)a = -ca$.
2. If $a \epsilon V$ and c is a real number and $ac = 0$, then $a = 0$ or $c = 0$.
3. If c, d are real numbers and $a \epsilon V$ $(a \neq 0)$ and $ca = da$, then $c = d$.
4. If $a, b \epsilon V$ and c is a nonzero real number such that $ca = cb$, then $a = b$.
5. If a_1, a_2, and a_3 are fixed real numbers, then the set of all three component vectors $(x_1\, x_2\, x_3)$ such that $a_1x_1 + a_2x_2 + a_3x_3 = 0$ is a subspace of $V(3)$ over the set of real numbers.
6. Show that any vector in $V(3)$ can be expressed as a sum of the form

$$x_1(1 \quad 0 \quad 0) + x_2(0 \quad 1 \quad 0) + x_3(0 \quad 0 \quad 1)$$

Can you generalize to $V(n)$?

10.7 LINEAR DEPENDENCE

For clarity in reading we shall denote the elements (i.e., the vectors) of a vector space by capital letters. There will be no confusion with the notation for matrices or sets, since which is meant will be evident from the context. We now study an important relation that may exist between elements of a vector space. In what follows, the reader will recall that the null or 0 (zero) vector, denoted by 0, is a vector all of whose components are 0 and that the unit vector E_i is a vector whose ith component is 1, all other components being 0.

Definition 10.36. A subset $\{A_1, A_2, \ldots, A_m\}$ of vectors of V is linearly dependent if there exists a subset $\{r_1, r_2, \cdots, r_m\}$ of real numbers at least one of which is not zero, such that

$$\sum_{i=1}^{m} r_i A_i = 0 \qquad 0 \text{ the zero vector}$$

The set $\{A_1, A_2, \ldots, A_m\}$ is linearly independent if $\sum_{i=1}^{m} r_i A_i = 0$ implies $r_i = 0$ for all $i = 1, \ldots, m$.

Example 10.37. Consider the vector space designated by $V(2)$. The set $\{(1 \quad 0), (2 \quad 3)\}$ is a linearly independent subset of $V(2)$, since

$$r_1(1 \quad 0) + r_2(2 \quad 3) = (0 \quad 0)$$
$$(r_1 \quad 0) + (2r_2 \quad 3r_2) = (0 \quad 0)$$
$$r_1 + 2r_2 = 0$$
$$0 + 3r_2 = 0$$

Therefore $r_2 = 0 = r_1$.

Example 10.38. Is the set $\{(2 \quad 4), (3 \quad 6)\}$ of $V(2)$ a linearly dependent set?

Solution. We need to see whether $r_1(2 \quad 4) + r_2(3 \quad 6) = (0 \quad 0)$ is possible with either r_1 or $r_2 \neq 0$. We have

$$2r_1 + 3r_2 = 0$$
$$4r_1 + 6r_2 = 0$$

Therefore $r_1 = -\frac{3}{2}r_2$. Evidently, if $r_2 = 2$, $r_1 = -3$ will do. Hence $\{(2 \quad 4), (3 \quad 6)\}$ is a linearly dependent subset of $V(2)$. Note that $r_2(3 \quad 6) = 3r_2(1 \quad 2) = \frac{3}{2}r_2(2 \quad 4)$.

Example 10.39. Is the subset $\{(1 \quad 0 \quad 0), (0 \quad 1 \quad 0), (0 \quad 0 \quad 1)\}$ of $V(3)$ a linearly dependent set?

Solution. The answer is "no." Note that this set is also a subspace of $V(3)$. The proofs are left to the student.

Example 10.40. Any set of vectors containing the null vector will be a linearly dependent set.

Let $\{A_1, 0, A_2, \ldots, A_n\}$ be such a set. Then

$$0 \cdot A_1 + 0 \cdot A_2 + \cdots + 0A_n + c0 = 0$$

Example 10.41. The n unit vectors of the vector space $V(n)$ are linearly independent, since

$$c_1 E_1 + c_1 E_2 + \cdots + c_1 E_n = 0$$

if and only if all $c_i = 0$.

We now prove a few theorems.

Theorem 10.42

If the set $A = \{A_1, A_2, \ldots, A_m\}$ of vectors of a vector space V is linearly independent, then any nonempty subset of this set is linearly independent.

Proof. Let $B = \{A_{i_1}, A_{i_2}, \ldots, A_{i_k}\}$ $(k < m)$ be a subset of A. Assume the set B to be linearly dependent. Then there exists a set of real numbers $\{r_1, r_2, \ldots, r_k\}$ not all zero such that $\sum_{j=1}^{k} A_{i_j} r_j = 0$. In that case

$$\sum_{j=1}^{k} A_{i_j} r_j + \sum_{j=k+1}^{m} A_{i_j} \cdot 0 = \sum_{j=1}^{m} A_j r_j = 0$$

and the original set is linearly dependent. This contradicts the assumption and proves the theorem.

Theorem 10.43

If $A = \{A_1, A_2, \ldots, A_m\}$ is a set of linearly dependent vectors of a vector space V, then, if $B = \{B_1, B_2, \ldots, B_n\} \, \epsilon \, V$, the set $C = \{A_1, A_2, \ldots, A_m, B\}$ is also linearly dependent.

Proof. The proof is left to the student.

Theorem 10.44

If $\{A_1, A_2, \ldots, A_m\}$ is a set of m linearly independent vectors in $V(n)$ and we form a set of m vectors in $V(n + k)$ by introducing k additional components in each A_i, then the set of m vectors $B = \{B_1, B_2, \ldots, B_m\}$ so formed is also linearly independent.

Proof. We denote the elements of A_i and B_i by

$$A_i = (a_{i1} \quad a_{i2} \quad \cdots \quad a_{in}) \qquad\qquad i = 1, \ldots, m$$
$$B_i = (a_{i1} \quad a_{i2} \quad \cdots \quad a_{in} \quad a_{in+1} \quad \cdots \quad a_{in+k}) \qquad i = 1, \ldots, m$$

Assume, for the moment, that a set of scalars $\{s_1, s_2, \ldots, s_m\}$ exists such that $\sum_{i=1}^{m} s_i B_i = 0$ with some $s \neq 0$. This implies that

$$\sum_{i=1}^{m} a_{i1} s_i = 0$$
$$\sum_{i=1}^{m} a_{i2} s_i = 0 \qquad\qquad (10.16)$$
$$\cdot \ \cdot \ \cdot \ \cdot \ \cdot \ \cdot$$
$$\sum_{i=1}^{m} a_{in+k} s_i = 0$$

with some $s \neq 0$. However, since $\{A_1, \ldots, A_m\}$ is linearly independent, $r_i = 0$ $(i = 1, \ldots, m)$ are the only real numbers for which $\sum_{i=1}^{m} r_i A_i = 0$. This means that $r_i = 0$ are the only r_i's satisfying

$$\sum_{i=1}^{m} a_{ij} r_i = 0 \qquad j = 1, \ldots, n$$

Since this fact is contradicted by the first n equations in (10.16), the theorem is proved.

Example 10.45.   Given

$$E_1 = (1 \quad 0 \quad 0) \qquad E_2 = (0 \quad 1 \quad 0) \qquad E_3 = (0 \quad 0 \quad 1)$$

in $V(3)$. These are linearly independent. Let us form

$$B_1 = (1 \quad 0 \quad 0 \quad 2) \qquad B_2 = (0 \quad 1 \quad 0 \quad 3) \qquad B_3 = (0 \quad 0 \quad 1 \quad 5)$$

Then $\{B_1, B_2, B_3\}$ is also linearly independent, since

$$r_1 \bar{B}_1 + r_2 \bar{B}_2 + r_3 \bar{B}_3 = \bar{0}$$

implies that $r_1 \cdot 1 + r_2 \cdot 0 + r_3 \cdot 0 = 0$ so that $r_1 = 0$, and so on, for r_2 and r_3.

Definition 10.46. g is the *maximum number* of linearly independent vectors in a set of k vectors of V if there exists at least one subset of g linearly independent vectors and if no subset of more than g vectors is linearly independent.

PROBLEM SET 10.5

1. Determine whether or not this set of vectors of $V(3)$ $\{(1 \quad 0 \quad 0), (0 \quad 1 \quad 0), (0 \quad 0 \quad 1), (3 \quad 2 \quad 1)\}$ is linearly dependent.

2. Prove that the set of vectors $\{A_1, A_2, \ldots, A_m\}$ of V is a linearly dependent set if at least one of the vectors A_i is the zero vector.

3. Prove: If $\{A_1, \ldots, A_m\}$ is a set of vectors of a vector space V and if $\{r_1, \ldots, r_m\}$ is a set of real numbers such that $\{A_2 + r_2 A_1, A_3 + r_3 A_1, \ldots, A_m + r_m A_1\}$ is a linearly dependent set, then $\{A_1, \ldots, A_m\}$ is also.

4. For the purposes of vector spaces, column vectors are indistinguishable from row vectors. We therefore operate with the column vectors precisely as if they were row vectors. Determine whether the following vectors are linearly dependent:

a.

$$\begin{pmatrix} 1 \\ -1 \\ 4 \\ 2 \end{pmatrix} \quad \begin{pmatrix} 4 \\ 1 \\ 1 \\ 1 \end{pmatrix} \quad \begin{pmatrix} 2 \\ -1 \\ 0 \\ 1 \end{pmatrix}$$

b.

$$\begin{pmatrix} 1 \\ 0 \\ 0 \\ 0 \end{pmatrix} \quad \begin{pmatrix} 0 \\ 1 \\ 0 \\ 0 \end{pmatrix} \quad \begin{pmatrix} 0 \\ 0 \\ 1 \\ 0 \end{pmatrix} \quad \begin{pmatrix} 0 \\ 0 \\ 0 \\ 0 \end{pmatrix} \quad \begin{pmatrix} 2 \\ -4 \\ 3 \\ 0 \end{pmatrix}$$

5. Prove: If $A = \{A_1, A_2, \ldots, A_m\}$ is a set of linearly independent vectors and $X \epsilon A$, then $\{A_1, A_2, \ldots, A_m, X\}$ is also linearly independent.

10.8 LINEAR COMBINATIONS

It should be evident that, if we have a set of linearly dependent vectors, then some one of these vectors can be written in terms of the others. We develop this idea for its usefulness in solving equations. As before, capital letters denote vectors.

Definition 10.47. Linear combination $= \{\langle X, Y \rangle | X = \{A_1, A_2, \ldots, A_m\}$ & $Y = \sum_{i=1}^{m} a_i A_i$ & a_i are real numbers$\}$.

We speak of Y as a linear combination of the vectors $\{A_1, A_2, \ldots, A_m\}$.

Example 10.48. Let $X = \{(1 \quad 3), (4 \quad 1)\}$. Then

$$Y = (2(1 \quad 3) + 3(4 \quad 1)) = (2 \quad 6) + (12 \quad 3) = (14 \quad 9)$$

is a linear combination of the elements of X. Note that there are an infinite number of linear combinations possible if we allow the a's to be any real numbers.

The student will observe that, if the linear combination of a set of vectors is zero when not all a_i's are 0, the set of vectors is linearly dependent. If it is zero only when all a_i's are zero, it is linearly independent.

Example 10.49. Let $X = \{(1 \quad 3), (4 \quad 1), (1 \quad 0), (0 \quad 1)\}$. Among the linear combinations of these vectors we find

$$1(1 \quad 3) + 0(4 \quad 1) + (-1)(1 \quad 0) + (-3)(0 \quad 1) = (0 \quad 0)$$

Evidently the two vectors $(1 \quad 3)$, $(4 \quad 1)$ can be written as a linear combination of $(1 \quad 0)$ and $(0 \quad 1)$.

We prove the following theorem

Theorem 10.50

If a set of vectors $V = \{A_1, \ldots, A_m\}$ is linearly dependent, at least one $A_i \epsilon V$ can be written as a linear combination of the remaining vectors in V.

Proof. The proof is left to the student.

Corollary 10.51. If an element of V can be written as a linear combination of the other elements of V, V is a linearly dependent set.

Now we have the following important theorem.

Theorem 10.52

If $A = \{A_1, A_2, \ldots, A_m\}$ is a set of vectors in a vector space V, then the set L of all linear combinations of the elements of A is a subspace of V.

Proof. By Theorem 10.34, we need to prove only that L is closed under addition and scalar multiplication. We leave the proof to the student.

Definition 10.53. The subspace S of V containing all linear combinations of the subset A of V is called the *subspace generated by* A.

PROBLEM SET 10.6

1. Given the set of vectors $\{(1 \quad 2), (3 \quad 4)\}$ and the possible set of coefficients $\{1 \quad 3\}$. Write all linear combinations of $\{(1 \quad 2), (3 \quad 4)\}$.

2. Given $V(2)$. Show that any set of three vectors of $V(2)$ is a linearly dependent set.

3. Show that the vectors $(1 \quad 0)$ and $(0 \quad 1)$ generate $V(2)$, that is, the two-component vector space.

4. Show that the set of all linear combinations of

$$\{(1 \quad 0 \quad 0), (0 \quad 1 \quad 0), (0 \quad 0 \quad 1)\}$$

is a vector space.

10.9 BASIS

The student will have noticed that, in a given vector space, we can often select a subset of linearly independent vectors such that every other vector can be written as a linear combination of them. Such a set of vectors of a vector space V is of particular interest to us.

Definition 10.54. A set $A = \{A_1, A_2, \ldots, A_m\}$ of elements of a vector space V is a basis of V if

1. $A = \{A_1, A_2, \ldots, A_m\}$ is a linearly independent set.

2. The set of all vectors generated by A is the set V (that is, every vector in V can be written as a linear combination of A).

If a set of vectors A satisfies condition 2, then A is said to *span* V.

Example 10.55. The set $\{(1 \quad 1 \quad 1), (1 \quad 2 \quad 0), (1 \quad 1 \quad -1)\}$ forms a basis for $V(3)$.

We leave the proof to the student.

Theorem 10.56

The n unit vectors $A = \{E_1, E_2, \ldots, E_n\}$ are a basis for $V(n)$.

Proof. Condition 1 of Definition 10.54 is satisfied from Example 10.41. To show that condition 2 is satisfied, take any vector

$$B = (b_1 \quad b_2 \quad \cdots \quad b_n)$$

from $V(n)$. We can always express B as a linear combination of A by using the set of scalars $\{\lambda_i | \lambda_i = b_i (i = 1, \ldots, n)\}$, ·

$$(b_1 \quad b_2 \quad \cdots \quad b_n) = \lambda_1(1 \quad 0 \quad 0 \quad \cdots \quad 0) + \lambda_2(0 \quad 1 \quad 0 \quad \cdots \quad 0)$$
$$+ \cdots + \lambda_n(0 \quad 0 \quad 0 \quad \cdots \quad 1)$$

This proves the theorem.

Theorem 10.57

If $A = \{A_1, A_2, \ldots, A_m\}$ is a basis for $V(n)$, then any vector B of $V(n)$ can be uniquely expressed in terms of the elements of A.

Proof. We need prove only the uniqueness. Let $B = \sum\limits_{i=1}^{m} a_i A_i$ be a linear combination of the A_i expressing B (not all $a_i = 0$). Let $B = \sum\limits_{i=1}^{m} b_i A_i$ be any other linear combination of A_i expressing B. Then

$$\sum_{i=1}^{m} a_i A_i = \sum_{i=1}^{m} b_i A_i \quad \text{or} \quad \sum_{i=1}^{m} (a_i - b_i) A_i = 0$$

Since $A_i \neq 0$ by hypothesis,

$$a_i - b_i = 0$$
$$a_i = b_i$$

Theorem 10.58

Given the following conditions:
    1. The set of vectors $\{A_1, A_2, \ldots, A_k\}$ is a basis for $V(n)$.
    2. Any other nonnull vector

$$B = \sum_{i=1}^{k} \lambda_i A_i \tag{10.17}$$

replaces any vector A_i for which $\lambda_i \neq 0$.

Then the newly formed set of k vectors is also a basis for $V(n)$.

Proof. Since $B \neq 0$, at least one of the $\lambda_i \neq 0$. Arrange the A_i's so that $\lambda_k \neq 0$. We must prove that the set $\{A_1, \ldots, A_{k-1}, B\}$ is a basis for $V(n)$. The proof proceeds in two steps:

    1. The set $\{A_1, \ldots, A_{k-1}, B\}$ is linearly independent. To show this, assume that the set is dependent. Then

$$\sum_{i=1}^{k-1} \alpha_i A_i + \alpha B = 0 \tag{10.18}$$

with at least one α_i or $\alpha \neq 0$. However, α cannot be 0, since if it were, one or more of the α_i's would not be 0 (on the assumption that the $k - 1$

A_i's and B are linearly dependent) and this would contradict the fact that the k A_i's are linearly independent (Theorem 10.42). Substituting (10.17) into (10.18), we obtain

$$\sum_{i=1}^{k-1} \alpha_i A_i + \alpha \sum_{i=1}^{k} \lambda_i A_i = \sum_{i=1}^{k-1} \alpha_i A_i + \sum_{i=1}^{k} \alpha\lambda_i A_i = 0$$

$$\sum_{i=1}^{k-1} (\alpha_i + \alpha\lambda_i) A_i + \alpha\lambda_k A_k = 0$$

Since α and λ_k are not zero, $\alpha\lambda_k \neq 0$. But this contradicts the fact that the set $\{A_1, \ldots, A_k\}$ is linearly independent. Since this contradiction stems from the assumption that the set $\{A_1, \ldots, A_{k-1}, B\}$ is linearly dependent, the set $\{A_1, \ldots, A_{k-1}, B\}$ must be linearly independent.

2. The set $\{A_1, \ldots, A_{k-1}, B\}$ spans $V(n)$. To show this, take any vector C in $V(n)$. Since the set $\{A_1, \ldots, A_k\}$ is a basis, we can write C as a linear combination of these basis vectors,

$$C = \sum_{i=1}^{k} \delta_i A_i \tag{10.19}$$

From (10.17) we obtain

$$A_k = \frac{1}{\lambda_k} B - \sum_{i=1}^{k-1} \frac{\lambda_i}{\lambda_k} A_i$$

which, when substituted in (10.19), gives

$$C = \sum_{i=1}^{k-1} \delta_i A_i + \frac{\delta_k}{\lambda_k} B - \sum_{i=1}^{k-1} \frac{\delta_k\lambda_i}{\lambda_k} A_i$$

$$= \sum_{i=1}^{k-1} \left(\delta_i - \frac{\delta_k\lambda_i}{\lambda_k}\right) A_i + \frac{\delta_k}{\lambda_k} B \tag{10.20}$$

Since (10.20) expresses any vector C from $V(n)$ as a linear combination of $\{A_1, \ldots, A_{k-1}, B\}$, these vectors generate $V(n)$. Since the set of vectors $\{A_1, \ldots, A_{k-1}, B\}$ is linearly independent (part 1) and since it generates $V(n)$ (part 2), it is a basis of $V(n)$.

Theorem 10.59

Every basis for $V(n)$ contains exactly n vectors.

Proof. The proof proceeds in two steps:

1. Every basis for $V(n)$ has the same number of basis vectors. To show this, take any two bases for $V(n)$, for example, $\{A_1, \ldots, A_k\}$ and

$\{B_1, \ldots, B_g\}$. We must show that $k = g$. Number the A_i's in such a way that when B_g is expressed as a linear combination of the A_i's,

$$B_g = \sum_{i=1}^{k} \lambda_i A_i$$

we have $\lambda_k \neq 0$ (we know that some $\lambda_i \neq 0$, since, from Example 10.40, no linearly independent set of vectors can contain the null vector, and therefore $B_j, A_i \neq 0, j = 1, \ldots, g; i = 1, \ldots, k$). Applying Theorem 10.58, we know that $\{A_1, \ldots, A_{k-1}, B_g\}$ is a basis for $V(n)$. Thus we can write

$$B_{g-1} = \sum_{i=1}^{k-1} \alpha_i A_i + \alpha B_g$$

At least one α_i must be different from 0, since if all the $\alpha_i = 0$, α would have to be different from 0 (since none of the vectors are the null vector), implying that B_{g-1} is a linear combination of B_g and thereby contradicting the fact that the B_j's ($j = 1, \ldots, g$) are linearly independent. Arranging the vectors so that $\alpha_{k-1} \neq 0$, we form another basis for $V(n)$, that is, $\{A_1, \ldots, A_{k-2}, B_{g-1}, B_g\}$.

Continuing this procedure until all the B_j's have been used up, we obtain a basis which must take one of the two forms

$$\{A, \ldots, A_{k-g}, B_1, \ldots, B_g\} \qquad \text{or} \qquad \{B_1, \ldots, B_g\}$$

The first form implies that $k > g$. The second form, as it stands, would seem to indicate that $k \leq g$. However, k cannot be less than g, since if it were, we would find that, after all the A_i's had been replaced, the B_m's ($m = 1, \ldots, g - k$) would be linear combinations of the B_n's ($n = g - k + 1, \ldots, g$) (Theorem 10.58 plus the fact that the A_i's formed a basis) and this contradicts the fact that the B_j's ($j = 1, \ldots, g$) are independent. Therefore $k \geq g$. However, we could have started by inserting the A_i's into the B_j's, which, by similar reasoning, would lead to the conclusion that $g \geq k$. Since, when we inserted the B_j's, we showed that k cannot be less than g, we conclude that $g = k$.

2. Thus we can determine the actual number of vectors in a basis for $V(n)$ by finding any one basis and counting the number of vectors in it. In Theorem 10.56 we showed that the n unit vectors form a basis for $V(n)$. Therefore, every basis for $V(n)$ contains exactly n vectors.

Theorem 10.60

Any set of n linearly independent vectors from $V(n)$ is a basis for $V(n)$.

Proof. If $\{A_1, \ldots, A_n\}$ is any set of n linearly independent vectors from $V(n)$, we can start with the basis $\{E_1, \ldots, E_n\}$ containing the n unit vectors and insert each of the A_i's as in part 1 of the proof of Theorem 10.59. After n insertions we have a basis made up of the vectors $\{A_1, \ldots, A_n\}$.

Theorem 10.61

Any set of $k > n$ vectors from $V(n)$ is linearly dependent; that is, n is the maximum number (Definition 10.46) of linearly independent vectors in any set of k $(k > n)$ vectors from $V(n)$.

Proof. Let $\{A_1, \ldots, A_k\}$ be the set of k vectors from $V(n)$. Assume this set to be linearly independent. After n insertions into the basis $\{E_1, \ldots, E_n\}$ we would have the new basis $\{A_{k-n+1}, \ldots, A_k\}$. Since $\{A_{k-n+1}, \ldots, A_k\}$ is a basis, each of the vectors $\{A_1, \ldots, A_{k-n}\}$ can be expressed as a linear combination of the vectors $\{A_{k-n+1}, \ldots, A_k\}$. But this means that the set of vectors $\{A_1, \ldots, A_k\}$ is linearly dependent (Theorem 10.50). Therefore the assumption that a set of k $(k > n)$ vectors can be linearly independent is false.

Theorem 10.62

There are an infinite number of bases for $V(n)$.

Proof. We know the n unit vectors E_i form a basis for $V(n)$. Therefore any set of vectors of the form $c_i E_i$, where c_i is any real number, forms a basis. But there are an infinite number of c_i. Therefore the theorem is proved.

PROBLEM SET 10.7

1. Given the basis $(1 \quad 0)$ and $(0 \quad 1)$ for $V(2)$. Find two other bases, not merely scalar products of these two.

2. If $(1 \quad 0 \quad 0)$, $(0 \quad 1 \quad 0)$, $(0 \quad 0 \quad 1)$ is a basis for $V(3)$, find a basis for $V(4)$.

3. Can the set of vectors $\{(1 \quad 0 \quad 0), (0 \quad 1 \quad 0)(0 \quad 0 \quad 1)(3 \quad 2 \quad 1)\}$ be a basis for $V(3)$?

4. Find a basis for $V(3)$ which contains the vectors $(1 \quad -1 \quad 0)$ and $(2 \quad 1 \quad 3)$.

5. Is the set $\{(1 \quad 3), (1 \quad 2)\}$ a basis for $V(2)$?

6. Given the set of vectors generated by $\{(2 \quad 3 \quad 1), (1 \quad 2 \quad 3), (1 \quad 1 \quad 1)\}$. Does the vector $(2 \quad 1 \quad 5)$ belong to this set?

11 RANK AND THE GENERAL SOLUTION TO LINEAR EQUATIONS

11.1 MOTIVATION

In this chapter, we shall apply the theory of matrices, determinants and vector spaces developed in the preceding chapters to the solution of simultaneous linear equations. We have already shown how to write a set of n simultaneous linear equations in n variables as a single matrix equation. We have also indicated the conditions under which such a matrix equation has a solution. We wish to expand this theory to take care of m linear equations in n variables. First, however, we need the concept of the rank of a matrix and a few theorems connected with the determination of the rank of a matrix.

11.2 RANK

We first define the dimension of a vector space.

Definition 11.1. If V is a vector space and $A = \{A_1, A_2, \ldots, A_m\}$ is a basis for V, then m is the dimension of V. We write dim $V = m$.

Thus dim V is the number of vectors which form a basis for V. Since we proved that the number of vectors forming a basis for a given vector space V is unique, dim V is a function from the set of vector spaces to the set of nonnegative integers.

We have also seen that if $A = (a_{ij})$ denotes a matrix of shape $m \times n$, we can consider the rows and columns of the matrix as vectors, using the names row vectors and column vectors.

Evidently, in a given matrix we can use the set of row vectors (or column vectors) to generate a vector space. We shall designate this vector space as the row space (column space). Since this vector space will have a basis, we write the following definition.

Definition 11.2. If the set of vectors R is the row space of a matrix $A = (a_{ij})_{m\times n}$ then dim R is the *row rank* of $A = (a_{ij})_{m\times n}$. We use $r_r(A)$ to denote the row rank of A.

Definition 11.3. If C is the column space of a matrix $A = (a_{ij})_{m\times n}$, then dim C is the *column rank* of $A = (A_{ij})_{m\times n}$. We use $r_c(A)$ to denote the column rank of A.

Theorem 11.4

If $A = (a_{ij})$ is a matrix of shape $m \times n$, dim $R = r_r(A) \leq m$.

Proof. By definition of row space, each vector in R is a linear combination of the m row vectors in A. If k $(k = 1, 2, \ldots, m)$ is the maximum number of linearly independent rows in A, then the remaining $m - k$ rows can be expressed as linear combinations of them. This means that each vector in R can be expressed as a linear combination of k $(k = 1, \ldots, m)$ rows in A. Q.E.D.

Corollary 11.5. $r_r(A)$ is the maximum number of linearly independent rows in A.

The above theorem and corollary can be proved in the same way for $r_c(A)$.

Example 11.6

$$A = \begin{pmatrix} 2 & 0 & 0 & 0 \\ 0 & 2 & 0 & 0 \\ 0 & 0 & 2 & 0 \\ 0 & 0 & 0 & 2 \end{pmatrix}$$

has dim R = dim C = 4.

For convenience we shall now adopt a notation somewhat different from that used before. An $m \times n$ matrix will be denoted by capital letters, as earlier. However, a column vector will be denoted by a bold-face small letter, usually without subscript, e.g.,

$$\mathbf{x} = \begin{pmatrix} x_1 \\ x_2 \\ \cdot \\ \cdot \\ \cdot \\ x_m \end{pmatrix}$$

A boldface small letter with a subscript, for example, $\mathbf{x}_1$, will identify a particular column vector. Ordinary small letters will be used for the components of vectors or matrices. A row vector will be noted by a boldface small letter with a prime, for example, $\mathbf{x}' = (x_1 \ x_2 \ \ldots \ x_n)$. To identify a particular row vector, a subscript will be used, for example, $\mathbf{x}'_j$.

We now prove the following theorem.

Theorem 11.7

Let A be any $m \times n$ matrix and B any $n \times t$ matrix. Then each row of $AB = C$ is a linear combination of the rows of B.

  Proof.   Let

$$\mathbf{a}_j = \begin{pmatrix} a_{1j} \\ a_{2j} \\ \cdot \\ \cdot \\ \cdot \\ a_{mj} \end{pmatrix} \qquad j = 1, 2, \ldots, n$$

$$\mathbf{b}'_i = (b_{i1} \ b_{i2} \ \ldots \ b_{it}) \qquad i = 1, 2, \ldots, n$$
$$c_{ij} = a_{i1}b_{1j} + a_{i2}b_{2j} + \cdots + a_{in}b_{nj}$$
$$\qquad \qquad i = 1, \ldots, m; j = 1, \ldots, t \quad (11.1)$$
$$\mathbf{c}'_i = (c_{i1} \ c_{i2} \ \cdots \ c_{it}) \qquad i = 1, \ldots, m \qquad (11.2)$$

Substituting (11.1) into (11.2), we obtain

$$\mathbf{c}'_i = (a_{i1}b_{11} + a_{i2}b_{21} + \cdots + a_{in}b_{n1} \quad a_{i1}b_{12} + a_{i2}b_{22} + \cdots$$
$$\qquad \qquad + a_{in}b_{n2} \cdots a_{i1}b_{1t} + a_{i2}b_{2t} + \cdots + a_{in}b_{nt})$$
$$= (a_{i1}b_{11} \quad a_{i1}b_{12} \cdots a_{i1}b_{1t}) + (a_{i2}b_{21} \quad a_{i2}b_{22} \cdots a_{i2}b_{2t})$$
$$\qquad \qquad + \cdots + (a_{in}b_{n1} \quad a_{in}b_{n2} \cdots a_{in}b_{nt})$$
$$= a_{i1}\mathbf{b}'_1 + a_{i2}\mathbf{b}'_2 + \cdots + a_{in}\mathbf{b}'_n \qquad (11.3)$$

which proves the theorem

Theorem 11.8

The row space of an $m \times n$ matrix A contains the row space of a matrix product BA.

Proof. Each linear combination of the rows of A with the coefficients $w_1, \ldots, w_m$ is a matrix product $w'A$, where the row space of A includes all products $w'A$, with w' varying over V. From Theorem 11.7, we know that each row of a product BA can be expressed as one of the products $w'A$. Therefore, the rows of BA lie in the row space R of A. Since linear combinations of the rows of BA are linear combinations of vectors belonging to R, row space of $BA \leq$ row space of A.

Theorem 11.9

Let A be an $n \times n$ matrix. Then, if A is nonsingular, the row rank of A is n.

Proof. Let $\bar{B}$ be the inverse of A. Then $BA = I$, where B, A, and I are each $n \times n$ (Theorem 10.29). The rows of BA are contained in the row space of A (Theorem 11.8), and since $BA = I$, the rows of I are contained in the row space of A. Therefore, since the n rows of I are linearly independent (Example 10.41), $r_r(A) \geq n$. But there are only n rows in A, and, by definition of row space, all vectors in the row space V of A are linear combinations of the n vectors in A, so that $r_r(A)$ cannot exceed n. Therefore $r_r(A) = n$.

As a result of this theorem we can assert that the n rows of a nonsingular matrix are linearly independent.

Definition 11.10. The *determinant rank*, denoted by $r_d(A)$, of an $m \times n$ matrix A is k if each of the following conditions holds:

1. The determinant of at least one $k \times k$ submatrix in A is not zero.
2. The determinant of every $t \times t$ $(t = k + 1)$ submatrix in A is zero.

If all elements of A are 0, $r_d(A) = 0$.

Example 11.11. Let A be an $m \times n$ matrix. Show that, if $r_d(A) = k$, the determinant of every square submatrix of order s $(s > k)$ is zero.

Solution. By definition, the determinant of every $s \times s$ $(s = k + 1)$ is 0. We must show that the determinant of every $s \times s$ $(s > k + 1)$ submatrix is also 0. Let B be any square submatrix of order $k + 2$. If the determinant of B is obtained by the cofactor expansion of any row (or column), every cofactor is the determinant of a $(k + 1) \times (k + 1)$ submatrix of A and therefore has a value of 0. Hence the determinant of B is 0. By the same argument, any square submatrix of order $k + 3$ must be zero, and, by the process of induction, any square submatrix of order $k + r$ $(r = 1, 2, \ldots, v$, where v is the smaller of $m - k$ and $n - k)$ is 0.

Theorem 11.12

Let A be any $m \times n$ matrix. Then its determinant rank $r_d(A)$ equals its row rank $r_r(A)$.

Proof. Let $r_d(A) = k$. If $k = 0$, all the elements of A are 0 by definition. From Example 10.40 we know that no set of linearly independent vectors can contain the null vector, so that $r_r(A) = 0$. For $k > 0$, the proof is a little more complex.

Since we can interchange rows and columns of a matrix without affecting the absolute value of $r_r(A)$ or $r_d(A)$ (Theorem 10.11), we can, without loss of generality and for ease of notation, assume that the square $k \times k$ submatrix, denoted by B, in the upper left-hand corner of A has a determinant $\neq 0$ [since we take $r_d(A) = k$, there must be, by definition of $r_d(A)$, at least one $k \times k$ submatrix in A with determinant $\neq 0$]. From Definition 10.26, we know, since det $B \neq 0$, that B is nonsingular. From Theorem 11.9, we know, since B is nonsingular, that the row rank of B equals k. Then, by definition of $r_r(B)$, the k rows of B are linearly independent. Since

$$
B = \begin{pmatrix} a_{11} & a_{12} & \cdots & a_{1k} \\ a_{21} & a_{22} & \cdots & a_{2k} \\ \cdots & \cdots & \cdots & \cdots \\ a_{k1} & a_{k2} & \cdots & a_{kk} \end{pmatrix} \quad \text{and}
$$

$$
A = \begin{pmatrix} a_{11} & a_{12} & \cdots & a_{1k} & \cdots & a_{1n} \\ a_{21} & a_{22} & \cdots & a_{2k} & \cdots & a_{2n} \\ \cdots & \cdots & & \cdots & & \cdots \\ a_{k1} & a_{k2} & \cdots & a_{kk} & \cdots & a_{kn} \\ \cdots & \cdots & & \cdots & & \cdots \\ a_{m1} & a_{m2} & \cdots & a_{mk} & \cdots & a_{mn} \end{pmatrix}
$$

we know (Theorem 10.44) that the first k rows of A are also linearly independent. If $k = m$, then it is evident that $r_r(A) = r_d(A) = k$. Therefore we take $k < m$.

Let t be any fixed integer such that $k < t < m$. If we can show that any $\mathbf{a}'_t$ is a linear combination of $\mathbf{a}'_1, \mathbf{a}'_2, \ldots, \mathbf{a}'_k$, then we have proved that $r_r(A) = k$. For each integer $s = 1, 2, \ldots, n$, consider the $(k + 1) \times (k + 1)$ matrix C_s, defined as follows:

$$
C_s = \begin{pmatrix} a_{11} & a_{12} & \cdots & a_{1k} & a_{1s} \\ a_{21} & a_{22} & \cdots & a_{2k} & a_{2s} \\ \cdots & \cdots & \cdots & \cdots & \cdots \\ a_{k1} & a_{k2} & \cdots & a_{kk} & a_{ks} \\ a_{t1} & a_{t2} & \cdots & a_{tk} & a_{ts} \end{pmatrix}
$$

If $s \leq k$, C_s has two identical columns and therefore det $C_s = 0$ (Corollary 10.12). If $s > k$, C_s is a $(k + 1) \times (k + 1)$ submatrix of A and again det $C_s = 0$ [since it is given that $r_d(A) = k$]. Therefore, det $C_s = 0$ for $s = 1, 2, \ldots, n$. The cofactors, denoted by d_i $(i = 1, \ldots, t)$, of the elements of the last column of C_s do not depend on s, so that the cofactor expansion of C_s by its last column gives

$$\det C_s = a_{1s}d_1 + a_{2s}d_2 + \cdots + a_{ks}d_k + a_{ts}d_t = 0 \qquad s = 1, 2, \ldots, n$$

which can be written in terms of row vectors as

$$d_1\mathbf{a}_1' + d_2\mathbf{a}_2' + \cdots + d_k\mathbf{a}_k' + d_t\mathbf{a}_t' = 0$$

Now, $d_t \neq 0$, since it is the determinant of B. Therefore, the $k + 1$ row vectors $\mathbf{a}_1' + \cdots + \mathbf{a}_k' + \mathbf{a}_t'$ are linearly dependent for each t satisfying $k < t \leq m$, and we have proved that $r_r(A) = k = r_d(A)$.

Theorem 11.13

The column rank $r_c(A)$ of an $m \times n$ matrix A is equal to $r_r(A) = r_d(A)$.

   Proof.   Suppose that the row rank of A is k and the column rank k'. The row rank of the transpose A' of A is then equal to k', the column rank of A. Since $r_r(A') = r_d(A')$, all determinants of order $k' + 1$ in A' vanish. Since the determinant of a square matrix equals the determinant of its transpose (Theorem 10.4), this means that all determinants of order $k' + 1$ in A also vanish, so that $r_r(A) = k \leq k'$. Finally, since there is at least one nonzero $k' \times k'$ determinant in A', there is at least one nonzero $k' \times k'$ determinant in A, so that $r_r(A) = k \geq k'$. We therefore conclude that $r_r(A) = k = k' = r_c(A)$.

   Since we have already shown that $r_r(A) = r_d(A)$, we have

$$r_r(A) = r_c(A) = r_d(A)$$

That is, the rank of a matrix, whether it be defined by Definition 11.2, 11.3, or 11.10, is unique, and for this reason we shall from this point on refer only to the *rank*, denoted by $r(A)$, of a matrix. This leads to the following theorem

Theorem 11.14

The rank $r(A)$ of a matrix A, that is, dim R or dim C, can be computed by determining the order of the largest nonvanishing determinant in A.
Example 11.15.   What is the rank of

$$A = \begin{pmatrix} 2 & 4 \\ 3 & 5 \end{pmatrix}$$

Solution. Since

$$\det \begin{pmatrix} 1 & 4 \\ 3 & 5 \end{pmatrix} = -7 \neq 0 \qquad r(A) = 2$$

Example 11.16. What is the rank of

$$A = \begin{pmatrix} 0 & 0 & 0 \\ 1 & 3 & 5 \\ 2 & 4 & 6 \end{pmatrix}$$

Solution. Since

$$\det \begin{pmatrix} 0 & 0 & 0 \\ 1 & 4 & 5 \\ 2 & 4 & 6 \end{pmatrix} = 0$$

but since

$$\det \begin{pmatrix} 4 & 5 \\ 4 & 6 \end{pmatrix} = 4 \neq 0 \qquad r(A) = 2$$

Example 11.17. Determine the rank of an $n \times n$ identity matrix I.

Solution. We can write $I = (e_1 \ldots e_n)$. From Example 10.41, we know that the n e_i's are linearly independent so that $r(I) = n$.

Theorem 11.18

If the $n \times n$ matrix A is nonsingular, its n rows (or columns) form a basis for $V(n)$.

Proof. Since A is nonsingular, $r(A) = n$ (Theorem 11.9). Since there are n linearly independent rows (columns) from $V(n)$ in A, A is a basis for $V(n)$.

Corollary 11.19. Any n linearly independent vectors from $V(n)$ can be combined to form a matrix which is nonsingular.

PROBLEM SET 11.1

1. Find the dimensions of:

   a. $\begin{pmatrix} -1 & 2 & 1 \\ 1 & -1 & 2 \\ 1 & 1 & 4 \end{pmatrix}$

   b. $\begin{pmatrix} 1 & 0 & 0 \\ 0 & 1 & 0 \\ 0 & 0 & 1 \end{pmatrix}$

   c. $\begin{pmatrix} 1 & 2 & 1 & 1 \\ 0 & 1 & 2 & 1 \\ 0 & 0 & -5 & 3 \\ 0 & 0 & 0 & -2 \end{pmatrix}$

2. Find the dimension of the space generated by the set of vectors

$$\{(1\ 2-1),(3\ 1\ 2),(1-2\ 4)\}$$

(*Hint:* Find the rank of the matrix formed by these vectors.)

3. Prove that the transpose of a matrix has the same rank as the matrix itself.

4. Two $m \times n$ matrices are equivalent if they have the same rank. Prove that every 3×5 matrix will be equivalent to one of four 3×5 matrices. (*Hint:* What are the possible ranks of 3×5 matrices?)

11.3 SIMULTANEOUS LINEAR EQUATIONS

We can now use the preceding notions for the complete solution of the problem of solving any set of m linear equations in n variables. We do this by using matrices formed from various elements of the set of linear equations.

As we know from Chap. 10, we can express a set of m simultaneous linear equations in n variables by $A\mathbf{x} = \mathbf{b}$, where A is the $m \times n$ coefficients matrix, $\mathbf{x}$ is the column vector formed from the variables, and $\mathbf{b}$ is the column vector formed from the constants. We shall now determine the conditions which must be satisfied if the solution set of

$$A\mathbf{x} = \mathbf{b} \tag{11.4}$$

is to be nonempty. By a solution set of (11.4), we mean a set of vectors $\mathbf{a}$ such that, if $\mathbf{x}$ is replaced by any $\mathbf{a}$, (11.4) is true.

Assume that there are no restrictions on the value of m, that is, that m can be less than, equal to, or greater than n. We form the $m \times (n + 1)$ *augmented* matrix A_b by annexing to A the vector $\mathbf{b}$, which becomes column $n + 1$ in A_b; that is, $A_b = (A\ \mathbf{b}) = (\mathbf{a}_1\ \mathbf{a}_2\ \cdot\ \cdot\ \cdot\ \mathbf{a}_n\ \mathbf{b})$. Since every column in A also appears in A_b, $r(A_b) \geq r(A)$.

Theorem 11.20

If $r(A_b) > r(A)$, there is no solution to (11.4).

Proof. If $r(A_b) = k > r(A)$, every set of k linearly independent columns from A_b must contain $\mathbf{b}$, since A_b differs from A only by the annexing of $\mathbf{b}$. We take the two possible cases with respect to the values of k and n; that is, we consider $k = n + 1$ and $k < n + 1$ (k cannot exceed $n + 1$—why?).

1. $k = n + 1$. Since $k = r(A_b) = n + 1$, the set of $n + 1$ linearly independent vectors in A_b includes all the n vectors of A. From Theorem 10.50, $\mathbf{b}$ cannot therefore be written as a linear combination of the

columns of A—that is, there is no $\mathbf{x}$ such that

$$(\mathbf{a}_1 \; \cdots \; \mathbf{a}_n) \begin{pmatrix} x_1 \\ x_2 \\ \cdot \\ \cdot \\ \cdot \\ x_n \end{pmatrix} = \mathbf{b}$$

2. $k < n + 1$.   In this case each of the n vectors in A can be written as a linear combination of the $k - 1$ linearly independent vectors in A. Without loss of generality, we take the first $k - 1$ vectors to be linearly independent, so that

$$A =$$
$$(\mathbf{a}_1 \; \cdots \; \mathbf{a}_{k-1} \underbrace{(\alpha_1\mathbf{a}_1 + \cdots + \alpha_{k-1}\mathbf{a}_{k-1}) \; \cdots \; (\lambda_1\mathbf{a}_1 + \cdots + \lambda_{k-1}\mathbf{a}_{k-1}))}_{n-k+1 \text{ vectors}}$$

If we attempt to express $\mathbf{b}$ as a linear combination of the $\mathbf{a}_i$'s ($i = 1$, $\ldots$, n), we would therefore obtain

$$\mathbf{b} = \delta_1\mathbf{a}_1 + \cdots + \delta_{k-1}\mathbf{a}_{k-1} + \delta_k(\alpha_1\mathbf{a}_1 + \cdots + \alpha_{k-1}\mathbf{a}_{k-1}) + \cdots$$
$$+ \delta_n(\lambda_1\mathbf{a}_1 + \cdots + \lambda_{k-1}\mathbf{a}_{k-1})$$
$$= (\delta_1 + \delta_k\alpha_1 + \cdots + \delta_n\lambda_1)\mathbf{a}_1 + \cdots + (\delta_{k-1} + \delta_k\alpha_{k-1} + \cdots$$
$$+ \delta_n\lambda_{k-1})\mathbf{a}_{k-1}$$
$$= x_1\mathbf{a}_1 + \cdots + x_{k-1}\mathbf{a}_{k-1} \tag{11.5}$$

(the α_i's, λ_i's, δ_i's, x_i's are scalars).   That is, if $k < n + 1$, any vector which can be expressed as a linear combination of the n vectors from A can equivalently be expressed as a linear combination of the $k - 1$ linearly independent vectors from A.   But since the vectors $\mathbf{a}_1, \ldots$, $\mathbf{a}_{k-1}$, $\mathbf{b}$ are linearly independent, there is no vector $\mathbf{x}$ for which (11.5) holds.

The reader should recall from Chap. 7 that if a system of equations has no solution the equations are said to be *inconsistent*.

Example 11.21.   Does the following set of equations have a solution?

$$\begin{aligned} x_1 - 2x_2 + x_3 - x_4 &= 1 \\ 3x_i \quad\quad - 2x_3 + 3x_4 &= 4 \\ 5x_1 - 4x_2 \quad\quad + x_4 &= 3 \end{aligned}$$

Solution.   We write these in form $A\mathbf{x} = b$, where

$$\mathbf{x} = \begin{pmatrix} x_1 \\ x_2 \\ x_3 \\ x_4 \end{pmatrix}$$

$$b = \begin{pmatrix} 1 \\ 4 \\ 3 \end{pmatrix}$$

The coefficient matrix is

$$A = \begin{pmatrix} 1 & -2 & 1 & -1 \\ 3 & 0 & -2 & 3 \\ 5 & -4 & 0 & 1 \end{pmatrix}$$

The augmented matrix is

$$A_b = \begin{pmatrix} 1 & -2 & 1 & -1 & 1 \\ 3 & 0 & -2 & 3 & 4 \\ 5 & -4 & 0 & 1 & 3 \end{pmatrix}$$

Calculation will show that

$$r(A) = 2$$
$$r(A_b) = 3$$

Therefore, there is no solution.

Theorem 11.22

If $r(A) = r(A_b) = k$, there is at least one solution to (11.4).

Proof. Since $r(A) = r(A_b) = k$, every column of A_b, including **b**, can be expressed as a linear combination of k linearly independent columns of A. This implies that

$$(\mathbf{a}_1 \cdot \cdot \cdot \ \mathbf{a}_k \ \mathbf{a}_{k+1} \cdot \cdot \cdot \ \mathbf{a}_n) \begin{pmatrix} x_1 \\ x_2 \\ \cdot \\ \cdot \\ \cdot \\ x_k \\ x_{k+1} \\ \cdot \\ \cdot \\ \cdot \\ x_n \end{pmatrix} = \mathbf{b}$$

from some scalars $x_1, \ldots, x_k$, with $x_{k+1}, \ldots, x_n = 0$.

Note that this theorem is valid for $k < m$ and/or $k < n$; that is, there is no restriction on the value of k relative to m or n (except, of course, that k cannot exceed m or n—why?).

We shall now examine in more detail systems of equations for which $r(A) = r(A_b) = k$. We shall pay particular attention to the relationship between k, m, and n.

Theorem 11.23

Given that $r(A) = r(A_b) = k = m = n$. Then (11.4) has a unique solution.

   Proof. Since $r(A) = r(A_b)$, there is at least one solution (Theorem 11.22). Since $r(A) = n$, A is nonsingular (Theorem 11.9) so that $\det A \neq 0$ (Definition 10.26) and therefore A has an inverse A^{-1} (Corollary 10.27) which will give a unique (Theorem 10.30) solution $\mathbf{x} = A^{-1}\mathbf{b}$.

Theorem 11.24

Given that $r(A) = r(A_b) = k < m$. Then any $\mathbf{x}$ which satisfies the k equation $\mathbf{a}'_i\mathbf{x} = b_i$ corresponding to the k linearly independent rows in A satisfies all m equations.

   Proof. We denote the rows of A_b by

$$(\mathbf{a}'_i\, b_i) = (a_{i1}\, a_{i2}\, \cdots\, a_{in}\, b_i)$$

If we select k linearly independent rows from A, the corresponding rows of A_b will also be linearly independent (Theorem 10.44). Assume that these are the first k rows of A_b. Then any other row v in A_b is a linear combination of these first k rows, that is,

$$(\mathbf{a}'_v\, b_v) = \alpha_{1v}(\mathbf{a}'_1\, b_1) + \alpha_{2v}(\mathbf{a}'_2\, b_2) + \cdots + \alpha_{kv}(\mathbf{a}^k\, b_k)$$
$$v = k + 1, \ldots, m$$

Separating out b_v, we have

$$\mathbf{a}'_v = \sum_{i=1}^{k} \alpha_{iv}\mathbf{a}'_i \tag{11.6}$$

$$b_v = \sum_{i=1}^{k} \alpha_{iv}b_i \tag{11.7}$$

Since $r(A) = r(A_b)$, we know there is at least one solution to (11.4). This means that there is an $\mathbf{x}$ which satisfies the first k equations of (11.4), that is, an $\mathbf{x}$ such that

$$\begin{pmatrix} \mathbf{a}'_1 \\ \mathbf{a}'_2 \\ \cdot \\ \cdot \\ \cdot \\ \mathbf{a}'_k \end{pmatrix} \begin{pmatrix} x_1 \\ x_2 \\ \cdot \\ \cdot \\ \cdot \\ x_n \end{pmatrix} = \begin{pmatrix} b_1 \\ b_2 \\ \cdot \\ \cdot \\ \cdot \\ b_k \end{pmatrix}$$

or $\qquad\qquad \mathbf{a}'_i\mathbf{x} = b_i \qquad i = 1, \ldots, k \qquad\qquad$ (11.8)

If we multiply (11.6) by $\mathbf{x}$, we obtain

$$\mathbf{a}_v'\mathbf{x} = \sum_{i=1}^{k} \alpha_{iv}\mathbf{a}_i'\mathbf{x} \qquad v = k + 1, \ldots, m$$

which, upon substitution of (11.8) into the right-hand side, gives

$$\mathbf{a}_v'\mathbf{x} = \sum_{i=1}^{k} \alpha_{iv}b_i \qquad v = k + 1, \ldots, m$$

But when (11.7) is substituted into the right-hand side of the preceding equation, we obtain

$$\mathbf{a}_v'\mathbf{x} = b_v \qquad v = k + 1, \ldots, m$$

Thus we have shown that any $\mathbf{x}$ which satisfies k equations $\mathbf{a}_i'\mathbf{x} = b_i$ (corresponding to the k linearly independent rows in A) also satisfies the remaining $m - k$ equations in A.

As this implies, in seeking solutions to $A\mathbf{x} = \mathbf{b}$, given that

$$r(A) = r(A_b) = k < m$$

all equations except those corresponding to the k linearly independent rows in A can be ignored without affecting the solution in any way. Since these $m - k$ equations place no additional constraints on the variables, we call them *redundant*.

Theorem 11.25

Given that $r(A) = r(A_b) = k = n < m$. Then (11.4) has a unique solution.

Proof. From Theorem 11.24 we know that all but the k equations corresponding to the k linearly independent rows in A can be ignored in obtaining a solution. But this is the situation described in Theorem 11.23. *Q.E.D.*

Theorems 11.23 and 11.25 together imply that, if

$$r(A) = r(A_b) = k = n \le m$$

then there is a unique solution to $A\mathbf{x} = \mathbf{b}$. Note that, if

$$r(A) = r(A_b) = k = n$$

then n cannot exceed m, since $r(A) = r_c(A) = r_r(A)$ and there are only m rows. Furthermore, since there are only n columns in A, $r(A)$ cannot exceed n. Since we have treated the cases where $r(A) = r(A_b) = k = n$ and since $r(A) = r(A_b) = k$ cannot exceed n, we shall now examine the cases in which $r(A) = r(A_b) = k < n$.

Theorem 11.26

Given that $r(A) = r(A_b) = k < n$, then (11.4) has an infinite number of solutions.

Proof. Without loss of generality, we assume that the first k rows and columns in A form a nonsingular matrix B [we can make this assumption, since $r(A) = r_d(A) = k$]. This implies that the first k rows of A are linearly independent (Theorem 10.44), and we can therefore work just with these k rows, since we know (Theorem 11.24) that any solution which satisfies them will also satisfy all m rows. Let C denote a $k \times (n - k)$ matrix formed from the first k rows and last $n - k$ columns of A,

$$\mathbf{x}_b = \begin{pmatrix} x_1 \\ x_2 \\ \cdot \\ \cdot \\ \cdot \\ x_k \end{pmatrix}$$

$$\mathbf{x}_c = \begin{pmatrix} x_{k+1} \\ \cdot \\ \cdot \\ \cdot \\ x_n \end{pmatrix}$$

and $\mathbf{b}^*$ a column vector which contains the k elements of $\mathbf{b}$ which correspond to the k linearly independent rows in B. Thus we can write the first k equations as

$$B\mathbf{x}_b + C\mathbf{x}_c = \mathbf{b}^* \tag{11.9}$$

Since B is nonsingular, it has an inverse, so that we can write (11.9) as

$$\mathbf{x}_b = B^{-1}\mathbf{b}^* - B^{-1}C\mathbf{x}_c \tag{11.10}$$

Thus, if we are given any $\mathbf{x}_c$ we can solve uniquely for $\mathbf{x}_b$ in terms of x_c. That is, we can assign arbitrary values to the $n - k$ variables in $\mathbf{x}_c$, and the remaining k variables in $\mathbf{x}$ can be determined from (11.10) so that $\mathbf{x} = \begin{pmatrix} \mathbf{x}_b \\ \mathbf{x}_c \end{pmatrix}$ is a solution to $A\mathbf{x} = b$. Since an infinite number of values can be assigned to the variables in $\mathbf{x}_c$, there are an infinite number of solutions to (11.4).

Example 11.27. Determine the solution set of the set of linear equations,

$$\begin{aligned} x_1 - x_2 + x_3 &= 1 \\ 2x_1 - 2x_2 + 4x_3 &= 4 \\ x_1 - x_2 + 3x_3 &= 3 \end{aligned}$$

Solution. We have then

$$A = \begin{pmatrix} 1 & -1 & 1 \\ 2 & -2 & 4 \\ 1 & -1 & 3 \end{pmatrix}$$

$$A_b = \begin{pmatrix} 1 & -1 & 1 & 1 \\ 2 & -2 & 4 & 4 \\ 1 & -1 & 3 & 3 \end{pmatrix}$$

$$r(A) = r(A_b) = 2 < n \; (=3)$$

Moreover, the 2×2 submatrices of coefficients of x_1 and x_2 have determinants 0, but not the submatrix for coefficients of x_1 and x_3. We therefore solve for x_1 and x_3 in terms of x_2 and obtain

$$x_1 = x_2$$
$$x_3 = 1$$

The solution set consists of all triples $\langle c,c,1 \rangle$, where c is any constant.

Table 11.1 summarizes the results of this section thus far. It shows that, for those conditions which are theoretically possible, there are three mutually exclusive and collectively exhaustive possibilities: (1) the set of equations is inconsistent; (2) the set of equations has a unique solution; (3) the set of equations has an infinite number of solutions. These results, of course, agree with those of Chap. 7.

Assume that we have a set of m linear equations in n $(n > m)$ variables represented by $Ax = b$ in which $r(A) = r(A_b) = k = m < n$. Since $k = m$, none of the equations are redundant. Arrange the first $k = m$ columns in A so that the $m \times m$ submatrix formed from them is nonsingular [this can be done because $r(A) = r_d(A) = k$]. Then, from Theorem 11.26, we can generate an infinite number of solutions to $Ax = b$ by: (1) assigning arbitrary values to the $n - k$ variables not associated with the first k columns, and (2) solving (11.10). If we set these $n - k$

TABLE 11.1 IMPLICATIONS OF RANK FOR SOLUTIONS OF m SIMULTANEOUS LINEAR EQUATIONS IN n VARIABLES

Condition	*Implication*
1. $r(A) < r(A_b)$	Inconsistent
2. $r(A) > r(A_b)$	Impossible
3. $r(A) = r(A_b) = k$	
$\quad k = n = m$	Unique solution
$\quad k = n < m$	Unique solution
$\quad k = n > m$	Impossible
$\quad k > n$	Impossible
$\quad k < n, k \leq m$	Infinite number of solutions
$\quad k < n, k > m$	Impossible

variables all equal to 0, (11.10) becomes (since $B^{-1}C\mathbf{x}_c = B^{-1}C\mathbf{o} = 0$)

$$\mathbf{x}_b = \begin{pmatrix} x_1 \\ x_2 \\ \cdots \\ x_m \end{pmatrix} = B^{-1}\mathbf{b} = \begin{pmatrix} a_{11} & a_{12} & \cdots & a_{1m} \\ a_{21} & a_{22} & \cdots & a_{2m} \\ \cdots\cdots\cdots\cdots\cdots\cdots \\ a_{m1} & a_{m2} & \cdots & a_{mm} \end{pmatrix}^{-1} \begin{pmatrix} b_1 \\ b_2 \\ \cdots \\ b_m \end{pmatrix} \quad (11.11)$$

so that a solution to $A\mathbf{x} = \mathbf{b}$ is

$$\mathbf{x} = \begin{pmatrix} \mathbf{x}_b \\ \mathbf{o} \end{pmatrix}$$

This result, which is of fundamental importance in linear programming, leads to the following definition.

Definition 11.28. Given a set $A\mathbf{x} = \mathbf{b}$ of m simultaneous linear equations in n $(n > m)$ variables with $r(A) = m$. If any $m \times m$ nonsingular matrix is selected from A, and if all the $n - m$ variables not associated with the m columns of this matrix are set equal to 0, the resulting solution, containing no more than m nonzero variables, to the set of equations $A\mathbf{x} = \mathbf{b}$ is a *basic solution*. The m variables which can be different from 0 are *basic variables*.

Example 11.29. In a set of m equations in n variables, what is the maximum number of basic solutions possible?

    Solution. From Chap. 3 we know that the total number of combinations of m columns (variables) taken from n columns (variables) is given by $c = n!/m!(n - m)!$. However, for there to be exactly c distinct solutions, every set of m columns from A must be linearly independent, so that B^{-1} exists and a solution is defined for (11.11). If every set of m columns is not linearly independent, then the number of basic solutions is $<c$.

    It is theoretically possible that one or more of the basic variables, i.e., some of the x_i's in $\mathbf{x}_b$, vanish, so that more than $n - m$ variables will be 0 in the solution vector $\mathbf{x}$. We say that the basic solution is *degenerate* when this occurs.

PROBLEM SET 11.2

1. Show that the system

$$\begin{aligned} 2x_1 + 5x_2 - x_3 &= 2 \\ 3x_1 + 7x_2 - 2x_3 &= 7 \\ x_1 + 2x_2 - x_3 &= 5 \end{aligned}$$

has a solution by determining $r(A)$ and $r(A_b)$.

2. Analyze the set of linear homogeneous equations

$$2x_1 + 5x_2 - x_3 = 0$$
$$3x_1 + 7x_2 - 2x_3 = 0$$
$$x_1 + 2x_2 - x_3 = 0$$

by determining $r(A)$ and $r(A_b)$.

3. Solve the set in Prob. 1 for x_1 and x_2 in terms of x_3. Show that the set of solutions of Prob. 1 can be expressed in terms of the set of solutions of Prob. 2 (that is, if r_1, r_2, and r_3 are solutions of the set in Prob. 2, then the set of solutions in Prob. 1 consists of $r_1 + c_1$, $r_2 + c_2$, and $r_3 + c_3$).

4. Use the concepts of $r(A)$ and $r(A_b)$ to determine the nature of the solutions to the following systems:

a.
$$x_1 - 3x_2 + 2x_3 - 5x_4 = 7$$
$$x_1 - 3x_2 - x_3 - 5x_4 = 0$$

b.
$$x_1 - 2x_2 + x_3 = 0$$
$$x_1 - 2x_2 - x_3 = 0$$
$$2x_1 - 4x_2 - 5x_3 = 0$$

12 SIMPLEX METHOD OF LINEAR PROGRAMMING: THEORY[1]

12.1 MOTIVATION

Before beginning this chapter, the reader should review thoroughly Secs. 6.6 and 6.7, in which the general linear-programming problem is formulated and the graphical method of solution presented. The reader will recall that this method of solution is applicable only in situations involving two or at most three variables. Since almost all the situations that arise in practice involve more than two or three variables, the graphical method of solution is mainly of pedagogical importance. The reason why linear programming receives so much attention today is that methods of solution to the general linear-programming problem involving n variables have been developed.

---

[1] The reader may omit this chapter on first reading, or he may study it and omit the proofs.

The best-known and most widely used of these methods is called the *simplex method*, which was developed by George Dantzig in 1947 and made generally available in 1951. We shall now develop the theory and computational aspects of this procedure, which is essentially an iterative technique based on the algebra of vector spaces. The general problem we seek to solve is the maximization of the linear objective function

$z = \sum_{j=1}^{s} c_j x_j$, subject to m linear inequalities of the form

$$\sum_{j=1}^{s} a_{ij} x_j \leq b_i \qquad i = 1, \ldots, m$$

with $x_j, b_i \geq 0$ $(j = 1, \ldots, s; i = 1, \ldots, m)$.

The simplex method which we shall develop in this chapter is lengthy and somewhat involved. We outline the course of development so that the student may see the overall picture.

We shall proceed as follows:

1. We introduce the concept of *slack variables* to convert the set of "less than or equal to" constraints into a set of linear equalities.

2. We examine the effect of this conversion on the objective function.

3. We examine feasible solutions involving not more than m positive variables.

4. We consider methods of generating solutions containing not more than m positive variables which successively "improve" the objective function.

5. We study problems with no maximum solutions.

6. Finally, we determine the conditions which must be satisfied if a given solution is to be maximal and describe how to arrive at such a solution, if one exists.

12.2 SLACK VARIABLES

The first step in the simplex procedure is to convert the m inequalities in s variables,

$$\sum_{j=1}^{s} a_{ij} x_j \leq b_i \qquad i = 1, \ldots, m \qquad (12.1)$$

which represent the structural constraints into a system of m simultaneous linear equations in n $(n > s)$ variables. We do this by introducing additional variables called slack variables. We assume that $b_i \geq 0$.

While this assumption corresponds to the actual fact in almost all situations that arise in practice, it is not a crucial assumption, since if some $b_i < 0$, multiplication of the relevant inequalities by -1 would make these $b_i > 0$ (of course, if the inequalities were $\leq$, this multiplication would transform the inequalities to $\geq$; however, inequalities of this type are readily handled by the general simplex method).

Consider a typical constraint, say the rth constraint,

$$\sum_{j=1}^{s} a_{rj} x_j \leq b_r$$

We introduce the *slack* variable $x_{s+r} \geq 0$ where

$$x_{s+r} = b_r - \sum_{j=1}^{s} a_{rj} x_j \geq 0$$

When this slack variable is added to the rth inequality, we obtain the equation

$$\sum_{j=1}^{s} a_{rj} x_j + x_{s+r} = b_r$$

We call x_{s+r} a slack variable since it represents the difference between the available amount (b_r) of the resource corresponding to the rth constraint and the amount $\left(\sum_{j=1}^{s} a_{rj} x_j \right)$ actually used.

By introducing slack variables for each of the m constraints, we can convert the original m inequalities into a set of m simultaneous linear equations in $n = s + m$ variables,

$$\sum_{j=1}^{s} a_{ij} x_j + x_{s+i} = b_i \qquad i = 1, 2, \ldots, m \qquad (12.2)$$

We can write (12.2) in matrix form as

$$A\mathbf{x} = \mathbf{b} \qquad (12.3)$$

where

$$\mathbf{x} = \begin{pmatrix} x_1 \\ x_2 \\ \cdot \\ \cdot \\ \cdot \\ x_n \end{pmatrix} \qquad \mathbf{b} = \begin{pmatrix} b_1 \\ b_2 \\ \cdot \\ \cdot \\ \cdot \\ b_m \end{pmatrix}$$

$$A = (\mathbf{a}_1 \, \mathbf{a}_2 \, \cdots \, \mathbf{a}_s \, \mathbf{e}_1 \, \mathbf{e}_2 \, \cdots \, \mathbf{e}_m) \qquad \mathbf{a}_i = \begin{pmatrix} a_{1i} \\ a_{2i} \\ \cdot \\ \cdot \\ \cdot \\ a_{mi} \end{pmatrix}$$

$$A = \begin{pmatrix} a_{11} & a_{12} & \cdots & a_{1s} & 1 & 0 & \cdots & 0 \\ a_{21} & a_{22} & \cdots & a_{2s} & 0 & 1 & \cdots & 0 \\ \cdot & \cdot & \cdots & \cdot & \cdot & \cdot & \cdots & \cdot \\ a_{m1} & a_{m2} & \cdots & a_{ms} & 0 & 0 & \cdots & 1 \end{pmatrix} \qquad (12.4)$$

$$\underbrace{\phantom{a_{11} \quad a_{12} \quad \cdots \quad a_{1s} \quad 1 \quad 0 \quad \cdots \quad 0}}_{m \text{ columns}}$$

Note that $\mathbf{e}_i$, the ith m-component unit vector, is the column of A which corresponds to variable x_{s+i}; in this way x_{s+i} can appear only in Eq. (i), where it was introduced to remove an inequality.

Example 12.1. Convert the following set of $m = 3$ linear inequalities in $s = 4$ variables into a set of $m = 3$ simultaneous linear equations in $n = s + m = 4 + 3 = 7$ variables. Use the notation of (12.2), (12.3), and (12.4).

$$2x_1 + 3x_2 + x_3 + 4x_4 \leq 8$$
$$x_1 + 2x_2 + 3x_3 + 9x_4 \leq 3$$
$$5x_1 + 4x_3 + x_4 \leq 16$$

Solution. We have, employing (12.2),

$$2x_1 + 3x_2 + x_3 + 4x_4 + x_5 = 8$$
$$x_1 + 2x_2 + 3x_3 + 9x_4 + x_6 = 3$$
$$5x_1 + 4x_3 + x_4 + x_7 = 16$$

Employing (12.3) and (12.4), we obtain $A\mathbf{x} = \mathbf{b}$, where

$$\mathbf{x} = \begin{pmatrix} x_1 \\ x_2 \\ x_3 \\ x_4 \\ x_5 \\ x_6 \\ x_7 \end{pmatrix} \qquad \mathbf{b} = \begin{pmatrix} 8 \\ 3 \\ 16 \end{pmatrix} \qquad A = \begin{pmatrix} 2 & 3 & 1 & 4 & 1 & 0 & 0 \\ 1 & 2 & 3 & 9 & 0 & 1 & 0 \\ 5 & 0 & 4 & 1 & 0 & 0 & 1 \end{pmatrix}$$

Example 12.2. To make the preceding example concrete, assume that x_1, x_2, x_3, and x_4 represent, respectively, the number of units of products 1, 2, 3, and 4 produced daily; that a_{ij} $(i = 1, \ldots, 3; j = 1, \ldots, 4)$ represents the number of hours required on machine i to produce product j; and that b_i $(i = 1, \ldots, 3)$ denotes the number of hours available on machine i. Then, if $x_1 = 1$, $x_2 = \frac{1}{2}$, $x_3 = \frac{1}{3}$, and $x_4 = 0$, upon substituting into the first constraint we find that $3\frac{5}{6}$ hours of machine 1 will be used, so that $x_5 = 8 - 3\frac{5}{6} = 4\frac{1}{6}$ hours remain idle or slack. Similarly, all the hours of machine 2 are used ($x_6 = 0$); and only $6\frac{1}{3}$ hours of machine 3, so $x_7 = 16 - 6\frac{1}{3} = 9\frac{2}{3}$ hours of machine 3 remain slack or idle.

We must now examine the effect of the introduction of the slack variables on the objective function,

$$z = \sum_{j=1}^{s} c_j x_j \qquad (12.5)$$

to be maximized. Let $c_{s+i} = 0$ ($i = 1, \ldots, m$). Then

$$\sum_{j=1}^{n} c_j x_j = c_1 x_1 + \cdots + c_s x_s + 0 x_{s+1} + \cdots + 0 x_n = \sum_{j=1}^{s} c_j x_j \qquad (12.6)$$

Theorem 12.3

Given that $\mathbf{x}^*$ is a maximal feasible solution to the transformed constraints (12.2) and objective function (12.6), the maximum value being z^*. Then the first s elements $x_1^*, \ldots, x_s^*$ of $\mathbf{x}^*$ represent a maximal feasible solution to (12.1) and (12.5), the maximum value being z^*.

Proof. A direct comparison of (12.5) and (12.6) shows that, if $\mathbf{x}^*$ yields a value for (12.6) of z^*, then the solution $x_1^*, \ldots, x_s^*$ yields a value for (12.5) of z^*. We must show that z^* is also the maximal value for (12.1) and (12.5). Note, first, that, if we have any feasible solution to (12.1) into which we introduce slack variables, our method of introducing slack variables will yield a feasible solution to (12.2). Conversely, if we have any feasible solution $\mathbf{x}$ to (12.2), the first s elements of $\mathbf{x}$ yield a feasible solution to (12.1). Thus, there is a 1–1 correspondence between the set of feasible solutions to (12.1) and the set of feasible solutions to (12.2), or, putting it another way, we have described a function

$$f = \left\{ \langle D, E \rangle | D = \langle x_1, \ldots, x_s \rangle \ \& \ E = \langle x_1, \ldots, x_s, x_{s+1}, \ldots, x_n \rangle \right.$$
$$\left. \& \ x_j \geq 0 (j = 1, \ldots, n) \ \& \ x_{s+i} = b_i - \sum_{j=1}^{s} a_{ij} x_j (i = 1, \ldots, m) \right\}$$

which has an inverse

$$f^{-1} = \left\{ \langle E, D \rangle | E = \langle x_1, \ldots, x_s, x_{s+1}, \ldots, x_n \rangle \ \& \ D = \langle x_1, \ldots, x_s \rangle \right.$$
$$\left. \& \ x_j \geq 0 (j = 1, \ldots, n) \ \& \ x_{s+i} = b_i - \sum_{j=1}^{s} a_{ij} x_j (i = 1, \ldots, m) \right\}$$

Assume, now, that the theorem is false. That is, assume that a different feasible solution, say $\hat{x}_1, \ldots, \hat{x}_s$, to (12.1) gives a z value, denoted by $\hat{z}$, which exceeds the value z^* associated with the solution $x_1^*, \ldots, x_s^*$. We could then introduce nonnegative slack variables $\hat{x}_{s+1}, \ldots, \hat{x}_n$ such that $\hat{x}_1, \ldots, \hat{x}_n$ is a feasible solution to (12.2) with a z value of $\hat{z}$. But $\hat{z} > z^*$, and this contradicts the fact that $\mathbf{x}^*$ maximizes (12.2) and (12.6). Therefore the solution $x_1^*, \ldots, x_s^*$ maximizes (12.1) and (12.5). In a similar fashion, we can show that by adding slack variables to a maximal feasible solution to (12.1) we obtain a maximal feasible solution to (12.2). Thus there is a 1–1 correspondence between the sets of maximal feasible solutions to (12.2) and (12.1) which is described by

$$f = \left\{ \langle F, G \rangle \, | \, F = \langle x_1^*, \ldots, x_s^*, x_{s+1}^*, \ldots, x_n^* \rangle \text{ is a maximal} \right.$$
$$\text{solution to (12.2) \& } G = \langle x_1^*, \ldots, x_s^* \rangle \text{ is a maximal}$$
$$\text{solution to (12.1) \& } x_j^* \geq 0, j = 1, \ldots, n \, \&$$
$$\left. x_{s+i} = b_i - \sum_{j=1}^{s} a_{ij} x_j, \, i = 1, \ldots, m \right\}$$

We have therefore shown that: (1) each feasible solution $\mathbf{x}$ to (12.2) corresponds to one and only one feasible solution to (12.1), namely, the solution containing the first s elements of $\mathbf{x}$; (2) a maximal feasible solution $\mathbf{x}^*$ to (12.2) corresponds to a unique maximal feasible solution to (12.1), namely, the solution containing the first s element of $\mathbf{x}^*$; (3) the value of (12.6) associated with any $\mathbf{x}$ equals the value of (12.5) associated with the first s elements of $\mathbf{x}$. Thus, if we can find a solution which maximizes (12.2) and (12.6), we have solved the linear-programming problem summarized by (12.1) and (12.5).

12.3 SOME ASSUMPTIONS

We shall now comment on the implications of some of the assumptions that we shall make at the outset of our development of the simplex method. We assume, for the set of constraints (12.3), that $r(A) = r(A_b)$ so that the system is consistent and at least one solution exists. We also assume that $r(A) = m$ so that none of the constraint equations are redundant. Since $r(A) = r_r(A) = r_c(A)$, this assumption implies that there are at least as many variables as equations. In the typical situation, if the problem is properly formulated, both assumptions will be satisfied with the number of variables n exceeding the number of constraints m.

These assumptions do not restrict the generality of the simplex method, since the application of the method automatically provides a check on the validity of these assumptions, without the need ever actually to compute $r(A)$. Furthermore, the application of the simplex method will also indicate whether or not a feasible solution exists.

12.4 BASIC FEASIBLE SOLUTIONS

We shall now state and prove a very important theorem. But first we need the following definition.

Definition 12.4. A *basic* feasible solution to a linear-programming problem summarized by (12.3) is a feasible solution in which there are at most m variables with a value different from 0.

From the preceding chapter we know that if $r(A) = r(A_b)$ then (12.3) has a solution and, furthermore, if $r(A) = m$ then **b** can be written as a linear combination of m linearly independent columns of A; so there is a solution to (12.3) with at most m variables (not necessarily all nonnegative) different from 0. We now give the following Theorem.

Theorem 12.5

Given a set of m simultaneous linear equations in n variables $(n \geq m)$ in matrix form,

$$A\mathbf{x} = \mathbf{b}$$

with $r(A) = m$. Then, if there is a feasible solution $\mathbf{x}$, there is at least one basic feasible solution.

Proof. Assume that a feasible solution with $k \leq n$ positive variables exists. We number the variables so that the first k are positive. The feasible solution can then be written

$$\sum_{j=1}^{k} x_j \mathbf{a}_j = \mathbf{b}$$

with $x_j > 0$ for $j = 1, \ldots , k$ and $x_j = 0$ for $j = k + 1, \ldots , n$. The k vectors associated with the positive variables may be linearly independent or dependent. Assume, first, that the k vectors are linearly independent. Then, since $r(A) = m$, $k \leq m$. If $k = m$, the given solution is already a nondegenerate basic feasible solution. If $k < m$, the given solution is actually a degenerate basic feasible solution. This follows since [remember that $r(A) = m$] we can find $m - k$ columns in A which, together with the k columns, will form a basis for $V(m)$; the feasible solution with $k < m$ variables positive can thus be viewed as a degenerate basic feasible solution with $m - k$ of the basic variables equal to 0.

Assume, now, that the vectors corresponding to positive variables are linearly dependent. We shall introduce a procedure which will reduce the number of positive variables successively until the columns associated with the positive variables are linearly independent. Since the k vectors are linearly dependent, there exist λ_i's not all 0 such that

$$\sum_{j=1}^{k} \lambda_j \mathbf{a}_j = 0 \tag{12.7}$$

We shall use (12.7) to reduce some x_r in

$$\sum_{j=1}^{k} x_j \mathbf{a}_j = \mathbf{b} \qquad x_j > 0; j = 1, \ldots, k \tag{12.8}$$

to 0. Suppose that one, say $\mathbf{a}_r$, of the k vectors in (12.7) for which $\lambda_r > 0$ is expressed as a linear combination of the remaining $k - 1$ vectors

$$\mathbf{a}_r = -\sum_{\substack{j=1 \\ j \neq r}}^{k} \frac{\lambda_j}{\lambda_r} \mathbf{a}_j \tag{12.9}$$

[We can always find some $\lambda_r > 0$, since, even if all the original $\lambda_j \leq 0$, we can multiply (12.7) by -1 to obtain some new $\lambda_j > 0$.] Substituting (12.9) into (12.8) gives

$$\sum_{\substack{j=1 \\ j \neq r}}^{k} x_j \mathbf{a}_j - x_r \sum_{\substack{j=1 \\ j \neq r}}^{k} \frac{\lambda_j}{\lambda_r} \mathbf{a}_j = \sum_{\substack{j=1 \\ j \neq r}}^{k} \left(x_j - x_r \frac{\lambda_j}{\lambda_r} \right) \mathbf{a}_j = \mathbf{b} \tag{12.10}$$

Equation (12.10) is a solution with not more than $k - 1$ nonzero variables.

Although we have reduced the number of nonzero variables in the solution, it is possible that some of the nonzero variables are negative, so that the reduced solution is not feasible. We can make certain that the reduced solution is also feasible if we select $\mathbf{a}_r$ according to the following procedure.

From (12.10), in order to obtain a feasible solution we must have

$$x_j - x_r \frac{\lambda_j}{\lambda_r} \geq 0 \qquad j = 1, \ldots, k; j \neq r \tag{12.11}$$

Equation (12.11) will be automatically satisfied for any j for which $\lambda_j = 0$ (remember that the original x_j's form a feasible solution so that each $x_j \geq 0$). Moreover, since $\lambda_r > 0$, (12.11) will be satisfied for any j for which $\lambda_j < 0$. We are thus left with those j's for which $\lambda_j > 0$. In these cases, division of (12.11) by λ_j will give

$$\frac{x_j}{\lambda_j} - \frac{x_r}{\lambda_r} \geq 0 \qquad (12.12)$$

If we satisfy (12.12), we satisfy (12.11); that is, we can use (12.12) to determine which vector $\mathbf{a}_r$ in (12.7) to select so that the remaining $k - 1$ vectors in (12.10) correspond to variables which are nonnegative.

We compute all ratios $\alpha = x_j/\lambda_j$ for which $\lambda_j > 0$. There will be at most k such ratios. We take as $\mathbf{a}_r$ the vector which corresponds to the minimum value in the set

$$\left\{ \alpha \,\middle|\, \alpha = \frac{x_j}{\lambda_j} \text{ for all } j\text{'s for which } \lambda_j > 0 \right\} \qquad (12.13)$$

The variable x_r corresponding to the minimum α will vanish when $\mathbf{a}_r$, as given by (12.9), is substituted into (12.8) [see (12.10)]. Since x_r/λ_r is the minimum x_j/λ_j (for all j's corresponding to $\lambda_j > 0$), (12.12) will be satisfied (note that $x_j/\lambda_j \geq x_r/\lambda_r$) so that the $k - 1$ variables in (12.10) will be nonnegative. If the minimum in (12.13) is not unique—i.e., if two or more x_j/λ_j have the same minimum value—then in (12.12) some $x_j/\lambda_j = x_r/\lambda_r$ and more than one variable will vanish so that there may be less than $k - 1$ positive variables. (Since $\mathbf{b} \neq \mathbf{0}$, it is not possible for all k of the x_j's to vanish.)

In any event, at least one of the original k variables will vanish, and we shall have a solution with not more than $k - 1$ positive variables, all other variables being 0. If the columns associated with the positive variables are still linearly dependent, we repeat the reduction procedure just described. Eventually we shall derive a solution in which the columns corresponding to the positive variables are linearly independent (remember that none of the $\mathbf{a}_j = \mathbf{0}$ and that a set containing a single nonnull vector is linearly independent).

We examined this situation at the outset of this discussion. We showed then that, if we have a feasible solution in which the set of column vectors associated with the nonzero variables is linearly independent, we can form a basic feasible solution. We have just shown that, if the original set of column vectors associated with the feasible solution is linearly dependent, it can be transformed into a set which is linearly independent and which still gives a feasible solution. Theorem 12.5 is proved.

Basic feasible solutions are important because most of the simplex operations are in terms of these solutions.

Example 12.6.   Given the following set of $m = 2$ simultaneous linear equations in $n = 4$ unknowns, with the feasible solution $x_1 = 1$, $x_2 = 1$, $x_3 = 1$, $x_4 = 3$.   Obtain a basic feasible solution.

$$x_1 + 2x_2 + x_3 \qquad = 4$$
$$x_1 + 4x_2 \qquad + x_4 = 8$$

Solution.   We express the above system as

$$A\mathbf{x} = \mathbf{b}$$

where $\qquad A = \begin{pmatrix} 1 & 2 & 1 & 0 \\ 1 & 4 & 0 & 1 \end{pmatrix} \qquad \mathbf{x} = \begin{pmatrix} x_1 \\ x_2 \\ x_3 \\ x_4 \end{pmatrix} \qquad \mathbf{b} = \begin{pmatrix} 4 \\ 8 \end{pmatrix}$

From the results of the preceding chapter, the student should be able to determine that $r(A) = m = 2$, so that a basic feasible solution will contain no more than two positive variables.   Then, since the present solution contains $k = n = 4$ positive variables, the $k = 4$ vectors associated with them are linearly dependent.   Following (12.8), we can express the present feasible solution as

$$1\begin{pmatrix} 1 \\ 1 \end{pmatrix} + 1\begin{pmatrix} 2 \\ 4 \end{pmatrix} + 1\begin{pmatrix} 1 \\ 0 \end{pmatrix} + 3\begin{pmatrix} 0 \\ 1 \end{pmatrix} = \begin{pmatrix} 4 \\ 8 \end{pmatrix} \qquad (12.8a)$$

The student can verify that $\lambda_1 = 3$, $\lambda_2 = -1$, $\lambda_3 = -1$, $\lambda_4 = 1$ satisfy (12.7), so that

$$3\begin{pmatrix} 1 \\ 1 \end{pmatrix} - 1\begin{pmatrix} 2 \\ 4 \end{pmatrix} - 1\begin{pmatrix} 1 \\ 0 \end{pmatrix} + 1\begin{pmatrix} 0 \\ 1 \end{pmatrix} = \begin{pmatrix} 0 \\ 0 \end{pmatrix} \qquad (12.7a)$$

If we compute all ratios $\alpha = x_j/\lambda_j$ for which $\lambda_j > 0$, we obtain

$$\alpha_1 = \frac{x_1}{\lambda_1} = \frac{1}{3} \qquad \alpha_2 = \frac{x_4}{\lambda_4} = \frac{3}{1}$$

Following the analysis of this section, we take as the vector $\mathbf{a}_r$ to be removed that vector corresponding to the minimum α for which $\lambda_j > 0$; that is, we take the vector corresponding to $\alpha_1 = x_1/\lambda_1 = \frac{1}{3}$, namely, $\mathbf{a}_r = \mathbf{a}_1$.   Using (12.10), we find a new feasible solution involving $k - 1 = 4 - 1 = 3$ positive variables $x_1' = 0$, $x_2' = \frac{4}{3}$, $x_3' = \frac{4}{3}$, $x_4' = \frac{8}{3}$,

$$\frac{4}{3}\begin{pmatrix} 2 \\ 4 \end{pmatrix} + \frac{4}{3}\begin{pmatrix} 1 \\ 0 \end{pmatrix} + \frac{8}{3}\begin{pmatrix} 0 \\ 1 \end{pmatrix} = \begin{pmatrix} 4 \\ 8 \end{pmatrix} \qquad (12.8b)$$

We now repeat the procedure for the system (12.8b) and (12.7b) below (note that the new x_j and λ_j are designated with a prime),

$$2\begin{pmatrix} 2 \\ 4 \end{pmatrix} - 4\begin{pmatrix} 1 \\ 0 \end{pmatrix} - 8\begin{pmatrix} 0 \\ 1 \end{pmatrix} = \begin{pmatrix} 0 \\ 0 \end{pmatrix} \qquad (12.7b)$$

The reader can verify that $\lambda_2' = 2$, $\lambda_3' = -4$, $\lambda_4' = -8$ satisfy (12.7). Since only $\lambda_2' = 2$ is > 0, we let $\mathbf{a}_r = \mathbf{a}_2$, so that we obtain, using (12.10), a nondegenerate basic feasible solution $x_1'' = 0$, $x_2'' = 0$, $x_3'' = 4$, $x_4'' = 8$, which the reader can verify from

$$4 \binom{1}{0} + 8 \binom{0}{1} = \binom{4}{8} \tag{12.8c}$$

The reader can verify that, if we used $\lambda_2' = -1$, $\lambda_3' = 2$, $\lambda_4' = 4$ in (12.7b), we would have obtained a degenerate basic feasible solution with $x_1'' = 0$, $x_2'' = 2$, $x_3'' = 0$, $x_4'' = 0$.

12.5 SOME NOTATION

The general linear-programming problem summarized by (12.1) has been transformed, by the addition of slack variables, to (12.2) and (12.3). Since we are assuming that $r(A) = m$, there will be at least one set of m linearly independent columns in A. We shall denote by B any matrix composed of m linearly independent columns from A. We shall refer to B as the *basis* matrix, since the columns of $B = (\mathbf{b}_1 \ \mathbf{b}_2 \ \cdots \ \mathbf{b}_m)$ form a basis for $V(m)$. Any column $\mathbf{a}_j$ of A can then be written as a linear combination of the columns of B. We shall use the following notation to represent such a combination,

$$\mathbf{a}_j = y_{ij}\mathbf{b}_1 + \cdots + y_{mj}\mathbf{b}_m = \sum_{i=1}^{m} y_{ij}\mathbf{b}_i = B\mathbf{y}_j \tag{12.14}$$

where
$$\mathbf{y}_j = \begin{pmatrix} y_{1j} \\ y_{2j} \\ \cdot \\ \cdot \\ \cdot \\ y_{mj} \end{pmatrix} = B^{-1}\mathbf{a}_j \tag{12.15}$$

(B^{-1} exists, from Theorem 11.18). The subscript j refers to the vector $\mathbf{a}_j$ and the subscript i to the column of B which is multiplied by y_{ij} in (12.14). The vector $\mathbf{y}_j$ will change if the columns of A making up B change.

Any basis matrix B will yield a basic solution (Sec. 11.3) to $A\mathbf{x} = \mathbf{b}$. We denote this solution by

$$\mathbf{x}_B = \begin{pmatrix} x_{B1} \\ x_{B2} \\ \cdot \\ \cdot \\ \cdot \\ x_{Bm} \end{pmatrix}$$

where x_B is determined from

$$\mathbf{x}_B = B^{-1}\mathbf{b} \tag{12.16}$$

The subscript i in x_{Bi} indicates that x_{Bi} corresponds to column $\mathbf{b}_i$ of B.

Corresponding to any $\mathbf{x}_B$, we denote by $\mathbf{c}'_B$ the m-component row vector containing the constants, taken from the objective function (12.6), associated with the basic variables,

$$\mathbf{c}'_B = (c_{B1}\, c_{B2} \cdots c_{Bm})$$

The subscript i indicates that c_{Bi} is the objective function constant corresponding to variable x_{Bi}. This notation implies that for any basic feasible solution, since all nonbasic variables vanish, the value z of the objective function is given by

$$z = \mathbf{c}'_B\mathbf{x}_B \tag{12.17}$$

In linear-programming terminology, the constants $\mathbf{c}'_B$ are called *prices*, and this is how we shall refer to them in what follows.

Finally, we define a new variable z_j,

$$z_j = y_{ij}c_{B1} + \cdots + y_{mj}c_{Bm} = \sum_{i=1}^{m} y_{ij}c_{Bi} = \mathbf{c}'_B\mathbf{y}_j \tag{12.18}$$

There is a z_j for each $\mathbf{a}_j$, the z_j corresponding to $\mathbf{a}_j$ changing as the columns of A in B change. The variable z_j will assume importance in the subsequent analysis.

Example 12.7. Illustrate the above definitions, given the system $c_1 = 1$, $c_2 = 2$, $c_3 = 0$, $c_4 = 0$, and

$$
\begin{aligned}
x_1 + 2x_2 + x_3 \quad\;\; &= 4 \\
x_1 + 4x_2 \quad\;\; + x_4 &= 8
\end{aligned}
$$

Solution. We have $A\mathbf{x} = \mathbf{b}$, where

$$
A = \begin{pmatrix} 1 & 2 & 1 & 0 \\ 1 & 4 & 0 & 1 \end{pmatrix}
\qquad
x = \begin{pmatrix} x_1 \\ x_2 \\ x_3 \\ x_4 \end{pmatrix}
\qquad
\mathbf{b} = \begin{pmatrix} 4 \\ 8 \end{pmatrix}
$$

We form a basis matrix $B = (\mathbf{b}_1\, \mathbf{b}_2)$ using columns $\mathbf{a}_2$ and $\mathbf{a}_3$ of A so that

$$
\mathbf{b}_1 = \mathbf{a}_2 = \begin{pmatrix} 2 \\ 4 \end{pmatrix}
\qquad
\mathbf{b}_2 = \mathbf{a}_3 = \begin{pmatrix} 1 \\ 0 \end{pmatrix}
$$

Then, using (12.14) and (12.15), we have

$$\mathbf{a}_1 = \frac{1}{4}\begin{pmatrix}2\\4\end{pmatrix} + \frac{1}{2}\begin{pmatrix}1\\0\end{pmatrix} = \begin{pmatrix}1\\1\end{pmatrix} \qquad y_{11} = \frac{1}{4} \qquad y_{21} = \frac{1}{2} \qquad \mathbf{y}_1 = \begin{pmatrix}\frac{1}{4}\\\frac{1}{2}\end{pmatrix}$$

$$\mathbf{a}_2 = 1\begin{pmatrix}2\\4\end{pmatrix} + 0\begin{pmatrix}1\\0\end{pmatrix} = \begin{pmatrix}2\\4\end{pmatrix} \qquad y_{12} = 1 \qquad y_{22} = 0 \qquad \mathbf{y}_2 = \begin{pmatrix}1\\0\end{pmatrix}$$

$$\mathbf{a}_3 = 0\begin{pmatrix}2\\4\end{pmatrix} + 1\begin{pmatrix}1\\0\end{pmatrix} = \begin{pmatrix}1\\0\end{pmatrix} \qquad y_{13} = 0 \qquad y_{23} = 1 \qquad \mathbf{y}_3 = \begin{pmatrix}0\\1\end{pmatrix}$$

$$\mathbf{a}_4 = \frac{1}{4}\begin{pmatrix}2\\4\end{pmatrix} - \frac{1}{2}\begin{pmatrix}1\\0\end{pmatrix} = \begin{pmatrix}0\\1\end{pmatrix} \qquad y_{14} = \frac{1}{4} \qquad y_{24} = -\frac{1}{2} \qquad \mathbf{y}_4 = \begin{pmatrix}\frac{1}{4}\\-\frac{1}{2}\end{pmatrix}$$

We also have $x_{B1} = 2$, $x_{B2} = 0$, and $\mathbf{x}_B = \begin{pmatrix}2\\0\end{pmatrix}$ since $B\mathbf{x}_B = \mathbf{b}$. Since basis variables x_{B1} and x_{B2} correspond, respectively, to basis vectors $\mathbf{b}_1$ and $\mathbf{b}_2$, nonbasis vectors $\mathbf{a}_2$ and $\mathbf{a}_3$, nonbasis variables x_2 and x_3, and nonbasis prices c_2 and c_3, we have $c_{B1} = c_2 = 2$ and $c_{B2} = c_3 = 0$. Then, using (12.17), we obtain

$$z = (2 \quad 0)\begin{pmatrix}2\\0\end{pmatrix} = 4$$

and, using (12.18),

$$z_1 = (2 \quad 0)\begin{pmatrix}\frac{1}{4}\\\frac{1}{2}\end{pmatrix} = \frac{1}{2} \qquad z_2 = (2 \quad 0)\begin{pmatrix}1\\0\end{pmatrix} = 2$$

$$z_3 = (2 \quad 0)\begin{pmatrix}0\\1\end{pmatrix} = 0 \qquad z_4 = (2 \quad 0)\begin{pmatrix}\frac{1}{4}\\-\frac{1}{2}\end{pmatrix} = \frac{1}{2}$$

12.6 IMPROVING A BASIC FEASIBLE SOLUTION

Assume that we have a basic feasible solution to (12.3) which is given by $\mathbf{x}_B = B^{-1}\mathbf{b}$ and which yields a value for the objective function of $z = \mathbf{c}_B'\mathbf{x}_B$. We shall now develop a procedure for determining whether there exists another basic feasible solution which yields a greater z value and, if such a solution exists, for determining this solution.

Theorem 12.8

Given a nondegenerate basic feasible solution $x_B = B^{-1}b$ to (12.3) which yields a value for the objective function of $z = c_B' x_B$. If for any column a_j in A but not in B we have $c_j > z_j$, and if at least one $y_{ij} > 0$ ($i = 1,$ $\ldots, m$), then we can obtain a new basic feasible solution by replacing one of the columns in B by a_j.

Proof. We can compute for the given basic feasible solution the $y_j = B^{-1}a_j$ and $z_j = c_B' y_j$ for every column a_j of A not in B. In Theorem 10.58 we showed how to replace a single basis vector so that the resulting set of vectors was also a basis. The procedure is to replace any vector b_r for which $y_{rj} \neq 0$ with $a_j = \sum_{i=1}^{m} y_{ij} b_i$. Solving this last expression for b_r, we obtain

$$b_r = \frac{1}{y_{rj}} a_j - \sum_{\substack{i=1 \\ i \neq r}}^{m} \frac{y_{ij}}{y_{rj}} b_i \qquad (12.19)$$

We can write the original basic feasible solution as

$$\sum_{i=1}^{m} x_{Bi} b_i = b \qquad (12.20)$$

If we eliminate b_r from (12.20) by using (12.19), we obtain

$$\sum_{\substack{i=1 \\ i \neq r}}^{m} x_{Bi} b_i + x_{Br} \left(\frac{1}{y_{rj}} a_j - \sum_{\substack{i=1 \\ i \neq r}}^{m} \frac{y_{ij}}{y_{rj}} b_i \right) = \sum_{\substack{i=1 \\ i \neq r}}^{m} \left(x_{Bi} - x_{Br} \frac{y_{ij}}{y_{rj}} \right) b_i + \frac{x_{Br}}{y_{rj}} a_j = b$$

$$\qquad (12.21)$$

For the new basic solution to be feasible, we need [from (12.21)]

$$x_{Bi} - x_{Br} \frac{y_{ij}}{y_{rj}} \geq 0 \qquad i = 1, \ldots, m; i \neq r \qquad (12.22a)$$

$$\frac{x_{Br}}{y_{rj}} \geq 0 \qquad (12.22b)$$

From (12.22b) we see that we must have $y_{rj} > 0$ (remember that, since we start with a nondegenerate basic feasible solution, $x_{Bi} > 0$, $i = 1,$ $\ldots, m$). If $y_{rj} > 0$, and if $y_{ij} \leq 0$ ($i \neq r$), then (12.22) is satisfied. If $y_{rj} > 0$ and $y_{ij} > 0$ ($i \neq r$), then (12.22) is satisfied only if

$$\frac{x_{Bi}}{y_{ij}} - \frac{x_{Br}}{y_{rj}} \geq 0 \qquad (12.23)$$

[(12.23) is obtained by dividing (12.22a) by y_{ij}]. This will be the case only if x_{Br}/y_{rj} is the minimum α in the set,

$$\left\{ \alpha \middle| \alpha = \frac{x_{Bi}}{y_{ij}} \ \& \ y_{ij} > 0 \right\} \tag{12.24}$$

We use θ to denote the minimum α. Thus, if we select for replacement by $\mathbf{a}_j$ that column $\mathbf{b}_r$ of B which corresponds to the minimum $\alpha = \theta$ in (12.24), the new basic solution will be feasible. Theorem 12.8 is proved.

We denote the new nonsingular matrix, obtained from B by replacing $\mathbf{b}_r$ with $\mathbf{a}_j$, by $\hat{B} = (\hat{\mathbf{b}}_1 \cdots \hat{\mathbf{b}}_m)$, where

$$\hat{\mathbf{b}}_i = \mathbf{b}_i \qquad i \neq r \qquad \hat{\mathbf{b}}_r = \mathbf{a}_j \tag{12.25}$$

If we denote the new basic feasible solution by $\hat{\mathbf{x}}_B$, then $\hat{\mathbf{x}}_B = \hat{B}^{-1}\mathbf{b}$, and, from (12.21), the values of the new basic variables are given by

$$\hat{x}_{Bi} = x_{Bi} - x_{Br}\frac{y_{ij}}{y_{rj}} \qquad i \neq r$$

$$\hat{x}_{Br} = \frac{x_{Br}}{y_{rj}} = \theta \tag{12.26}$$

If the minimum in (12.24) is not unique, the new basic solution will be degenerate (see discussion at end of Sec. 12.4).

Example 12.9. Given the nondegenerate basic feasible solution $x_3 = 4$ and $x_4 = 8$ to the following set of equations, obtain a new basic feasible solution:

$$\begin{aligned} x_1 + 2x_2 + x_3 \qquad &= 4 \\ x_1 + 4x_2 \qquad + x_4 &= 8 \end{aligned}$$

Solution. The given solution can be expressed as

$$B\mathbf{x}_B = \mathbf{b} = 4\begin{pmatrix} 1 \\ 0 \end{pmatrix} + 8\begin{pmatrix} 0 \\ 1 \end{pmatrix} = \begin{pmatrix} 4 \\ 8 \end{pmatrix}$$

$$\mathbf{x}_B = \begin{pmatrix} 4 \\ 8 \end{pmatrix} \qquad B = \begin{pmatrix} 1 & 0 \\ 0 & 1 \end{pmatrix} \qquad \mathbf{b} = \begin{pmatrix} 4 \\ 8 \end{pmatrix} \qquad A = \begin{pmatrix} 1 & 2 & 1 & 0 \\ 1 & 4 & 0 & 1 \end{pmatrix}$$

$$\mathbf{x} = \begin{pmatrix} 0 \\ 0 \\ 4 \\ 8 \end{pmatrix}$$

The $\mathbf{y}_j$'s for every column $\mathbf{a}_j$ in A but not in B are

$$\mathbf{y}_1 = \begin{pmatrix} 1 \\ 1 \end{pmatrix} \qquad \mathbf{y}_2 = \begin{pmatrix} 2 \\ 4 \end{pmatrix}$$

Since $y_{11} = 1$ and $y_{21} = 1$ are > 0, we can insert $\mathbf{a}_1$ in B. We select for replacement by $\mathbf{a}_1$ that column in B which corresponds to the minimum $\alpha = \theta$ in (12.24). Since

$$\alpha_1 = \frac{x_{B1}}{y_{11}} = \frac{4}{1} = 4 \qquad \alpha_2 = \frac{x_{B2}}{y_{21}} = \frac{8}{1} = 8$$

we shall remove $\mathbf{b}_1$. The new basis is $\hat{B} = (\hat{\mathbf{b}}_1 \hat{\mathbf{b}}_2)$, where $\hat{\mathbf{b}}_1 = \mathbf{a}_1$, $\hat{\mathbf{b}}_2 = \mathbf{b}_2$ [see (12.25)]. Using (12.26), we find the new basic feasible solution $\hat{x}_{B1} = 4$ and $\hat{x}_{B2} = 4$, so that the solution to the original system of equations is $x_1 = x_{B1} = 4$, $x_2 = 0$, $x_3 = 0$, $x_4 = x_{B2} = 4$. Note that, if we had decided to insert $\mathbf{a}_2$ instead of $\mathbf{a}_1$, the new basic feasible solution would have been degenerate.

Now that we know how to obtain a new basic feasible solution, we must next determine whether the value of the objective function has improved—i.e., whether $\hat{z} > z$, where $\hat{z}$ denotes the new value of the objective function. We state the following theorem.

Theorem 12.10

Assume that we have a nondegenerate basic feasible solution $\mathbf{x}_B = B^{-1}\mathbf{b}$ to $A\mathbf{x} = \mathbf{b}$ which yields a value for the objective function of $z = \mathbf{c}_B'\mathbf{x}_B$. Assume, further, that we have obtained a new basic feasible solution $\hat{\mathbf{x}}_B = \hat{B}^{-1}\mathbf{b}$ to $A\mathbf{x} = \mathbf{b}$ by replacing one of the columns in B by a column $\mathbf{a}_j$ (for which some $y_{ij} > 0$) in A but not in B. Then, if $c_j > z_j$, the new value (denoted by $\hat{z}$) of the objective function will be greater than z.

Proof. The value of the objective function for the original basic feasible solution is $z = \mathbf{c}_B'\mathbf{x}_B = \sum_{i=1}^{m} c_{Bi}x_{Bi}$. The new value is

$$\hat{z} = \hat{\mathbf{c}}_B'\hat{\mathbf{x}}_B = \sum_{i=1}^{m} \hat{c}_{Bi}\hat{x}_{Bi}$$

where $\hat{c}_{Bi} = c_{Bi}$ $(i \neq r)$ and $\hat{c}_{Br} = c_j$. Substituting (12.26) into the last expression gives

$$\hat{z} = \sum_{\substack{i=1 \\ i \neq r}}^{m} c_{Bi}\left(x_{Bi} - x_{Br}\frac{y_{ij}}{y_{rj}}\right) + \frac{x_{Br}}{y_{rj}}c_j \qquad (12.27)$$

Since the term for which $i = r$ is

$$c_{Br}\left(x_{Br} - x_{Br}\frac{y_{rj}}{y_{rj}}\right) = 0$$

we can include it in the summation in (12.27) without changing $\hat{z}$, so that

$$\hat{z} = \sum_{i=1}^{m} c_{Bi}\left(x_{Bi} - x_{Br}\frac{y_{ij}}{y_{rj}}\right) + \frac{x_{Br}}{y_{rj}}c_j$$

$$= \sum_{i=1}^{m} c_{Bi}x_{Bi} - \frac{x_{Br}}{y_{rj}}\sum_{i=1}^{m} c_{Bi}y_{ij} + \frac{x_{Br}}{y_{rj}}c_j \qquad (12.28)$$

Note that the second term in (12.28) is $-x_{Br}/y_{rj}$ times z_j [Eq. (12.18)] and the first term is z, so that

$$\hat{z} = z + \frac{x_{Br}}{y_{rj}}(c_j - z_j) = z + \theta(c_j - z_j) \qquad (12.29)$$

From (12.29) we see that the new value of the objective function is the original value plus the quantity $\theta(c_j - z_j)$. If $\hat{z}$ is to exceed z, then $\theta(c_j - z_j)$ must be greater than 0; since $\theta > 0$, this means that $c_j - z_j$ must be >0 or $c_j > z_j$. That is, if $c_j > z_j$, the value of the objective function is improved and we have proved Theorem 12.10.

Example 12.11. In Example 12.9, assume that $c_1 = 1$, $c_2 = 2$, $c_3 = 0$, $c_4 = 0$. Then the original solution $x_3 = 4$ and $x_4 = 8$ yields

$$z = 0(4) + 0(8) = 0$$

In the new feasible solution x_1 replaces x_3. Since

$$z_1 = \mathbf{c}_B'\mathbf{y}_1 = 0(1) + 0(1) = 0$$

and since $c_1 = 1 > z_1 = 0$, $\hat{z}$ should exceed $z = 0$. We see from (12.29) that this is the case,

$$\hat{z} = 0 + 4(1 - 0) = 4 > z = 0$$

Up to this point we have assumed that the original basic feasible solution is nondegenerate. We shall now examine the implications of original basic feasible solutions which are degenerate.

Theorem 12.12

Given a degenerate basic feasible solution $\mathbf{x}_B = B^{-1}\mathbf{b}$ to $A\mathbf{x} = \mathbf{b}$. If for any column $\mathbf{a}_j$ in A but not in B we have at least one $y_{ij} > 0$ ($i = 1$, . . . , m), then we can obtain a new basic feasible solution, which may or may not be degenerate, by replacing one of the columns in B by $\mathbf{a}_j$.

Proof. Follow the proof of Theorem 12.8 down to (12.24). If some of the $y_{ij} > 0$ correspond to $x_{Bi} = 0$, then $\theta = 0 = x_{Br}$ and a basic feasible solution will exist which will also be degenerate. Since $x_{Br} = 0$, we see from (12.26) that the values of the variables which have been retained in the new solution are unchanged ($\hat{x}_{Bi} = x_{Bi}$, $i \neq r$). On the other hand, if all the $y_{ij} > 0$ correspond to $x_{Bi} > 0$, none of the $x_{Bi} = 0$ enter into (12.24), so that $\theta > 0$ and, from (12.26), the new solution will be nondegenerate (provided, also, that the minimum α is unique).

Theorem 12.13

Given a degenerate basic feasible solution $\mathbf{x}_B = B^{-1}\mathbf{b}$ to $A\mathbf{x} = \mathbf{b}$. If for any column $\mathbf{a}_j$ in A but not in B we have at least one $y_{ij} \neq 0$ ($i = 1$, . . . , m) and if the corresponding $x_{Bi} = 0$, then we can obtain a new degenerate basic feasible solution.

Proof. Follow the proof of Theorem 12.8 to (12.22). If $x_{Br} = 0$, then as long as $y_{rj} \neq 0$ (12.22) is satisfied an $\mathbf{a}_j$ can be substituted for $\mathbf{b}_r$ to yield a new degenerate ($x_{Br}/y_{rj} = 0$) basic feasible solution in which $\hat{x}_{Bi} = x_{Bi}$ ($i \neq r$).

Theorem 12.14

Assume that we have a degenerate basic feasible solution $\mathbf{x}_B = B^{-1}\mathbf{b}$ to $A\mathbf{x} = \mathbf{b}$ which yields a value for the objective function of $z = \mathbf{c}'_B\mathbf{x}_B$. Assume, further, that we have obtained a new basic feasible solution $\mathbf{x}_B = B^{-1}\mathbf{b}$ to $A\mathbf{x} = \mathbf{b}$ by replacing one of the columns in B by a column $\mathbf{a}_j$ (for which some $y_{ij} > 0$) in A but not in B. Then, if $c_j > z_j$, the new value of the objective function will be such that $\hat{z} \geq z$.

Proof. Follow the proof of Theorem 12.10 to (12.29). From Theorem 12.12 we know that $\theta(c_j + z_j) \geq 0$, implying that $\hat{z} \geq z$.

To sum up this section, we have shown that *given a basic (degenerate or nondegenerate) feasible solution* $\mathbf{x}_B = B^{-1}\mathbf{b}$ *to* $A\mathbf{x} = \mathbf{b}$ *which yields a value for the objective function of* $z = \mathbf{c}'_B\mathbf{x}_B$, *if for any column* $\mathbf{a}_j$ *in* A *but not in* B *we have* $c_j > z_j$, *and if at least one* $y_{ij} > 0$ ($i = 1$, . . . , m), *then we can obtain a new basic feasible solution by replacing one of the columns in* B *by* $\mathbf{a}_j$ *and the new value* $\hat{z}$ *of the objective function will be such that* $\hat{z} \geq z$.

12.7 UNBOUNDED SOLUTIONS

The results obtained in the preceding section require that for the $\mathbf{a}_j$ inserted into the basis matrix B there is at least one $y_{ij} > 0$, $i = 1$, . . . , m. This raises the question of the implication of a situation in which, for at least one $\mathbf{a}_j$, all $y_{ij} \leq 0$. This leads to the following definition and theorem.

Definition 12.15. A linear-programming problem has an unbounded solution if the value z of the objective function can be made arbitrarily large, so that the problem has no finite maximum value of z.

Theorem 12.16

Given any basic feasible solution $\mathbf{x}_B = B^{-1}\mathbf{b}$ to $A\mathbf{x} = \mathbf{b}$. If for this solution there is some column $\mathbf{a}_j$ in A but not in B for which $c_j > z_j$ and $y_{ij} \leq 0$ $(i = 1, \ldots, m)$, then, if the objective function is to be maximized, the problem has an unbounded solution.

Proof. Let us insert $\mathbf{a}_j$ in B. Since it is given that the vector $\mathbf{a}_j$ has all $y_{ij} \leq 0$, x_j must enter the basis at a value of 0; otherwise, the solution will not be feasible [see (12.22)]. To maintain a feasible solution and still have $x_j > 0$, let us form a feasible solution with $m + 1$ variables, x_j and the m x_{Bi}'s, positive. To accomplish this, consider the basic feasible solution

$$\sum_{i=1}^{m} x_{Bi}\mathbf{b}_i = \mathbf{b} \tag{12.30}$$

with $z = \mathbf{c}_B'\mathbf{x}_B$. Let λ be any scalar. If we add and subtract $\lambda\mathbf{a}_j$ in (12.30) we have

$$\sum_{i=1}^{m} x_{Bi}\mathbf{b}_i - \lambda\mathbf{a}_j + \lambda\mathbf{a}_j = \mathbf{b} \tag{12.31}$$

Since $\mathbf{a}_j = \sum_{i=1}^{m} y_{ij}\mathbf{b}_i$, we have

$$-\lambda\mathbf{a}_j = -\lambda \sum_{i=1}^{m} y_{ij}\mathbf{b}_i$$

which, when substituted in (12.31), yields

$$\sum_{i=1}^{m} (x_{Bi} - \lambda y_{ij})\mathbf{b}_i + \lambda\mathbf{a}_j = \mathbf{b} \tag{12.32a}$$

Since all $y_{ij} \leq 0$, when $\lambda > 0$ we have $x_{Bi} - \lambda y_{ij} \geq 0$, so that (12.32a) is a feasible solution with the number of positive variables less than or equal to $m + 1$ (we say less than $m + 1$ since some $x_{Bi} - \lambda y_{ij}$ may be 0).

Denoting the variables in the new feasible solution by $\hat{x}_i$, and noting from (12.32a) that

$$\hat{x}_i = x_{Bi} - \lambda y_{ij} \qquad i = 1, \ldots, m$$
$$\hat{x}_{m+1} = \lambda \tag{12.32b}$$

we can obtain the new value, denoted by $\hat{z}$, of the objective function from

$$\hat{z} = \sum_{i=1}^{m} c_{Bi}\hat{x}_i + c_j\lambda = \sum_{i=1}^{m} c_{Bi}(x_{Bi} - \lambda y_{ij}) + c_j\lambda$$

$$= \sum_{i=1}^{m} c_{Bi}x_{Bi} - \lambda \sum_{i=1}^{m} c_{Bi}y_{ij} + c_j\lambda$$

$$= z + \lambda(c_j - z_j) \qquad (12.33)$$

Since it is given that $c_j > z_j$ so that $c_j - z_j > 0$, we see from (12.33) that we can make $\hat{z}$ as large as we like by setting λ sufficiently large. Theorem 12.16 is proved; if there is some $\mathbf{a}_j$ not in B such that $c_j > z_j$ and all $y_{ij} \leq 0$, we can form a new feasible solution, in which the number of positive variables is less than or equal to $m + 1$, which is unbounded.

Example 12.17. Show that the system

$$\begin{aligned} x_1 - x_2 + x_3 \quad &= 4 \\ x_1 - 5x_2 \quad + x_4 &= 8 \end{aligned}$$

with $c_1 = 1$, $c_2 = 2$, $c_3 = 0$, $c_4 = 0$, has an unbounded solution.

Solution. Let

$$A = \begin{pmatrix} 1 & -1 & 1 & 0 \\ 1 & -5 & 0 & 1 \end{pmatrix} \qquad \mathbf{b} = \begin{pmatrix} 4 \\ 8 \end{pmatrix} \qquad \mathbf{x} = \begin{pmatrix} x_1 \\ x_2 \\ x_3 \\ x_4 \end{pmatrix}$$

Take the basic solution $B\mathbf{x}_B = \mathbf{b}$, where

$$B = (\mathbf{b}_1\ \mathbf{b}_2) = (\mathbf{a}_1\ \mathbf{a}_4) = \begin{pmatrix} 1 & 0 \\ 1 & 1 \end{pmatrix} \qquad \mathbf{x}_B = \begin{pmatrix} 4 \\ 4 \end{pmatrix}$$

Then $\qquad \mathbf{a}_2 = -1\begin{pmatrix} 1 \\ 1 \end{pmatrix} - 4\begin{pmatrix} 0 \\ 1 \end{pmatrix} = \begin{pmatrix} -1 \\ -5 \end{pmatrix}$

so that $y_{12} = -1 < 0$ and $y_{22} = -4 < 0$. We also have

$$z_2 = c_{B1}y_{12} + c_{B2}y_{22} = (1)(-1) + (0)(-4) = -1$$

so that $c_2 = 2 > z_2 = -1$. Thus an unbounded solution exists (Theorem 12.16).

12.8 MAXIMIZING THE OBJECTIVE FUNCTION

We start with the following definition.

Definition 12.18. Given a linear-programming problem with n variables and m $(m \leq n)$ structural constraints $A\mathbf{x} = \mathbf{b}$ and objective function $z = \mathbf{c}'\mathbf{x}$. A *maximal* basic feasible solution to this problem is one which makes the value of $z = c'x$ a maximum and which contains not more than m nonzero variables.

In this section we shall examine the conditions which must be satisfied if a given basic feasible solution is to be maximal. We shall show that, in the absence of degeneracy, if there is a maximal feasible solution to a linear-programming problem, one of the basic feasible solutions will be maximal. We shall discuss the circumstances under which it is possible to arrive at a solution which satisfies the maximal conditions.

Theorem 12.19

Given a basic (degenerate or nondegenerate) feasible solution $x_B = B^{-1}b$ to $Ax = b$ with $z^* = c'_B x_B$. If $c_j \leq z_j$ for every column a_j in A but not in B, then z^* is the maximum value of the objective function $z = c'x$ and x_B is a maximal basic feasible solution.

Proof. Let

$$\sum_{j=1}^{n} x_j a_j = b \qquad x_j \geq 0 \qquad (12.34)$$

be any feasible solution to $Ax = b$, the corresponding value, denoted by z', of the objective function being

$$z' = \sum_{j=1}^{n} c_j x_j \qquad (12.35)$$

Since any vector a_j in A can be written as a linear combination of the m basis vectors in B, we have

$$a_j = \sum_{i=1}^{m} y_{ij} b_i \qquad (12.36)$$

When (12.36) is substituted in (12.34), we obtain

$$x_1 \sum_{i=1}^{m} y_{i1} b_i + \cdots + x_n \sum_{i=1}^{m} y_{in} b_i = b$$

which is equivalent to

$$(x_1 y_{11} b_1 + x_1 y_{21} b_2 + \cdots + x_1 y_{m1} b_m) + \cdots$$
$$+ (x_n y_{1n} b_1 + x_n y_{2n} b_2 + \cdots + x_n y_{mn} b_m)$$
$$= \left(\sum_{j=1}^{n} x_j y_{1j} \right) b_1 + \cdots + \left(\sum_{j=1}^{n} x_j y_{mj} \right) b_m = b \qquad (12.37)$$

Since the vector b can be expressed as a linear combination of the basis vectors B in only one way (Theorem 10.57), and since it is given that

x_B is a basic feasible solution to the problem, we conclude, using (12.37), that

$$x_{Bi} = \sum_{j=1}^{n} x_j y_{ij} \qquad i = 1, \ldots, m \tag{12.38}$$

Let a_j now denote the column in A that represents column i in B; that is, $a_j = b_i$ ($i = 1, \ldots, m$; j taking on m values from the set of integers $\{1, \ldots, n\}$, $m \le n$). Since B is a basis, we have

$$(b_1 \cdots b_i \cdots b_m)y_j = a_j$$

However, since $a_j = b_i$, we see that $y_j = e_i$. Therefore, from (12.18), for those a_j's in B

$$z_j = c_B' y_j = c_B' e_i = c_{Bi}$$

But since $b_i = a_j$, $c_{Bi} = c_j$. Thus, for the columns of A in B, it is always true that $c_j = z_j$. Since it is given that $c_j \le z_j$ for every column a_j of A not in B, we see that, for the situation described by Theorem 12.19, $c_j \le z_j$ for every column in A. Using this result in (12.35), we obtain

$$z' \le \sum_{j=1}^{n} z_j x_j \tag{12.39}$$

From (12.18) we have

$$z_j = \sum_{i=1}^{m} y_{ij} c_{Bi}$$

which, when substituted in (12.39), yields

$$z' \le \left(\sum_{i=1}^{m} y_{i1} c_{Bi} \right) x_1 + \cdots + \left(\sum_{i=1}^{m} y_{in} c_{Bi} \right) x_n$$

or

$$z' \le \left(\sum_{j=1}^{n} x_j y_{1j} \right) c_{B1} + \cdots + \left(\sum_{j=1}^{n} x_j y_{mj} \right) c_{Bm} \tag{12.40}$$

Substituting (12.38) into (12.40), we obtain

$$z' \le x_{B1} c_{B1} + \cdots + x_{Bm} c_{Bm} = c_B' x_B = z^* \tag{12.41}$$

This result shows that z^* is at least as large as the value z' of the objective function for any other feasible solution. We therefore conclude that z^* is the maximum value of the objective function. Furthermore, since z^* was determined from a basic feasible solution, x_B is a maximal basic feasible solution. Theorem 12.19 is proved. Note that our proof did not require x_B to be nondegenerate, so that the theorem holds for both degenerate and nondegenerate solutions.

We know, then, that, if we ever obtain a basic feasible solution with $c_j \le z_j$ for every column in A but not in B, the solution is a maximal basic feasible solution. We can state the very important theorem which follows.

Theorem 12.20

In the absence of degeneracy in all but the maximal basic feasible solution, if there is a maximal feasible solution to a linear-programming problem, then there is a maximal basic feasible solution which can be determined in a finite number of steps.

Proof. Let

$$\sum_{j=1}^{n} x_j \mathbf{a}_j = \mathbf{b} \qquad x_j \geq 0$$

be a maximal feasible solution to $A\mathbf{x} = \mathbf{b}$, the corresponding value z' of the objective function being

$$z' = \sum_{j=1}^{n} c_j x_j$$

The proof of Theorem 12.19 from the first line after (12.35) through (12.41) shows that, if we can find a basic feasible solution $B\mathbf{x}_B = \mathbf{b}$ such that $c_j \leq z_j$ for all $\mathbf{a}_j$'s in A but not in B, then this solution is a maximal basic feasible solution. We shall now show that such a solution always exists and can always be found.

All basic feasible solutions fall into one of three mutually exclusive and completely exhaustive categories:

1. All $c_j \leq z_j$
2. At least one $c_j > z_j$ with all corresponding $y_{ij} \leq 0$ $(i = 1, \ldots, m)$
3. At least one $c_j > z_j$ with at least one of the corresponding $y_{ij} > 0$ $(i = 1, \ldots, m)$

Category 2 will never be encountered, since this category indicates an unbounded solution and it is given that a maximal feasible solution exists. Consider, then, category 3.

We know that, if we start with a basic feasible solution [and one exists, from Theorem 12.5, since it is given that a feasible (maximal) solution exists] and if for some vector $\mathbf{a}_j$ in A but not in B we have $c_j > z_j$ with at least one $y_{ij} > 0$ $(i = 1, \ldots, m)$, then there exists another basic feasible solution such that $\hat{z} > z$ (Theorem 12.10). We can generate a series of basic feasible solutions by changing the basis by one vector at a time. Upon assuming that we never encounter degeneracy, the value of the objective function associated with each new basis will be increased as long as for each $\mathbf{a}_j$ not in the present basis

$c_j > z_j$ with at least one $y_{ij} > 0$ $(i = 1, \ldots, m)$. Since each basis gives a single z value, and since successive bases yield successively higher z values, no basis can ever be repeated. This implies, since there are (Example 11.29) a finite number of bases, that the process of generating new bases cannot be continued indefinitely; i.e., it is possible to examine, in a finite number of steps, all possible basic feasible solutions (on assuming that degeneracy never occurs).

This means that we shall eventually form a basis which does not fall in category 3. We can see why this is so if we denote the finite number of possible bases by q. Then, by assuming the extreme case, if the first $q - 1$ bases fall in category 3, the qth base cannot, since if it did this would imply that another basis could be formed which would improve the objective function, and this contradicts the fact that q is the maximum number of possible bases. We have already shown that no basis can fall in category 2. Therefore, we must eventually obtain a basis which falls in category 1. But, from Theorem 12.19, such a basis represents a maximal basic feasible solution. Theorem 12.20 is proved. Note that it is not at all necessary that q bases be formed before the maximal basis is obtained; if any basis, say the tth $(t < q)$, cannot be improved by the insertion of another $\mathbf{a}_j$ not in B, then this basis does not fall in category 2 or 3 and must therefore belong to category 1.

We can use the same method to prove the following corollary.

Corollary 12.21.   In the absence of degeneracy, if there is an unbounded solution we shall be able to discover it in a finite number of steps.

Theorem 12.20 assumed the absence of degeneracy in all but the maximal basic feasible solution. The reason for this is that, if degeneracy is present, it is theoretically possible that some of the basic feasible solutions (including, perhaps, the maximal solution) will never be examined if the procedures we have developed are employed. This possibility occurs because the value of the objective function *may* remain unchanged (Theorem 12.14) when a new basis is generated, given that the old basis was degenerate. This means that it is possible for a basis to be repeated, with the further possibility that a cycle may be generated in which the same sequence of bases is repeated indefinitely without changing the value of the objective function and without examining all possible bases. In this case we may never reach a basis which indicates a maximal or an unbounded solution.

The procedures and theorems we have presented can be adjusted to resolve the difficulty created by the possibility of degeneracy. We shall not do this, however, since the adjustment is time- and space-consuming and is actually not worth the effort, for cycling, while a theoretical possibility, never seems to occur in practice. Most linear-programming applications are made on the assumption that cycling never occurs, so that all solutions have an opportunity to be examined. We shall make this negligibly restrictive assumption in what follows. As this implies, Theorem 12.20 will be assumed valid even if degeneracy is encountered as bases are generated.

Theorem 12.22

If we have a basic feasible solution which is not maximal or indicative of an unbounded solution, then it is possible to generate new bases until we reach one which we can recognize as maximal or indicative of an unbounded solution.

Proof. Following the method of proof used in the preceding theorem, the given basic feasible solution must fall in category 3 (since it is neither maximal nor indicative of an unbounded solution). We know that only a finite number, say q, of bases can be generated (proof to Theorem 12.20), so that, in the extreme case, if the first $q - 1$ bases are in category 3, the qth must be in category 1 or 2, since if it were in category 3 this would indicate that another basis could be formed which improves the objective function by a unique amount and this contradicts the fact that there are only q bases. Since we must eventually come to a basis which falls in category 1 or 2, the theorem is proved. Note that the maximal or unbounded solution may be indicated before q bases have been generated. (Why?)

Example 12.23. Obtain a maximal basic feasible solution to the system

$$x_1 + 2x_2 + x_3 \qquad = 4$$
$$x_1 + 4x_2 \qquad + x_4 = 8$$

with $c_1 = 1$, $c_2 = 2$, $c_3 = 0$, $c_4 = 0$.

Solution. Take the basic feasible solution $B\mathbf{x}_B = \mathbf{b}$ to $A\mathbf{x} = \mathbf{b}$ where

$$A = \begin{pmatrix} 1 & 2 & 1 & 0 \\ 1 & 4 & 0 & 1 \end{pmatrix} \quad B = \begin{pmatrix} 1 & 0 \\ 1 & 1 \end{pmatrix} \quad \mathbf{b} = \begin{pmatrix} 4 \\ 8 \end{pmatrix} \quad \mathbf{x} = \begin{pmatrix} 4 \\ 0 \\ 0 \\ 4 \end{pmatrix}$$

$$\mathbf{x}_B = \begin{pmatrix} 4 \\ 4 \end{pmatrix}$$

We compute

$$z_2 = c_{B1}y_{12} + c_{B2}y_{22} = (1)(2) + (0)(2) = 2$$
$$z_3 = c_{B1}y_{13} + c_{B2}y_{23} = (1)(1) - (0)(0) = 1$$

Since $c_2 = 2 = z_2$ and $c_3 = 0 < z_3 = 1$, the present solution is optimal (Theorem 12.19).

PROBLEM SET 12.1

The student is advised to keep the appropriate text material before him as he works through these problems.

1. Convert the following set of $m = 4$ linear inequalities in $s = 8$ variables into a set of $m = 4$ simultaneous linear equations in $n = s + m$ variables. Use the notation of (12.2), (12.3), and (12.4).

$$3x_1 + 2x_2 + 19x_3 - 2x_4 + x_5 + 2x_6 + 8x_7 + x_8 \leq 92$$
$$2x_1 + 3x_2 \qquad + 3x_4 + 2x_5 \qquad + 6x_8 \leq 46$$
$$x_1 + 3x_2 - 4x_3 + x_4 \qquad + 6x_6 \qquad + x_8 \leq 16$$
$$5x_1 + 6x_2 + x_3 + 4x_4 \qquad + 6x_6 + x_7 + 3x_8 \leq 50$$

2. Given the following set of two simultaneous linear equations in five variables, with feasible solution $x_1 = 1$, $x_2 = 1$, $x_3 = 1$, $x_4 = 11$, $x_5 = 4$, form a basic feasible solution using the method of proof of Theorem 12.5:

$$2x_1 + 2x_2 + x_3 + x_4 \qquad = 16$$
$$8x_1 + 4x_2 + 4x_3 \qquad + x_5 = 20$$

3. Given the following set of three simultaneous linear equations in six variables, with feasible solution $x_1 = 1$, $x_2 = 2$, $x_3 = 2$, $x_4 = 33$, $x_5 = 8$, $x_6 = 1$, form a basic feasible solution using the method of proof of Theorem 12.5:

$$x_1 + 2x_2 + x_3 + x_4 \qquad = 40$$
$$2x_1 + 4x_2 + x_3 \qquad + x_5 \qquad = 20$$
$$x_1 + x_2 + 4x_3 \qquad + x_6 = 12$$

4. In Prob. 2, if $c_1 = 2$, $c_2 = 4$, $c_3 = 5$, $c_4 = 0$, and $c_5 = 0$, determine the y_{ij} and z_j ($i = 1, 2; j = 1, \ldots, 5$) from (12.14), (12.15), and (12.18). Use the basic feasible solution obtained in Prob. 2.

5. In Prob. 3, if $c_1 = 1$, $c_2 = 2$, $c_3 = 6$, $c_4 = 0$, $c_5 = 0$, and $c_6 = 0$, determine the y_{ij} and z_j ($i = 1, 2, 3; j = 1, \ldots, 6$) from (12.14), (12.15), and (12.18). Use the basic feasible solution obtained in Prob. 3.

6. Form a new basic feasible solution from the basic feasible solution obtained in Prob. 2. Use the method introduced in the proof of Theorem 12.8.

7. Form a new basic feasible solution from the basic feasible solution obtained in Prob. 3. Use the method introduced in the proof of Theorem 12.8.

8. Can you form a degenerate basic feasible solution to the system given in Probs. 4 and 5?

9. Given the basic feasible solution obtained in Prob. 6, determine a new basic feasible solution (if it exists) which improves the objective function (use the c_j given in Prob. 4). Use the method introduced in the proof of Theorem 12.10.

10. Given the basic feasible solution obtained in Prob. 7, determine a new basic feasible solution (if it exists) which improves the objective function (use the c_j given in Prob. 5). Use the method introduced in the proof of Theorem 12.10.

11. Does the system given in Prob. 4 have an unbounded solution? If so, give such a solution [use (12.32b)]. Does the system have a maximal basic feasible solution? If so, what is it? Use Theorems 12.16 and 12.19.

12. Does the system given in Prob. 5 have an unbounded solution? If so, give one such solution. Does the system have a maximal basic feasible solution? If so, what is it? Use Theorems 12.16 and 12.19.

13 SIMPLEX METHOD OF LINEAR PROGRAMMING: APPLICATION

13.1 SUMMARY OF THEORETICAL RESULTS

In this chapter we shall apply the theory developed in Chap. 12. The general problem we seek to solve is the maximization of the linear objective function $z = \sum\limits_{j=1}^{s} c_j x_j$, subject to m linear inequalities of the form

$$\sum_{j=1}^{s} a_{ij}x_j \leq b_i \qquad i = 1, \ldots, m$$

with $x_j, b_i \geq 0$ $(j = 1, \ldots, s; i = 1, \ldots, m)$.

From Chap. 12 we have the following important results:

1. We can solve the problem formulated above by adding slack variables and maximizing $z = \sum_{j=1}^{n} c_j x_j$ subject to m linear equalities of the form

$$\sum_{j=1}^{n} a_{ij} x_j = b_i \qquad i = 1, \ldots, m$$

or $A\mathbf{x} = \mathbf{b}$, with the components of $\mathbf{x}$ nonnegative real numbers (Sec. 12.2).

2. If there is a feasible solution there is a basic feasible solution (Theorem 12.5).

3. If a maximal feasible solution exists, one of the basic feasible solutions will be maximal (Theorem 12.20).

4. If we have a basic feasible solution which is not maximal or indicative of an unbounded solution, then it is possible to generate new bases until we reach one which we can recognize as maximal or as indicative of an unbounded solution to the problem (Theorem 12.22). Given any basic feasible solution:

a. If all $c_j \leq z_j$, the solution is maximal.

b. If any vector for which $c_j > z_j$ has all $y_{ij} \leq 0$ $(i = 1, \ldots, m)$, there is an unbounded solution.

c. If no vector for which $c_j > z_j$ has all $y_{ij} \leq 0$ $(i = 1, \ldots, m)$, we can insert any of these vectors into the basis and form a new basic feasible solution with a new value of the objective function at least as large as the old value.

13.2 TRANSFORMATION FORMULAS FOR y_j AND z_j

Assume that we have a basic feasible solution $\mathbf{x}_B$ for which some $c_j > z_j$ with at least one $y_{ij} > 0$. This implies that we should form a new basic feasible solution $\hat{\mathbf{x}}_B$ with a new value $\hat{z}$ for the objective function. To determine whether $\hat{z}$ is maximal, we must determine the value of $\hat{z}_j$, where $\hat{z}_j$ denotes the value of the z_j associated with the new basis. If all $c_j \leq \hat{z}_j$, the new solution is maximal, and if $c_j > \hat{z}_j$ with at least one $\hat{y}_{ij} > 0$ for some $\mathbf{a}_j$ in A but not in B, the new solution should be changed. To compute $\hat{z}_j$, we need new y_{ij} (denoted by $\hat{y}_{ij}$).

We shall now develop formulas for transforming the old y_{ij} into $\hat{y}_{ij}$ and the old z_j into $\hat{z}_j$. These transformation formulas will greatly enhance the ease with which these values can be computed [the $\hat{y}_{ij}$ could be alternatively calculated, from (12.14), by solving a system of m simultaneous linear equations in m variables]. In what follows, all values associated with the new basis will be distinguished from those associated with the original basis by a caret.

Theorem 13.1

If a new basis is formed by replacing $\mathbf{b}_r$ with $\mathbf{a}_k$, the new y_{ij} (denoted by $\hat{y}_{ij}$) can be calculated from

$$\hat{y}_{ij} = y_{ij} - y_{rj} \frac{y_{ik}}{y_{rk}} \qquad i \neq r \tag{13.1}$$

$$\hat{y}_{rj} = \frac{y_{rj}}{y_{rk}} \tag{13.2}$$

Proof. In terms of the original basis, we have for any a_j in A but not in B

$$\mathbf{a}_j = \sum_{i=1}^{m} y_{ij}\mathbf{b}_i \tag{13.3}$$

For a particular $\mathbf{a}_k$, (13.3) becomes

$$\mathbf{a}_k = \sum_{i=1}^{m} y_{ik}\mathbf{b}_i$$

which, when solved for $\mathbf{b}_r$ $(y_{rk} \neq 0)$, gives

$$\mathbf{b}_r = - \sum_{\substack{i=1 \\ i \neq r}}^{m} \frac{y_{ik}}{y_{rk}} \mathbf{b}_i + \frac{1}{y_{rk}} \mathbf{a}_k \tag{13.4}$$

Equation (13.4) expresses $\mathbf{b}_r$, the vector removed from the original basis, as a linear combination of the new basis composed of $m - 1$ of the original vectors plus the newly inserted vector $\mathbf{a}_k$.

If (13.4) is substituted into (13.3), we obtain

$$\mathbf{a}_j = \sum_{\substack{i=1 \\ i \neq r}}^{m} y_{ij}\mathbf{b}_i - y_{rj} \sum_{\substack{i=1 \\ i \neq r}}^{m} \frac{y_{ik}}{y_{rk}} \mathbf{b}_i + \frac{y_{rj}}{y_{rk}} \mathbf{a}_k$$

$$= \sum_{\substack{i=1 \\ i \neq r}}^{m} \left(y_{ij} - y_{rj} \frac{y_{ik}}{y_{rk}} \right) \mathbf{b}_i + \frac{y_{rj}}{y_{rk}} \mathbf{a}_k \tag{13.5}$$

$$\mathbf{a}_j = \sum_{i=1}^{m} \hat{y}_{ij}\hat{\mathbf{b}}_i \tag{13.6}$$

where $\hat{\mathbf{b}}_i = \mathbf{b}_i$ $(i \neq r)$ and $\hat{\mathbf{b}}_r = \mathbf{a}_k$.

From (13.5) we see that

$$\hat{y}_{ij} = y_{ij} - y_{rj}\frac{y_{ik}}{y_{rk}} \qquad i \neq r$$

$$\hat{y}_{rj} = \frac{y_{rj}}{y_{rk}}$$

This proves the theorem.

Theorem 13.2

If a new basis is formed by replacing $\mathbf{b}_r$ with $\mathbf{a}_k$, the new z_i (denoted by $\hat{z}_j$) can be calculated from

$$\hat{z}_j = z_j - \frac{y_{rj}}{y_{rk}}(z_k - c_k) \tag{13.7}$$

Proof. From [12.18] we have

$$\hat{z}_j = \hat{\mathbf{c}}_B'\hat{\mathbf{y}}_j = \sum_{i=1}^{m} \hat{c}_{Bi}\hat{y}_{ij} \tag{13.8}$$

We can use (13.1) and (13.2) plus the fact that $\hat{c}_{Bi} = c_{Bi}\ (i \neq r)$ and $\hat{c}_{Br} = c_k$ to obtain [from (13.8)]

$$\hat{z}_j = \sum_{\substack{i=1\\i\neq r}}^{m} c_{Bi}\left(y_{ij} - y_{rj}\frac{y_{ik}}{y_{rk}}\right) + c_k\frac{y_{rj}}{y_{rk}} \tag{13.9}$$

For convenience we include in the summation in (13.9) the term

$$c_{Br}\left(y_{rj} - y_{rj}\frac{y_{rk}}{y_{rk}}\right) = 0$$

We can then write (13.9) as

$$\hat{z}_j = \sum_{i=1}^{m} c_{Bi}y_{ij} - \frac{y_{rj}}{y_{rk}}\sum_{i=1}^{m} c_{Bi}y_{ik} + c_k\frac{y_{rj}}{y_{rk}}$$

$$= \sum_{i=1}^{m} c_{Bi}y_{ij} - \frac{y_{rj}}{y_{rk}}\left(\sum_{i=1}^{m} c_{Bi}y_{ik} - c_k\right)$$

$$= z_j - \frac{y_{rj}}{y_{rk}}(z_k - c_k)$$

which proves the theorem.

Example 13.3. Given the system

$$x_1 + 2x_2 + x_3 \qquad = 4$$
$$x_1 + 4x_2 \qquad + x_4 = 8$$

equivalent to the matrix equation $A\mathbf{x} = \mathbf{b}$, with $c_1 = 1$, $c_2 = 2$, $c_3 = 0$, $c_4 = 0$, and with basic solution $B\mathbf{x}_B = \mathbf{b}$, where $A = \begin{pmatrix} 1 & 2 & 1 & 0 \\ 1 & 4 & 0 & 1 \end{pmatrix}$, $B = (\mathbf{b}_1\,\mathbf{b}_2) = (\mathbf{a}_3\,\mathbf{a}_4) = \begin{pmatrix} 1 & 0 \\ 0 & 1 \end{pmatrix}$, $\mathbf{x}_B = \begin{pmatrix} 4 \\ 8 \end{pmatrix}$, $\mathbf{b} = \begin{pmatrix} 4 \\ 8 \end{pmatrix}$. Form a new basic feasible solution, and determine the new y_{ij} and z_j from Theorems 13.1 and 13.2.

Solution. We have $y_{12} = 2$, $y_{22} = 4$, $z_2 = 0$, $y_{11} = 1$, $y_{21} = 1$, $z_1 = 0$. If we form a new basis by replacing $\mathbf{b}_1$ with $\mathbf{a}_1$, we can compute (using Theorems 13.1 and 13.2)

$$\hat{y}_{12} = \frac{y_{12}}{y_{11}} = \frac{2}{1} = 2 \qquad \hat{y}_{22} = y_{22} - y_{12}\frac{y_{21}}{y_{11}} = 4 - (2)\left(\frac{1}{1}\right) = 2$$

$$\hat{z}_2 = z_2 - \frac{y_{12}}{y_{11}}(z_1 - c_1) = 0 - \frac{2}{1}(0 - 1) = 2$$

The reader can verify these answers by employing definitions (12.15) and (12.18).

13.3 THE INITIAL BASIC FEASIBLE SOLUTION

The preceding results have been based on the assumption that we are somehow able to obtain a basic feasible solution with which to start the analysis. We shall now show how an initial basic feasible solution can always be found.

Any basic feasible solution will be of the form

$$B\mathbf{x}_B = \mathbf{b}$$

where B contains any m linearly independent columns from the $m \times n$ matrix A and $x_{Bi} \geq 0$ $(i = 1, \ldots, m)$, all other variables $= 0$. From Sec. 12.2 we know that columns $\mathbf{a}_{s+1}, \ldots, \mathbf{a}_n$ in the $m \times n$ matrix A form an $m \times m$ identity matrix I_m (the reader should recall that the column corresponding to the slack variable x_{s+i} is $\mathbf{e}_i$). If we set the variables $x_1, \ldots, x_s$ equal to 0 and form an initial solution from the m columns $\mathbf{a}_{s+j}$ $(j = 1, \ldots, m)$, we obtain $B\mathbf{x}_B = \mathbf{b}$, where $B = I_m$. Since $B = I_m$, $B^{-1} = I_m$, so that

$$\mathbf{x}_B = B^{-1}\mathbf{b} = \mathbf{b} \tag{13.10}$$

Equation (13.10) is a basic feasible solution since it satisfies the conditions of Definition 11.28, and since $\mathbf{b} \geq \mathbf{0}$ (Sec. 12.2).

This initial solution is especially convenient to work with since the

y_j and z_j can be easily determined without recourse to Theorems 13.1 and 13.2,

$$\mathbf{y}_j = B^{-1}\mathbf{a}_j = I_m\mathbf{a}_j = \mathbf{a}_j \qquad j = 1, \ldots, n$$
$$\mathbf{c}_B = \mathbf{0} \tag{13.11}$$

(since only slack variables are employed in the initial solution)

$$z_j = \mathbf{c}'_B\mathbf{y}_j = 0$$
$$z = \mathbf{c}'_B\mathbf{x}_B = 0 \tag{13.12}$$

Thus for the type of linear-programming problem formulated in the preceding discussion, we can always find an initial basic feasible solution. This result justifies all the assumptions made in Sec. 12.3.

Example 13.4.   Add slack variables to the following system of linear inequalities, and, for the resulting system of linear equalities, form an initial basic feasible solution and determine the $\mathbf{y}_j$ and $\mathbf{z}_j$:

$$2x_1 + 3x_2 + 2x_3 + x_4 \leq 24$$
$$x_1 + x_2 + 6x_3 + 4x_4 \leq 100$$
$$8x_1 + 2x_2 + 3x_3 + 2x_4 \leq 36$$

with $\qquad c_1 = 5 \qquad c_2 = 4 \qquad c_3 = 6 \qquad c_4 = 2$

Solution.   Adding slack variables, we obtain

$$2x_1 + 3x_2 + 2x_3 + x_4 + x_5 \qquad\qquad = 24$$
$$x_1 + x_2 + 6x_3 + 4x_4 \qquad + x_6 \qquad = 100$$
$$8x_1 + 2x_2 + 3x_3 + 2x_4 \qquad\qquad + x_7 = 36$$

with $c_5 = c_6 = c_7 = 0$.   Forming an initial basic feasible solution from the slack variables, we obtain $B\mathbf{x} = \mathbf{b}$, where

$$A = \begin{pmatrix} 2 & 3 & 2 & 1 & 1 & 0 & 0 \\ 1 & 1 & 6 & 4 & 0 & 1 & 0 \\ 8 & 2 & 3 & 2 & 0 & 0 & 1 \end{pmatrix} \qquad B = (\mathbf{b}_1\,\mathbf{b}_2\,\mathbf{b}_3) = (\mathbf{a}_5\,\mathbf{a}_6\,\mathbf{a}_7) = \begin{pmatrix} 1 & 0 & 0 \\ 0 & 1 & 0 \\ 0 & 0 & 1 \end{pmatrix}$$

$$\mathbf{b} = \begin{pmatrix} 24 \\ 100 \\ 36 \end{pmatrix} \qquad \mathbf{x}_B = \begin{pmatrix} 24 \\ 100 \\ 36 \end{pmatrix}$$

Employing (13.11) and (13.12), we find

$$\mathbf{y}_1 = \begin{pmatrix} 2 \\ 1 \\ 8 \end{pmatrix} \qquad \mathbf{y}_2 = \begin{pmatrix} 3 \\ 1 \\ 2 \end{pmatrix} \qquad \mathbf{y}_3 = \begin{pmatrix} 2 \\ 6 \\ 3 \end{pmatrix} \qquad \mathbf{y}_4 = \begin{pmatrix} 1 \\ 4 \\ 2 \end{pmatrix}$$

$$z_j = 0, j = 1, \ldots, 4$$

13.4 SIMPLEX PROCEDURE

We can now describe the simplex method for solving the linear-programming problem formulated in Sec. 13.1. It is an iterative procedure composed of the following steps:

1. Form an initial basic feasible solution (Sec. 13.3), and determine the y_j and z_j from (13.11) and (13.12).

2. Examine the relationship between the z_j and c_j, there being three mutually exclusive and collectively exhaustive possibilities:

 a. All $c_j \leq z_j$. In this case, the given basic feasible solution is maximal.

 b. Some $c_j > z_j$, and for at least one of the corresponding $\mathbf{a}_j$ all $y_{ij} \leq 0$. In this case, there is an unbounded solution.

 c. Some $c_j > z_j$, and all the corresponding $\mathbf{a}_j$'s have at least one $y_{ij} > 0$. In this case, we form another basic feasible solution by replacing one of the vectors at present in the basis by one outside the basis.

3. When (2c) holds, select the vector to be inserted into the basis. While any vector for which $c_j > z_j$ can be selected, actual practice indicates that the most efficient computational procedure is to select the vector which corresponds to the maximum λ in the set

$$\{\lambda | \lambda = c_j - z_j \text{ for all variables for which } c_j > z_j\}$$

If the maximum λ is obtained from more than one distinct vector, any one of these vectors can be arbitrarily selected.

From Eq. (12.29), the change in the value of the objective function is given by $\theta(c_j - z_j)$, where θ denotes the value of the new basis variable. This suggests that $c_j - z_j$ can be interpreted as the increase in the value of the objective function for each unit of the added basis variable. Thus the criterion suggested implies that we select the vector which maximizes the unit contribution of the corresponding variable. This criterion appears, in practice, to be the most efficient computationally, because no other criterion seems to arrive at a maximal (or unbounded) solution faster, and those which appear to be as fast [e.g., choosing the vector corresponding to the maximum $\theta(c_j - z_j)$] require more time-consuming arithmetic operations.

4. When (2c) holds, select the vector to be removed from the basis. Following the results of Sec. 12.6, we select that vector $\mathbf{b}_r$ which corresponds to the minimum α, denoted by θ, in the set

$$\left\{\alpha | \alpha = \frac{y_{Bi}}{y_{ij}} \ \& \ y_{ij} > 0 \ (i = 1, \ldots, m) \ \& \ j \text{ denotes the column } \mathbf{a}_j \text{ which is to be inserted}\right\}$$

If θ is obtained from more than one distinct vector, any one of the vectors corresponding to the minimum $\alpha = \theta$ may be removed arbitrarily.

5. Compute $\hat{\mathbf{x}}_B$, $\hat{z}$, $\hat{\mathbf{y}}_j$, and $\hat{z}_j$ for all j's. This requires, respectively, the use of formulas (12.26) and (12.29) and formulas (13.1), (13.2), and (13.7).

6. Return to step 2.

These six steps describe the simplex method of linear programming. In the absence of the negligible possibility of cycling associated with degeneracy, this iterative procedure will, in a finite number of steps, result in a maximal solution, if one exists, or an unbounded solution if such is the case. It can be shown that, in general, the number of iterations required to reach a maximal solution is between m and $2m$, where m denotes the number of constraints.

13.5 SIMPLEX TABLEAU

The method just described can be most efficiently implemented if a systematic procedure is followed. Such a procedure involves the construction of a simplex tableau for each iteration or basis. Table 13-1 illustrates the format of such a tableau:

1. Column 1 indicates which vectors from A are in B. Thus $\mathbf{b}_i$ is the vector from A which is in the ith column of B. For example, if $\mathbf{a}_8$ is in the third column of B, we would write $\mathbf{a}_8$ where $\mathbf{b}_3$ appears in Table 16-1.

2. Column 2 gives $\mathbf{c}_B$ for the current basis.

3. The first m rows of column 3 give $\mathbf{x}_B$ for the current basis.

TABLE 13.1 THE SIMPLEX TABLEAU

Column / Row	1	2	3	4	5	$\cdots$	$j+3$	$\cdots$	$n+3$
	Vectors from A in B	c_B	x_B & z	\multicolumn{5}{l}{y_j, c_j, & z_j $\cdots$ corresponding to:}			
				$\mathbf{a}_1$	$\mathbf{a}_2$	$\cdots$	$\mathbf{a}_j$	$\cdots$	$\mathbf{a}_n$
1	$\mathbf{b}_1$	c_{B1}	x_{B1}	y_{11}	y_{12}	$\cdots$	y_{1j}	$\cdots$	y_{1n}
2	$\mathbf{b}_2$	c_{B2}	x_{B2}	y_{21}	y_{22}	$\cdots$	y_{2j}	$\cdots$	y_{2n}
$\cdots$	$\cdots$	$\cdots$	$\cdots$	$\cdots$	$\cdots$	$\cdots$	$\cdots$	$\cdots$	$\cdots$
m	$\mathbf{b}_m$	c_{Bm}	x_{Bm}	y_{m1}	y_{m2}	$\cdots$	y_{mj}	$\cdots$	y_{mn}
$m+1$			z	z_1	z_2	$\cdots$	z_j	$\cdots$	z_n
$m+2$				c_1	c_2	$\cdots$	c_j	$\cdots$	c_n
$m+3$				$c_1 - z_1$	$c_2 - z_2$	$\cdots$	$c_j - z_j$	$\cdots$	$c_n - z_n$

4. The last row of column 3 gives the value of the objective function for the current basis.

5. The first m rows of each of the remaining n columns give $\mathbf{y}_j$ for each of the $\mathbf{a}_j$'s in A.

6. For each of these remaining n columns, row $m + 1$ gives the z_j corresponding to $\mathbf{a}_j$, row $m + 2$ gives the c_j, and row $m + 3$ gives $c_j - z_j$.

Column 1 is required so that the c_j and x_j corresponding, respectively, to c_{Bi} and x_{Bi} can be determined   For example, if $\mathbf{a}_j$ is in row i of column 1, the ith row of column 2 would show the value of c_j in place of c_{Bi} and the ith row of column 3 would show the value of x_j in place of x_{Bi}.

13.6 AN EXAMPLE

We shall illustrate the results of Secs. 13.4 and 13.5 with an example. Assume that a firm produces four products, each of which requires a fixed number of hours in each of three processing operations as given in the table.   The numbers 1, 2, 3, 4 in the column Product and the numbers 1,

Product	Process			Unit profit
	1	2	3	
1	2	1	8	5
2	3	1	2	4
3	2	6	3	6
4	1	4	2	2

2, 3 directly under Process are used simply as *indices*.   All other numbers are quantities.   This schedule also shows the profit earned on each unit of each product.   Assume that, for the coming week, the firm will have 24 hours available in process 1, 100 hours in process 2, and 36 hours in process 3.   What is the most profitable combination of products for the firm to produce in the coming week?

We denote the number of units produced of product i by x_i ($i = 1$, . . . , 4), and the unit profit of each product by c_i.   We seek nonnegative values of x_i which satisfy the three processing constraints and also maximize total profit $\left(= \sum_{i=1}^{4} c_i x_i \right)$.   This is a linear-programming problem which can be represented by a system of $m = 3$ linear inequalities in $s = 4$ variables,

$$2x_1 + 3x_2 + 2x_3 + x_4 \leq 24$$
$$x_1 + x_2 + 6x_3 + 4x_4 \leq 100$$
$$8x_1 + 2x_2 + 3x_3 + 2x_4 \leq 36$$

with $c_1 = 5$, $c_2 = 4$, $c_3 = 6$, and $c_4 = 2$. We want a maximal basic feasible solution.

First, we add slack variables and form a system of $m = 3$ linear equalities in $n = s + 3 = 4 + 3 = 7$ variables,

$$2x_1 + 3x_2 + 2x_3 + x_4 + x_5 = 24$$
$$x_1 + x_2 + 6x_3 + 4x_4 + x_6 = 100$$
$$8x_1 + 2x_2 + 3x_3 + 2x_4 + x_7 = 36$$

with $c_5 = c_6 = c_7 = 0$. x_5, x_6, and x_7 denote the number of idle (i.e., slack, unused) hours in, respectively, processes 1, 2, and 3. In matrix notation the above system becomes $Ax = \mathbf{b}$, where

$$A = \begin{pmatrix} 2 & 3 & 2 & 1 & 1 & 0 & 0 \\ 1 & 1 & 6 & 4 & 0 & 1 & 0 \\ 8 & 2 & 3 & 2 & 0 & 0 & 1 \end{pmatrix} \qquad \mathbf{x} = \begin{pmatrix} x_1 \\ x_2 \\ x_3 \\ x_4 \\ x_5 \\ x_6 \\ x_7 \end{pmatrix} \qquad \mathbf{b} = \begin{pmatrix} 24 \\ 100 \\ 36 \end{pmatrix}$$

Using the $\mathbf{y}_j$ and z_j determined in Example 13.4 (since this is the same example), we then construct simplex tableau 1 (Table 13-2) according to the format specified in Sec. 13.5. In this case $z = \mathbf{c}'_B \mathbf{x}_B = 0$ (column 3, row 4).

Following step 2 of Sec. 13.4, we examine the relationship between the c_j and z_j. Since $c_1 > z_1$, $c_2 > z_2$, $c_3 > z_3$, and $c_4 > z_4$, and since each

TABLE 13.2 SIMPLEX TABLEAU 1

Column Row	1	2	3	4	5	6	7	8	9	10
	Vectors from A in B	c_B	$\mathbf{x}_B$ & z	$\mathbf{y}_j$, c_j, & z_j corresponding to:						
				$\mathbf{a}_1$	$\mathbf{a}_2$	$\mathbf{a}_3$	$\mathbf{a}_4$	$\mathbf{a}_5$	$\mathbf{a}_6$	$\mathbf{a}_7$
1	$\mathbf{a}_5$	0	24	2	3	2	1	1	0	0
2	$\mathbf{a}_6$	0	100	1	1	6	4	0	1	0
3	$\mathbf{a}_7$	0	36	8	2	3	2	0	0	1
4			0	0	0	0	0	0	0	0
5				5	4	6	2	0	0	0
6				5	4	6	2	0	0	0

$\mathbf{y}_j$ ($j = 1, \ldots, 4$) has at least one $y_{ij} > 0$ ($i = 1, \ldots, 3$), this solution is neither maximal nor indicative of an unbounded solution (category 3), so that we must form a new basis. Proceeding to step 3, we find that the maximum $c_j - z_j$ ($j = 1, \ldots, 4$) is $c_3 - z_3 = 6$, which indicates that we should form the new basis by inserting $\mathbf{a}_k = \mathbf{a}_3$.

The vector which will be removed (step 4 of Sec. 13.4) will be the one which corresponds to the minimum α, denoted by θ, in the set

$$\left\{ \alpha \,\middle|\, \alpha = \frac{y_{Bi}}{y_{ik}} \ \& \ y_{ik} > 0 \ \& \ i = 1, \ldots, 3 \ \& \ k = 3 \right\}$$

Since

$$\frac{x_{B1}}{y_{13}} = \frac{24}{2} = 12 \qquad \frac{x_{B2}}{y_{23}} = \frac{100}{6} = 16\frac{2}{3} \qquad \frac{x_{B3}}{y_{33}} = \frac{36}{3} = 12$$

we see that the minimum is obtained in two ways. We can therefore remove either the vector corresponding to x_{B1}/y_{13} (that is, $\mathbf{b}_1 = \mathbf{a}_5$) or that corresponding to x_{B3}/y_{33} (that is, $\mathbf{b}_3 = \mathbf{a}_7$). Arbitrarily, we shall remove $\mathbf{b}_r = \mathbf{b}_1 = \mathbf{a}_5$, so that $\theta = x_{B1}/y_{13} = 12$. The α's are determined by dividing row i of column 3 by row i of the column corresponding to the vector being inserted (in this case $\mathbf{a}_3$) for those i for which $y_{ik} > 0$ ($i = 1, \ldots, m$). The new value, $\hat{z}$, of the objective function can now be determined from (12.29),

$$\hat{z} = z + \theta(c_k - z_k) = 0 + 12(c_3 - z_3) = (12)(6) = 72$$

In the above expression we use the subscript k to denote the vector which is being inserted, rather than the subscript j originally employed when the expression was derived. We shall follow this convention in what follows, for ease in notation. In particular, the reader should note this change in (12.29), (12.26), and (12.22) as we employ these expressions. To facilitate the following computations, we circle the column ($\mathbf{a}_3$) that will be inserted and the row corresponding to the vector ($\mathbf{b}_1 = \mathbf{a}_5$) that will be removed.

Step 5 of Sec. 13.4 requires that new $\mathbf{x}_B$, $\mathbf{y}_j$, and z_j be computed. We shall display these new values in simplex tableau 2 (Table 13.3; remember, from Sec. 13.5, that we construct a new tableau for each basis or iteration). Columns 1 and 2 and row 5 can be filled in immediately: the new $\mathbf{b}_i$'s equal the old $\mathbf{b}_i$'s for $i \neq r = 1$, and the new $\mathbf{b}_r = \mathbf{b}_1 = \mathbf{a}_k = \mathbf{a}_3$; the c_j's ($j = 1, \ldots, 7$) are the same for each tableau so that row 5 is simply reproduced from the preceding tableau; and the new c_{Bi}'s equal the old c_{Bi}'s for $i \neq r = 1$, and the new $c_{Br} = c_{B1} = c_k = c_3$. The circled row and column in tableau 1 make it possible speedily to identify these required changes in the tableau, since the only changes in columns 1

TABLE 13.3   SIMPLEX TABLEAU 2

Column Row	1	2	3	4	5	6	7	8	9	10
	Vectors from A in B	c_B	x_B & z	y_j, c_j, & z_j corresponding to:						
				a_1	a_2	a_3	a_4	a_5	a_6	a_7
1	a_3	6	12	1	1.5	1	0.5	0.5	0	0
2	a_6	0	28	−5	−8	0	1	−3	1	0
3	a_7	0	0	5	−2.5	0	0.5	−1.5	0	1
4			72	6	9	6	3	3	0	0
5				5	4	6	2	0	0	0
6				−1	−5	0	−1	−3	0	0

and 2 involve the replacement of the circled entries in these columns by, respectively, the heading of the circled column and the fifth row entry in the circled column.

Since $\hat{x}_{Br} = \theta = 12$ has already been calculated, we also know the entry in the row of column 3 of tableau 2 (Table 13. 3) which corresponds to the circled entry in column 3 of tableau 1 (Table 13.2). (We designate the new values of x_B, z, y_j, and z_j with a caret.)

We obtain the remaining $\hat{x}_{Bi}$'s (i.e., the values of rows 2 and 3) in tableau 2 from (12.26),

$$\hat{x}_{Bi} = x_{Bi} - x_{Br}\frac{y_{ik}}{y_{rk}} = x_{Bi} - \theta y_{ik} = x_{Bi} - 12y_{i3} \qquad i \neq r = 1$$

The necessary computations are conveniently made from tableau 1 by multiplying each of the entries in rows 2 and 3 (that is, $i \neq r$) of the circled column by θ, and subtracting each of these products from the corresponding row entry in column 3. The resulting differences represent the entries in the corresponding rows of column 3 of tableau 2. The reader should be able to generalize this computational procedure for any problem involving $m = 1, 2, \ldots$ basis variables. In this case, since the minimum α was not unique, $x_{B3} = 0$ and the new basic feasible solution is degenerate.

The remaining entries in rows 1 through 3 and columns 4 through 10 can be determined from (13.1) and (13.2). It is most convenient to fill in one row at a time, starting with row $r = 1$. From (13.2), we see that each entry in row 1 (columns 4 through 10) in tableau 2 is determined by dividing the corresponding column entry in the circled row of tableau 1 by the double circled entry (row 1 and the column corresponding to a_3) of tableau 1.

The column entries of each of the remaining $m - 1 = 2$ rows are determined from (13.1). $y_{ik}/y_{rk} = y_{i3}/y_{13}$ is a constant for each row, determined by dividing the entry in the circled column and ith row by the double circled entry in tableau 1. If we let $\lambda_i = y_{ik}/y_{rk} = y_{i3}/y_{13}$ we can find the new entry (tableau 2) in each column (4 through 10) of the ith row by multiplying λ_i by the entry in the corresponding column of the circled row of tableau 1 and subtracting this product from the entry in the corresponding column of row i of tableau 1.

We determine the z_j from (13.7). The entry in each column of row $m + 1 = 4$ in tableau 2 is determined by multiplying the entry of the corresponding column of row $r = 1$ of tableau 2 (why?) by the constant $z_k - c_k = -6$ (determined from rows 4 and 5 of the circled column in tableau 1) and subtracting this product from the entry in the corresponding column of row 4 of tableau 1.

Tableau 2 is now complete. Using this tableau, we return to step 2 (Sec. 13.4) and repeat the computational procedure just described. Since no $c_j > z_j$, we have carried at a maximal basic feasible solution in just two iterations. The maximal value of the objective function is 72, and the values of the variables are $x_1 = 0$, $x_2 = 0$, $x_3 = 12$, $x_6 = 28$, and $x_7 = 0$.

For our present problem the optimum product mix is 12 units of just one product—product 3. There will be 28 hours of idle capacity in process 2 ($x_6 = 28$), but all other processes will be fully employed.

If, in tableau 2, some $c_j > z_j$ with at least one $y_{ij} > 0$, we would have formed a new basis. This would involve circling, in tableau 2, the column corresponding to the vector to be inserted and the row corresponding to the vector to be removed. A new tableau—tableau 3—would be constructed, according to the computational procedure just described, to represent this new basis.

13.7 GENERALIZATION OF COMPUTATIONAL PROCEDURE

The reader may wonder why we presented such an extended discussion of computational technique. The reason is that the format of the simplex tableaux permits a purely mechanical and straightforward procedure for the determination of a maximal feasible solution (if one exists). Such a procedure can be and has been readily programmed on electronic digital computers. Even if the computations are carried out by hand, the procedure described permits a high degree of computational speed and accuracy which can be achieved by purely clerical labor. For this reason we now generalize the computational procedure for generating simplex tableaux for a problem involving m constraints (and therefore $m + 3$ rows in the tableau) and n variables (and therefore $n + 3$ columns in the tableau):

1. For any given tableau, if some nonnegative value in row $m + 3$ corresponds to a column in which, over the first m rows, no value is > 0, the linear-programming problem has an unbounded solution. If no value in row $m + 3$ is > 0, the present solution is a maximal basic feasible solution. If row $m + 3$ has at least 1 nonnegative value and if, for each of the corresponding columns, at least one value in the first m rows is > 0, a new tableau must be constructed. The remaining steps describe how to use the tableau format to do this efficiently and mechanically.

2. We insert the vector, denoted by $\mathbf{a}_k$, which corresponds to the maximum value in row $m + 3$. If this maximum value appears more than once in row $m + 3$, any of the corresponding vectors can be selected arbitrarily. Circle the column corresponding to $\mathbf{a}_k$.

3. To find the vector which will be removed, we compute ratios, denoted by α, by dividing the value in row i of column 3 by the value in row i $(i = 1, \ldots, m)$ of the circled column for those values in the circled column which are greater than 0. The vector corresponding to the minimum α, denoted by θ, will be removed. If more than one α yields θ, any one of the corresponding vectors can be removed arbitrarily. Circle the row corresponding to the vector (determined from column 1) being removed.

4. Column 1 of the new tableau is identical to column 1 of the present tableau for rows which are not circled. The row in the new tableau which corresponds to the circled row will have, in column 1, the heading associated with the circled column.

5. Column 2 of the new tableau is identical to column 2 of the present tableau for rows which are not circled. The row in the new tableau which corresponds to the circled row will have, in column 2, the value in row $m + 2$ of the circled column.

6. In column 3 of the new tableau, the entry in the row corresponding to the circled row in the present tableau is θ. Each entry in the remaining rows (except row $m + 1$) is determined by multiplying the entry in the same row of the circled column by θ and subtracting the product from the entry in column 3 of the same row. The entry in row $m + 1$ can be determined by multiplying θ by the value in row $m + 3$ and the circled column and adding the product to the entry in row $m + 1$ and column 3 of the present tableau.

7. Columns 4 through $n + 3$ of the row corresponding to the circled row in the present tableau can be determined by dividing the corresponding column entries in the circled row by the double circled entry. Columns 4 through $n + 3$ of each of the remaining rows (except rows

$m + 1$, $m + 2$, and $m + 3$) are determined by dividing the entry in the circled column of the given row by the double circled entry, multiplying this ratio by the entries in the corresponding columns of the circled row, and subtracting these products from the entries in the corresponding columns of the given row.

8. Columns 4 through $m + 3$ of row $m + 1$ are determined by multiplying the entries in the corresponding columns of the row in the *new* tableau which corresponds to the circled row in the old tableau, by the entry in row $m + 3$ of the circled column, and adding these products to the entries in the corresponding columns of row $m + 1$.

9. Row $m + 2$ of the new tableau is identical to row $m + 2$ of the present tableau. Row $m + 3$ is determined by subtracting row $m + 1$ from row $m + 2$.

The reader should be able to justify mathematically all the mechanics of the preceding computational procedure.

PROBLEM SET 13.1

1. Find a maximal feasible solution to the system

$$2x_1 + 3x_2 + 4x_3 + 5x_4 + x_5 \leq 5$$
$$x_1 + 2x_2 \quad\quad + 4x_4 \quad\quad \leq 10$$
$$2x_1 + 4x_2 + 2x_3 \quad\quad + x_5 \leq 20$$

with $c_1 = 2$, $c_2 = 3$, $c_3 = 10$, $c_4 = 1$, $c_5 = 1$.

2. Find a maximal feasible solution to the system

$$x_1 + 2x_2 + x_3 + x_4 + 16x_5 + 2x_6 + x_7 \leq 40$$
$$2x_1 + 3x_2 \quad\quad + 4x_4 \quad\quad + x_6 + 4x_7 \leq 100$$

with $c_1 = 1$, $c_2 = 2$, $c_3 = 4$, $c_4 = 12$, $c_5 = 4$, $c_6 = 2$, $c_7 = 1$.

3. A firm produces three products which require processing time (in hours) in

Product	Department				Unit profit
	1	2	3	4	
1	2	4	6	4	$50
2	3	1	8	1	40
3	2	0	0	12	10
Available hours for coming week.........	300	400	200	200	

each of four departments as given in the tabulation. Also shown are the unit profits yielded by each product and the available time in each department for the coming week. Determine a product mix which maximizes total profit.

4. In the preceding problem, assume that each product requires a specified amount, given in the tabulation, of a special wrapping material. One hundred square

Product	Number of square feet of wrapping required
1	1
2	2
3	0.5

feet of this covering is available. Since products left unwrapped spoil, the firm does not want to produce products which it cannot wrap. What is the optimum product mix now?

5. Solve Prob. 2 in Problem Set 6.4 and Examples 6.32 and 6.33, using the simplex method.

APPENDIX

TABLE 1 LOGARITHMS OF FACTORIALS, 1-2,000*

n	log n!	n	log n!	n	log n!	n	log n!
1	0.000,0000	51	66.190,6450	101	159.974,3250	151	264.935,8704
2	0.301,0300	52	67.906,6484	102	161.982,9252	152	267.117,7139
3	0.778,1513	53	69.630,9243	103	163.995,7624	153	269.302,4054
4	1.380,2112	54	71.363,3180	104	166.012,7958	154	271.489,9261
5	2.079,1812	55	73.103,6807	105	168.033,9851	155	273.680,2578
6	2.857,3325	56	74.851,8687	106	170.059,2909	156	275.873,3824
7	3.702,4305	57	76.607,7436	107	172.088,6747	157	278.069,2820
8	4.605,5205	58	78.371,1716	108	174.122,0985	158	280.267,9391
9	5.559,7630	59	80.142,0236	109	176.159,5250	159	282.469,3363
10	6.559,7630	60	81.920,1748	110	178.200,9176	160	284.673,4562
11	7.601,1557	61	83.705,5047	111	180.246,2406	161	286.880,2821
12	8.680,3370	62	85.497,8964	112	182.295,4586	162	289.089,7971
13	9.794,2803	63	87.297,2369	113	184.348,5371	163	291.301,9847
14	10.940,4084	64	89.103,4169	114	186.405,4419	164	293.516,8286
15	12.116,4996	65	90.916,3303	115	188.436,1398	165	295.734,3125
16	13.320,6196	66	92.735,8742	116	190.530,5978	166	297.954,4206
17	14.551,0685	67	94.561,9490	117	192.598,7836	167	300.177,1371
18	15.806,3410	68	96.394,4579	118	194.670,6656	168	302.402,4464
19	17.085,0946	69	98.233,3070	119	196.746,2126	169	304.630,3331
20	18.386,1246	70	100.078,4050	120	198.825,3938	170	306.860,7820
21	19.708,3439	71	101.929,6634	121	200.908,1792	171	309.093,7781
22	21.050,7666	72	103.786,9959	122	202.994,5390	172	311.329,3066
23	22.412,4944	73	105.650,3187	123	205.084,4442	173	313.567,3527
24	23.792,7057	74	107.519,5505	124	207.177,8658	174	315.807,9019
25	25.190,6457	75	109.394,6117	125	209.274,7759	175	318.050,9400
26	26.605,6190	76	111.275,4253	126	211.375,1464	176	320.296,4526
27	28.036,9828	77	113.161,9160	127	213.478,9501	177	322.544,4259
28	29.484,1408	78	115.054,0106	128	215.586,1601	178	324.794,8459
29	30.946,5388	79	116.951,6377	129	217.696,7498	179	327.047,6989
30	32.423,6601	80	118.854,7277	130	219.810,6932	180	329.302,9714
31	33.915,0218	81	120.763,2127	131	221.927,9645	181	331.560,6500
32	35.420,1717	82	122.677,0266	132	224.048,5384	182	333.820,7214
33	36.938,6857	83	124.596,1047	133	226.172,3900	183	336.083,1725
34	38.470,1646	84	126.520,3840	134	228.299,4948	184	338.347,9903
35	40.014,2326	85	128.449,8029	135	230.429,8286	185	340.615,1620
36	41.570,5351	86	130.384,3013	136	232.563,3675	186	342.884,6750
37	43.138,7369	87	132.323,8206	137	234.700,0881	187	345.156,5166
38	44.718,5205	88	134.268,3033	138	236.839,9672	188	347.430,6744
39	46.309,5851	89	136.217,6933	139	238.982,9820	189	349.707,1362
40	47.911,6451	90	138.171,9358	140	241.129,1100	190	351.985,8898
41	49.524,4289	91	140.130,9772	141	243.278,3291	191	354.266,9232
42	51.147,6782	92	142.094,7650	142	245.430,6174	192	356.550,2244
43	52.781,1467	93	144.063,2480	143	247.585,9535	193	358.835,7817
44	54.424,5993	94	146.036,3758	144	249.744,3160	194	361.123,5835
45	56.077,8119	95	148.014,0994	145	251.905,6840	195	363.413,6181
46	57.740,5697	96	149.996,3707	146	254.070,0368	196	365.705,8742
47	59.412,6676	97	151.983,1424	147	256.237,3542	197	368.000,3404
48	61.093,9088	98	153.974,3865	148	258.407,6159	198	370.297,0056
48	62.784,1049	99	155.970,0037	149	260.580,8022	199	372.595,8586
50	64.483,0749	100	157.970,0037	150	262.756,8934	200	374.896,8886

* From H. Arkin and R. R. Colton, "Tables for Statisticians," 2d ed., pp. 113–118, Barnes & Noble, New York, 1963.

TABLE 1 (CONTINUED)

n	log $n!$	n	log $n!$	n	log $n!$	n	log $n!$
201	377.200,0847	251	494.909,2601	301	616.964,3695	351	742.637,2813
202	379.505,4361	252	497.310,6607	302	619.444,3765	352	745.183,8240
203	381.812,9321	253	499.713,7812	303	621.925,8191	353	747.731,5987
204	384.122,5623	254	502.118,6149	304	624.408,6927	354	750.280,6020
205	386.434,3161	255	504.525,1551	305	626.892,9925	355	752.830,8303
206	388.748,1834	256	506.933,3950	306	629.378,7140	356	755.382,2803
207	391.064,1537	257	509.343,3282	307	631.865,8523	357	757.934,9485
208	393.382,2170	258	511.754,9479	308	634.354,4031	358	760.488,8316
209	395.702,3633	259	514.168,2476	309	636.844,3615	359	763.043,9260
210	398.024,5826	260	516.583,2210	310	639.335,7232	360	765.600,2285
211	400.348,8651	261	518.999,8615	311	641.828,4836	361	768.157,7357
212	402.675,2009	262	521.418,1628	312	644.322,6382	362	770.716,4443
213	405.003,5805	263	523.838,1185	313	646.818,1825	363	773.276,3509
214	407.333,9943	264	526.259,7225	314	649.315,1122	364	775.837,4523
215	409.666,4328	265	528.682,9683	315	651.813,4227	365	778.399,7452
216	412.000,8865	266	531.107,8500	316	654.313,1098	366	780.963,2262
217	414.337,3463	267	533.534,3612	317	656.814,1691	367	783.527,8923
218	416.675,8027	268	535.962,4960	318	659.316,5962	368	786.093,7401
219	419.016,2469	269	538.392,2483	319	661.820,3869	369	788.660,7665
220	421.358,6695	270	540.823,6121	320	664.325,5369	370	791.228,9682
221	423.703,0618	271	543.256,5814	321	666.832,0419	371	793.798,3421
222	426.049,4148	272	545.691,1503	322	669.339,8978	372	796.368,8851
223	428.397,7197	273	548.127,3129	323	671.849,1003	373	798.940,5939
224	430.747,9677	274	550.565,0635	324	674.359,6453	374	801.513,4655
225	433.100,1502	275	553.004,3962	325	676.871,5287	375	804.087,4968
226	435.454,2586	276	555.445,3052	326	679.384,7463	376	806.662,6846
227	437.810,2845	277	557.887,7850	327	681.899,2940	377	809.239,0260
228	440.168,2193	278	560.331,8298	328	684.415,1679	378	811.816,5178
229	442.528,0548	279	562.777,4340	329	686.932,3638	379	814.395,1570
230	444.889,7827	280	565.224,5920	330	689.450,8777	380	816.974,9406
231	447.253,3946	281	567.673,2984	331	691.970,7057	381	819.555,8655
232	449.618,8826	282	570.123,5475	332	694.491,8438	382	822.137,9289
233	451.986,2835	283	572.575,3339	333	697.014,2880	383	824.721,1277
234	454.355,4544	284	575.028,6523	334	699.538,0345	384	827.305,4589
235	456.726,5223	285	577.483,4971	335	702.063,0793	385	829.890,9196
236	459.099,4343	286	579.939,8631	336	704.589,4186	386	832.477,5069
237	461.474,1826	287	582.397,7450	337	707.117,0485	387	835.065,2179
238	463.850,7596	288	584.857,1375	338	709.645,9652	388	837.654,0496
239	466.229,1575	289	587.318,0354	339	712.176,1649	389	840.243,9992
240	468.609,3687	290	589.780,4334	340	714.707,6438	390	842.835,0638
241	470.991,3857	291	592.244,3264	341	717.240,3982	391	845.427,2406
242	473.375,2011	292	594.709,7092	342	719.774,4243	392	848.020,5267
243	475.760,8074	293	597.176,5768	343	722.309,7184	393	850.614,9192
244	478.148,1972	294	599.644,9242	344	724.846,2768	394	853.210,4154
245	480.537,3633	295	602.114,7462	345	727.384,0959	395	855.807,0125
246	482.928,2984	296	604.586,0379	346	729.923,1720	396	858.404,7077
247	485.320,9954	297	607.058,7943	347	732.463,5015	397	861.003,4982
248	487.715,4470	298	609.533,0106	348	735.005,0807	398	863.603,3813
249	490.111,6464	299	612.008,6818	349	737.547,9062	399	866.204,3542
250	492.509,5864	300	614.485,8030	350	740.091,9742	400	868.806,4142

TABLE 1 (CONTINUED)

n	$\log n!$	n	$\log n!$	n	$\log n!$	n	$\log n!$
401	871.409,5586	451	1002.893,0675	501	1136.786,2463	551	1272.848,0029
402	874.013,7846	452	1005.548,2059	502	1139.486,9500	552	1275.589,9419
403	876.619,0896	453	1008.204,3041	503	1142.188,5180	553	1278.332,6671
404	879.225,4710	454	1010.861,3600	504	1144.890,9485	554	1281.076,1768
405	881.832,9260	455	1013.519,3714	505	1147.594,2399	555	1283.820,4698
406	884.441,4521	456	1016.178,3362	506	1150.298,3904	556	1286.565,5446
407	887.051,0465	457	1018.838,2524	507	1153.003,3984	557	1289.311,3998
408	889.661,7066	458	1021.499,1179	508	1155.709,2621	558	1292.058,0340
409	892.273,4300	459	1024.160,9306	509	1158.415,9798	559	1294.805,4458
410	894.886,2138	460	1026.823,6884	510	1161.123,5500	560	1297.553,6338
411	897.500,0556	461	1029.487,3893	511	1163.831,9709	561	1300.302,5967
412	900.114,9528	462	1032.152,0313	512	1166.541,2409	562	1303.052,3330
413	902.730,9029	463	1034.817,6123	513	1169.251,3583	563	1305.802,8414
414	905.347,9032	464	1037.484,1303	514	1171.962,3214	564	1308.554,1205
415	907.965,9513	465	1040.151,5832	515	1174.674,1286	565	1311.306,1690
416	910.585,0447	466	1042.819,9692	516	1177.386,7783	566	1314.058,9854
417	913.205,1807	467	1045.489,2860	517	1180.100,2688	567	1316.812,5684
418	915.826,3570	468	1048.159,5319	518	1182.814,5986	568	1319.566,9168
419	918.448,5710	469	1050.830,7047	519	1185.529,7660	569	1322.322,0290
420	921.071,8203	470	1053.502,8026	520	1188.245,7693	570	1325.077,9039
421	923.696,1024	471	1056.175,8235	521	1190.962,6070	571	1327.834,5400
422	926.321,4149	472	1058.849,7655	522	1193.680,2775	572	1330.591,9360
423	928.947,7552	473	1061.524,6266	523	1196.398,7792	573	1333.350,0907
424	931.575,1211	474	1064.200,4050	524	1199.118,1105	574	1336.109,0026
425	934.203,5100	475	1066.877,0986	525	1201.838,2698	575	1338.868,6704
426	936.832,9196	476	1069.554,7056	526	1204.559,2556	576	1341.629,0929
427	939.463,3475	477	1072.233,2239	527	1207.281,0662	577	1344.390,2687
428	942.094,7913	478	1074.912,6518	528	1210.003,7001	578	1347.152,1965
429	944.727,2486	479	1077.592,9873	529	1212.727,1558	579	1349.914,8751
430	947.360,7170	480	1080.274,2286	530	1215.451,4316	580	1352.678,3031
431	949.995,1943	481	1082.956,3737	531	1218.176,5262	581	1355.442,4792
432	952.630,6780	482	1085.639,4207	532	1220.902,4378	582	1358.207,4022
433	955.267,1659	483	1088.323,3678	533	1223.629,1650	583	1360.973,0708
434	957.904,6557	484	1091.008,2132	534	1226.356,7063	584	1363.739,4836
435	960.543,1449	485	1093.693,9549	535	1229.085,0600	585	1366.506,6395
436	963.182,6314	486	1096.380,5912	536	1231.814,2248	586	1369.274,5371
437	965.823,1128	487	1099.068,1202	537	1234.544,1991	587	1372.043,1752
438	968.464,5869	488	1101.756,5400	538	1237.274,9814	588	1374.812,5525
439	971.107,0515	489	1104.445,8488	539	1240.006,5702	589	1377.582,6678
440	973.750,5041	490	1107.136,0449	540	1242.738,9639	590	1380.353,5198
441	976.394,9427	491	1109.827,1264	541	1245.472,1612	591	1383.125,1073
442	979.040,3650	492	1112.519,0915	542	1248.206,1605	592	1385.897,4290
443	981.686,7687	493	1115.211,9384	543	1250.940,9603	593	1388.670,4837
444	984.334,1517	494	1117.905,6654	544	1253.676,5592	594	1391.444,2702
445	986.982,5117	495	1120.600,2706	545	1256.412,9557	595	1394.218,7871
446	989.631,8466	496	1123.295,7523	546	1259.150,1483	596	1396.994,0334
447	992.282,1541	497	1125.992,1086	547	1261.888,1357	597	1399.770,0077
448	994.933,4321	498	1128.689,3380	548	1264.626,9162	598	1402.546,7089
449	997.585,6784	499	1131.387,4385	549	1267.366,4886	599	1405.324,1357
450	1000.238,8910	500	1134.086,4085	550	1270.106,8513	600	1408.102,2870

TABLE 1 (CONTINUED)

n	log n!	n	log n!	n	log n!	n	log n!
601	1410.881,1614	651	1550.721,4519	701	1692.229,8994	751	1835.287,3949
602	1413.660,7579	652	1553.535,6995	702	1695.076,2365	752	1838.163,6127
603	1416.441,0752	653	1556.350,6126	703	1697.923,1918	753	1841.040,4077
604	1419.222,1122	654	1559.166,1904	704	1700.770,7644	754	1843.917,7790
605	1422.003,8676	655	1561.982,4317	705	1703.618,9536	755	1846.795,7260
606	1424.786,3402	656	1564.799,3355	706	1706.467,7583	756	1849.674,2478
607	1427.569,5289	657	1567.616,9009	707	1709.317,1777	757	1852.553,3437
608	1430.353,4324	658	1570.435,1268	708	1712.167,2109	758	1855.433,0129
609	1433.138,0497	659	1573.254,0122	709	1715.017,8572	759	1858.313,2546
610	1435.923,3796	660	1576.073,5561	710	1717.869,1155	760	1861.194,0682
611	1438.709,4208	661	1578.893,7576	711	1720.720,9851	761	1864.075,4529
612	1441.496,1722	662	1581.714,6156	712	1723.573,4651	762	1868.957,4079
613	1444.283,6327	663	1584.536,1291	713	1726.426,5546	763	1869.839,9324
614	1447.071,8011	664	1587.358,2972	714	1729.280,2529	764	1872.723,0258
615	1449.860,6762	665	1590.181,1188	715	1732.134,5589	765	1875.606,6872
616	1452.650,2569	666	1593.004,5931	716	1734.989,4719	766	1878.490,9160
617	1455.440,5420	667	1595.828,7189	717	1737.844,9911	767	1881.375,7113
618	1458.231,5305	668	1598.653,4954	718	1740.701,1155	768	1884.261,0726
619	1461.023,2212	669	1601.478,9215	719	1743.557,8444	769	1887.146,9989
620	1463.815,6129	670	1604.304,9963	720	1746.415,1769	770	1890.033,4896
621	1466.608,7045	671	1607.131,7188	721	1749.273,1122	771	1892.920,5440
622	1469.402,4948	672	1609.959,0881	722	1752.131,6494	772	1895.808,1613
623	1472.196,9829	673	1612.787,1031	723	1754.990,7877	773	1898.698,3408
624	1474.992,1675	674	1615.615,7630	724	1757.850,5262	774	1901.585,0817
625	1477.788,0475	675	1618.445,0668	725	1760.710,8642	775	1904.474,3835
626	1480.584,6218	676	1621.275,0135	726	1763.571,8009	776	1907.364,2452
627	1483.381,8894	677	1624.105,6022	727	1766.433,3353	777	1910.254,6662
628	1486.179,8490	678	1626.936,8319	728	1769.295,4667	778	1913.145,6458
629	1488.978,4997	679	1629.768,7016	729	1772.158,1942	779	1916.037,1832
630	1491.777,8402	680	1632.601,2106	730	1775.021,5170	780	1918.929,2778
631	1494.577,8696	681	1635.434,3577	731	1777.885,4344	781	1921.821,9289
632	1497.378,5866	682	1638.268,1420	732	1780.749,9455	782	1924.715,1356
633	1500.179,9904	683	1641.102,5627	733	1783.615,0495	783	1927.608,8974
634	1502.982,0796	684	1643.937,6189	734	1786.480,7455	784	1930.503,2135
635	1505.784,8533	685	1646.773,3094	735	1789.347,0329	785	1933.398,0831
636	1508.588,3105	686	1649.609,6335	736	1792.213,9107	786	1936.293,5057
637	1511.392,4499	687	1652.446,5903	737	1795.081,3782	787	1939.189,4804
638	1514.197,2706	688	1655.284,1787	738	1797.949,4345	788	1942.086,0066
639	1517.002,7714	689	1658.122,3979	739	1800.818,0790	789	1944.983,0836
640	1519.808,9514	690	1660.961,2470	740	1803.687,3107	790	1947.880,7107
641	1522.516,8094	691	1663.800,7251	741	1806.557,1289	791	1950.778,8872
642	1525.423,3445	692	1666.640,8312	742	1809.427,5328	792	1953.677,6124
643	1528.231,5554	693	1669.481,5644	743	1812.298,5216	793	1956.576,8856
644	1531.040,4413	694	1672.322,9239	744	1815.170,0946	794	1959.476,7061
645	1533.850,0010	695	1675.164,9087	745	1818.042,2508	795	1962.377,0732
646	1536.660,2335	696	1678.007,5179	746	1820.914,9897	796	1965.277,9863
647	1539.471,1378	697	1680.850,7507	747	1823.788,3103	797	1968.179,4446
648	1542.282,7128	698	1683.694,6061	748	1826.662,2119	798	1971.081,4475
649	1545.094,9575	699	1686.539,0833	749	1829.536,6937	799	1973.983,9943
650	1547.907,8709	700	1689.384,1813	750	1832.411,7549	800	1976.887,0842

TABLE 1 (CONTINUED)

n	$\log n!$	n	$\log n!$	n	$\log n!$	n	$\log n!$
801	1979.790,7168	851	2125.649,5488	901	2272.784,2010	951	2421.123,8376
802	1982.694,8911	852	2128.579,9884	902	2275.739,4075	952	2424.102,4745
803	1985.599,6067	853	2131.510,9374	903	2278.695,0953	953	2427.081,5674
804	1988.504,8627	854	2134.442,3953	904	2281.651,2637	954	2430.061,1158
805	1991.410,6586	855	2137.374,3614	905	2284.607,9123	955	2433.041,1192
806	1994.316,9936	856	2140.306,8352	906	2287.565,0405	956	2436.021,5771
807	1997.223,8672	857	2143.239,8160	907	2290.522,6478	957	2439.002,4890
808	2000.131,2785	858	2146.173,3033	908	2293.480,7336	958	2441.983,8545
809	2003.039,2271	859	2149.107,2964	909	2296.439,2975	959	2444.965,6731
810	2005.947,7121	860	2152.041,7949	910	2299.398,3389	960	2447.947,9443
811	2008.856,7329	861	2154.976,7980	911	2302.357,8573	961	2450.930,6677
812	2011.766,2890	862	2157.912,3053	912	2305.317,8521	962	2453.913,8428
813	2014.676,3795	863	2160.848,3161	913	2308.278,3229	963	2456.897,4691
814	2017.587,0039	864	2163.784,8298	914	2311.239,2691	964	2459.881,5461
815	2020.498,1615	865	2166.721,8459	915	2314.200,6902	965	2462.886,0734
816	2023.409,8517	866	2169.659,3638	916	2317.162,5856	966	2465.851,0506
817	2026.322,0737	867	2172.597,3829	917	2320.124,9550	967	2468.836,4770
818	2029.234,8270	868	2175.535,9027	918	2323.087,7977	968	2471.822,3524
819	2032.148,1109	869	2178.474,9224	919	2326.051,1132	969	2474.808,6762
820	2035.061,9248	870	2181.414,4417	920	2329.014,9010	970	2477.795,4479
821	2037.976,2679	871	2184.354,4598	921	2331.979,1606	971	2480.782,6671
822	2040.891,1398	872	2187.294,9763	922	2334.943,8915	972	2483.770,3334
823	2043.806,5396	873	2190.235,9906	923	2337.909,0932	973	2486.758,4462
824	2046.722,4668	874	2193.177,5020	924	2340.874,7652	974	2489.747,0052
825	2049.638,9208	875	2196.119,5101	925	2343.840,9069	975	2492.736,0098
826	2052.555,9008	876	2199.062,0142	926	2346.807,5179	976	2495.725,4596
827	2055.473,4063	877	2202.005,0138	927	2349.774,5977	977	2498.715,3542
828	2058.391,4367	878	2204.948,5083	928	2352.742,1456	978	2501.705,6930
829	2061.309,9912	879	2207.892,4971	929	2355.710,1614	979	2504.696,4757
830	2064.229,0693	880	2210.836,9798	930	2358.678,6443	980	2507.687,7018
831	2067.148,6703	881	2213.781,9557	931	2361.647,5940	981	2510.679,3708
832	2070.068,7936	882	2216.727,4243	932	2364.617,0099	982	2513.671,4823
833	2072.989,4386	883	2219.673,3850	933	2367.586,8915	983	2516.664,0358
834	2075.910,6047	884	2222.619,8373	934	2370.557,2384	984	2519.657,0309
835	2078.832,2912	885	2225.566,7805	935	2373.528,0500	985	2522.650,4672
836	2081.754,4974	886	2228.514,2143	936	2376.499,3259	986	2525.644,3441
837	2084.677,2229	887	2231.462,1379	937	2379.471,0655	987	2528.638,6612
838	2087.600,4669	888	2234.410,5509	938	2382.443,2683	988	2531.633,4182
839	2090.524,2289	889	2237.359,4526	939	2385.415,9339	989	2534.628,6145
840	2093.448,5082	890	2240.308,8426	940	2388.389,0618	990	2537.624,2497
841	2096.373,3042	891	2243.258,7203	941	2391.362,6514	991	2540.620,3233
842	2099.298,6162	892	2246.209,0852	942	2394.336,7023	992	2543.616,8350
843	2102.224,4438	893	2249.159,9366	943	2397.311,2140	993	2546.613,7842
844	2105.150,7863	894	2252.111,2742	944	2400.286,1860	994	2549.611,1706
845	2108.077,6430	895	2255.063,0972	945	2403.261,6178	995	2552.608,9937
846	2111.005,0133	896	2258.015,4052	946	2406.237,5089	996	2555.706,2530
847	2113.932,8967	897	2260.968,1976	947	2409.213,8589	997	2558.605,9482
848	2116.861,2926	898	2263.921,4740	948	2412.190,6672	998	2561.605,0787
849	2119.790,2003	899	2266.875,2337	949	2415.167,9334	999	2564.604,6442
850	2122.719,6192	900	2269.829,4762	950	2418.145,6570	1000	2567.604,6442

TABLE 1 (CONTINUED)

n	$\log n!$	n	$\log n!$	n	$\log n!$	n	$\log n!$
1005	2582.611,1467	1255	3345.706,7417	1505	4130.567,1194	1755	4933.540,7804
1010	2597.628,4473	1260	3361.205,1436	1510	4146.459,1251	1760	4949.765,8740
1015	2612.656,4924	1265	3376.712,1590	1515	4162.358,3188	1765	4965.997,1349
1020	2627.695,2292	1270	3392.227,7539	1520	4178.264,6767	1770	4982.234,5455
1025	2642.744,6053	1275	3407.751,8946	1525	4194.178,1753	1775	4998.478,0885
1030	2657.804,5688	1280	3423.284,5475	1530	4210.098,7911	1780	5014.727,7466
1035	2672.875,0683	1285	3438.825,6795	1535	4226.026,5010	1785	5030.983,5026
1040	2687.956,0531	1290	3454.375,2575	1540	4241.961,2818	1790	5047.245,3395
1045	2703.047,4726	1295	3469.933,2488	1545	4257.903,1105	1795	5063.513,2403
1050	2718.149,2771	1300	3485.499,6210	1550	4273.851,9643	1800	5079.787,1881
1055	2733.261,4170	1305	3501.074,3418	1555	4289.807,8207	1805	5096.067,1660
1060	2748.383,8434	1310	3516.657,3792	1560	4305.770,6571	1810	5112.353,1575
1065	2763.516,5078	1315	3532.248,7016	1565	4321.740,4511	1815	5128.645,1458
1070	2778.659,3621	1320	3547.848,2774	1570	4337.717,1805	1820	5144.943,1146
1075	2793.812,3589	1325	3563.456,0754	1575	4353.700,8232	1825	5161.247,0473
1080	2808.975,4508	1330	3579.072,0645	1580	4369.691,3574	1830	5177.556,9276
1085	2824.148,5912	1335	3594.696,2140	1585	4385.688,7611	1835	5193.872,7393
1090	2839.331,7339	1340	3610.328,4934	1590	4401.693,0127	1840	5210.194,4662
1095	2854.524,8329	1345	3625.968,8723	1595	4417.704,0907	1845	5226.522,0922
1100	2869.727,8428	1350	3641.617,3205	1600	4433.721,9737	1850	5242.855,6014
1105	2884.940,7185	1355	3657.273,8083	1605	4449.746,6405	1855	5259.194,9778
1110	2900.163,4156	1360	3672.938,3060	1610	4465.778,0699	1860	5275.540,2058
1115	2915.395,8896	1365	3688.610,7841	1615	4481.816,2409	1865	5291.891,2694
1120	2930.638,0969	1370	3704.291,2134	1620	4497.861,1327	1870	5308.248,1532
1125	2945.889,9940	1375	3719.979,5650	1625	4513.912,7244	1875	5324.610,8414
1130	2961.151,5378	1380	3735.675,8099	1630	4529.970,9956	1880	5340.979,3187
1135	2976.422,6856	1385	3751.379,9197	1635	4546.035,9257	1885	5357.353,5697
1140	2991.703,3953	1390	3767.091,8659	1640	4562.107,4944	1890	5373.733,5791
1145	3006.993,6248	1395	3782.811,6023	1645	4578.185,6814	1895	5390.119,3315
1150	3022.293,3325	1400	3798.539,1551	1650	4594.270,4667	1900	5406.510,8120
1155	3037.602,4774	1405	3814.274,4423	1655	4610.361,8301	1905	5422.908,0053
1160	3052.921,0186	1410	3830.017,4545	1660	4626.459,7520	1910	5439.310,8966
1165	3068.248,9156	1415	3845.768,1642	1665	4642.564,2124	1915	5455.719,4708
1170	3083.586,1282	1420	3861.526,5443	1670	4658.675,1919	1920	5472.133,7133
1175	3098.932,6167	1425	3877.292,5677	1675	4674.792,6708	1925	5488.553,6091
1180	3114.288,3416	1430	3893.056,2077	1680	4690.916,6298	1930	5504.979,1437
1185	3129.653,2638	1435	3908.847,4376	1685	4707.047,0496	1935	5521.410,3023
1190	3145.027,3444	1440	3924.636,2310	1690	4723.183,9111	1940	5537.847,0706
1195	3160.410,5451	1445	3940.432,5616	1695	4739.327,1951	1945	5554.289,4341
1200	3175.802,8277	1450	3956.236,4034	1700	4755.476,8828	1950	5570.737,3782
1205	3191.204,1543	1455	3972.047,7304	1705	4771.632,9553	1955	5587.190,8889
1210	3206.614,4875	1460	3987.866,5170	1710	4787.795,3939	1960	5603.649,9518
1215	3222.033,7900	1465	4003.692,7376	1715	4803.964,1799	1965	5620.114,5527
1220	3237.462,0250	1470	4019.526,3669	1720	4820.139,2950	1970	5636.584,6776
1225	3252.899,1558	1475	4035.367,3796	1725	4836.320,7207	1975	5653.060,3125
1230	3268.345,1462	1480	4051.215,7508	1730	4852.508,4386	1980	5669.541,4434
1235	3283.799,9602	1485	4067.071,4556	1735	4868.702,4307	1985	5686.028,0564
1240	3299.263,5620	1490	4082.934,4693	1740	4884.109,6789	1990	5702.520,1377
1245	3314.735,9162	1495	4098.804,7673	1745	4901.109,1651	1995	5719.017,6737
1250	3330.216,9878	1500	4114.682,3254	1750	4917.321,8715	2000	5735.520,6505

TABLE 2 FOUR-PLACE COMMON LOGARITHMS OF NUMBERS*

N	0	1	2	3	4	5	6	7	8	9	Proportional parts 1	2	3	4	5
10	0000	0043	0086	0128	0170	0212	0253	0294	0334	0374	4	8	12	17	21
11	0414	0453	0492	0531	0569	0607	0645	0682	0719	0755	4	8	11	15	19
12	0792	0828	0864	0899	0934	0969	1004	1038	1072	1106	3	7	10	14	17
13	1139	1173	1206	1239	1271	1303	1335	1367	1399	1430	3	6	10	13	16
14	1461	1492	1523	1553	1584	1614	1644	1673	1703	1732	3	6	9	12	15
15	1761	1790	1818	1847	1875	1903	1931	1959	1987	2014	3,	6	8	11	14
16	2041	2068	2095	2122	2148	2175	2201	2227	2253	2279	3	5	8	11	13
17	2304	2330	2355	2380	2405	2430	2455	2480	2504	2529	2	5	7	10	12
18	2553	2577	2601	2625	2648	2672	2695	2718	2742	2765	2	5	7	9	12
19	2788	2810	2833	2856	2878	2900	2923	2945	2967	2989	2	4	7	9	11
20	3010	3032	3054	3075	3096	3118	3139	3160	3181	3201	2	4	6	8	11
21	3222	3243	3263	3284	3304	3324	3345	3365	3385	3404	2	4	6	8	10
22	3424	3444	3464	3483	3502	3522	3541	3560	3579	3598	2	4	6	8	10
23	3617	3636	3655	3674	3692	3711	3729	3747	3766	3784	2	4	6	7	9
24	3802	3820	3838	3856	3874	3892	3909	3927	3945	3962	2	4	5	7	9
25	3979	3997	4014	4031	4048	4065	4082	4099	4116	4133	2	4	5	7	9
26	4150	4166	4183	4200	4216	4232	4249	4265	4281	4298	2	3	5	7	8
27	4314	4330	4346	4362	4378	4393	4409	4425	4440	4456	2	3	5	6	8
28	4472	4487	4502	4518	4533	4548	4564	4579	4594	4609	2	3	5	6	8
29	4624	4639	4654	4669	4683	4698	4713	4728	4742	4757	1	3	4	6	7
30	4771	4786	4800	4814	4829	4843	4857	4871	4886	4900	1	3	4	6	7
31	4914	4928	4942	4955	4969	4983	4997	5011	5024	5038	1	3	4	5	7
32	5051	5065	5079	5092	5105	5119	5132	5145	5159	5172	1	3	4	5	7
33	5185	5198	5211	5224	5237	5250	5263	5276	5289	5302	1	3	4	5	7
34	5315	5328	5340	5353	5366	5378	5391	5403	5416	5428	1	2	4	5	6
35	5441	5453	5465	5478	5490	5502	5514	5527	5539	5551	1	2	4	5	6
36	5563	5575	5587	5599	5611	5623	5635	5647	5658	5670	1	2	4	5	6
37	5682	5694	5705	5717	5729	5740	5752	5763	5775	5786	1	2	4	5	6
38	5798	5809	5821	5832	5843	5855	5866	5877	5888	5899	1	2	3	5	6
39	5911	5922	5933	5944	5955	5966	5977	5988	5999	6010	1	2	3	4	5
40	6021	6031	6042	6053	6064	6075	6085	6096	6107	6117	1	2	3	4	5
41	6128	6138	6149	6160	6170	6180	6191	6201	6212	6222	1	2	3	4	5
42	6232	6243	6253	6263	6274	6284	6294	6304	6314	6325	1	2	3	4	5
43	6335	6345	6355	6365	6375	6385	6395	6405	6415	6425	1	2	3	4	5
44	6435	6444	6454	6464	6474	6484	6493	6503	6513	6522	1	2	3	4	5
45	6532	6542	6551	6561	6571	6580	6590	6599	6609	6618	1	2	3	4	5
46	6628	6637	6646	6656	6665	6675	6684	6693	6702	6712	1	2	3	4	5
47	6721	6730	6739	6749	6758	6767	6776	6785	6794	6803	1	2	3	4	5
48	6812	6821	6830	6839	6848	6857	6866	6875	6884	6893	1	2	3	4	5
49	6902	6911	6920	6928	6937	6946	6955	6964	6972	6981	1	2	3	4	4
50	6990	6998	7007	7016	7024	7033	7042	7050	7059	7067	1	2	3	3	4
51	7076	7084	7093	7101	7110	7118	7126	7135	7143	7152	1	2	3	3	4
52	7160	7168	7177	7185	7193	7202	7210	7218	7226	7235	1	2	3	3	4
53	7243	7251	7259	7267	7275	7284	7292	7300	7308	7316	1	2	2	3	4
54	7324	7332	7340	7348	7356	7364	7372	7380	7388	7396	1	2	2	3	4
N	0	1	2	3	4	5	6	7	8	9	1	2	3	4	5

* From R. S. Burington, "Handbook of Mathematical Tables and Formulas," 4th ed., pp. 386–387, McGraw-Hill Book Company, New York, 1965.

TABLE 2 (**CONTINUED**)

N	0	1	2	3	4	5	6	7	8	9	Proportional parts				
											1	2	3	4	5
55	7404	7412	7419	7427	7435	7443	7451	7459	7466	7474	1	2	2	3	4
56	7482	7490	7497	7505	7513	7520	7528	7536	7543	7551	1	2	2	3	4
57	7559	7566	7574	7582	7589	7597	7604	7612	7619	7627	1	1	2	3	4
58	7634	7642	7649	7657	7664	7672	7679	7686	7694	7701	1	1	2	3	4
59	7709	7716	7723	7731	7738	7745	7752	7760	7767	7774	1	1	2	3	4
60	7782	7789	7796	7803	7810	7818	7825	7832	7839	7846	1	1	2	3	4
61	7853	7860	7868	7875	7882	7889	7896	7903	7910	7917	1	1	2	3	3
62	7924	7931	7938	7945	7952	7959	7966	7973	7980	7987	1	1	2	3	3
63	7993	8000	8007	8014	8021	8028	8035	8041	8048	8055	1	1	2	3	3
64	8062	8069	8075	8082	8089	8096	8102	8109	8116	8122	1	1	2	3	3
65	8129	8136	8142	8149	8156	8162	8169	8176	8182	8189	1	1	2	3	3
66	8195	8202	8209	8215	8222	8228	8235	8241	8248	8254	1	1	2	3	3
67	8261	8267	8274	8280	8287	8293	8299	8306	8312	8319	1	1	2	3	3
68	8325	8331	8338	8344	8351	8357	8363	8370	8376	8382	1	1	2	3	3
69	8388	8395	8401	8407	8414	8420	8426	8432	8439	8445	1	1	2	3	3
70	8451	8457	8463	8470	8476	8482	8488	8494	8500	8506	1	1	2	3	3
71	8513	8519	8525	8531	8537	8543	8549	8555	8561	8567	1	1	2	3	3
72	8573	8579	8585	8591	8597	8603	8609	8615	8621	8627	1	1	2	3	3
73	8633	8639	8645	8651	8657	8663	8669	8675	8681	8686	1	1	2	2	3
74	8692	8698	8704	8710	8716	8722	8727	8733	8739	8745	1	1	2	2	3
75	8751	8756	8762	8768	8774	8779	8785	8791	8797	8802	1	1	2	2	3
76	8808	8814	8820	8825	8831	8837	8842	8848	8854	8859	1	1	2	2	3
77	8865	8871	8876	8882	8887	8893	8899	8904	8910	8915	1	1	2	2	3
78	8921	8927	8932	8938	8943	8949	8954	8960	8965	8971	1	1	2	2	3
79	8976	8982	8987	8993	8998	9004	9009	9015	9020	9025	1	1	2	2	3
80	9031	9036	9042	9047	9053	9058	9063	9069	9074	9079	1	1	2	2	3
81	9085	9090	9096	9101	9106	9112	9117	9122	9128	9133	1	1	2	2	3
82	9138	9143	9149	9154	9159	9165	9170	9175	9180	9186	1	1	2	2	3
83	9191	9196	9201	9206	9212	9217	9222	9227	9232	9238	1	1	2	2	3
84	9243	9248	9253	9258	9263	9269	9274	9279	9284	9289	1	1	2	2	3
85	9294	9299	9304	9309	9315	9320	9325	9330	9335	9340	1	1	2	2	3
86	9345	9350	9355	9360	9365	9370	9375	9380	9385	9390	1	1	2	2	3
87	9395	9400	9405	9410	9415	9420	9425	9430	9435	9440	1	1	2	2	3
88	9445	9450	9455	9460	9465	9469	9474	9479	9484	9489	0	1	1	2	2
89	9494	9499	9504	9509	9513	9518	9523	9528	9533	9538	0	1	1	2	2
90	9542	9547	9552	9557	9562	9566	9571	9576	9581	9586	0	1	1	2	2
91	9590	9595	9600	9605	9609	9614	9619	9624	9628	9633	0	1	1	2	2
92	9638	9643	9647	9652	9657	9661	9666	9671	9675	9680	0	1	1	2	2
93	9685	9689	9694	9699	9703	9708	9713	9717	9722	9727	0	1	1	2	2
94	9731	9736	9741	9745	9750	9754	9759	9763	9768	9773	0	1	1	2	2
95	9777	9782	9786	9791	9795	9800	9805	9809	9814	9818	0	1	1	2	2
96	9823	9827	9832	9836	9841	9845	9850	9854	9859	9863	0	1	1	2	2
97	9868	9872	9877	9881	9886	9890	9894	9899	9903	9908	0	1	1	2	2
98	9912	9917	9921	9926	9930	9934	9939	9943	9948	9952	0	1	1	2	2
99	9956	9961	9965	9969	9974	9978	9983	9987	9991	9996	0	1	1	2	2
N	0	1	2	3	4	5	6	7	8	9	1	2	3	4	5

TABLE 3 NATURAL LOGARITHMS OF NUMBERS*

NATURAL LOGARITHMS OF NUMBERS—0.00 to 5.99
(Base $e = 2.718 \cdots$)

N	0	1	2	3	4	5	6	7	8	9
0.0	*(Take tabular value −10)*	5.395	6.088	6.493	6.781	7.004	7.187	7.341	7.474	7.592
0.1	7.697	7.793	7.880	7.960	8.034	8.103	8.167	8.228	8.285	8.339
0.2	8.391	8.439	8.486	8.530	8.573	8.614	8.653	8.691	8.727	8.762
0.3	8.796	8.829	8.861	8.891	8.921	8.950	8.978	9.006	9.032	9.058
0.4	9.084	9.108	9.132	9.156	9.179	9.201	9.223	9.245	9.266	9.287
0.5	9.307	9.327	9.346	9.365	9.384	9.402	9.420	9.438	9.455	9.472
0.6	9.489	9.506	9.522	9.538	9.554	9.569	9.584	9.600	9.614	9.629
0.7	9.643	9.658	9.671	9.685	9.699	9.712	9.726	9.739	9.752	9.764
0.8	9.777	9.789	9.802	9.814	9.826	9.837	9.849	9.861	9.872	9.883
0.9	9.895	9.906	9.917	9.927	9.938	9.949	9.959	9.970	9.980	9.990
1.0	0.0 0000	0995	1980	2956	3922	4879	5827	6766	7696	8618
1.1	9531	*0436	*1333	*2222	*3103	*3976	*4842	*5700	*6551	*7395
1.2	0.1 8232	9062	9885	*0701	*1511	*2314	*3111	*3902	*4686	*5464
1.3	0.2 6236	7003	7763	8518	9267	*0010	*0748	*1481	*2208	*2930
1.4	0.3 3647	4359	5066	5767	6464	7156	7844	8526	9204	9878
1.5	0.4 0547	1211	1871	2527	3178	3825	4469	5108	5742	6373
1.6	7000	7623	8243	8858	9470	*0078	*0682	*1282	*1879	*2473
1.7	0.5 3063	3649	4232	4812	5389	5962	6531	7098	7661	8222
1.8	8779	9333	9884	*0432	*0977	*1519	*2058	*2594	*3127	*3658
1.9	0.6 4185	4710	5233	5752	6269	6783	7294	7803	8310	8813
2.0	9315	9813	*0310	*0804	*1295	*1784	*2271	*2755	*3237	*3716
2.1	0.7 4194	4669	5142	5612	6081	6547	7011	7473	7932	8390
2.2	8846	9299	9751	*0200	*0648	*1093	*1536	*1978	*2418	*2855
2.3	0.8 3291	3725	4157	4587	5015	5442	5866	6289	6710	7129
2.4	7547	7963	8377	8789	9200	9609	*0016	*0422	*0826	*1228
2.5	0.9 1629	2028	2426	2822	3216	3609	4001	4391	4779	5166
2.6	5551	5935	6317	6698	7078	7456	7833	8208	8582	8954
2.7	9325	9695	*0063	*0430	*0796	*1160	*1523	*1885	*2245	*2604
2.8	1.0 2962	3318	3674	4028	4380	4732	5082	5431	5779	6126
2.9	6471	6815	7158	7500	7841	8181	8519	8856	9192	9527
3.0	9861	*0194	*0526	*0856	*1186	*1514	*1841	*2168	*2493	*2817
3.1	1.1 3140	3462	3783	4103	4422	4740	5057	5373	5688	6002
3.2	6315	6627	6938	7248	7557	7865	8173	8479	8784	9089
3.3	9392	9695	9996	*0297	*0597	*0896	*1194	*1491	*1788	*2083
3.4	1.2 2378	2671	2964	3256	3547	3837	4127	4415	4703	4990
3.5	5276	5562	5846	6130	6413	6695	6976	7257	7536	7815
3.6	8093	8371	8647	8923	9198	9473	9746	*0019	*0291	*0563
3.7	1.3 0833	1103	1372	1641	1909	2176	2442	2708	2972	3237
3.8	3500	3763	4025	4286	4547	4807	5067	5325	5584	5841
3.9	6098	6354	6609	6864	7118	7372	7624	7877	8128	8379
4.0	8629	8879	9128	9377	9624	9872	*0118	*0364	*0610	*0854
4.1	1.4 1099	1342	1585	1828	2070	2311	2552	2792	3031	3270
4.2	3508	3746	3984	4220	4456	4692	4927	5161	5395	5629
4.3	5862	6094	6326	6557	6787	7018	7247	7476	7705	7933
4.4	8160	8387	8614	8840	9065	9290	9515	9739	9962	*0185
4.5	1.5 0408	0630	0851	1072	1293	1513	1732	1951	2170	2388
4.6	2606	2823	3039	3256	3471	3687	3902	4116	4330	4543
4.7	4756	4969	5181	5393	5604	5814	6025	6235	6444	6653
4.8	6862	7070	7277	7485	7691	7898	8104	8309	8515	8719
4.9	8924	9127	9331	9534	9737	9939	*0141	*0342	*0543	*0744
5.0	1.6 0944	1144	1343	1542	1741	1939	2137	2334	2531	2728
5.1	2924	3120	3315	3511	3705	3900	4094	4287	4481	4673
5.2	4866	5058	5250	5441	5632	5823	6013	6203	6393	6582
5.3	6771	6959	7147	7335	7523	7710	7896	8083	8269	8455
5.4	8640	8825	9010	9194	9378	9562	9745	9928	*0111	*0293
5.5	1.7 0475	0656	0838	1019	1199	1380	1560	1740	1919	2098
5.6	2277	2455	2633	2811	2988	3166	3342	3519	3695	3871
5.7	4047	4222	4397	4572	4746	4920	5094	5267	5440	5613
5.8	5786	5958	6130	6302	6473	6644	6815	6985	7156	7326
5.9	7495	7665	7834	8002	8171	8339	8507	8675	8842	9009
N	0	1	2	3	4	5	6	7	8	9

$\log_e 0.10 = 7.69741\ 49070 - 10$

* From R. S. Burington, "Handbook of Mathematical Tables and Formulas," 4th ed., pp. 311–314, McGraw-Hill Book Company, New York, 1965.

TABLE 3 (CONTINUED)

NATURAL LOGARITHMS OF NUMBERS—6.00 to 10.09

N	0	1	2	3	4	5	6	7	8	9
6.0	1.7 9176	9342	9509	9675	9840	*0006	*0171	*0336	*0500	*0665
6.1	1.8 0829	0993	1156	1319	1482	1645	1808	1970	2132	2294
6.2	2455	2616	2777	2938	3098	3258	3418	3578	3737	3896
6.3	4055	4214	4372	4530	4688	4845	5003	5160	5317	5473
6.4	5630	5786	5942	6097	6253	6408	6563	6718	6872	7026
6.5	7180	7334	7487	7641	7794	7947	8099	8251	8403	8555
6.6	8707	8858	9010	9160	9311	9462	9612	9762	9912	*0061
6.7	1.9 0211	0360	0509	0658	0806	0954	1102	1250	1398	1545
6.8	1692	1839	1986	2132	2279	2425	2571	2716	2862	3007
6.9	3152	3297	3442	3586	3730	3874	4018	4162	4305	4448
7.0	4591	4734	4876	5019	5161	5303	5445	5586	5727	5869
7.1	6009	6150	6291	6431	6571	6711	6851	6991	7130	7269
7.2	7408	7547	7685	7824	7962	8100	8238	8376	8513	8650
7.3	8787	8924	9061	9198	9334	9470	9606	9742	9877	*0013
7.4	2.0 0148	0283	0418	0553	0687	0821	0956	1089	1223	1357
7.5	1490	1624	1757	1890	2022	2155	2287	2419	2551	2683
7.6	2815	2946	3078	3209	3340	3471	3601	3732	3862	3992
7.7	4122	4252	4381	4511	4640	4769	4898	5027	5156	5284
7.8	5412	5540	5668	5796	5924	6051	6179	6306	6433	6560
7.9	6686	6813	6939	7065	7191	7317	7443	7568	7694	7819
8.0	7944	8069	8194	8318	8443	8567	8691	8815	8939	9063
8.1	9186	9310	9433	9556	9679	9802	9924	*0047	*0169	*0291
8.2	2.1 0413	0535	0657	0779	0900	1021	1142	1263	1384	1505
8.3	1626	1746	1866	1986	2106	2226	2346	2465	2585	2704
8.4	2823	2942	3061	3180	3298	3417	3535	3653	3771	3889
8.5	4007	4124	4242	4359	4476	4593	4710	4827	4943	5060
8.6	5176	5292	5409	5524	5640	5756	5871	5987	6102	6217
8.7	6332	6447	6562	6677	6791	6905	7020	7134	7248	7361
8.8	7475	7589	7702	7816	7929	8042	8155	8267	8380	8493
8.9	8605	8717	8830	8942	9054	9165	9277	9389	9500	9611
9.0	9722	9834	9944	*0055	*0166	*0276	*0387	*0497	*0607	*0717
9.1	2.2 0827	0937	1047	1157	1266	1375	1485	1594	1703	1812
9.2	1920	2029	2138	2246	2354	2462	2570	2678	2786	2894
9.3	3001	3109	3216	3324	3431	3538	3645	3751	3858	3965
9.4	4071	4177	4284	4390	4496	4601	4707	4813	4918	5024
9.5	5129	5234	5339	5444	5549	5654	5759	5863	5968	6072
9.6	6176	6280	6384	6488	6592	6696	6799	6903	7006	7109
9.7	7213	7316	7419	7521	7624	7727	7829	7932	8034	8136
9.8	8238	8340	8442	8544	8646	8747	8849	8950	9051	9152
9.9	9253	9354	9455	9556	9657	9757	9858	9958	*0058	*0158
10.0	2.3 0259	0358	0458	0558	0658	0757	0857	0956	1055	1154
N	0	1	2	3	4	5	6	7	8	9

NATURAL LOGARITHMS OF NUMBERS—10 to 99

N	0	1	2	3	4	5	6	7	8	9
1	2.30259	39790	48491	56495	63906	70805	77259	83321	89037	94444
2	99573	*04452	*09104	*13549	*17805	*21888	*25810	*29584	*33220	*36730
3	3.40120	43399	46574	49651	52636	55535	58352	61092	63759	66356
4	68888	71357	73767	76120	78419	80666	82864	85015	87120	89182
5	91202	93183	95124	97029	98898	*00733	*02535	*04305	*06044	*07754
6	4.09434	11087	12713	14313	15888	17439	18965	20469	21951	23411
7	24850	26268	27667	29046	30407	31749	33073	34381	35671	36945
8	38203	39445	40672	41884	43082	44265	45435	46591	47734	48864
9	49981	51086	52179	53260	54329	55388	56435	57471	58497	59512

$$\log_e 10 = 2.30258\ 50930$$

TABLE 3 (CONTINUED)

NATURAL LOGARITHMS OF NUMBERS

100 to 609

N	0	1	2	3	4	5	6	7	8	9
10	4.6 0517	1512	2497	3473	4439	5396	6344	7283	8213	9135
11	4.7 0048	0953	1850	2739	3620	4493	5359	6217	7068	7912
12	8749	9579	*0402	*1218	*2028	*2831	*3628	*4419	*5203	*5981
13	4.8 6753	7520	8280	9035	9784	*0527	*1265	*1998	*2725	*3447
14	4.9 4164	4876	5583	6284	6981	7673	8361	9043	9721	*0395
15	5.0 1064	1728	2388	3044	3695	4343	4986	5625	6260	6890
16	7517	8140	8760	9375	9987	*0595	*1199	*1799	*2396	*2990
17	5.1 3580	4166	4749	5329	5906	6479	7048	7615	8178	8739
18	9296	9850	*0401	*0949	*1494	*2036	*2575	*3111	*3644	*4175
19	5.2 4702	5227	5750	6269	6786	7300	7811	8320	8827	9330
20	9832	*0330	*0827	*1321	*1812	*2301	*2788	*3272	*3754	*4233
21	5.3 4711	5186	5659	6129	6598	7064	7528	7990	8450	8907
22	9363	9816	*0268	*0717	*1165	*1610	*2053	*2495	*2935	*3372
23	5.4 3808	4242	4674	5104	5532	5959	6383	6806	7227	7646
24	8064	8480	8894	9306	9717	*0126	*0533	*0939	*1343	*1745
25	5.5 2146	2545	2943	3339	3733	4126	4518	4908	5296	5683
26	6068	6452	6834	7215	7595	7973	8350	8725	9099	9471
27	9842	*0212	*0580	*0947	*1313	*1677	*2040	*2402	*2762	*3121
28	5.6 3479	3835	4191	4545	4897	5249	5599	5948	6296	6643
29	6988	7332	7675	8017	8358	8698	9036	9373	9709	*0044
30	5.7 0378	0711	1043	1373	1703	2031	2359	2685	3010	3334
31	3657	3979	4300	4620	4939	5257	5574	5890	6205	6519
32	6832	7144	7455	7765	8074	8383	8690	8996	9301	9606
33	9909	*0212	*0513	*0814	*1114	*1413	*1711	*2008	*2305	*2600
34	5.8 2895	3188	3481	3773	4064	4354	4644	4932	5220	5507
35	5793	6079	6363	6647	6930	7212	7493	7774	8053	8332
36	8610	8888	9164	9440	9715	9990	*0263	*0536	*0808	*1080
37	5.9 1350	1620	1889	2158	2426	2693	2959	3225	3489	3754
38	4017	4280	4542	4803	5064	5324	5584	5842	6101	6358
39	6615	6871	7126	7381	7635	7889	8141	8394	8645	8896
40	9146	9396	9645	9894	*0141	*0389	*0635	*0881	*1127	*1372
41	6.0 1616	1859	2102	2345	2587	2828	3069	3309	3548	3787
42	4025	4263	4501	4737	4973	5209	5444	5678	5912	6146
43	6379	6611	6843	7074	7304	7535	7764	7993	8222	8450
44	8677	8904	9131	9357	9582	9807	*0032	*0256	*0479	*0702
45	6.1 0925	1147	1368	1589	1810	2030	2249	2468	2687	2905
46	3123	3340	3556	3773	3988	4204	4419	4633	4847	5060
47	5273	5486	5698	5910	6121	6331	6542	6752	6961	7170
48	7379	7587	7794	8002	8208	8415	8621	8826	9032	9236
49	9441	9644	9848	*0051	*0254	*0456	*0658	*0859	*1060	*1261
50	6.2 1461	1661	1860	2059	2258	2456	2654	2851	3048	3245
51	3441	3637	3832	4028	4222	4417	4611	4804	4998	5190
52	5383	5575	5767	5958	6149	6340	6530	6720	6910	7099
53	7288	7476	7664	7852	8040	8227	8413	8600	8786	8972
54	9157	9342	9527	9711	9895	*0079	*0262	*0445	*0628	*0810
55	6.3 0992	1173	1355	1536	1716	1897	2077	2257	2436	2615
56	2794	2972	3150	3328	3505	3683	3859	4036	4212	4388
57	4564	4739	4914	5089	5263	5437	5611	5784	5957	6130
58	6303	6475	6647	6819	6990	7161	7332	7502	7673	7843
59	8012	8182	8351	8519	8688	8856	9024	9192	9359	9526
60	9693	9859	*0026	*0192	*0357	*0523	*0688	*0853	*1017	*1182
N	0	1	2	3	4	5	6	7	8	9

$$\log_e 100 = 4.60517\ 01860$$

T A B L E 3 (C O N T I N U E D)

NATURAL LOGARITHMS OF NUMBERS

600 to 1109

N	0	1	2	3	4	5	6	7	8	9
60	6.3 9693	9859	*0026	*0192	*0357	*0523	*0688	*0853	*1017	*1182
61	6.4 1346	1510	1673	1836	1999	2162	2325	2487	2649	2811
62	2972	3133	3294	3455	3615	3775	3935	4095	4254	4413
63	4572	4731	4889	5047	5205	5362	5520	5677	5834	5990
64	6147	6303	6459	6614	6770	6925	7080	7235	7389	7543
65	7697	7851	8004	8158	8311	8464	8616	8768	8920	9072
66	9224	9375	9527	9677	9828	9979	*0129	*0279	*0429	*0578
67	6.5 0728	0877	1026	1175	1323	1471	1619	1767	1915	2062
68	2209	2356	2503	2649	2796	2942	3088	3233	3379	3524
69	3669	3814	3959	4103	4247	4391	4535	4679	4822	4965
70	5108	5251	5393	5536	5678	5820	5962	6103	6244	6386
71	6526	6667	6808	6948	7088	7228	7368	7508	7647	7786
72	7925	8064	8203	8341	8479	8617	8755	8893	9030	9167
73	9304	9441	9578	9715	9851	9987	*0123	*0259	*0394	*0530
74	6.6 0665	0800	0935	1070	1204	1338	1473	1607	1740	1874
75	2007	2141	2274	2407	2539	2672	2804	2936	3068	3200
76	3332	3463	3595	3726	3857	3988	4118	4249	4379	4509
77	4639	4769	4898	5028	5157	5286	5415	5544	5673	5801
78	5929	6058	6185	6313	6441	6568	6696	6823	6950	7077
79	7203	7330	7456	7582	7708	7834	7960	8085	8211	8336
80	8461	8586	8711	8835	8960	9084	9208	9332	9456	9580
81	9703	9827	9950	*0073	*0196	*0319	*0441	*0564	*0686	*0808
82	6.7 0930	1052	1174	1296	1417	1538	1659	1780	1901	2022
83	2143	2263	2383	2503	2623	2743	2863	2982	3102	3221
84	3340	3459	3578	3697	3815	3934	4052	4170	4288	4406
85	4524	4641	4759	4876	4993	5110	5227	5344	5460	5577
86	5693	5809	5926	6041	6157	6273	6388	6504	6619	6734
87	6849	6964	7079	7194	7308	7422	7537	7651	7765	7878
88	7992	8106	8219	8333	8446	8559	8672	8784	8897	9010
89	9122	9234	9347	9459	9571	9682	9794	9906	*0017	*0128
90	6.8 0239	0351	0461	0572	0683	0793	0904	1014	1124	1235
91	1344	1454	1564	1674	1783	1892	2002	2111	2220	2329
92	2437	2546	2655	2763	2871	2979	3087	3195	3303	3411
93	3518	3626	3733	3841	3948	4055	4162	4268	4375	4482
94	4588	4694	4801	4907	5013	5118	5224	5330	5435	5541
95	5646	5751	5857	5961	6066	6171	6276	6380	6485	6589
96	6693	6797	6901	7005	7109	7213	7316	7420	7523	7626
97	7730	7833	7936	8038	8141	8244	8346	8449	8551	8653
98	8755	8857	8959	9061	9163	9264	9366	9467	9568	9669
99	9770	9871	9972	*0073	*0174	*0274	*0375	*0475	*0575	*0675
100	6.9 0776	0875	0975	1075	1175	1274	1374	1473	1572	1672
101	1771	1870	1968	2067	2166	2264	2363	2461	2560	2658
102	2756	2854	2952	3049	3147	3245	3342	3440	3537	3634
103	3731	3828	3925	4022	4119	4216	4312	4409	4505	4601
104	4698	4794	4890	4986	5081	5177	5273	5368	5464	5559
105	5655	5750	5845	5940	6035	6130	6224	6319	6414	6508
106	6602	6697	6791	6885	6979	7073	7167	7261	7354	7448
107	7541	7635	7728	7821	7915	8008	8101	8193	8286	8379
108	8472	8564	8657	8749	8841	8934	9026	9118	9210	9302
109	9393	9485	9577	9668	9760	9851	9942	*0033	*0125	*0216
110	7.0 0307	0397	0488	0579	0670	0760	0851	0941	1031	1121
N	0	1	2	3	4	5	6	7	8	9

$$\log_e 1000 = 6.90775\ 52790$$

To find the logarithm of a number which is 10 (or 1/10) times a number whose logarithm is given, add to (or subtract from) the given logarithm the logarithm of 10.

ANSWERS TO PROBLEMS

1. *a, c.*   Statements are declarative sentences.

Problem Set 1.2

1.

p	q	$-p \lor q$
T	T	T
T	F	F
F	T	T
F	F	T

3. *a, b.*

p	q	$(p \to q) \,\&\, (q \to p)$
T	T	T
T	F	F
F	T	F
F	F	T

5a.

p	q	$(p \lor q) \mathrel{\&} (-p \lor -q)$
T	T	F
T	F	T
F	T	T
F	F	F

b.

p	$-p$	$p \mathrel{\&} -p$
T	F	F
F	T	F

c.

p	$-p$	$p \lor -p$
T	F	T
F	T	T

d.

p	q	r	$(p \mathrel{\&} q) \lor (p \mathrel{\&} r)$
T	T	T	T
T	T	F	T
T	F	T	T
T	F	F	F
F	T	T	F
F	T	F	F
F	F	T	F
F	F	F	F

e.

p	q	$q \mathrel{\&} p$
T	T	T
T	F	F
F	T	F
F	F	F

f.

p	q	$(p \mathrel{\&} q) \to p$
T	T	T
T	F	T
F	T	T
F	F	T

g.

p	q	$q \lor p$
T	T	T
T	F	T
F	T	T
F	F	F

h.

p	q	$(p \to q) \to -(p \mathrel{\&} -q)$
T	T	T
T	F	T
F	T	T
F	F	T

i.

p	q	r	$p \mathrel{\&} (q \mathrel{\&} r)$
T	T	T	T
T	T	F	F
T	F	T	F
T	F	F	F
F	T	T	F
F	T	F	F
F	F	T	F
F	F	F	F

j.

p	q	$-(p \mathrel{\&} q) \leftrightarrow -p \lor q$
T	T	F
T	F	F
F	T	T
F	F	T

k.

p	q	$[p \ \& \ (p \to q)] \to p$
T	T	T
T	F	T
F	T	T
F	F	T

l.

p	q	$[-q \ \& \ (p \to q)] \to -p$
T	T	T
T	F	T
F	T	T
F	F	T

Logically equivalent: d, e, g, i
Tautologies: c, h, k, l, f

PROBLEM SET 1.3

1. We must not trade with and not aid foreign nations.
3. Our tariffs are lowered and our exports will not increase.
5. Either our national income is growing rapidly enough or our government policies are sufficiently resolute.
7. Government should not regulate monopoly, and government should not allow free trade in monopolized commodities.

9.

p	q	$-p \to -q$
T	T	T
T	F	,T
F	T	F
F	F	T

PROBLEM SET 1.4

1. p: Consumers buy more at higher incomes.
   q: Consumers buy less at higher prices.
   $(p \ \& \ q) \to -(q \ \& \ p)$ is invalid:

p	q	$(p \ \& \ q) \to -(q \ \& \ p)$
T	T	Ⓕ
T	F	T
F	T	T
F	F	T

3. p: Investments fail to increase per period.
   q: Income will decline several periods later.
   $[(p \to q) \ \& \ -p] \to -q$ is invalid:

p	q	$[(p \to q) \ \& \ -p] \to -q$
T	T	T
T	F	T
F	T	Ⓕ
F	F	T

5. p: A country is poor.
    q: A country cannot devote much of its income to technological development
    r: A country's income will not change.
    $[(p \rightarrow q) \& (q \rightarrow r)] \rightarrow (p \rightarrow r)$ is valid by (1.6).
7. If real-estate values will not fall, then property taxes are lessened.
9. p: Income increases.
    q: Consumers' buying increases.
    r: Businessmen invest more.
    $[(p \rightarrow q) \& (q \rightarrow r)] \rightarrow (r \rightarrow p)$ is invalid:

p	q	r	$[(p \rightarrow q) \& (q \rightarrow r)] \rightarrow (r \rightarrow p)$
T	T	T	T
T	T	F	T
T	F	T	T
T	F	F	T
F	T	T	Ⓕ
F	T	F	T
F	F	T	Ⓕ
F	F	F	T

PROBLEM SET 1.5

1.

p	q
T	F
F	T
F	F

3. Let s_1 and s_2 denote superintendents 1 and 2, respectively.
    p_1: The path from p to $v.p._1$ is open.
    p_2: The path from p to $v.p._2$ is open.
    q_1: The path from $v.p._1$ to s_1 is open.
    q_2: The path from $v.p._2$ to s_2 is open.
    r_1: The path from s_1 to w is open.
    r_2: The path from s_2 to w is open.
    q_3: The path from $v.p._1$ to s_2 is open.
    q_4: The path from $v.p._2$ to s_1 is open.
Then communication is possible if

$$(p_1 \& q_1 \& r_1) \lor (p_2 \& q_2 \& r_2) \lor (p_1 \& q_3 \& r_2) \lor (p_2 \& q_4 \& r_1)$$

5a. If it is true that communication is possible via the vice-president, then th
path from the president to the vice-president must be open.
   b. Given that (1) if the path from p to $v.p.$ is open then the path from $v.p.$ to
is open, and that (2) if the path from $v.p.$ to w is open then the direct path from p to
is open, it follows that if the path from p to $v.p.$ is open then the path from p to w
open.
   c. $(p \& q) \rightarrow -(-p \lor -q)$: If communication is possible via the vice-presiden

hen it is false that either the path from p to $v.p.$ is closed or the path from $v.p.$ to w is
losed.

$(p \lor q) \to -(-p \,\&\, -q)$: If either of the paths from p to $v.p.$ or $v.p.$ to w is open,
hen it is false that both the paths from p to $v.p.$ and $v.p.$ to w are closed.

d. Given that if the path from p to $v.p.$ is open then the path from $v.p.$ to w is
pen, it follows that either the path from p to $v.p.$ is closed or the path from $v.p.$ to w
s open.

PROBLEM SET 1.6

1. Let p: 20 per cent or less of the advertising budget is at present being spent
on the product.

q: The unit profit margin of this product is less than 3 per cent.

r: The sales revenue of this product is less than \$100,000 per year.

he statement which must be true before a product can be considered for elimination:

a. All products except A and B:

$$[p \,\&\, (q \,\&\, r)] \lor [-p \,\&\, (q \lor r)] \tag{1.15}$$

b. Products A and B:

et s_1: (1.15) is true for product A.

s_2: (1.15) is true for product B.

s_3: (1.15) is true for product D.

s_4: (1.15) is true for product E.

hen A and B can be considered for elimination if $s_1 \,\&\, s_3$ and $s_2 \,\&\, s_4$, respectively, are
rue.

Product	p	q	r	$[p \,\&\, (q \,\&\, r)] \lor [-p \,\&\, (q \lor r)]$
A	F	T	F	T
B	T	T	T	T
C	T	T	T	T
D	T	F	F	F
E	T	T	T	T
F	T	T	T	T
G	T	F	F	F
H	T	F	T	F
I	F	F	F	F
J	T	T	F	F
K	T	T	T	T

s_1	s_2	s_3	s_4	$s_1 \,\&\, s_3$	$s_2 \,\&\, s_4$
T	T	F	T	F	T

roducts that can be considered for elimination: B, C, E, F, K

3. *a*, Condition 2; *d*, Conditions 2, 3, 4; *g*, Conditions 2, 3, 4.

PROBLEM SET 2.1

1. $S = \{x | x \text{ is less than } 25 \,\&\, x \text{ is divisible by } 3\} = \{3,6,9,12,15,18,21,24\}$.

3. Finite.

5. Let F denote failure to pass the quality test, and let S denote success. Let the first item listed in the following sets denote the result of testing the first product, the second item the result for the second product, and the third item the result for the third product. Two possible sets are: $Q_1 = \{F,S,S\}$, $Q_2 = \{S,S,S\}$.

PROBLEM SET 2.2

1*a.* Every set contains zero or more elements. Therefore every set contains the empty set.

b. Since every element in A is contained in B, and since every element in B is contained in C, then every element in A must be contained in C.

c. Since U contains all possible elements in the group presently under study, all sets of elements formed from this group must be contained in U.

3. $B - A = \emptyset \neq A - B = \{1,2,5\}$. 5. a, c, e, h.

7. $W \subseteq A$, $M \subseteq A$, $P \in A$, $P \notin W$, $r \in A$, $r \notin W$, $P \notin M$, $r \notin M$, $P \in \bar{W}$, $r \in \bar{W}$, $P \notin \bar{W}$, $r \notin \bar{W}$, $P \notin \bar{A}$, $r \notin \bar{A}$.

$A - W$: male employees of G.M.
$A - \{p\}$: employees of G.M. other than the president.
$W - M$: women employees of G.M. other than managers.
$\bar{W}$: male employees of G.M.

9. Denote the four members by a, b, c, d. Then winning coalitions are: $\{a,b,c\}$, $\{a,b,d\}$, $\{a,c,d\}$, $\{b,c,d\}$, $\{a,b,c,d\}$.

Losing coalitions are: $\{a\}$, $\{b\}$, $\{c\}$, $\{d\}$, $\emptyset$.

Blocking coalitions are: $\{a,b\}$, $\{a,c\}$, $\{a,d\}$, $\{b,c\}$, $\{b,d\}$, $\{c,d\}$.

PROBLEM SET 2.3

1. We use membership tables (cf. solution to Prob. 4 of Problem Set 2.2). Each element of U belongs in one and only one of the four categories symbolized in the four rows to the left of the double vertical line.

a.

A	B	$A \cap B$	$B \cap A$
∈	∈	∈	∈
∈	∉	∉	∉
∉	∈	∉	∉
∉	∉	∉	∉

b.

A	B	$A \cup B$	$B \cup A$
∈	∈	∈	∈
∈	∉	∈	∈
∉	∈	∈	∈
∉	∉	∉	∉

c.

A	B	C	$B \cap C$	$A \cap (B \cap C)$	$A \cap B$	$(A \cap B) \cap C$
∈	∈	∈	∈	∈	∈	∈
∈	∈	∉	∉	∉	∈	∉
∈	∉	∈	∉	∉	∉	∉
∈	∉	∉	∉	∉	∉	∉
∉	∈	∈	∈	∉	∉	∉
∉	∈	∉	∉	∉	∉	∉
∉	∉	∈	∉	∉	∉	∉
∉	∉	∉	∉	∉	∉	∉

d. Same method of proof, with column headings:

$$A \mid B \mid C \mid B \cup C \mid A \cup (B \cup C) \mid A \cup B \mid (A \cup B) \cup C$$

3. $A \cap B \neq \emptyset$ implies that one or more products with a profit margin of over 10 per cent are being sold overseas. Since $A \cap \bar{B} = \emptyset$ implies that no high-profit products are being sold at home, the term *milking* could be loosely applied.

5. *a, b, f, g.*

7. $Z = \{x \mid (x \, \epsilon \, U) \, \& \, (x \text{ is an industrial stock or a rail stock or a utility stock})\}$.

9. $\{C\}, \{I\}, \{C,I\}$.

PROBLEM SET 2.4

1*a.*

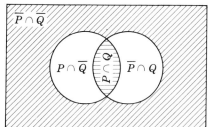

b.

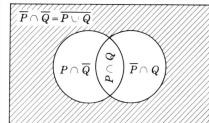

c.

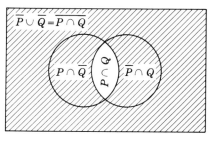

d.

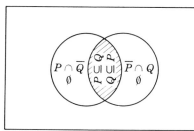

e.

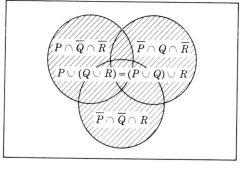

f.

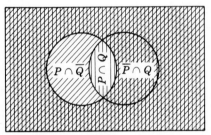

$P = \emptyset$

g.

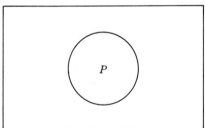

$\overline{P} \cap Q$: Slanted lined area
$\overline{P} \cup Q$: Vertical lined area

h.

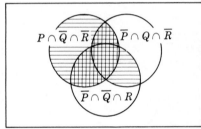

$(P \cap Q) \cup (P \cap R)$: Vertical lined area
$P \cup (Q \cap R)$: Horizontal lined area

i.

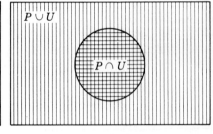

$P \cap \overline{P} = \emptyset$
$P \cup P = P$

j.

3.

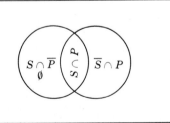

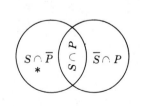

PROBLEM SET 2.5

1*a.*   *b.*

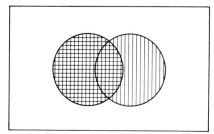

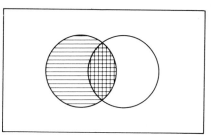

P: Horizontal lined area   P: Horizontal lined area
P ∪ Q: Vertical lined area   P ∩ Q: Vertical lined area

3.   5.

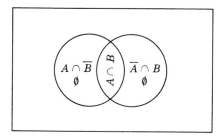

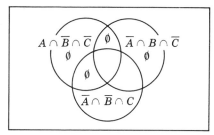

PROBLEM SET 2.6

1. $A \cap Y \cap \bar{X}$ and $B \cap X \cap \bar{Y}$.

   3*a.* This country has relatively little labor and capital and large quantities of land, and desires commodities requiring much labor and capital and little land.

   b. This country has relatively large quantities of labor and capital and little land, and desires commodities requiring little labor and much land.

   5. Let: $C = \{x|x$ is a country which requires much food and raw materials in order to survive$\}$

$$D = \{x|x \text{ is a country which refuses to engage in world trade}\}$$

Then conflict could well arise between $A \cap C$ and $B \cap D$.

PROBLEM SET 2.7

   1. Let S_1, S_2, and S_3 be subsets which contain, respectively, plus, negative, and zero errors.   Let T_1, T_2, and T_3 be subsets which contain, respectively, errors associated with upper turning points, lower turning points, and no turning points.   Let M_1, M_2, and M_3 denote subsets which contain, respectively, large, moderate, and negligible errors.   Let A_1 and A_2 be subsets which contain, respectively, errors which appear correlated with time and errors which are completely random.   Then the following are partitions: S = $\{S_1, S_2, S_3\}$, T = $\{T_1, T_2, T_3\}$, M = $\{M_1, M_2, M_3\}$, and A = $\{A_1, A_2\}$.

3. P = {2 of clubs, 3 of clubs, . . . , ace of clubs, 2 of diamonds, 3 of diamonds, . . . , ace of diamonds, 2 of hearts, . . . , ace of hearts, 2 of spades, . . . , ace of spades}. P contains 52 elements.

PROBLEM SET 3.1

1a. 15. **b.** 16.

PROBLEM SET 3.2

1a. 31. **b.** 1,0,0,0,0; 0,1,0,0,0; 0,0,1,0,0; 0,0,0,1,0; 0,0,0,0,1; 1,1,0,0,0; 1,0,1,0,0; 1,0,0,1,0; 1,0,0,0,1; 1,1,1,0,0; 1,1,0,1,0; 1,1,0,0,1; 0,1,1,1,0; 0,1,0,1,1; 0,1,1,0,1; 0,0,1,1,1.
3. Three: 1,1,0; 1,0,1; 0,1,1.
5a. 50. **b.** 0. **c.** 0. **d.** 25. **e.** 40.   Start with $n(W \cap M \cap$ 0) = 10.

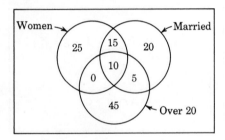

PROBLEM SET 3.3

1a. 20. **b.** 2. **3.** 12.

PROBLEM SET 3.4

1a. The possible results from the toss of a pair of pennies.
b. The possible results from the spinning of the wheels of the familiar gambling device known as the "one-armed bandit."
3. Fill the second job first: 3 × 4 = 12. Assume that the second job can be filled only by men 1, 2, and 3, and that the first element in each ordered couple (below) refers to the man holding the first job. Then the entries with asterisks in the following table show the 12 relevant possibilities:

Man	1	2	3	4	5
1	$\langle 1,1 \rangle$	*$\langle 1,2 \rangle$	*$\langle 1,3 \rangle$	$\langle 1,4 \rangle$	$\langle 1,5 \rangle$
2	*$\langle 2,1 \rangle$	$\langle 2,2 \rangle$	*$\langle 2,3 \rangle$	$\langle 2,4 \rangle$	$\langle 2,5 \rangle$
3	*$\langle 3,1 \rangle$	*$\langle 3,2 \rangle$	$\langle 3,3 \rangle$	$\langle 3,4 \rangle$	$\langle 3,5 \rangle$
4	*$\langle 4,1 \rangle$	*$\langle 4,2 \rangle$	*$\langle 4,3 \rangle$	$\langle 4,4 \rangle$	$\langle 4,5 \rangle$
5	*$\langle 5,1 \rangle$	*$\langle 5,2 \rangle$	*$\langle 5,3 \rangle$	$\langle 5,4 \rangle$	$\langle 5,5 \rangle$

PROBLEM SET 3.5

1. Three: $\{3,5\}$, $\{1,2,5\}$, $\{1,3,4\}$.
3. $5 \times 4 \times 3 = 60$. $5 \times 4 \times 3 \times 2 = 120$.   10.   5.
5. 326.   Subsets containing one and zero elements.
7. $1 \times 3 \times 2 = 6$.
9. $10 \times 9 \times 8 \times 7 \times 6 \times 5 \times 4 \times 3 \times 2 \times 1 = 3,628,800$.
11. Seven: $\{A,B,C\}$, $\{A,B,\}$, $\{A,C\}$, $\{B,C\}$, $\{A\}$, $\{B\}$, $\{C\}$.
13. $5 \times 4 \times 3 \times 2 \times 1 = 120$. $1 \times 4 \times 3 \times 2 \times 1 = 24$.

PROBLEM SET 3.6

1a. 10.   **b.** 20.   **c.** 1.   **d.** 1.   **e.** 5.   **f.** 5.

3.

$$\binom{n-1}{r-1} + \binom{n-1}{r} = \frac{(n-1)!}{(r-1)![(n-1)-(r-1)]!} + \frac{(n-1)!}{r![(n-1)-r]!}$$

$$= \frac{(n-1)\cdots(r)}{(n-r)!} + \frac{(n-1)\cdots(n-r)}{r!}$$

$$= \frac{[(n-1)\cdots r]r! + [(n-1)\cdots(n-r)](n-r)!}{(n-r)!r!}$$

$$= \frac{(n-1)![r+(n-r)]}{(n-r)!r!} = \frac{n!}{r!(n-r)!} = \binom{n}{r}$$

$$\binom{5}{3} + \binom{5}{4} = \frac{5!}{3!2!} + \frac{5!}{4!1!} = 15 = \frac{6!}{4!2!} = \binom{6}{4}$$

5. $\dfrac{40!}{5!35!} \times \dfrac{10!}{0!10!} \times \dfrac{35!6!}{41!} = \dfrac{6}{41}$

7. 20; 8; 5040.

9. $10 \times 10 \times 10 \times 10 \times 10 = 100,000$. $26 \times 26 \times 26 \times 10 \times 10 \times 10 \times 10 \times 10 = 1,757,600,000$.

PROBLEM SET 3.7

1a. 120.   **b.** 20.   **c.** 46,558,512.   **d.** 120.

3. $8,237 \times 10^5$.   5. $\dbinom{4}{2}\dbinom{5}{2} = 60$.   7. $\dbinom{x}{4,3,x-7}$.

9a. $\dbinom{15}{3} = 455$.   **b.** $455 - \dbinom{11}{3}\dbinom{4}{0} = 455 - 165\,(1) = 290$.

PROBLEM SET 3.8

1. $\dbinom{10}{3} = 120$.   3. -21.

5. $(1 + 0.02)^{10} = 1^{10} + \dbinom{10}{1}(1)^9(0.02)^1 + \dbinom{10}{2}(1)^8(0.02)^2 + \cdots = 1.218$.

$(100 - 1)^3 = 100^3 + \dbinom{3}{1}100^2(-1)^1 + \dbinom{3}{2}100^1(-1)^2 + (-1)^3 = 970,299$.

7. From Prob. 2 we know that

$$\binom{n}{0} + \binom{n}{1} + \cdots + \binom{n}{r} + \cdots + \binom{n}{n} = 2^n$$

Thus

$$\frac{\binom{n}{0}}{2^n} + \frac{\binom{n}{1}}{2^n} + \cdots + \frac{\binom{n}{r}}{2^n} + \cdots + \frac{\binom{n}{n}}{2^n} = \frac{1}{2^n}\left[\binom{n}{0} + \binom{n}{1} + \cdots\right] = \frac{1}{2^n}(2^n) = 1$$

9. $\binom{10}{4} = 210.$ 11. $\binom{6}{3,1,2} = 60.$

PROBLEM SET 3.9

1.

$$\frac{540!}{18!522!}\frac{60!}{2!58!} = \log 540! + \log 60! - (\log 18! + \log 522! + \log 2! + \log 58!)$$

$$= 36.50031$$

$$\text{antilog } 36.50031 = 3165 \times 10^{33}$$

3.

$$\log 540! + \log 60! - (\log 20! + \log 520! + \log 0! + \log 60!) = 36.10707$$
$$\text{antilog } 36.10707 = 1{,}280 \times 10^{33}$$

PROBLEM SET 4.1

1a. 0.3.   **b.** 0.7.   **c.** 0.02.   **d.** 0.08.

3. $\dfrac{\binom{4}{2}\binom{5}{1}}{\binom{9}{3}} = \dfrac{5}{14}$ 5. $\dfrac{\binom{4}{2}\binom{4}{0}\binom{4}{0}}{\binom{12}{2}} = \dfrac{1}{11}$

7. $\dfrac{\binom{10}{2}\binom{10}{0}\binom{40}{0}\binom{40}{0}}{\binom{100}{2}} = \dfrac{1}{110}$ **9a.** $\frac{1}{10}.$ **b.** $\frac{3}{20}.$

11a. $\dfrac{10^{33} \times 7{,}392}{10^{33} \times 10{,}910} = 0.68.$ **b.** $7{,}496/15{,}504 = 0.48.$

PROBLEM SET 4.2

1. Since $\bar{E}$ is the complement of $E = S$, then $m(\bar{E}) = 0$.   Thus

$$P(E) \cdot P(\bar{E}) = \frac{m(E)}{m(S)} \cdot \frac{m(\bar{E})}{m(S)} = 1 \cdot \frac{0}{m(S)} = 0$$

3. Probability of obtaining a double is

$$P(D) = \frac{6 \times 1}{6 \times 6} = \frac{1}{6}$$
$$P(\bar{D}) = 1 - P(D) = \tfrac{5}{6}$$

5. No. The sum of the probabilities of mutually exclusive events cannot exceed 1.

7. 0.5.   **9.** $\frac{17}{31}$.

PROBLEM SET 4.3

1. $\frac{1}{3}$.   **3.** $\dfrac{\dbinom{4}{3}\dbinom{1}{0}\dbinom{1}{0}}{\dbinom{6}{3}} = \dfrac{1}{5}$ **5.** 0.8.

PROBLEM SET 4.4.

1. No:

$$S = \{\langle H\ \ H\rangle, \langle H\ \ T\rangle, \langle T\ \ H\rangle, \langle T\ \ T\rangle\} \qquad E_1 = \{\langle H\ \ H\rangle, \langle H\ \ T\rangle\}$$
$$E_2 = \{\langle H\ \ H\rangle, \langle T\ \ H\rangle\} \qquad E_3 = \{\langle H\ \ H\rangle, \langle T\ \ T\rangle\}$$
$$E_1 \cap E_2 \cap E_3 = \{\langle H\ \ H\rangle\}$$
$$P(E_1 \cap E_2 \cap E_3) = \tfrac{1}{4} \neq P(E_1) \cdot P(E_2) \cdot P(E_3) = (\tfrac{2}{4})(\tfrac{2}{4})(\tfrac{2}{4}) = \tfrac{1}{8}$$

3. $(0.005)^3$.   **5.** $0.97 \times 0.98 \times 0.99$.   **7.** $\frac{1}{15}$.

9. Assuming independence, $(0.01)^6$.   **11.** 0.02.

PROBLEM SET 4.5

1. Let

$$E_1 = \{x | x \text{ is an employee who favors affiliation}\}$$
$$E_2 = \{x | x \text{ is a pieceworker}\}$$
$$P(E_2|E_1) = \tfrac{25}{30} = \tfrac{5}{6}$$

3. Since E_1 and E_2 are independent, $P(E_1 \cap E_2) = P(E_1) \cdot P(E_2)$. From Theorem 4.31,

$$P(E_1|E_2) = \frac{P(E_1 \cap E_2)}{P(E_2)} = \frac{P(E_1)P(E_2)}{P(E_2)} = P(E_1)$$

Similarly for $P(E_2|E_1)$.

5. $\frac{7}{20}$.   **7.** $\frac{3}{4}$.   **9.** 0.77.

PROBLEM SET 4.6

1. 0.4325.   **3a.** $\frac{1}{3}$.   **b.** 0.2.

PROBLEM SET 4.7

1a. 0.9801.   **b.** $\dbinom{10}{0}(0.01)^0(0.99)^{10}$.   **3.** 0.9619.

5a. $\frac{1}{9}$.   **b.** $\frac{1}{729}$.   **c.** $\frac{1}{6561}$.

7. Cf. Prob. 12 of Problem Set 3.8 and Example 4.46.   **9.** 0.0846.

PROBLEM SET 4.8

1. 7.1.

PROBLEM SET 5.1

1*a*. $r = \{\langle x,y\rangle | x \in S \ \& \ y \in T \ \& \ y > x\}$.
b.   Domain is all of S, range is $R = \{3,2,1,19,20\}$.
c. $f = \{\langle x,y\rangle | x \in S \ \& \ y \in T \ \& \ y = x\} = \{\langle 1,1\rangle, \langle 2,2\rangle, \langle 3,3\rangle\}$.
3*a*.   Yes.   *b*.   Yes.   *c*. R and D are the set of real numbers.
5.   Let $T = \{t | t$ is zero or a positive integer$\}$, $V = \{v | v$ is zero or a positive real number$\}$. t denotes time in years, r denotes the annual interest rate, and P the principal.   Then

$$f = \{\langle t,v\rangle | t \in T \ \& \ v \in V \ \& \ v = P(1 + r)^t\}$$

7*a*.   No: $f = \{\langle x,y\rangle | x \ \& \ y$ are real numbers $\& \ y = x^2\}$.   *b*.   Yes.
9*a*. D is a subset of the set of positive real numbers. R is the set of positive real numbers.
b. D is a subset, of the set of positive real numbers, whose elements are greater in value than those in a. R is the set of positive real numbers.

PROBLEM SET 5.2

1.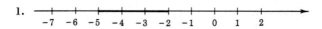

3.   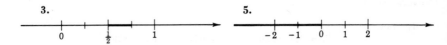   5.

PROBLEM SET 5.3

1.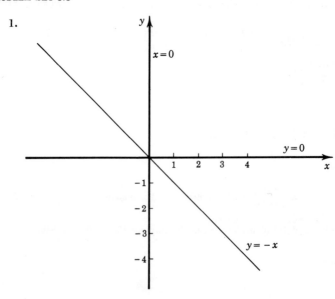

3.

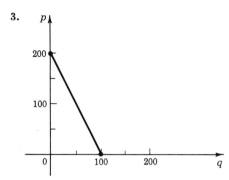

5. $m = \dfrac{20 - 0}{0 - 25} = -0.8.$ $y = 20 - 0.8x,\ x = 25 - 1.25y.$ Cost of a military good is 1.25 units of civilian goods.

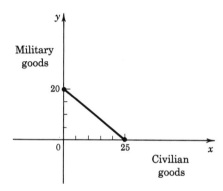

PROBLEM SET 5.4

1a. $\sqrt{10}.$ **b.** $\sqrt{65}.$ **c.** $\sqrt{34}.$ **d.** 14.   **e.** 5.

3. $d = 10 = \sqrt{(y - 5)^2 + (-3 + 3)^2} = \sqrt{(y - 5)^2} = y - 5,\ y = 15.$

5. $P_1P_2 = \sqrt{(P_1P_3)^2 + (P_2P_3)^2}.$ $\sqrt{145} = \sqrt{29 + 116}.$

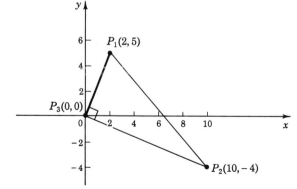

PROBLEM SET 5.5

1a. $x = 0$, m is undefined, $\alpha = 90°$.　　**b.** $y = 0$, $m = 0$, $\alpha = 0°$.　　**c.** $y = -x$, $m = -1$, $\alpha = 135°$, line falls.　　**d.** $y = -\frac{2}{3}x + \frac{1}{3}$, $m = -\frac{2}{3}$, $\alpha = 146°$, line falls.
e. $y = -x/3 + \frac{2}{7}$, $m = -\frac{1}{3}$, $\alpha = 162°$, line falls.　　**f.** $y = -\frac{1}{2}x$, $m = -\frac{1}{2}$, $\alpha = 153°$, line falls.

3. a and c.　　**5.** $m = \dfrac{7 - 3}{-5 - 2} = -\dfrac{4}{7}$.

7. Denote the number of units bought of each product by x and y. Then two points on the budget line are $(5,0)$ and $(0,10)$, so that $m = (10 - 0)/(0 - 5) = -2$.

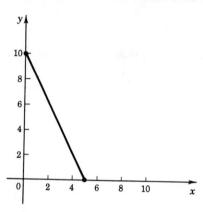

PROBLEM SET 5.6

1a. 5.　　**b.** 5.　　**c.** a, if a is positive; $-a$, if a is negative.　　**d.** a, if a is positive; $-a$, if a is negative.　　**e.** $x - y$, if $x > y$; $-(x - y)$, if $x < y$.
f. $-ab$.　　**g.** ab.

3.

P**ROBLEM** S**ET** 5.7

1. c_1 more profitable over $0 \le q < q_e$.

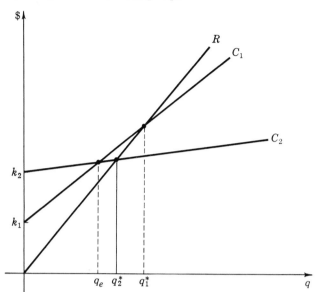

3a. Plant 2. Its total fixed cost is double that of plant 1, yet its capacity is only 50 per cent greater. This implies that such items as interest and depreciation, which are associated with capital equipment, are higher than would be expected because of the greater capacity alone. In addition, the unit variable cost, of which labor is a big component, is lower in plant 2, again implying that the output is produced with relatively less labor and more capital equipment than in plant 1.

b.

$$q_1^* = \frac{100}{5 - 2} = 33\tfrac{1}{3} \qquad q_2^* = \frac{200}{5 - \tfrac{5}{7}} = 46\tfrac{2}{3}$$

c. $c_1 = c_2 = 2q + 100 = \tfrac{5}{7}q + 200$, $q = 77\tfrac{7}{9}$. Plant 2 is more profitable for $q > 77\tfrac{7}{9}$.

d. $P_1 = 5(100) - 2(100) - 100 = 200$, $P_2 = 5(150) - \tfrac{5}{7}(150) - 200 = 442\tfrac{6}{7}$, $P_1 + P_2 = 642\tfrac{6}{7}$.

e. $2(46\tfrac{2}{3}) = 93\tfrac{1}{3}$.

f.

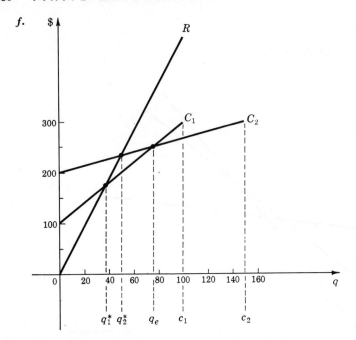

PROBLEM SET 6.1

1a. By (3) of Definition 6.1, $(a - 0) \epsilon R^+$ or $-(a - 0) \epsilon R^+$ $(a \neq 0)$. By Definition 6.2, if $-(a - 0) = (-a + 0) \epsilon R^+$ then $-a > 0$. But it is given that $a > 0$. Thus $(a - 0) \epsilon R^+$, which means $a > 0$ (from Definition 6.2).

b. Part 2 of Corollary 6.5 is proved similarly.

c. Theorem 6.6: Since $a > 0$, $b > 0$, a, $b \epsilon R^+$ by Corollary 6.5. Thus by (1) and (2) of Definition 6.1, $a + b \epsilon R^+$ and $ab \epsilon R^+$.

3. $|x| \leq 5$.

5. From Theorem 6.11,

$$a + c < b + c$$

and
$$b + a < c + a$$

so that
$$b + a < b + c$$

Thus
$$(b + a) + (-b) < (b + c) + (-b)$$

or
$$a < c$$

PROBLEM SET 6.2

1a. $y > \frac{5}{2} - x/2$.   **b.** $y > -x$.   **c.** $y < 4 - 2x$.
d. $y > \frac{2}{3}x + \frac{5}{3}$.   **e.** $y > -\frac{2}{3}x + \frac{5}{3}$.

3.

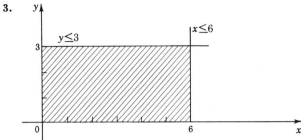

5. $5x + 3y \geq 50.$ $y \geq \frac{50}{3} - \frac{5}{3}x.$

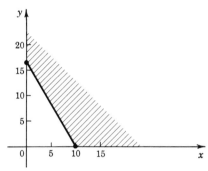

PROBLEM SET 6.3

1a.

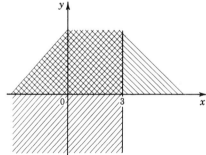

b.

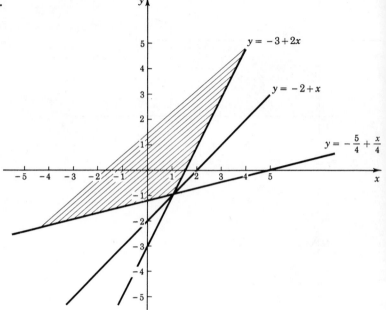

c.

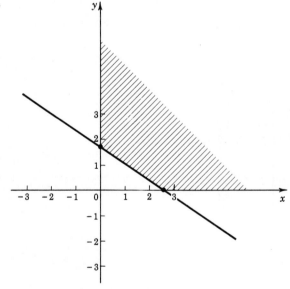

d.

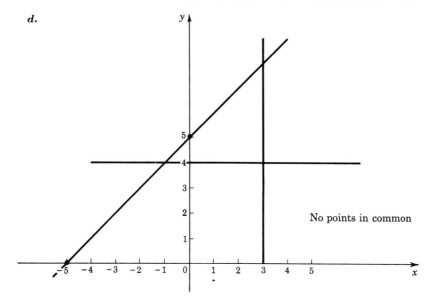

No points in common

3.

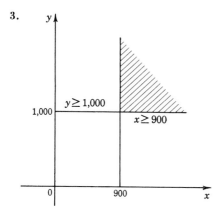

5. Meet requirements: *c, d, g.* *a* violates all 3 constraints. *b* violates $10x + 30y = 120$ & $10x + 5y = 40$. *e* violates $10x + 30y = 120$ & $10x + 5y = 40$. *f* violates all three constraints.

7. $x_A + y_A \geq 6$, $x_B + y_B \geq 8$, $x + y \geq 14$, $y \geq 14 - x$. $x + 2y \leq 20$, $y \leq 10 - x/2$. $x + 2y \geq 8$, $y \geq 4 - x/2$.

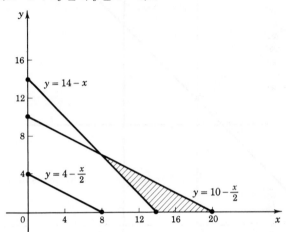

9. $y \geq 6 - 2x$. $y \geq \frac{8}{3} - x/3$.

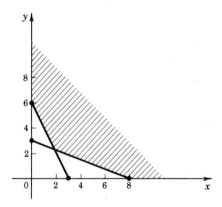

PROBLEM SET 6.4

1a. Any point along $10x_1 + 30x_2 = 120$ between the intersections of this line with each of the other constraints.

b. $x_1 = 9$, $x_2 = 1$.

3. $x_2 = -\frac{2}{3}x_1 + \frac{k}{3}$.

a. No labor constraints: $x_1 = 14$, $x_2 = 0$, $c = 28$. *b.* First labor constraint: $x_1 = 14$, $x_2 = 0$, $c = 28$. *c.* Second labor constraint: $x_1 = 14$, $x_2 = 0$, $c = 28$.

5. $x_1 = 2$, $x_2 = 2$, $c = 10$.

PROBLEM SET 7.1

1a. $f = \{\langle x,y \rangle | y = -\frac{35}{8} + \frac{5}{8}x\}$. *b.* $S = \{\langle x,y \rangle | \frac{2}{3}x - \frac{4}{5}y - \frac{7}{2} = 0\}$.

c. $\frac{21}{4}$. *d.* $(\frac{21}{4}, 0)$. *e.* x intercept is $\frac{21}{4}$, y intercept is $-\frac{35}{8}$.

3. $Q = 25$.

5. Since the intersection of the solution sets is empty, the two equations graph as parallel lines. This means their slopes are equal, and thus $m_1 = a_{11}/a_{12} = m_2 = a_{21}/a_{22}$, or $a_{11}a_{22} - a_{12}a_{21} = \Delta = 0$, which by definition means the equations are not consistent.

7a. $p = 11, q = 2.$ **b.** $p = 21.$ **c.** $q_s - q_d = 4\frac{1}{2} - 1 = 3\frac{1}{2}.$

Problem Set 7.2

1. $x = \frac{119}{11}, y = -\frac{18}{11}, z = -\frac{23}{11}.$

3. $x = 1, y = -\frac{27}{33}, z = \frac{19}{11}.$

Problem Set 7.3

1. See answers to Probs. 1 and 3 of Problem Set 7.2.

Problem Set 7.4

1a. $\begin{pmatrix} 3 & 3 & 5 \\ 1 & 0 & 0 \\ 3 & 2 & 2 \\ 4 & 4 & 3 \end{pmatrix}$ **b.** $\begin{pmatrix} 7 & 8 \\ -2 & -5 \\ 10 & 9 \end{pmatrix}$ **c.** $\begin{pmatrix} 10 & 4 & 4 \\ 21 & 9 & 9 \\ 40 & 28 & 28 \end{pmatrix}$

d. $\begin{pmatrix} -1 & 0 & 1 & 2 \\ 2 & 1 & 3 & 4 \\ 5 & 1 & -1 & 0 \\ 2 & 1 & 3 & 1 \end{pmatrix}$ **e.** $(24).$

3. $A + (-A) = (a_{ij} - a_{ij})_{m \times n} = (0_{ij})_{m \times n}$

5. $A \times B = \begin{pmatrix} -3 + 3 & -3 + 3 \\ -6 + 6 & -6 + 6 \end{pmatrix} = (0_{ij})_{2 \times 2}$

7a.

	Total requirements	Raw material

$$R = A' \times B = \begin{pmatrix} 2 & 1 & 4 & 4 \\ 1 & 0 & 3 & 1 \\ 4 & 1 & 2 & 2 \end{pmatrix} \begin{pmatrix} 4 \\ 5 \\ 6 \\ 2 \end{pmatrix} = \begin{pmatrix} 45 \\ 24 \\ 37 \end{pmatrix} \quad \begin{matrix} 1 \\ 2 \\ 3 \end{matrix}$$

b. $K = (A' \times B)' \times C = (45 \quad 24 \quad 37) \begin{pmatrix} 2 \\ 3 \\ 6 \end{pmatrix} = 384.$

Problem Set 7.5

1. The determinant of a 3×3 matrix can be determined by taking the sum of the products of each element and its cofactor in any single row or column.

3. $\det A = a_{11}A_{11} + a_{12}A_{12} + a_{13}A_{13} = 2(1) + 0(-4) + 1(1) = 3.$

$$C = \begin{pmatrix} A_{11} & A_{12} & A_{13} \\ A_{21} & A_{22} & A_{23} \\ A_{31} & A_{32} & A_{33} \end{pmatrix} = \begin{pmatrix} 1 & -4 & 1 \\ 1 & 2 & -2 \\ -1 & 1 & 2 \end{pmatrix} \quad A_{\text{adj}} = C' = \begin{pmatrix} 1 & 1 & -1 \\ -4 & 2 & 1 \\ 1 & -2 & 2 \end{pmatrix}$$

$$A^{-1} = \frac{A_{\text{adj}}}{\det A} = \frac{1}{3} \begin{pmatrix} 1 & 1 & -1 \\ -4 & 2 & 1 \\ 1 & -2 & 2 \end{pmatrix} = \begin{pmatrix} \frac{1}{3} & \frac{1}{3} & -\frac{1}{3} \\ -\frac{4}{3} & \frac{2}{3} & \frac{1}{3} \\ \frac{1}{3} & -\frac{2}{3} & \frac{2}{3} \end{pmatrix}$$

$$A \times A^{-1} = \begin{pmatrix} 2 & 0 & 1 \\ 3 & 1 & 1 \\ 2 & 1 & 2 \end{pmatrix} \begin{pmatrix} \frac{1}{3} & \frac{1}{3} & -\frac{1}{3} \\ -\frac{4}{3} & \frac{2}{3} & \frac{1}{3} \\ \frac{1}{3} & -\frac{2}{3} & \frac{2}{3} \end{pmatrix} = \begin{pmatrix} 1 & 0 & 0 \\ 0 & 1 & 0 \\ 0 & 0 & 1 \end{pmatrix}$$

5. Zero, because the sum of the products of each element in the zero row and its cofactor are zero.

7. No, since $A \times A^{-1} \times B = 0 \times A^{-1} = I \times B = B = 0$, which is impossible since it is given that $B \neq 0$. The same conclusion follows if we take $A \times B \times B^{-1} = 0 \times B^{-1}$.

9. Let

$$A = \begin{pmatrix} a_{11} & a_{12} & a_{13} \\ a_{21} & a_{22} & a_{23} \\ a_{31} & a_{32} & a_{33} \end{pmatrix} \qquad B = \begin{pmatrix} a_{21} & a_{22} & a_{23} \\ a_{11} & a_{12} & a_{13} \\ a_{31} & a_{32} & a_{33} \end{pmatrix}$$

B is formed by interchanging rows 1 and 2 of A. Note that det A computed by using the second row and its cofactors is identical, except for sign, to det B computed by using its first row and cofactors. This result follows in the same way for any interchange of two rows or columns.

11. Let

$$A = \begin{pmatrix} a_{11} & a_{12} & a_{13} \\ a_{21} & a_{22} & a_{23} \\ a_{31} & a_{32} & a_{33} \end{pmatrix} \qquad B = \begin{pmatrix} ka_{21} + a_{11} & ka_{22} + a_{12} & ka_{23} + a_{13} \\ a_{21} & a_{22} & a_{23} \\ a_{31} & a_{32} & a_{33} \end{pmatrix}$$

$$\det B = (ka_{21} + a_{11})(a_{22}a_{33} - a_{23}a_{32}) - (ka_{22} + a_{12})(a_{21}a_{33} - a_{23}a_{31})$$
$$+ (ka_{23} + a_{13})(a_{21}a_{32} - a_{22}a_{31})$$
$$= ka_{21}a_{22}a_{33} + a_{11}a_{22}a_{33} - ka_{21}a_{23}a_{32} - a_{11}a_{23}a_{32} - ka_{22}a_{21}a_{33} - a_{12}a_{21}a_{33}$$
$$+ ka_{22}a_{23}a_{31} + a_{12}a_{23}a_{31} + ka_{23}a_{21}a_{32} + a_{13}a_{21}a_{32} - ka_{23}a_{22}a_{31} - a_{13}a_{22}a_{31}$$
$$= \det A$$

PROBLEM SET 7.6

1a. $\Delta_1 = -6$, $\Delta_2 = -21$, $\Delta_3 = -43$, $\Delta = -8$, $x_1 = \frac{3}{4}$, $x_2 = \frac{21}{8}$, $x_3 = \frac{43}{8}$.
b. $\Delta_1 = -58$, $\Delta_2 = 93$, $\Delta_3 = 20$, $\Delta = 7$, $x_1 = -\frac{58}{7}$, $x_2 = \frac{93}{7}$, $x_3 = \frac{20}{7}$.
c. $\Delta_1 = 3$, $\Delta_2 = 4$, $\Delta_3 = 5$, $\Delta = 11$, $x_1 = \frac{3}{11}$, $x_2 = \frac{4}{11}$, $x_3 = \frac{5}{11}$.

3. No (see d and e of Prob. 2). Prove this by using the results of Probs. 10 and 6 of Problem Set 7.5, and the fact that if det $B = k$ det A and if det $B = 0$, then det $A = 0$.

5. Let

$$A = \begin{pmatrix} 1 & 0 & 0 \\ 0 & 1 & 0 \\ 0 & 0 & 1 \end{pmatrix} \qquad B = \begin{pmatrix} 5 & 0 & 0 \\ 0 & 5 & 0 \\ 0 & 0 & 5 \end{pmatrix}$$

Then det $A = 1$ and det $B = 125$, so that 5^3 det $A =$ det B, and $5A = B$.

7. Yes. See Prob. 11 of Problem Set 7.5, and compare the determinant of the original matrix in Prob. 6 of this Problem Set with the determinant of the transformed matrix.

9.

$$\begin{pmatrix} x_1 \\ x_2 \\ x_3 \end{pmatrix} = \frac{1}{\Delta} \begin{pmatrix} A_{11} & A_{21} & A_{31} \\ A_{12} & A_{22} & A_{32} \\ A_{13} & A_{23} & A_{33} \end{pmatrix} \begin{pmatrix} b_1 \\ b_2 \\ b_3 \end{pmatrix}$$

$$= \frac{1}{0.154} \begin{pmatrix} 0.34 & 0.08 & 0.19 \\ 0.08 & 0.20 & 0.09 \\ 0.38 & 0.18 & 0.62 \end{pmatrix} \begin{pmatrix} 2 \\ 3 \\ 0.5 \end{pmatrix} = \begin{pmatrix} 6.6 \\ 5.2 \\ 10.5 \end{pmatrix}$$

$$\begin{pmatrix} x_1 \\ x_2 \\ x_3 \end{pmatrix} = \frac{1}{0.154} \begin{pmatrix} 0.34 & 0.08 & 0.19 \\ 0.08 & 0.20 & 0.09 \\ 0.38 & 0.18 & 0.62 \end{pmatrix} \begin{pmatrix} 4 \\ 5 \\ 2 \end{pmatrix} = \begin{pmatrix} 13.9 \\ 9.7 \\ 23.8 \end{pmatrix}$$

PROBLEM SET 8.1

1. $(-3.35, 0)$, $(-0.15, 0)$

3.

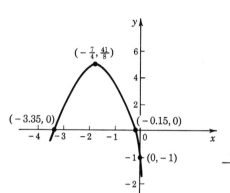

5.

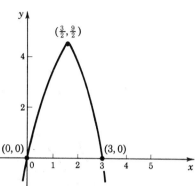

7.

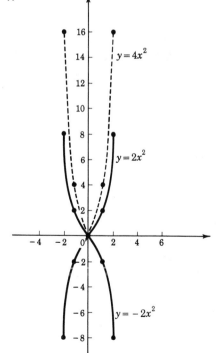

As the absolute value of the constant increases, the graph of the function "closes up."
Constants identical except for sign graph as "mirror images."

9.

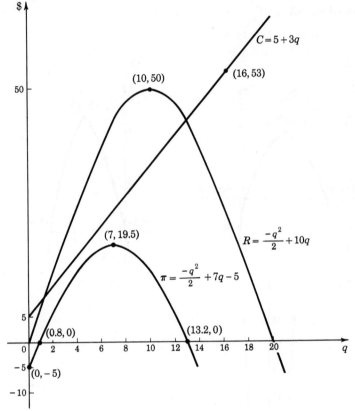

11. No, since R is a maximum at $q = 10$, while π is a maximum at $q = 7$.

13. $50/p = 25p - 25$, $25p^2 - 25p - 50 = 0$, $p = 2$, $q = 25$.

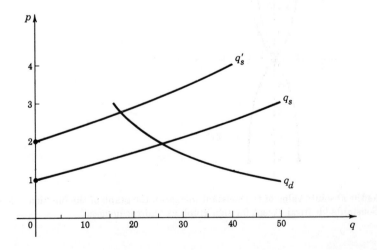

PROBLEM SET 8.2

1.

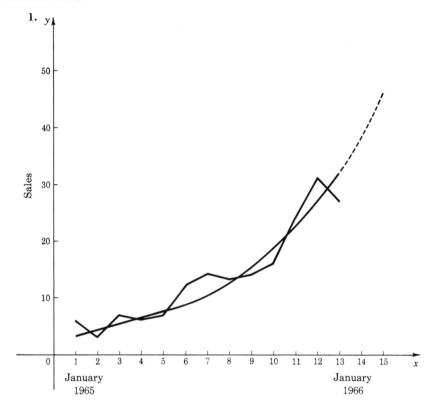

$y = 3(1.2)^{15} = 46.2.$ Monthly proportionate change: $b^1 - 1 = (1.2)^1 - 1 = 0.2 = 20$ per cent.

3.

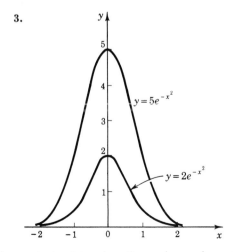

The constant a determines the maximum element of the function.

5.   Number which were 100 inches: $y = 1,000e^{-0.5(0)^2} = 1,000$.
Number which were 98 inches: $y = 1,000e^{-0.5(2)^2} = 135$.
Number which were 102 inches: $y = 1,000e^{-0.5(-2)^2} = 135$.

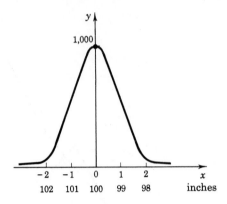

7a. $y = 22,000 + [10,000 - 10,000e^{-0.001(3,000)}] = 31,500$.
  b.   If the firm spends \$4,000, $y = 31,800$; thus a \$1,000 increase in advertising causes sales to increase by only \$300 and is therefore not worthwhile.

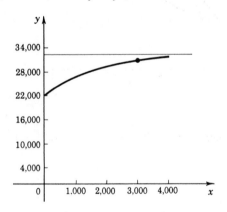

9. $y = 500 - 500e^{-0.2(5)} = 315$, $315 \times 3 = 945$ units. Z weekly requirement function is $y = 3(500 - 500e^{-0.2x})$.

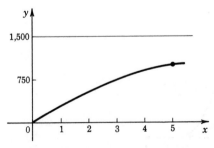

PROBLEM SET 8.3

1. Inverse is $y = 2^x$.

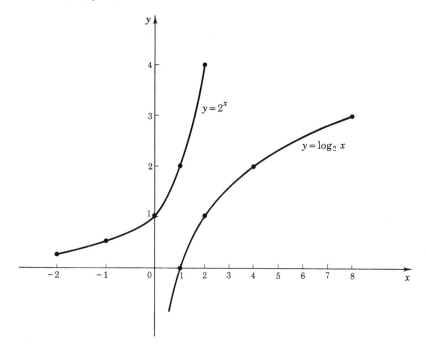

3. Let $y_1 = a^{x_1}$, $y = a^{x_2}$, $y_1 y_2 = a^{x_3}$. Then $a^{x_3} = y_1 y_2 = a^{x_1} a^{x_2} = a^{x_1 + x_2}$, so that $x_3 = x_1 + x_2$. But $x_3 = \log_a (y_1 y_2)$, $x_1 = \log_a y_1$, $x_2 = \log_a y_2$. Q.E.D.

5a. 3,4,1. **b.** 1. **7a.** $\log y = \frac{1}{2} \log (a^2 + x^2)$.

b. $\log y = \frac{9}{2} \log x$. **c.** $\log y = \log (25 - x^2)/2$.

9. $M_G = \sqrt[5]{2 \times 4 \times 8 \times 16 \times 32}$, $\log_2 M_G = \frac{1}{5}(\log_2 2 + \log_2 4 + \log_2 8 + \log_2 16 + \log_2 32) = \frac{1}{5}(1 + 2 + 3 + 4 + 5) = 3$, $M_G = 8$.

11. $M_G = \sqrt[5]{\frac{6}{3} \cdot \frac{12}{6} \cdot \frac{50}{12} \cdot \frac{300}{50} \cdot \frac{729}{300}} = \sqrt[5]{243}$, $\log_3 M_G = \frac{1}{5} \log_3 243 = \frac{1}{5}(5) = 1$, $M_G = 3$.

PROBLEM SET 9.1

1a. $\{1, \frac{1}{2}, \frac{1}{3}, \ldots, 1/n, \ldots\}$.

b. $\{1, 2, 3, \ldots, n, \ldots\}$ $d = 1$.

c. $\{1, -1, 1, -1, \ldots\}$ $r = -1$.

d. $\{1, \frac{1}{2}, \frac{1}{6}, \frac{1}{24}, \ldots, 1/n!, \ldots\}$.

e. $\{2, \frac{9}{4}, \frac{64}{27}, \ldots, (1 + 1/n)^n, \ldots\}$.

f. $\{\frac{1}{2}, \frac{1}{4}, \frac{1}{8}, \ldots, 1/2^n, \ldots\}$ $r = \frac{1}{2}$.

g. $\{1, \frac{3}{2}, \frac{7}{4}, \ldots, 2 - 1/2^{n-1}, \ldots\}$.

h. $\{\frac{3}{10}, \frac{3}{100}, \frac{3}{1,000}, \ldots, 3/10^n, \ldots\}$ $r = \frac{1}{10}$.

i. $\{2, 4, 8, \ldots, 2^n, \ldots\}$ $r = 2$.

3. b, e, g, i.

5.

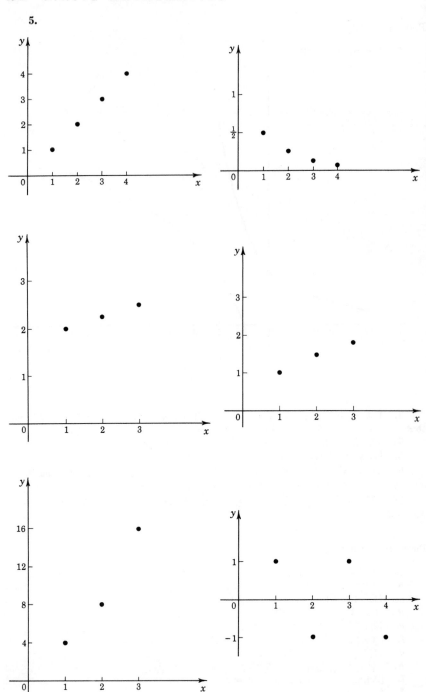

7a.

$a_1 = P(1 + i)^1$ is the value at end of 1st period

$a_2 = [P(1 + i)](1 + i) = P(1 + i)^2$ is the value at end of second period

$a_3 = [P(1 + i)^2](1 + i) = P(1 + i)^3$ is the value at end of third period

. . . .

$a_n = [P(1 + i)^{n-1}](1 + i) = P(1 + i)^n$ is the value at end of nth period

b. $a_8 = 1,000(1.0025)^8 = 1020.20.$ **c.** $a_2 = 1,000(1.01)^2 = 1,020.10.$

9a. $a_5 = 100(1.1)^5 = 161.05.$ Should take alternative investment since it yields more (\$170) than you can now earn over a 5-year period by investing \$100 at $i = 0.1$.

b. $P = 170(1.1)^{-5} = 106.$ Should take alternative investment since it would take \$106 at $i = 0.1$ to yield 170 over 5 years, and you can obtain the \$170 by investing only \$100 if you take the alternative investment.

PROBLEM SET 9.2

1a. 1. **b.** No limit. **c.** No limit. **d.** 2. **e.** No limit.
f. 0. **g.** 0. **h.** No limit.

3. Let $a_1 = C, a_2 = C, \ldots, a_n = C$, so that $S = \{C,C,C, \ldots, C, \ldots\}$. $\lim_{n \to \infty} \{a_n\} = C$ because $|a_n - C| = 0$ for $n \geq N = 1$, and thus for any $\epsilon > 0$ we can take $N = 1$ and be sure that $|a_n - C| < \epsilon$.

5. Let $\lim_{n \to \infty} a_n = L_a$, $\lim_{n \to \infty} b_n = L_b$. Then by definition of a limit

$$-\epsilon_1 < a_n - L_a < \epsilon_1 \qquad n > N_1$$
$$-\epsilon_1 < b_n - L_b < \epsilon_1 \qquad n > N_2$$

These two inequalities will also be satisfied for $n > N$ where N is the greater of N_1 and N_2. Adding the inequalities we obtain

$$-2\epsilon_1 < (a_n + b_n) - (L_a + L_b) < 2\epsilon_1 \qquad n > N$$

If for any $\epsilon > 0$ we set $\epsilon_1 = \epsilon/2$, then $|(a_n + b_n) - (L_a + L_b)| < \epsilon$.

PROBLEM SET 9.3

1a. 6. **b.** 12. **c.** 58. **d.** 6. **e.** 12.
3. $S_1 = 2, S_2 = \frac{17}{4}, S_3 = \frac{715}{108}.$
5a. $r = 0.1, \lim_{n \to \infty} S_n = 0.3/0.9 = \frac{1}{3}.$ **b.** $r = 0.1, \lim_{n \to \infty} S_n = 0.6/0.9 = \frac{2}{3}.$
7. $d = 8, \quad S = \{-22, -14, -6, 2, 10, 18, 26, 34, \ldots\}. \quad S_1 = -22, \quad S_2 = -36,$
$S_3 = -42.$
9a. $\{-1, -4, -7, -10, -13, \ldots\}.$

b. $2n - 3 \sum_{i=1}^{n} i = 2n - 3(n + n^2)/2 = [n(1 - 3n)]/2.$ (See Sec. 9.10.)

11a. 122,500. **b.** $a_{10} = 14,500.$ **13a.** 588.23. **b.** 666.67.

PROBLEM SET 9.4

1. $\sum_{i=1}^{n} (2i + 1) = n(2 + n).$ This formula gives the sum of the second through $(n + 1)$th odd numbers. Theorem 9.42 gives the sum of the first n odd numbers.

3. $d = [2(n + 1) - 1] - [2n - 1] = 2$ for any $n \geq 1$. Similarly for $d = [2(n + 1) + 1] - [2n + 1]$. $S_n = (n/2)[2(1) + (n - 1)2] = n^2$. $T_n = (n/2)[2(3) + (n - 1)2] = n(2 + n)$.

PROBLEM SET 9.5

1.

$$\frac{\bar{P}[(1 + i)^n - 1]}{i} = I(1 + i)^n \qquad \bar{P} = \frac{iI(1 + i)^n}{(1 + i)^n - 1}$$

An investment of I should be undertaken, at an interest rate of i, if it will return more than $\bar{P}$ each period for n periods. (If $P > \bar{P}$, $S_{\overline{n}|i} > C_{\overline{n}|i}$.)

3.

Present value of first payment is $P(1 + i)^{-1}$
Present value of second payment is $P(1 + i)^{-2}$
. . . .
Present value of nth payment is $P(1 + i)^{-n}$

Sum of present values is

$$Q_{\overline{n}|i} = P(1 + i)^{-1} + P(1 + i)^{-2} + \cdots + P(1 + i)^{-n}$$

This is a geometric sequence with $r = (1 + i)^{-1}$, $a_1 = P(1 + i)^{-1}$; its sum, from Theorem 9.34, is

$$\frac{P(1 + i)^{-1}[1 - (1 + i)^{-n}]}{1 - (1 + i)^{-1}} = \frac{P[1 - (1 + i)^{-n}]}{i}$$

Undertake the investment if $Q_{\overline{n}|i} > I$. (If $Q_{\overline{n}|i} > I$, $S_{\overline{n}|i} > C_{\overline{n}|i}$.)

5. $Q_{\overline{n'}|i} = P[1 - (1 + i)^{-n'}]/i = Z$, $P = iZ/[1 - (1 + i)^{-n'}]$

PROBLEM SET 9.6

1. $P(x) = e^{-(x/\theta)} = P(3) = e^{-(3/3)} = 0.37$.

3.

$$P = s^x f(1 + s + s^2 + \cdots) = s^x f \frac{1}{1 - s} \qquad \text{since } 0 < s < 1$$

$$= s^x \qquad \text{since } f = 1 - s$$

Or $\qquad P = 1 - f(1 + s + s^2 + \cdots + s^{x-1}) = 1 - f \frac{1 - s^x}{1 - s} = s^x$

PROBLEM SET 10.1

3a. $\det A = c^4$.

b. Since row 4 is 2 times row 1, $\det A = 0$ (Corollary 10.13).

c. Since each term in $\det A = \sum_{i=1}^{n!} (-1)^\alpha a_{1i_1} \cdots a_{ni_n}$ has one factor from each row (column), each term is 0 if one row (column) is composed only of zeros. *Q.E.D.*

d. $\det A = -2$, $\det B + \det C = 5 - 2 = 3$.

e. $\det A = -10$, $\det B \times \det C = 5x - 2 = -10$.

5. Each term in $\det A = \sum_{i=1}^{n!} (-1)^\alpha a_{1i_1} \cdots a_{ni_n}$ is 0, except the term $(-1)^0$

$a_{11} a_{22} \cdots a_{nn} = ck_1 \cdot ck_2 \cdots ck_n = c^n k_1 k_2 \cdots k_n$.

PROBLEM SET 10.2

1. $\det A = a_{31} A_{31} + a_{32} A_{32} + \cdots + a_{3n} A_{3n}$.
3. $\det I = (0)A_{31} + (0)A_{32} + (1)A_{33} + (0)A_{34} + \cdots + (0)A_{3n} = (1)(1) = 1$.
5a. $x(0) - y(-1) + 1(-1) = 0$, $y = 1$.

b. $\det \begin{pmatrix} 1 - i & 2 \\ i & 1 + i \end{pmatrix} = 1 - i^2 - 2i$

PROBLEM SET 10.3

1.

$$A = \begin{pmatrix} 2 & -3 & 1 \\ 1 & 2 & -4 \\ 3 & -1 & 3 \end{pmatrix} \quad B = \begin{pmatrix} 5 \\ -2 \\ 4 \end{pmatrix} \quad \det A = 42 \quad A_{\mathrm{adj}} = \begin{pmatrix} 2 & 8 & 10 \\ -15 & 3 & 9 \\ -7 & -7 & 7 \end{pmatrix}$$

$$A^{-1} = \begin{pmatrix} \frac{2}{42} & \frac{8}{42} & \frac{10}{42} \\ -\frac{15}{42} & \frac{3}{42} & \frac{9}{42} \\ -\frac{7}{42} & -\frac{7}{42} & \frac{7}{42} \end{pmatrix} \quad X = \begin{pmatrix} x_3 \\ x_2 \\ x_3 \end{pmatrix} = A^{-1}B = \begin{pmatrix} \frac{17}{21} \\ -\frac{15}{14} \\ \frac{1}{6} \end{pmatrix}$$

3.

$$\det A = a_{11}a_{22}a_{33} \quad A_{\mathrm{adj}} = \begin{pmatrix} a_{22}a_{33} & 0 & 0 \\ -a_{21}a_{33} & a_{11}a_{33} & 0 \\ a_{21}a_{32} - a_{22}a_{31} & -a_{11}a_{32} & a_{11}a_{22} \end{pmatrix}$$

$$A^{-1} = \begin{pmatrix} \dfrac{1}{a_{11}} & 0 & 0 \\ \dfrac{-a_{21}}{a_{11}a_{22}} & \dfrac{1}{a_{22}} & 0 \\ \dfrac{a_{21}a_{32} - a_{22}a_{31}}{a_{11}a_{22}a_{33}} & \dfrac{-a_{32}}{a_{22}a_{33}} & \dfrac{1}{a_{33}} \end{pmatrix}$$

PROBLEM SET 10.4

1. $(-c)a = (-c)1 \cdot a$ (Condition 8, Definition 10.31) $= -ca$ (Condition 7, Definition 10.31).

3. $(c + d)a = ca + da$ (Condition 6, Definition 10.31) $= 2ca$ (since $ca = da$). Thus $c = d$.

5. If $a = (x_1' \ \ x_2' \ \ x_3')$ and $b = (x_1'' \ \ x_2'' \ \ x_3'')$ belong to

$$U = \{(x_1 \ \ x_2 \ \ x_3) | a_1x_1 + a_2x_2 + a_3x_3 = 0\}$$

then
$$a + b = (x_1' + x_1'' \ \ x_2' + x_2'' \ \ x_3' + x_3'')$$

belongs to U, since

$$a_1(x_1' + x_1'') + a_2(x_2' + x_2'') + a_3(x_3' + x_3'')$$
$$= (a_1x_1' + a_2x_2' + a_3x_3') + (a_1x_1'' + a_2x_2'' \ a_3x_3'') = 0$$

Also $ka = (kx_1' \quad kx_2' \quad kx_3') \, \epsilon \, U$, since $a_1kx_1' + a_2kx_2' + a_3kx_3' = k(a_1x_1' + a_2x_2' + a_3x_3')$ $= k(0) = 0$. Thus Theorem 10.34 is satisfied.

PROBLEM SET 10.5

1.
$$r_1(1 \quad 0 \quad 0) + r_2(0 \quad 1 \quad 0) + r_3(0 \quad 0 \quad 1) + r_4(3 \quad 2 \quad 1) = (0 \quad 0 \quad 0)$$
$$(r_1 \quad 0 \quad 0) + (0 \quad r_2 \quad 0) + (0 \quad 0 \quad r_3) + (3r_4 \quad 2r_4 \quad r_4) = (0 \quad 0 \quad 0)$$
$$r_1 + 0 + 0 + 3r_4 = 0$$
$$0 + r_2 + 0 + 2r_4 = 0$$
$$0 + 0 + r_3 + r_4 = 0$$

Linearly dependent since for any specified r_4, $r_1 = -3r_4$, $r_2 = -2r_4$, and $r_3 = -r_4$ satisfies the first part of Definition 10.36.

3. Because of the given linear dependence,

$$k_2(A_2 + r_2A_1) + k_3(A_3 + r_3A_1) + \cdots + k_m(A_m + r_mA_1) = 0$$

for some $k_i \neq 0$. But this expression is equivalent to

$$(k_2A_2 + k_2r_2A_1) + (k_3A_3 + k_3r_3A_1) + \cdots + (k_mA_m + k_mr_mA_1)$$
$$= (k_2r_2 + k_3r_3 + \cdots + k_mr_m)A_1 + k_2A_2 + k_3A_3 + \cdots + k_mA_m = 0 \qquad Q.E.D.$$

5. Assume $\{A_1, A_2, \ldots, A_m, X\}$ is linearly dependent, and let $X = A_i$. Then $r_1A_1 + r_2A_2 + \cdots + 2r_iA_i + \cdots + r_mA_m = 0$ for some $r_i \neq 0$. But this contradicts the fact that $\{A_1, A_2, \ldots, A_m\}$ is linearly independent. $Q.E.D.$

PROBLEM SET 10.6

1. $y = 1(1 \quad 2) + 1(3 \quad 4) = (4 \quad 6)$, $y = 1(1 \quad 2) + 3(3 \quad 4) = (10 \quad 14)$. $y = 3(1 \quad 2) + 1(3 \quad 4) = (6 \quad 10)$, $y = 3(1 \quad 2) + 3(3 \quad 4) = (12 \quad 18)$.

3. Definition 10.53 plus the fact that any element $(x_1 \quad x_2)$ of $V(2)$ can be obtained as a linear combination of $(1 \quad 0)$ and $(0 \quad 1)$. $(x_1 \quad x_2) = x_1(1 \quad 0) + x_2(0 \quad 1)$.

PROBLEM SET 10.7

1. $(1 \quad 0)$ and $(2 \quad 3)$, $(2 \quad 3)$ and $(0 \quad 1)$. (Theorem 10.58.)
3. No (Theorem 10.59).
5. Yes, since $r_1(1 \quad 3) + r_2(1 \quad 2) = (0 \quad 0)$ only when $r_1 = r_2 = 0$.

PROBLEM SET 11.1

1a. 3. **b.** 3. **c.** 4.
3. Let $r_r(A) = k$. Since the columns of A^T are the rows of A, $r_c(A^T) = k$. Thus $r(A) = r(A^T)$ (Theorem 11.13).

PROBLEM SET 11.2

1. $r(A) = r(A_b) = 2 < n = m \rightarrow$ infinite number of solutions.
3. Prob. 1: $x_1 = 3x_3 + 21$, $x_2 = -x_3 - 8$. Prob. 2: $x_1 = 3x_3$, $x_2 = -x_3$. Thus $c_1 = 21$, $c_2 = -8$, $c_3 = 0$ in this case.

PROBLEM SET 12.1

1. $A\mathbf{x} = \mathbf{b}$:

$$A = \begin{pmatrix} 3 & 2 & 19 & -2 & 1 & 2 & 8 & 1 & 1 & 0 & 0 & 0 \\ 2 & 3 & 0 & 3 & 2 & 0 & 0 & 6 & 0 & 1 & 0 & 0 \\ 1 & 3 & -4 & 1 & 0 & 6 & 0 & 1 & 0 & 0 & 1 & 0 \\ 5 & 6 & 1 & 4 & 0 & 6 & 1 & 3 & 0 & 0 & 0 & 1 \end{pmatrix}$$

$$\mathbf{x} = \begin{pmatrix} x_1 \\ x_2 \\ x_3 \\ x_4 \\ x_5 \\ x_6 \\ x_7 \\ x_8 \\ x_9 \\ x_{10} \\ x_{11} \\ x_{12} \end{pmatrix} \qquad \mathbf{b} = \begin{pmatrix} 92 \\ 46 \\ 16 \\ 50 \end{pmatrix}$$

3. $x_1 = x_2 = x_3 = 0,\ x_4 = 40,\ x_5 = 20,\ x_6 = 12.$

5.

$$\mathbf{y}_1 = \begin{pmatrix} 1 \\ 2 \\ 1 \end{pmatrix} \quad \mathbf{y}_2 = \begin{pmatrix} 2 \\ 4 \\ 1 \end{pmatrix} \quad \mathbf{y}_3 = \begin{pmatrix} 1 \\ 1 \\ 4 \end{pmatrix} \quad \mathbf{y}_4 = \begin{pmatrix} 1 \\ 0 \\ 0 \end{pmatrix} \quad \mathbf{y}_5 = \begin{pmatrix} 0 \\ 1 \\ 0 \end{pmatrix} \quad \mathbf{y}_6 = \begin{pmatrix} 0 \\ 0 \\ 1 \end{pmatrix}$$

$$z_j = 0\ (j = 1, 2, \ldots, 6)$$

7. Arbitrarily insert $\mathbf{a}_1 = \begin{pmatrix} 1 \\ 2 \\ 1 \end{pmatrix}$. Then $x_1 = 10,\ x_2 = x_3 = x_5 = 0,\ x_4 = 30,$ $x_6 = 2.$

9. $x_1 = x_2 = x_5 = 0,\ x_3 = 5,\ x_4 = 11,\ \hat{z} = 25 > z = 5.$

11. Maximal basic feasible solution is $x_1 = x_2 = x_5 = 0,\ x_3 = 5,\ x_4 = 1,\ z = 25,$ since for this solution $c_1 = 2 < z_1 = 10,\ c_2 = 4 < z_2 = 5,\ c_5 = 0 < z_5 = \frac{5}{4}.$

PROBLEM SET 13.1

1. $x_1 = x_2 = x_4 = x_5 = x_6 = 0,\ x_3 = 1.25,\ x_7 = 10.00,\ x_8 = 17.50,\ z = 12.50.$

3. $x_1 = 33\frac{1}{3},\ x_2 = x_6 = x_7 = 0,\ x_3 = 5\frac{5}{9},\ x_4 = 222\frac{2}{9},\ x_5 = 266\frac{2}{3},\ z = 1{,}722\frac{2}{9}.$

5. Prob. 2, Problem Set 6.4: $x_1 = x_2 = 2,\ x_3 = x_4 = 0,\ z = 16.$

INDEX OF APPLIED TERMS

INDEX OF MATHEMATICAL TERMS